THE FMLA

Understanding The Family And Medical Leave Act
By Will Aitchison

LRIS PUBLICATIONS
PORTLAND, OREGON

Published by Labor Relations Information System
3021 NE Broadway
Portland OR 97232
503.282.5440
www.LRIS.com

Aitchison, William Bruce, 1951 -

ISBN 1-880607-20-4

Library of Congress Control No. 2003104566

Cover photograph by Mandy Green
Cover design by Appleton-Lloyd

ACKNOWLEDGMENTS

Writing a book like this requires a group effort and tremendous teamwork. Debbie Frields led our efforts, coordinating all aspects of the production of the book, and facing down the daunting task of formatting the final copy of the book. My assistant Carol Green, who has run my law practice for more than 10 years, not only proofread the book but also held my professional life together while the book was being written.

Marc Fuller at LRIS was responsible for advocating the idea of marketing the book in CD-ROM format and, once his ideas were accepted, designing the CD, developing an appropriate computer format, and formatting cases for inclusion in the CD. Anya Dahab King, the anchor of the Arbitration and Negotiations Service, put in diligent efforts at proofreading the book and formatting cases for the CD.

Three law clerks in my firm, Scott Preston, Michelle Acosta, and Denise Hurchanik, had the unenviable task of gathering cases for the book, and doing the tedious job of cite checking.

A special word of thanks is in order for Robert B. Gordon, an attorney with Ropes & Gray in Boston, Massachusetts. Robert gave greatly of his time in reviewing an early draft of the book, and his comments were invaluable in the rewriting process.

Lastly, a special word of appreciation is in order for my wife, Valerie, once a labor lawyer in her own right. The book was in large measure her idea, and her support and encouragement was invaluable throughout a writing process that was often arduous.

ABOUT THE AUTHOR

Will Aitchison is a Portland, Oregon attorney who has, over the course of his career, represented over 100 law enforcement and firefighter labor organizations in five western states.

Aitchison graduated from the University of Oregon (Honors College) in 1973, and received his Doctor of Jurisprudence Degree from Georgetown University Law Center in Washington, D.C. in 1976. After two years of clerking for the chief judge of the Oregon Court of Appeals, Aitchison entered private practice and has been representing labor organizations since that time. In addition to his private practice, Aitchison has served as both an arbitrator and a pro tem district court judge, and has contributed numerous articles to various periodicals.

Aitchison is the author of *Interest Arbitration (Second Edition)*, *The Rights of Law Enforcement Officers (Fourth Edition)*, *The Rights of Firefighters (Third Edition)*, *A Model Law Enforcement Contract: A Labor Perspective (Third Edition)*, and *A Model Firefighter's Contact: A Labor Perspective*, all published by the Labor Relations Information System. He has lectured on numerous occasions throughout the country on FLSA issues and topics concerning labor relations and personnel issues, and has served as an expert witness and consultant in a variety of employment matters.

Aitchison resides in Portland, Oregon with his wife Valerie, who appears on the cover of this book with their twin sons Alex and Luke. He is also the father of Michael, age 17, and Matthew, age 16.

TABLE OF CONTENTS

INTRODUCTION

A SHORT SUMMARY OF THE FMLA 2

Unraveling The Confusing FMLA 2

The Design Of This Book 4

Some Final Introductory Remarks 5

Notes 7

CHAPTER 1

THE ORIGINS AND HISTORY OF THE FMLA 9

The Drafting And Passage Of The FMLA 10

The Purposes Of The FMLA 11

The DOL's Role In The Enforcement Of The FMLA 13

Notes 15

CHAPTER 2

THE EMPLOYERS COVERED BY THE FMLA 17

The FMLA's Definition Of Covered Employers 18

Joint Employers And Temporary Employees 20

Successor Employers 22

Individual Managers And Supervisors Can Be Considered To Be "Employers" Potentially Subject To Liability 22

The Special Case Of Educational Employers 24

Notes 25

CHAPTER 3

THE EMPLOYEES COVERED BY THE FMLA 29

Who Is An "Eligible Employee" For Purposes Of The FMLA 30

To Be An "Eligible Employee" Under The FMLA, An Employee Must Have Been Employed By The Covered Employer For At Least 12 Months 30

To Be An "Eligible Employee" Under The FMLA, An Employee Must Have Been Employed By The Employer For At Least 1,250 Hours During The Previous 12 Months 31

What If The Employer Wrongfully Confirms That The Employee Has 1,250 Hours Of Service When Leave Is Requested 33

To Be A Covered Employee, The Employee Must Work At A Worksite Where, Within 75 Miles Of The Employee's Worksite, At Least 50 Other Employees Work For The Employer 35

How The FMLA Applies To Applicants And Former Employees   36

The FMLA Rights Of Federal Employees   36

Employees Versus Subcontractors   37

Notes   39

CHAPTER 4

BIRTH, ADOPTION, AND FOSTER CARE   43

The Birth Of A Child Or The Placement Of A Child With The Employee For Adoption Or Foster Care   44

Leave Standards Where A Husband And Wife Work For The Same Employer   46

Intermittent Leave In Connection With Birth, Adoption, Or Foster Care   47

Notes   49

CHAPTER 5

SERIOUS HEALTH CONDITION   51

What Is A Serious Health Condition   52

Incapacity – The Heart Of An FMLA Claim For A Serious Health Condition   55

Serious Health Conditions – What Qualifies And What Does Not   56

Colds, The Flu, Minor Ulcers, And Similar Conditions   67

The Family Members Covered By The FMLA   68

What Does It Mean To "Care For" A Seriously Ill Family Member   71

Alcohol And Substance Abuse   72

Treatment By A Chiropractor   73

If The Employer Initially Approves FMLA Leave For A Serious Health Condition, Can It Later Change Its Mind   74

Notes   75

CHAPTER 6

THE REQUIRED EXCHANGE OF INFORMATION ONCE FMLA LEAVE IS REQUESTED – THE NOTICES REQUIRED OF EMPLOYEES AND EMPLOYER   79

The FMLA's Notice Requirements, Part 1 – The Notice An Employee Is Required To Give   80

The FMLA's Notice Requirements, Part 2 – The Notice An Employer Is Required To Give In Addition To Posting   85

What Is The Significance Of An Employer Failing To Give Appropriate Notice Under The FMLA   91

Notes   93

CHAPTER 7

CERTIFICATION OF SERIOUS HEALTH CONDITION AND SECOND OPINIONS   99

An Employer's Right To Certification Of A Serious Health Condition   100

Certification When Leave Is Intermittent Or On A Reduced Leave Schedule   107

An Employer's Questions About The Adequacy Of Certification And The Employer's Right To A Second Opinion   108

Breaking The Tie Between Dueling Doctors – Resolving Conflicting Medical Opinions   109

The Rationale Behind The Certification Requirement   110

Recertification Of Health Conditions   111

Certification As A Condition Of Restoration To The Employee's Former Job   112

Certification When An Employee Is Unable To Return To Work   114

Notes   117

CHAPTER 8

DURATION OF FMLA LEAVE   121

The Entitlement To 12 Weeks Of FMLA Leave   122

In What 12-Month Period Is An Employee Entitled To 12 Workweeks Of Leave   123

Intermittent Leave And Leave On A Reduced-Leave Schedule   126

When Does FMLA Leave End   128

What Happens When FMLA Leave Ends And The Employee Does Not Return To Work   129

Intermittent Leave For Educational Employees   129

Instructional Employees And End-Of-School-Year Leave   131

Notes   133

CHAPTER 9

THE RELATIONSHIP OF FAMILY LEAVE TO OTHER FORMS OF PAID LEAVE AND OTHER FAMILY LEAVE LAWS 137

In General - The Relationship Of The FMLA To Other Leave Plans 138

The FMLA's Basic Requirement – 12 Weeks' Leave, Paid Or Unpaid 138

Designating FMLA Leave 141

Counting Leave That Qualifies Both As FMLA Leave And As Leave Under An Employer's Leave Plan 142

The Applicability Of The FMLA To Leave Benefits Provided By An Employer That Are More Generous Than The FMLA 143

The Integration Of The FMLA With Collective Bargaining Agreements 144

The Integration Of The FMLA With Disciplinary Systems 146

State Family And Medical Leave Laws 146

The Integration Of The FMLA With Workers' Compensation Laws 151

The Relationship Of The FMLA To The FLSA 152

The Relationship Of The FMLA To The Americans With Disabilities Act 153

The Relationship Of The FMLA To The Civil Rights Act 154

The Relationship Of The FMLA To Common-Law Civil Lawsuits 155

Notes 157

CHAPTER 10

THE FMLA'S PROTECTIONS OF EMPLOYMENT AND BENEFITS 163

The Right To Restoration To The Employee's Former Job 164

What Is An "Equivalent" Position 166

Periodic Reports During FMLA Leave As To The Employee's Status And Intention To Return To Work 167

What Happens If The Employee Indicates She Will Not Be Returning To Work 168

When Is An Employer Entitled To Refuse To Restore An Employee Or To Delay Restoration 168

The Transfer Of Employees Using Intermittent Leave 169

The Exemption For Key Employees 170

The Special Case Of Certain Educational Employers 172

Maintenance Of Health Benefits During Leave 173

THE RECOVERY OF HEALTH INSURANCE PREMIUMS FROM EMPLOYEES WHO DO NOT RETURN TO WORK AT THE END OF FMLA LEAVE   175

THE ACCRUAL OF OTHER BENEFITS WHILE ON FMLA LEAVE   176

NOTES   177

CHAPTER 11

DISCRIMINATION, INTERFERENCE, AND RETALIATION   181

THE FMLA'S ENFORCEMENT PROVISIONS   182

ENFORCING THE FIRST CORE PRINCIPLE OF THE FMLA – THE SUBSTANTIVE GRANT OF RIGHTS TO EMPLOYEES OF FAMILY LEAVE BENEFITS   183

THE STANDARDS FOR ENFORCING THE FMLA'S SECOND CORE PRINCIPLE: AN EMPLOYER MAY NOT TAKE INTO ACCOUNT THE EMPLOYEE'S USE OF FMLA LEAVE IN MAKING EMPLOYMENT DECISIONS   184

ENFORCING THE THIRD CORE PRINCIPLE OF THE FMLA – THE PROHIBITION AGAINST THE SPECIFIC TYPES OF DISCRIMINATION   187

DISCIPLINARY ACTION CONCURRENT WITH BUT INDEPENDENT OF FMLA LEAVE   187

THE COURTS' MISTAKEN USE OF THE TERM "ADVERSE EMPLOYMENT ACTION"   189

NOTES   191

CHAPTER 12

FMLA REMEDIES   197

DAMAGES UNDER THE FMLA   198

EQUITABLE RELIEF UNDER THE FMLA   203

ATTORNEY FEES UNDER THE FMLA   204

CLASS ACTIONS UNDER THE FMLA   205

ACTIONS BY THE SECRETARY OF LABOR   206

THE RELATIONSHIP BETWEEN PRIVATE LAWSUITS AND SUITS BY THE SECRETARY OF LABOR   207

THE STATUTES OF LIMITATIONS FOR FMLA ACTIONS   208

WHERE CAN FMLA LAWSUITS BE FILED   209

NEED AN EMPLOYEE "EXHAUST" ADMINISTRATIVE REMEDIES BEFORE BRINGING AN FMLA LAWSUIT   210

THE COMPULSORY ARBITRATION OF FMLA CLAIMS IN PRIVATE EMPLOYMENT CONTRACTS   210

THE SPECIAL CASE OF CERTAIN EDUCATIONAL EMPLOYERS   211

THE VALIDITY OF AGREEMENTS RELEASING AN EMPLOYER FROM LIABILITY UNDER THE FMLA   212

NOTES   215

CHAPTER 13

POSTING AND RECORDKEEPING REQUIREMENTS UNDER THE FMLA   221

The FMLA's Posting Requirements   222

The FMLA's Recordkeeping Requirements   225

Notes   227

APPENDIX A

A GLOSSARY OF TERMS AND WHERE TO FIND FMLA RESOURCES   229

Where To Find The Court Decisions Cited In This Book   230

On-Line FMLA Resources   232

APPENDIX B

THE TEXT OF THE FMLA   235

APPENDIX C

FMLA REGULATIONS   253

INDEX

INDEX   315

INTRODUCTION

A Short Summary Of The FMLA.

The heart of the Family and Medical Leave Act of 1993 (referred to in this book as "the FMLA") allows eligible employees the right to take leave from work for up to 12 workweeks in any 12-month period for the following reasons: The birth of a child, the placement of a child with the employee for adoption or foster care, where the employee is needed to care for a close family member with a serious health condition, or where the employee suffers from a serious health condition that makes the employee unable to perform the functions of his or her job. The FMLA mandates that an employee be allowed to take unpaid leave for such purposes and permits an employee or an employer to substitute paid leave for unpaid leave provided the employee has earned or accrued it.

The FMLA guarantees employees the right to return to the same or an equivalent position after the FMLA leave, with pay, benefits, and working conditions equivalent to those associated with the job held prior to the leave. During FMLA leave, the employee is entitled to the same level of health benefits on the same terms in existence at the commencement of the leave. The FMLA grants employers the right to advance notice of an employee's intention to use FMLA leave, where such notice is practicable. Employers may also establish a verification process to ensure that a serious health condition exists and that an employee returning from family leave is fit for duty.

The FMLA prohibits an employer from discriminating or retaliating against an employee using FMLA leave. An employer violating the FMLA will face the usual assortment of federal remedies, including private lawsuits for back wages and employment benefits, suits by the Department of Labor, possible injunctions, and potential liability for attorney fees. The law also requires an employer to post notices of compliance with the FMLA and to maintain records relevant to FMLA use.

Because the FMLA only applies to employers with 50 or more employees, it covers only two-thirds of American workers. The coverage of the FMLA is further reduced since it only applies to employees who have achieved certain tenure, leaving only 54.9% of employees that are covered. Since the "worksites" of employees must also meet certain minimum requirements per the FMLA, only 10.8% of private-sector worksites are actually covered by the FMLA, though this relatively small number of worksites actually employs 59.5% of private-sector American workers.[1]

Unraveling The Confusing FMLA.

It is no surprise that there have been difficulties interpreting and applying the FMLA. After all, the FMLA is a relatively new federal labor statute that came on the scene with little warning. What *is* surprising, however, is the degree of confusion about the requirements of the FMLA. Employers, employees, human resource specialists, labor organizations, attorneys, and the courts have all found at least portions of the FMLA particularly difficult to grasp. As a result, at least in part, there are thousands of FMLA lawsuits pending across the country, many arising out of simple misunderstandings of the law.

In the course of researching this book, I tried to read every possible document on the FMLA. That meant reading, among other things, all published federal and state court decisions concerning the FMLA, the Department of Labor's regulations, opinion letters and comments, articles in professional and not-so-professional journals on how the FMLA should be applied, historical documents showing the intent of Congress in passing the FMLA, and the contents of several dozen web pages dealing with FMLA issues. More than 30,000 pages later, I was left with the abiding belief that there are basically four reasons why the FMLA has been so particularly bedeviling.

First, the FMLA was the product of political compromise. Such compromise often breeds badly written laws, and the FMLA is no exception. While some portions of the FMLA are clear, others are confusing. More often, though, one encounters obvious "holes" in the law – gaps that leave significant questions unanswered. For example, the FMLA allows an employer to require the employee to use paid leave for the employee's absence from work. What happens if the employer simply does not tell the employee whether paid leave may be used *before* the employee begins using the leave, particularly if the unpaid status of the leave might impact the employee's decision to use FMLA leave and for how long? The FMLA does not answer this or scores of similar questions.

Second, the regulations of the Department of Labor (referred to in this book as the DOL) interpreting and applying the FMLA leave much to be desired. Admittedly, the DOL was given a Herculean job – it had only a short period of time in which to craft extensive regulations in an area of law that was, essentially, a blank slate. Part of the DOL's job was to fill in as many of the gaps left by Congress as it could. As the reader will see in this book, the DOL's gap-filling was not entirely satisfactory, as courts have since struck down several of the DOL's regulations for being beyond the agency's authority to enact.

Third, courts have hardly been models of consistency in their FMLA decisions. Courts have been deeply divided over some fundamental FMLA issues, such as whether an employer can retroactively give notice that paid leave will be substituted for FMLA leave, often reaching their decisions without a thorough consideration of the underlying purposes and history of the FMLA. The courts are, at best, not clear about even the most basic structure for determining whether an employee has been retaliated against for using FMLA leave. Even worse, some court decisions are poorly thought out and just plain wrong.[2]

Fourth, there has simply been too little training on the rights and responsibilities of employers and employees under the FMLA. Undoubtedly, some of the lack of training is due to the newness of the FMLA and some to complacency, for the FMLA does not pose the risks of multi-million dollar judgments associated with violations of the Fair Labor Standards Act, even though the FMLA does have significant risks for non-compliance.

In short, caution must be the watchword in handling FMLA issues. The law will continue to evolve and eventually settle down to a point where controversy is rare. In the meantime, the FMLA involves such important rights for employees and the potential for such significant liability for employers that competent advice – whether from the DOL, an attorney, or a human relations professional – should be sought before making any fundamental FMLA decision.

The Design Of This Book.

This book is written for a broad audience, attempting to reach everyone impacted by the FMLA in their work lives. The book is organized along the following lines:

Chapters 2 and 3	**Who** is covered by the FMLA. *The definitions of "employer" and "employee."*
Chapters 4 and 5	**What** is covered by the FMLA. *Leave for birth, adoption or foster care placement, and serious health conditions.*
Chapters 6 and 7	**Information sharing** under the FMLA. *The information employers and employees are required to provide each other about FMLA leave, and an employer's right to certification of serious health conditions.*
Chapters 8 and 9	**The duration** of FMLA leave and the **relationship** of FMLA leave to other types of leave benefits.
Chapters 10, 11, and 12	**Job restoration** after FMLA leave and an employee's **remedies** for violations of the FMLA.
Chapter 13	The FMLA's **posting and recordkeeping** requirements.
Appendix A	A **glossary** of terms and a list of FMLA resources.
Appendix B	The actual **text** of the FMLA.
Appendix C	The DOL's **regulations** on the FMLA.

Because of its design, the book attempts to relegate case names and legal citations to footnotes at the end of each chapter as much as possible. Though the legal authority for the statements made in this book has been deliberately minimized, the footnotes contain case references for the specific propositions in the book with citations made to hundreds of cases and DOL opinions.

Some Final Introductory Remarks.

In many ways, perhaps, the FMLA has been the victim of the tremendous political and media attention that accompanied its passage. The FMLA was never all-encompassing to begin with. It does not grant even one additional minute of paid leave to even one employee in the country. The FMLA merely guarantees that employees will be allowed to use their <u>own</u> paid leave for certain purposes and (usually) guarantees them a job at the end of the leave.

But that was not the press coverage that the FMLA received. Here is a sample of comments made during the time frame that began when the FMLA was being debated in Congress and ended when the FMLA became effective six months after President Clinton signed it into law:

> "I want an America that does more than talk about family values. I want an America that values families." President Bill Clinton.[3]

> "There's a great deal of confusion and fear among our members." Mary Reed, National Federation of Independent Business.[4]

> "This lessens the burden of choice. People no longer need to choose to take care of a family member or keep a job." Laurie Kane, Families and Work Institute.[5]

> "We have no idea how much it will cost business. We are talking about tens of thousands of jobs being lost or not created because of this bill." Senator Bob Dole.[6]

> "The revolutionary edicts of the new law . . ." The Dallas Morning News.[7]

> "The fact is, small businesses can't flourish when burdened by excessive regulation, like the provisions in the recently passed Family and Medical Leave Act." Senator Robert Bennett.[8]

> "When it comes to family values, the FMLA is basically where the rubber meets the road." Senator Bob Krueger.[9]

This kind of overwrought rhetoric primed the public to expect a law of significant moment, one that fundamentally changed the nature of the employer-employee relationship in this country. It is not surprising, then, that employees are shocked to learn that an employer has the unfettered right to force them to use up their FMLA allotments to account for an absence from work at the same time their paid leave accounts are being reduced; or that, because their employer employs fewer than 50 employees, the law does not apply at all.

The FMLA is a modest law rather than a sweeping one. To be sure, the FMLA has its share of technicalities – twists and turns that require an employer or employee to take special care to ensure that FMLA rights and responsibilities are being observed and met. While navigating the FMLA's road map, one also bumps up against some occasionally impenetrable DOL regulations and difficult court decisions. When all is said and done, however, the FMLA's requirements are as basic as they are simple. This book is intended to sweep away the mysteries of the FMLA and to lay bare its requirements in a manner that can be understood by all.

NOTES

[1] Commission on Family and Medical Leave, *A Workable Balance, Report To Congress On Family And Medical Leave Policies*, http://www.dol.gov/dol/esa/public/regs/compliance/whd/fmla/firstpa.pdf.

[2] *Walthall v. Fulton County School District*, 18 F.Supp.2d 1378 (N.D.Ga. 1998)(concluding that an employee must choose between sick leave and FMLA leave); *Mosley v. Hedges*, 1998 WL 182479 (N.D.Ill. 1998)(holding that "although an employee may take intermittent leave or reduced schedule leave when medically necessary, the FMLA does not protect an employee who is absent excessively from discharge"); *Kilcrease v. Coffee County, Alabama*, 951 F.Supp. 212 (M.D.Ala. 1996)(holding without analysis that an employee has no right to use sick leave donated from other employees for FMLA purposes); *Hicks v. Maytag Corporation*, 3 WH Cas.2d 992 (E.D.Tenn. 1995)(holding there is no right to a jury trial under the FMLA).

[3] Houston Chronicle, 1993 WL 9614202 (August 8, 1993).

[4] Washington Times, 1993 WL 5838759 (August 5, 1993).

[5] Dallas Morning News, 1993 WL 8816494 (August 9, 1993).

[6] Los Angeles Daily News, 1993 WL 3506106 (February 5, 1993).

[7] Dallas Morning News, 1993 WL 8816494 (August 9, 1993).

[8] Salt Lake Tribune, 1993 WL 5399867 (August 4, 1993).

[9] St. Louis Post Dispatch, 1993 WL 8000766 (February 4, 1993).

CHAPTER 1

THE ORIGINS AND HISTORY OF THE FMLA

The Drafting And Passage Of The FMLA.

The FMLA was born out of frustration that existing laws concerning maternity leave were inadequate to protect the jobs of women needing time off from work around the time of childbirth.[1] Drafted by Representative Howard Berman and a number of women's and family advocacy groups, what was then known as the Parental and Disability Act was first introduced into Congress in 1985 under the sponsorship of Representatives Patricia Schroeder and William Clay and Senator Christopher Dodd. The FMLA's road was a rocky one over the next eight years. There are several excellent summaries of the legislative history of the FMLA, with perhaps the best found in the book *Conflict and Compromise: How Congress Makes the Law*, by Ronald Elving.[2]

When first introduced in 1985, the FMLA successfully cleared a committee in the Democratic-controlled House but was never slated for a hearing in the Republican-controlled Senate. The following year, the FMLA died as a result of a filibuster in the Senate. In 1988, the bill's progress through Congress stopped after Senator Strom Thurmond attached an anti-pornography bill to it. By 1990, the proponents of the FMLA realized that the scope of the FMLA would have to be narrowed in order for the Act to become law. A key point of contention was the length of FMLA leave. Versions of the FMLA defeated in Congress before 1990 would have entitled employees to longer periods of protected leave. A 1986 version of the law, for example, would have entitled employees to up to 26 weeks of leave in a 12-month period for the employee's own serious health condition and up to 18 weeks in a two-year period for the birth or adoption of a child or to care for an ill family member.[3] A 1988 version would have entitled employees to up to ten weeks of leave in a two-year period for the birth or adoption of a child or to care for an ill family member, and up to 15 weeks of leave in a 12-month period for the employee's own serious health condition.[4]

The 1990 version of the law limited FMLA leave to 12 weeks and raised the exemption given to small employers.[5] The changes garnered enough support for the FMLA to pass both houses of Congress only to be promptly vetoed by President George Bush. In 1992, the FMLA passed Congress again only to be vetoed once more by President Bush. Not surprisingly, the FMLA became an important issue in the 1992 presidential election, with presidential candidate Bill Clinton stating he wanted the FMLA to be the first bill he signed into law as president.

And so it was in 1993. Within two weeks of President Clinton's inauguration, Congress held hearings on the FMLA, and both houses of Congress passed the law. On February 5, 1993, the day after the FMLA was adopted by Congress, President Clinton signed the FMLA.

The FMLA created a federal Commission on Family and Medical Leave, charged with reporting to Congress on the impact of the FMLA. The Commission's initial report was delivered in 1996 and gave the FMLA a fairly glowing review:

"The Family and Medical Leave Act has had a positive impact on employees overall. It has succeeded in replacing the piecemeal nature of voluntary employer leave policies and state leave statutes with a more consistent and uniform standard. The FMLA has not been the burden to business that some had feared. For most employers, compliance is easy, the costs are non-existent or small, and the effects are minimal. Most periods of leave are short, most employees return to work, and reduced turnover seems to be a tangible positive effect. The FMLA, with its signature features of guaranteed job protection and maintenance of health benefits, begins to emerge, even now, as a significant step in helping a larger cross-section of working Americans meet their medical and family care-giving needs while still maintaining their jobs and their economic security – achieving the workable balance intended by Congress."[6]

Notwithstanding this complimentary report, advocates for family leave decried what they perceived were the limited benefits of the FMLA – particularly the fact that the FMLA provided only a guarantee of unpaid leave, the exemption granted to smaller employers, and limited leave due to serious health conditions. On the other hand, advocates for employer groups felt that the law's benefits were too generous, requesting changes in the FMLA to narrow its definition of serious health conditions, to impose limitations on the use of intermittent leave, and to exclude additional employers from the law's coverage.

By 1996, even President Clinton was proposing changes in the FMLA, suggesting the law be expanded to cover short leaves for school activities, routine family medical services, and older relatives' health needs. Under the President's proposal, all employees would be entitled to up to 24 hours of unpaid leave per year for such purposes.[7]

Many of these proposals have enjoyed at least a modest reception in Congress. Indeed, in almost every year, a dozen or so proposed amendments to the FMLA are introduced in Congress. Thus far, none have passed and the FMLA remains as it was when first signed into law.[8]

The Purposes Of The FMLA.

Congress provided two prefaces to the FMLA containing statements of Congress' findings leading to the passage of the law and the Congressional purpose in enacting the FMLA. Congress' findings were as follows:

(1) The number of single-parent households and two-parent households in which the single parent or both parents work is increasing significantly;

(2) It is important for the development of children and the family unit that fathers and mothers be able to participate in early childrearing and the care of family members who have serious health conditions;

(3) The lack of employment policies to accommodate working parents can force individuals to choose between job security and parenting;

(4) There is inadequate job security for employees who have serious health conditions that prevent them from working for temporary periods;

(5) Due to the nature of the roles of men and women in our society, the primary responsibility for family caretaking often falls on women, and such responsibility affects the working lives of women more than it affects the working lives of men; and

(6) Employment standards that apply to one gender only have serious potential for encouraging employers to discriminate against employees and applicants for employment who are of that gender.[9]

These findings reflect two overall conclusions by Congress. Congress determined that the FMLA was necessary because of the changing makeup of the American workforce. Congress recognized that the large number of single-parent households and households in which both parents work demanded some provision for federally-guaranteed family leave. Congress also maintained that denying leave for parenting or other family care-taking purposes is a form of gender discrimination, and that without a law protecting the right to use family leave, women would suffer a disadvantage in the workplace.

Congress' statement of the purposes of the FMLA echoes its findings prior to passage, focusing on the stability and economic security of families and the potential for gender discrimination. Congress' list of the purposes of the FMLA was as follows:

(1) To balance the demands of the workplace with the needs of families, to promote the stability and economic security of families, and to promote national interests in preserving family integrity;

(2) To entitle employees to take reasonable leave for medical reasons, for the birth or adoption of a child, and for the care of a child, spouse, or parent who has a serious health condition;

(3) To accomplish the purposes described in paragraphs (1) and (2) in a manner that accommodates the legitimate interests of employers;

(4) To accomplish the purposes described in paragraphs (1) and (2) in a manner that, consistent with the Equal Protection Clause of the Fourteenth Amendment, minimizes the potential for employment discrimination on the basis of sex by ensuring generally that leave is available for eligible medical reasons (including maternity-related

disability) and for compelling family reasons, on a gender-neutral basis; and

(5) To promote the goal of equal employment opportunity for women and men, pursuant to such clause.[10]

Delving into the "legislative history" behind the FMLA, Congress recognized that, in an age when in many families all adults are in the workforce, the leave policies of employers often did not permit employees to perform necessary caregiver functions for their families. Congress found that the tensions between job responsibilities and family obligations place "a heavy burden on families, employees, employers and the broader society."[11] Congress also found that employees' lack of job security during serious illnesses that required them to miss work is particularly devastating to single-parent families as well as to families which need two incomes to make ends meet.[12] To this end, Congress concluded that "it is unfair for an employee to be terminated when he or she is struck with a serious illness and is not capable of working."[13] In its first significant pronouncement on the issue, the Supreme Court observed that Congress believed that the different treatment of men and women in the workplace with respect to family leave was "not attributable to any differential physical needs of men and women, but rather to the pervasive sex-role stereotype that caring for family members is women's work."[14]

Congress intended that the two core requirements of the FMLA – the entitlement to leave and the guarantee of a job on the expiration of the leave – would set "a minimum labor standard for leave," in the tradition of child labor and minimum wage laws, Social Security, safety and health laws, pension and welfare benefit laws, and other labor laws that establish minimum standards for employment.[15]

The DOL's Role In The Enforcement Of The FMLA.

The DOL has two key roles in enforcing the FMLA. The first is to enact regulations implementing the FMLA.[16] Courts defer to the DOL's regulations if they find them to be "reasonable."[17] In determining whether the DOL's regulations are valid, courts apply a two-step test. First, courts determine whether Congress has directly spoken on the particular issue. If it has, a court "must give effect to the unambiguously expressed intent of Congress."[18]

Second, if the statute is silent or ambiguous on the issue in dispute, a court must ask whether the DOL provided a permissible interpretation of the statute. Courts then defer to the DOL's interpretation unless they find the interpretation is "arbitrary, capricious, or manifestly contrary to the statute."[19] This deference to the DOL's regulations gives the DOL's interpretation of the FMLA as contained in its regulations great importance.

The second important role of the DOL is the FMLA's grant of authority to the DOL to bring lawsuits under the FMLA. Not only does the DOL have the authority to sue an employer demanding compliance with the FMLA, the DOL's involvement in an existing FMLA case may even eliminate the employee's right to continue a lawsuit.

These roles make the DOL the key player on the national scene under the FMLA. How the DOL interprets and applies the FMLA, and the positions the DOL takes in litigation in individual FMLA cases, has a tremendous impact on the continued shaping of the FMLA.

NOTES

[1] *See* D. Lenhoff, *What It Took To Pass The FMLA,*
http://www.nationalpartnership.org=275.

[2] *See also* Note, *The Failure of the Family and Medical Leave Act: Alternative Proposals for Contemporary American Families,* Hofstra Labor and Employment Law Journal (Spring, 2001); Comment, *Analysis Of The Political Dynamics Surrounding The Enactment Of The 1993 Family And Medical Leave Act,* Emory Law Journal (Winter, 1998).

[3] *See* H.R. 4300, 99th Cong. (1986).

[4] H.R. 925, 100th Cong. (1988).

[5] *See* H.R. 4300 §101 (covering employers with 15 or more employees); H.R. 925 §101(5)(A) (covering employers with 50 or more employees for the first three years the legislation would have been in effect, and thereafter, employers with 35 or more employees).

[6] Commission on Family and Medical Leave, *A Workable Balance, Report To Congress On Family And Medical Leave Policies,* http://www.dol.gov/dol/esa/public/regs/compliance/whd/flma/firstpa.pdf.

[7] *See Opinion Letter,* Wage and Hour Division, 1996 WL 1044779 (July 31, 1996).

[8] *See* Note, *Bridging The Gap Between Work And Family: Accomplishing The Goals Of The Family And Medical Leave Act Of 1993,* William and Mary Law Review (April, 2001).

[9] 29 U.S.C. §2601(a).

[10] 29 U.S.C. §2601(b).

[11] S.Rep. No. 103-3 at 4, 103d Cong., 2d Sess. (1993); *see Price v. City of Fort Wayne,* 117 F.3d 1022 (7th Cir. 1997).

[12] S.Rep. No. 103-3 at 11-12, 103d Cong., 2d Sess. (1993).

[13] S.Rep. No. 103-3 at 11-12, 103d Cong., 2d Sess. (1993).

[14] *Nevada Dept. of Human Resources v. Hibbs,* 123 S.Ct. 1972 (2003).

[15] S.Rep. No. 103-3 at 4; *see Stekloff v. St. John's Mercy Health Sys.,* 218 F.3d 858 (8th Cir. 2000).

[16] 29 U.S.C §2654; *see Toro v. Mastex Industries,* 32 F.Supp.2d 25 (D.Mass. 1999).

[17] *Chevron USA Inc. v. Natural Resources Defense Council,* 467 U.S. 837 (1984). *See Ninilchik Traditional Council v. United States,* 227 F.3d 1186 (9th Cir. 2000); *Duckworth v. Pratt & Whitney, Inc.,* 152 F.3d 1 (1st Cir. 1998).

[18] *New York Currency Research Corp. v. Commodity Futures Trading Comm'n,* 180 F.3d 83 (2nd Cir. 1999)

[19] *Chevron USA v. Natural Resources Defense Council,* 467 U.S. 837 (1984).

CHAPTER 2

THE EMPLOYERS COVERED BY THE FMLA

In A Nutshell . . .

To be covered by the FMLA, an employer must have 50 or more employees. In some circumstances — particularly with temporary employees — there may be multiple employers of the same individual. Because of the particular way the FMLA is worded, individual supervisors and managers can be considered to be employers subject to liability under the FMLA.

The FMLA's Definition Of Covered Employers.

The Statute: 29 U.S.C. §2611(4).

(A) In general the term "employer" -

(i) means any person engaged in commerce or in any industry or activity affecting commerce who employs 50 or more employees for each working day during each of 20 or more calendar workweeks in the current or preceding calendar year;

(ii) includes -

(I) any person who acts, directly or indirectly, in the interest of an employer to any of the employees of such employer; and

(II) any successor in interest of an employer;

(iii) includes -

any "public agency," as defined in section 203(x) of this title; and

(iv) includes the General Accounting Office and the Library of Congress.

(B) Public agency

For purposes of subparagraph (A)(iii), a public agency shall be considered to be a person engaged in commerce or in an industry or activity affecting commerce.

In crafting the FMLA, Congress intended a broad and inclusive definition of "employer."[1] There are essentially four pieces to the definition used by Congress: (1) A **person** who (2) is engaged in an activity **affecting commerce** who (3) employs **50 or more employees** for (4) each working day during each of **20 or more calendar workweeks** of the current or preceding calendar year. Each of these components will be discussed below.

> *The FMLA is applied to a broad class of employers, including individuals, corporations, partnerships, and any other "organized group of persons."*

Who or what is a "person" for purposes of the FMLA? The FMLA defines a "person" subject to the law by referring to the definition of "person" furnished in the Fair Labor Standards Act (FLSA). The FLSA's definition is a broad one, including an "individual, partnership, association, corporation, business trust, legal representative," **and** (if that were not enough) "any organized group of persons."[2]

Even legally separate business entities, such as a parent and a subsidiary corporation, may be part of a single employer for purposes of the FMLA *if they qualify as an "integrated employer."*[3] The "integrated employer" test was originally developed in a labor relations context[4] and was subsequently applied in civil rights cases.[5] The "integrated employer" test considers whether the two entities have:

- Common management.

- Interrelation between operations.

- Centralized control of labor relations.

- Common ownership and/or financial control.[6]

Not all four factors need be present for two entities to be considered an integrated employer.[7] Centralized control over labor relations is likely to be the most important factor.[8] Indeed, even in a situation where there is some degree of common ownership and management, a lack of centralized control over labor relations is likely to lead to the conclusion that an employer is not part of an "integrated employer."[9] As put by one court, "what entity made the final decisions regarding employment matters related to the person claiming discrimination" is the ultimate question in determining an integrated employer issue. [10]

A somewhat more difficult task is determining whether governmental bodies are the same governmental entity. The DOL's regulations provide that "a State or a political subdivision of a State constitutes a single public agency and, therefore, a single employer for purposes of determining employee eligibility. For example, a state is a single employer; a county is a single employer; a city or town is a single employer. Where there is any question about whether a public entity is a public agency, as distinguished from a part of another public agency, the U.S. Bureau of the Census *Census of Governments* will be determinative."[11] Under these principles, governmental bodies such as cities, counties and school districts are different entities for FMLA purposes.[12]

What does it mean to be engaged in an activity affecting commerce?
The second part of the FMLA's definition of "employer" is that the entity must be engaged in an activity "affecting commerce." The DOL's rules indicate that the term "affecting commerce" has the same definition as the one used in the Labor Management Relations Act of 1947. That definition, which includes "any industry or activity in commerce or in which a labor dispute would burden or obstruct commerce or tend to burden or obstruct commerce or the free flow of commerce,"[13] is considered by the Supreme Court to give the courts "the fullest jurisdictional breadth constitutionally permissible."[14] Given this broad definition, the DOL's regulations on the FMLA that specify that any employer with at least 50 employees will be deemed to be engaged in commerce or in an industry or activity affecting commerce will almost certainly be found valid.[15]

It is not clear whether churches and other religious institutions are covered by the FMLA. Though churches and many other religious institutions likely pass the "commerce" test, there may be freedom of religion implications that prevent FMLA coverage for their employees.[16]

How does one count employees towards the 50-employee threshold?
The third part of the FMLA's definition of "employer" requires that the person "employ" at least 50 employees.[17] Meeting the 50-employee test is a critical question in FMLA cases. In fact, if the employee does not cite in her court com-

The second part of the test of whether an employer is covered by the FMLA – that the entity must be engaged in an activity affecting commerce, is likely to be automatically met by employers.

The FMLA only applies to employers with 50 or more employees.

plaint that the employer has 50 employees, the complaint may be dismissed.[18] The DOL's regulations indicate that in counting employees, it will apply the broad definition of employment found in the FLSA.[19] Under that definition, to "employ" someone is also to "suffer or permit" them to work, meaning that mere knowledge on the part of an employer of a person's work done for the employer is enough to form an employment relationship.[20]

The most difficult question as to whether an individual is "employed" or not is when she may or may not be an independent contractor. The DOL's regulations distinguish between an independent contractor "who is engaged in a business of his/her own" and an employee who "follows the usual path of an employee and is dependent on the business which he/she serves."[21]

How does one calculate whether 50 employees have worked during a 20-calendar-workweek period? The fourth and last part of the FMLA's definition of "employer" specifies that the 50 employees must have been employed during each workday of 20 calendar weeks in the preceding or current calendar year. In general, any employee whose name is on the employer's payroll will be considered employed each working day of the calendar week, even if they receive no compensation for the week.[22] This "payroll method" of counting employees has been approved by the Supreme Court.[23] Even employees on paid or unpaid leave, such as disciplinary suspensions or leaves of absence, are counted as long as there is a reasonable expectation that they will later return to active employment.[24] The 20 calendar weeks do not need to be consecutive.[25]

Only individuals employed within the United States or any of its territories or possessions may be counted towards the 50-employee threshold.[26] New employees who begin work after the first day of a workweek, or terminating employees who do not work the last day of the workweek, are not counted towards the threshold.[27]

Joint Employers And Temporary Employees.

Two or more employers in "joint employment" can employ the same person for the purposes of the FMLA.[28] According to the DOL's rules, where two or more businesses exercise some control over the work or working conditions of an employee who performs work that benefits both during a workweek, the businesses may be considered to be joint employers *depending upon the following*:

- Whether there is an arrangement between employers to share an employee's services or to interchange employees;

- Whether one employer acts directly or indirectly in the interest of the other employer in relation to the employee; or,

- Whether the employers are not completely disassociated with respect to the employee's employment and may be deemed to share control of the employee, directly or indirectly, because one employer controls, is controlled by, or is under common control with the other employer.[29]

An employer's responsibilities under joint employment depend upon whether the employer is a "primary" or a "secondary" employer.[30] The primary employer is responsible for giving all FMLA notices, providing FMLA leave, the maintenance of health benefits while the employee is on leave, and job restoration at the conclusion of leave.[31] In determining primary status, the authority to hire and fire, the assignment of employees, who prepares payroll, and who furnishes employment benefits are considered. For example, where an employee works for a temporary agency, the temporary agency would be the primary employer. Being a "secondary employer" is significant in that employees who are jointly employed must be counted by *both* employers to determine whether the employers are subject to the FMLA.[32] This means that a temporary employee would count as an employee towards the 50-employee thresholds for both the temporary agency as well as the third-party employer.[33]

Because the FMLA is relatively new, courts are likely to turn to well-established principles for joint employment under the Fair Labor Standards Act.[34] Joint employment exists under the FLSA if one entity performs the lion's share of employer administration tasks or has the power to act on behalf of the employer with respect to its employees.[35] Courts analyzing the question of joint employment under the FLSA tend to focus on the "economic reality" of the relationship between two employers[36] and on the total employment situation.[37]

CASE IN POINT

Who Employs A Temporary Worker?

Marianna Shaff is employed by Workers On Call, an agency supplying temporary workers for employers with accounting needs. Workers On Call assigns Shaff to work for outside businesses and pays Shaff directly, billing the businesses for Shaff's time. During a busy tax season, Shaff spends three weeks on an assignment with Colombo Shades. At the start of the fourth week, and just before the height of the income tax season in April, Shaff requests FMLA leave because of her son's serious illness.

For purposes of the FMLA, who is Shaff's employer?

Both Workers On Call and Colombo Shades would be Shaff's employers under the FMLA. Workers On Call would be considered Shaff's primary employer, with the responsibility to restore Shaff to her job with Workers On Call at the end of her FMLA leave. Colombo Shades would be considered Shaff's secondary employer, meaning that Shaff would be counted as an employee for purposes of determining whether Colombo Shades is subject to the FMLA.

Successor Employers.

If a company takes over another company's business, the FMLA rights of employees are the same as if employment with the predecessor and successor employers was continuous employment by a single employer.

The DOL's regulations address what happens if an employer's operations are purchased or otherwise taken over by another employer. Under the regulations, if the new employer qualifies as a "successor in interest," the FMLA entitlements of employees are the same – as if the employment with the previous and succeeding employers was continuous.[38] Thus, the new employer must count periods of employment and hours worked for the previous employer to determine employee eligibility for FMLA leave.

The DOL's rules specify that an entity's status as new employer or "successor in interest" will be governed by the traditional factors used under Title VII of the Civil Rights Act and the Vietnam Era Veterans' Adjustment Act. Those factors include whether there is the following: (1) Substantial continuity of the same business operations; (2) use of the same physical plant; (3) continuity of the work force; (4) similarity of jobs and working conditions; (5) similarity of supervisory personnel; (6) similarity in machinery, equipment and production methods; (7) similarity of products or services; and (8) the ability of the predecessor to provide relief for the claimed violation.[39] Applying these standards, one court has found that an incoming sheriff is the "successor in interest" to his predecessor.[40] Along these same lines, another court found that a company purchasing another company's hotel, hiring one of the previous company's employees on the same day as the purchase, and promising the employee that her "original hire date will be honored for all benefits" was a successor employer.[41]

Individual Managers And Supervisors Can Be Considered To Be "Employers" Potentially Subject To Liability.

The Statute: 29 U.S.C. §2611(4).

(A) In general the term "employer" -

(i) means any person engaged in commerce or in any industry or activity affecting commerce who employs 50 or more employees for each working day during each of 20 or more calendar workweeks in the current or preceding calendar year;

(ii) includes -

(I) any person who acts, directly or indirectly, in the interest of an employer to any of the employees of such employer; and

(II) any successor in interest of an employer . . .

By its terms, the FMLA defines an employer as "any person who acts, directly or indirectly, in the interest of an employer." In interpreting this definition, courts and the DOL have drawn reference from a similar definition of "employer" under the FLSA.[42] The FLSA addresses the possibility that there may be several simultaneous "employers" who are responsible for compliance with the FLSA, including an employer's managers or supervisors.[43] Courts have applied an "economic reality" test to determine liability under the FLSA,[44] finding that a corporate officer with operational control of a corporation's covered enterprise is an "employer" and is liable for damages along with the corporation.[45]

Applying these principles, the vast majority of courts have concluded that managers have potential liability under the FMLA.[46] A key factor is whether the corporate officer or manager has substantial control over the aspect of the employee's FMLA rights alleged to have been violated.[47] In one case, the DOL sued not only a company, but also one of the owners of the company for FMLA violations. The court hearing the case allowed the lawsuit to proceed, citing the facts that the owner and his wife were the "sole owners, the sole directors, and the sole officers" of the company and that the owner oversaw the general day-to-day operations of the company.[48] In another case, a court allowed a lawsuit to proceed against a vice-president of a corporation, holding that the employee's contention that the vice-president was acting in the course and scope of his duties when he elected to terminate the employee was sufficient to file a claim against the vice-president as well as the corporation.[49] However, in a third case a court refused to hold a human resources manager potentially liable for an FMLA claim where the manager did not have ultimate authority over the employee's FMLA leave and played no part in the decision to terminate the employee.[50]

A different case may exist where the employer is a public agency. The unusual way in which the FMLA's definition of employer is structured has led to "disarray" among the courts as to whether supervisors of public employers are liable under the FMLA.[51] As Section 2611(4) of the FMLA is written, the term "employer" . . .

> "(i) means any person engaged in commerce or in any industry or activity affecting commerce who employs 50 or more employees for each working day during each of 20 or more calendar workweeks in the current or preceding calendar year;

> "(ii) includes -

> "(I) any person who acts, directly or indirectly, in the interest of an employer to any of the employees of such employer; and

> "(II) any successor in interest of an employer;

> "(iii) includes

"any 'public agency,' as defined in section 203(x) of this title; and

"(iv) includes the General Accounting Office and the Library of Congress."

Some courts have concluded that the "any person" language in subsection (ii) of the statute modifies only subsection (i) of the statute, and that because the "any person" language precedes the "public agency" language in subsection (iii), it cannot modify the "public agency" language. Under this fairly tortured analysis, public sector supervisors cannot be liable under the FMLA.[52] The majority of courts demur, finding that "common logic and the rules of grammar" demand the conclusion that public sector supervisors are just as personally liable under the FMLA as their private sector counterparts.[53]

The Special Case Of Educational Employers.

A variety of special rules apply to "local educational agencies," defined as public school boards and the schools under their jurisdiction and private elementary and secondary schools. The special rules do not apply to other kinds of educational institutions such as colleges, universities, trade schools, preschools, and day care centers.[54] Congress enacted these special rules because "the entitlement to leave for family reasons presents unique challenges to schools, as the teachers' right to leave must be balanced against the students' right to continuity in the classroom."[55]

The first of the special rules for such educational employers is that the 50-employee minimum employee test does not apply.[56] However, as discussed in the following chapter, for an employee to be eligible under the FMLA, the employee must work at a worksite within 75 miles of at least 50 other employees working for the employer. This 75-mile rule does apply to educational employees. Educational employers are also subject to special rules concerning the taking of intermittent leave, the taking of leave near the end of a school term, and job restoration after FMLA leave is complete. They also have a partial exemption from the award of liquidated damages.

NOTES

[1] *Torrez-Lopez v. May* 111 F.3d 633 (9th Cir. 1997); *Salgado v. CDW Computer Centers, Inc.*, 1998 WL 60779 (N.D.Ill. 1998); *Miller v. Defiance Metal Products, Inc.*, 989 F.Supp. 945 (N.D.Ohio 1997).

[2] 29 U.S.C. §203(a).

[3] One court has rejected the application of the "integrated employer" test to the FMLA, albeit in a somewhat tentative opinion. *See Diangi v. Valex, Inc.*, 56 F.Supp.2d 1023 (N.D.Ill. 1999).

[4] *See Radio & Television Broadcast Technicians Local 1264 v. Broadcast Service of Mobile Inc.*, 380 U.S. 255 (1965).

[5] *Armbruster v. Quinn*, 711 F.2d 1332 (6th Cir. 1983).

[6] 29 C.F.R. §825.104; *see Keene v. Teco Energy Corp.*, 141 Lab. Cas. ¶34,078 (M.D.Fla. 2000).

[7] *Opinion Letter*, Wage and Hour Division, 2000 WL 33157365 (September 11, 2000).

[8] *Schweitzer v. Advanced Telemarketing Corp.*, 104 F.3d 761 (5th Cir. 1997); *see Hukill v. Auto Care, Inc.*, 192 F.3d 437 (4th Cir. 1999).

[9] *Hukill v. Auto Care, Inc.*, 192 F.3d 437 (4th Cir. 1999); *see Glunt v. GES Exposition Services, Inc.*, 123 F.Supp.2d 847 (D.Md. 2000). *See generally Kinsey v. E & G Pizza Corp.*, 2000 WL 1911885 (S.D.Ind. 2000).

[10] *Trevino v. Celanese Corp.*, 701 F.2d 397 (5th Cir. 1983); *cf. Siko v. Kassab, Archbold & O'Brien*, 4 WH Cas.2d 1547 (E.D.Pa. 1998); *Locklin v. Headstart Family Hair Care Salons*, 743 So.2d 474 (Ala.App. 1999).

[11] 29 C.F.R. §825.108(c)(1).

[12] *Rollins v. Wilson County Government*, 967 F.Supp. 990 (M.D.Tenn. 1997), *affirmed* 154 F.3d 626 (6th Cir. 1998).

[13] 29 U.S.C. §142(1).

[14] *NLRB v. Reliance Fuel Oil Corp.*, 371 U.S. 224 (1963).

[15] *IAFF, Local 3683 v. South Johnson County Volunteer Fire & Rescue, Inc.*, 5 F.Supp.2d 1230 (D.Kan. 1998)(business with a $50,000 contract performing solely in-state services is in an industry affecting commerce).

[16] *Opinion Letter,* Wage and Hour Division, 1995 WL 1036747 (November 30, 1995); *see Catholic Bishop of Chicago*, 440 U.S. 490 (1979); *NLRB v. St. Louis Christian Home*, 663 F.2d 60 (8th Cir. 1981).

[17] *Conte v. Restaurant Management Services, Inc.*, 7 WH Cas.2d 315 (S.D.N.Y. 2001); *Sousa v. Orient Arts Inc.*, 5 WH Cas.2d 383 (S.D.N.Y. 1999).

[18] *Reddinger v. Hospital Central Services, Inc.*, 4 F.Supp.2d 405 (E.D.Pa. 1998); *Thurston v. Borden Waste-Away Service, Inc.*, 1998 WL 456441 (N.D.Ind. 1998).

See generally Jane Rigler, *Analysis and Understanding of the Family and Medical Leave Act of 1993*, 45 Case W. Res. L. Rev. 457 (1995).

[19] 29 C.F.R. §825.105(a).

[20] *See* 29 U.S.C. §203(g); *Cunningham v. Gibson Electric Co.*, 43 F.Supp.2d 965 (N.D.Ill. 1999).

[21] 29 C.F.R. §825.105(a); *see Sousa v. Orient Arts Inc.*, 5 WH Cas.2d 383 (S.D.N.Y. 1999).

[22] 29 C.F.R. §825.105(b).

[23] *Walters v. Metropolitan Educational Enterprises, Inc.*, 519 U.S. 202 (1997).

[24] 29 C.F.R. §825.105(c).

[25] 29 C.F.R. §825.105(e).

[26] 29 C.F.R. §825.105(b).

[27] 29 C.F.R. §825.105(d).

[28] *Sherry v. Protection, Inc.*, 981 F.Supp. 1133 (N.D.Ill. 1997); *see Karr v. Strong Detective Agency, Inc.*, 787 F.2d 1205 (7th Cir. 1986).

[29] 29 C.F.R. §825.106(a).

[30] *Salgado v. CDW Computer Centers, Inc.*, 1998 WL 60779 (N.D.Ill. 1998).

[31] 29 C.F.R. §825.106(c)(e).

[32] 29 C.F.R. §825.106(d). Employees seeking to sue an employer on the grounds that it is a joint employer required to count additional individuals as employees must be prepared to prove such joint employment by the most credible evidence – usually payroll records. *See Alderdice v. American Health Holding, Inc.*, 118 F.Supp.2d 856 (S.D.Ohio 2000).

[33] *Miller v. Defiance Metal Products, Inc.*, 989 F.Supp. 945 (N.D.Ohio 1997).

[34] *Sherry v. Protection, Inc.*, 981 F.Supp. 1133 (N.D.Ill. 1997); *see Opinion Letter, Department of Labor*, 2000 WL 33157365 (September 11, 2000).

[35] *E.g. Reich v. Circle C. Invs., Inc.*, 998 F.2d 324 (5th Cir. 1993); *Karr v. Strong Detective Agency, Inc.*, 787 F.2d 1205 (7th Cir. 1986).

[36] *U.S. Dept. of Labor v. Cole Enterprises, Inc.*, 62 F.3d 775 (6th Cir. 1995).

[37] *Welch v. Laney*, 57 F.3d 1004 (11th Cir. 1995).

[38] 29 C.F.R. §825.107(c).

[39] 29 C.F.R. §825.107(a).

[40] *Jolliffe v. Mitchell*, 971 F.Supp. 1039 (W.D.Va. 1997).

[41] *Barrilleaux v. Thayer Lodging Group, Inc.*, 5 WH Cas.2d 601 (E.D.La. 1999).

42 29 C.F.R. §825.104(d).

43 *Dole v. Elliott Travel & Tours, Inc.*, 942 F.2d 962 (6th Cir. 1991).

44 *Falk v. Brennan*, 414 U.S. 190 (1973); *Goldberg v. Whitaker House Cooperative*, 366 U.S. 28 (1961).

45 *Donovan v. Agnew*, 712 F.2d 1509 (1st Cir. 1983).

46 *See. e.g., Carter v. United States Postal Service*, 157 F.Supp.2d 726 (W.D.Ky. 2001); *Boriski v. City of College Station*, 65 F.Supp.2d 493 (S.D.Tex. 1999); *Carpenter v. Refrigeration Sales Corp.*, 49 F.Supp. 2d 1028 (N.D.Ohio 1999); *Llante v. American NTN Bearing Manufacturing Corp.*, 1999 WL 1045219 (N.D.Ill. 1999); *Meara v. Bennett*, 27 F.Supp.2d 288 (D.Mass. 1998); *Buser v. Southern Food Service, Inc.*, 73 F.Supp.2d 556 (M.D.N.C. 1999); *Divizio v. Elmwood Care, Inc.*, 1998 WL 292982 (N.D.Ill. 1998); *Bryant v. Delbar Prods., Inc.*, 18 F.Supp.2d 799 (M.D.Tenn 1998); *Mercer v. Borden*, 11 F.Supp.2d 1190 (C.D.Cal. 1998); *Rupnow v. TRC, Inc.*, 999 F.Supp. 1047 (N.D.Ohio 1998); *Enright v. CGH Medical Center*, 4 WH Cas.2d 1080 (N.D.Ill. 1998); *Beyer v. Elkay Manufacturing Co.*, 4 WH Cas.2d 984 (N.D.Ill. 1997); *Holt v. Welch Allyn, Inc.*, 3 WH Cas.2d 1622 (N.D.N.Y. 1997); *Waters v. Baldwin County*, 936 F.Supp. 860 (S.D.Ala. 1996); *Johnson v. A.P. Products, Ltd.*, 934 F.Supp. 625 (S.D.N.Y 1996); *Freemon v. Foley*, 911 F.Supp. 326 (N.D.Ill. 1995); *see Kilvitis v. County of Luzerne*, 52 F.Supp.2d 403 (M.D.Pa 1999); *Knussman v. Maryland*, 935 F.Supp. 659 (D.Md. 1996). *See generally Donovan v. Agnew*, 712 F.2d 1509 (1st Cir. 1983); Comment, *Supervisors Beware: The Family And Medical Leave Act May Be Hazardous To Your Health*, Journal of Contemporary Health Law and Policy (Winter, 1999). A minority of courts find no supervisory liability for FMLA violations. *See, e.g., Carter v. Rental Uniform Svc. of Culpeper, Inc.*, 977 F.Supp. 753 (W.D.Va. 1997); *Frizzell v. Southwest Motor Freight, Inc.*, 906 F.Supp. 441 (E.D.Tenn. 1995).

47 *Rollins v. Wilson County Government*, 154 F.3d 626 (6th Cir. 1998); *Blohm v. Dillard's Inc.*, 95 F.Supp.2d 473 (E.D.N.C. 2000); *Johnson v. A.P. Products, Inc., Ltd.*, 934 F.Supp. 625 (S.D.N.Y. 1996); *Freemon v. Foley*, 911 F.Supp. 326 (N.D.Ill 1995); *see* Note, *Individual Liability Under The Family And Medical Leave Act Of 1993: A Senseless Detour On The Road To A Flexible Workplace*, Brooklyn Law Review (Winter, 1997).

48 *Reich v. Midwest Plastic Engineering, Inc.*, 66 Empl.Prac. ¶43,701 (W.D.Mich. 1995).

49 *Buser v. Southern Food Service, Inc.*, 73 F.Supp.2d 556 (M.D.N.C. 1999).

50 *Johnson v. A.P. Products, Inc.*, 934 F.Supp. 625 (S.D.N.Y. 1996).

51 *Keene v. Rinaldi*, 127 F.Supp.2d 770 (M.D.N.C. 2000).

52 *Keene v. Rinaldi*, 127 F.Supp.2d 770 (M.D.N.C. 2000); *Johnson v. Runyan*, 1999 WL 893841 (W.D.Mich. 1999); *cf. Wascura v. Carver*, 169 F.3d 683 (11th Cir. 1999).

53 *Darby v. Bratch*, 287 F.3d 673 (8th Cir. 2002); *Cantley v. Simmons*, 179 F.Supp.2d 654 (S.D.W.Va. 2002); *Carter v. United States Postal Service*, 157 F.Supp.2d 726 (W.D.Ky. 2001); *see Morrow v. Putnam*, 142 F.Supp.2d 1271 (D.Nev. 2001); *Kilvitis v. County of Luzerne*, 52 F.Supp.2d 403 (M.D.Pa. 1999); *Meara v. Bennett*, 27 F.Supp.2d 288 (D.Mass. 1998); *Knussman v. State of Maryland*, 16 F.Supp.2d 601 (D.Md. 1998).

[54] 29 C.F.R. §825.600(a).

[55] S.Rep. No. 3, 103d Cong., 1st Ses. 3-5 (1993), *reprinted in* 1993 U.S.C.C.A.N. 3, 5-7.

[56] 29 C.F.R. §825.600(b).

CHAPTER 3

THE EMPLOYEES COVERED BY THE FMLA

In A Nutshell . . .

To be an "eligible employee" under the FMLA, an employee must meet the following three conditions:

⟶ *The employee must have worked for a covered employer for at least 12 months;*

⟶ *The employee must have been employed for at least 1,250 hours "of service" during the 12-month period immediately preceding the beginning of the leave; and*

⟶ *The employee must be employed at a worksite where 50 or more employees are employed by the employer within 75 miles of the worksite.[1]*

Who Is An "Eligible Employee" For Purposes Of The FMLA?

The Statute: 29 U.S.C. §2611(2).

(A) In general

The term "eligible employee" means an employee who has been employed -

for at least 12 months by the employer with respect to whom leave is requested under section 2612 of this title; and

for at least 1,250 hours of service with such employer during the previous 12-month period.

To Be An "Eligible Employee" Under The FMLA, An Employee Must Have Been Employed By The Covered Employer For At Least 12 Months.

The 12-month minimum employment period can consist of consecutive or non-consecutive months.

An employee remains unprotected under the FMLA until she works for at least 12 months for the employer.[2] In fact, if an employee uses leave for an FMLA qualifying purpose such as childbirth, and the employer responds by firing the employee for being absent from work, the FMLA will offer no protections to the employee unless the 12-month requirement is met.[3]

Under the DOL's rules, the 12 months of employment need not be consecutive to qualify for the minimum requirement.[4] If an employee is on the employer's payroll for any part of a week, the week counts as a full week of employment. Time spent on paid or unpaid leave during which time other benefits or compensation are paid counts as being "on the payroll" for purposes of the 12-month rule.[5] The 12-month period is measured retroactively from the first day qualifying FMLA leave is taken, *not* from a subsequent date such as when the employee filled out the employer's FMLA forms or sought additional leave.[6]

Case in Point

How To Count The 12 Months Necessary For FMLA Eligibility

Question: Peter Giese started work for Arbitration and Negotiations Service on July 1, 2001. On June 20, 2002, he requested 12 weeks of

---

FMLA leave starting on July 15, 2002 so he could care for his newborn child. His employer promptly fired him. Is Peter protected by the FMLA?

Answer: Yes. Peter's 12-month eligibility period would have been completed on July 1, 2002. When he requested the leave before July 1, 2002, two things happened: (1) His employer was required to advise him whether he would be eligible for the FMLA leave on July 15, 2002; and (2) His employer was prohibited from retaliating against him for requesting the leave.

A fair portion of requests for FMLA leave are made in advance of the taking of the leave. In some cases, the employee may not have met the 12-month minimum employment requirement at the time the request is made; however, she will have completed her first year on the job at the time the leave is anticipated to start. The DOL's regulations provide that in such circumstances, "the employer must either confirm the employee's eligibility based upon a projection that the employee will be eligible on the date leave would commence or must advise the employee when the eligibility requirement is met."[7] Moreover, the employee making the advance request for the leave is protected against reprisals by the employer because the employee is engaging in protected activity under the FMLA in requesting the leave.[8]

To Be An "Eligible Employee" Under The FMLA, An Employee Must Have Been Employed By The Employer For At Least 1,250 Hours During The Previous 12 Months.

The Statute: 29 U.S.C. §2611(2).

(C) Determination

For purposes of determining whether an employee meets the hours of service requirement specified in subparagraph (A)(ii), the legal standards established under section 207 of this title shall apply.

To qualify for FMLA protection, an employee must not only have worked for an employer during the previous 12 months, the employee must also have worked at least 1,250 hours during that period.[9] For a frame of reference, an employee working a 40-hour week will be scheduled to work 2,080 hours a year, less vacation and other paid leave. An employer claiming the employee has not met the 1,250-hour minimum requirement must "clearly demonstrate" the hours that the employee has actually worked.[10]

The 1,250-work hours requirement does not include any time spent on paid leave.

The 1,250-hour requirement for coverage under the FMLA is counted differently than the 12-month period described in the previous section. The FMLA provides that "for purposes of determining whether an employee meets the hours of service requirement…the legal standards established under section 207 of this title shall apply." "Section 207 of this title" means the Fair Labor Standards Act, found at 29 U.S.C. §207. Under the FLSA, only hours that an employee actually works are counted as "hours worked" for the purpose of determining eligibility for overtime compensation.[11] Neither paid leave such as vacation or sick leave nor unpaid leaves of absence are counted as "hours worked" under the FLSA. Thus, time spent on leave is not counted in calculating the 1,250-hour requirement for FMLA coverage,[12] though such time is counted in calculating the 12-month period.[13] Even when an employer is ordered by an arbitrator to reinstate an employee pursuant to a labor contract, the time the employee spent awaiting the arbitrator's decision while wrongfully discharged does not count towards the 1,250-hour requirement since the employee was not actually working.[14] In addition, even if an employee works overtime hours for which an overtime premium is paid, each overtime hour worked counts only as a single hour toward the 1,250-hour requirement.[15]

Also consistent with FLSA standards, any hours an employer "suffers or permits" an employee to work counts toward the 1,250-hour threshold.[16] For example, in one case an airline only paid flight attendants for the time between when they reported for a trip and the time the flight arrived at the gate at the end of the trip. Since flight attendants actually performed work on both sides of this span of time, a court counted the additional pre- and post-flight time toward the 1,250-hour threshold.[17]

As with other FLSA standards, the counting of hours worked by an employee does not entirely depend upon the employer's payroll system. "Any accurate accounting of actual hours worked under the FLSA's principles may be used."[18] If the employer has not complied with the FMLA's recordkeeping requirements (discussed in Chapter 13), the employer must prove that the employee has not worked the 1,250 hours. If the employer fails to do so, the employee is presumed to be covered by the FMLA. Because of their unusual work schedules, teachers are presumed to meet the 1,250-hour minimum requirement.[19]

The 1,250-hour requirement is actually two tests – the employee must have worked **1,250 hours** and must have worked them in the previous **12-month** period. The time frames involved with each test are evaluated on the date FMLA leave begins,[20] and an employee must prove she fits into both categories in order to have any claim under FMLA.[21] If FMLA leave is taken on an intermittent basis, the time frame is evaluated at the beginning of the series of absences, with the employee remaining eligible for FMLA leave throughout the following 12-month period.[22]

What If The Employer Wrongfully Confirms That The Employee Has 1,250 Hours Of Service When Leave Is Requested?

As detailed in Chapter 7, once an employee makes a request to use FMLA leave, an employer must furnish written notice to the employee of the employee's FMLA rights and obligations. Section 825.110(d) of the DOL's regulations states that if an employee notifies his employer of the need for FMLA leave before the employee has met the 1,250-hour requirement, the employer must inform the employee whether he is eligible to use FMLA leave or when the employee will become eligible. Under the regulation, if an employer confirms that an employee without the necessary qualifying hours is eligible for FMLA leave, the employer is prohibited from subsequently challenging the employee's eligibility to use FMLA leave even if it later develops that the employee has not, in fact, worked the requisite 1,250 hours.[23]

Most courts considering the validity of Section 825.110(d) have found the regulation invalid.[24] The courts striking down the regulation have generally reasoned as follows:

> "The statute straightforwardly defines an 'eligible employee' as 'an employee who has been employed * * * for at least 12 months by the employer with respect to whom leave is requested,' and who must have 'been employed * * * for at least 1,250 hours of service with such employer during the previous 12-month period.' The regulation impermissibly expands the scope of eligibility, however, because it compels employers to treat as eligible employees who have not met the twelve-month/1,250 hours requirement based on the regulation's additional set of notice requirements. Because 29 C.F.R. §825.110(d) would permit, under certain circumstances, employees who have not worked the statutorily defined minimum required hours to become eligible for the Act's benefits, it contradicts the expressed intent of Congress and therefore is invalid."[25]

Simply because Section 825.110(d) has been struck down by the court does not mean that the underlying principles behind the regulation do not have vigor if an employee makes the right argument. The law's principle of "equitable estoppel" exists where one party has made a misleading representation to another party, who in turn has reasonably relied to her detriment on that representation.[26] In such a case, the party making the misrepresentation will be "estopped" from taking a contrary position. Someone asserting equitable estoppel must generally prove (1) a misrepresentation by the party against whom estoppel is asserted, (2) reasonable reliance on the misrepresentation, and (3) some harm coming from that reliance.[27] The core idea behind equitable estoppel is that a person should not be allowed to change a statement that has been detrimentally relied upon.[28] In general, an employer's mere silence – neither confirming nor denying that the employee has accumulated the necessary 1,250 hours – will not be enough to establish that the employer made a misrepresentation sufficient to trigger estoppel rationale.[29]

CASE IN POINT

Question: Mike Edwards is in his first year of employment with the Philadelphia Police Department. When his first child is born, Edwards talks to Janice Corbin, the Department's Human Resources Manager to find out if he is eligible for FMLA leave. Quickly scanning Edwards' payroll records, Corbin tells Edwards he has the necessary 1,250 hours of employment and is eligible for 12 weeks of FMLA leave.

Based on Corbin's statements, Edwards requests family leave, which is granted. Six weeks into the leave, Edwards receives notice from the Department that he had not worked 1,250 hours and was, thus, not eligible for FMLA leave. When Edwards fails to return to work within the three days demanded by the Department (because he is unable to make alternate child care arrangements in such a short time frame), the Department fires him. In fact, Edwards had only worked 1,175 hours and was not eligible for coverage under the FMLA.

Does Edwards have a claim that his discharge violated the FMLA?

Answer: Edwards potentially has a claim. Though Section 825.110(d) of the Department of Labor's (DOL) regulations would prohibit the Department from firing Edwards because it mistakenly notified him he was eligible for FMLA leave, most courts have held the regulation unenforceable as beyond the DOL's ability to enact. Nonetheless, many courts would find protection for Edwards in the doctrine of "equitable estoppel," basing their decisions on (1) the inaccurate statement made by the Department to Edwards as to his FMLA eligibility, (2) Edwards' reasonable reliance on the misinformation, and (3) the harm resulting to Edwards from that reliance.

Therefore, Edwards may be able to take FMLA leave, depending on which court hears his case.

Equitable estoppel principles have been used for years under a variety of federal labor statutes to hold employers liable when the federal statute might not otherwise impose liability. For example, courts have applied equitable estoppel in cases under the Age Discrimination in Employment Act to allow employees to bring claims that otherwise might have been barred by a statute of limitations. In these instances, misrepresentations by the employer induced the employee not to file a timely claim.[30] Similarly, courts have applied equitable estoppel in cases arising under Title VII of the Civil Rights Act where an employer misled an employee concerning the nature of a Title VII claim.[31] Equitable estoppel has been applied in other areas of the FMLA. For example, in a case where an employer misrepresented the ending date of an employee's FMLA leave, a court allowed a trial to determine the question of whether the misrepresentation excused the employee's failure to return to work on the correct ending date.[32]

Some courts that have found Section 825.110(d) invalid have indicated a willingness to apply the principles of equitable estoppel in cases where an employer has incorrectly informed an employee of eligibility for FMLA leave, *and* the employee has relied on the employer's information to his detriment. As explained by one court:

> "Indeed, it is our view that even in the absence of a formal regulation, the doctrine of equitable estoppel itself may apply where an employer who has initially provided notice of eligibility for leave later seeks to challenge that eligibility. Thus, future employees who rely to their detriment upon the assurance of their employer that they qualify for leave under the FMLA may have recourse to the doctrine of equitable estoppel even without an enforceable regulation protecting their right to rely upon an employer's notice of eligibility."[33]

To Be A Covered Employee, The Employee Must Work At A Worksite Where, Within 75 Miles Of The Employee's Worksite, At Least 50 Other Employees Work For The Employer.

The Statute: 29 U.S.C. §2611(2).

(B) Exclusions

The term "eligible employee" does not include -

(i) any Federal officer or employee covered under subchapter V of chapter 63 of title 5; or

(ii) any employee of an employer who is employed at a worksite at which such employer employs less than 50 employees if the total number of employees employed by that employer within 75 miles of that worksite is less than 50.

Even if an employer has thousands of employees, it may not be covered by the FMLA unless it has at least 50 employees within a 75-mile distance.

The third part of FMLA's definition of "employee" requires that the employer employ at least 50 employees within 75 miles of the employee's worksite.[34] Under this rule, even if the employer employs thousands of individuals nationwide, an employee may still not be covered by the FMLA unless the 75-mile rule is met.[35] The assessment of whether the employer has the requisite 50 employees is made when the employee gives notice of the need for leave, and is measured by the number of employees on the employer's payroll.[36] The 75-mile distance is usually measured by calculating the shortest surface transportation route "over public streets, roads, highways and waterways."[37] If an employee is jointly employed, the employee's worksite for purposes of the 75-mile rule is the primary employer's office to which the employee is assigned or reports.[38] Once an employee is found eligible under the 75-mile rule, the employee's eligibility is not affected if the employer drops below 50 employees during the taking of the FMLA leave, even if the leave is taken on an intermittent or reduced leave basis.[39]

Some employees such as salespersons have no fixed worksite and leave for and return from work to their homes. Under the DOL's regulations, the worksite of such employees is the office to which they report and are assigned, not their homes or their employer's home office.[40] In making this determination, it is important to consider "the location of the personnel who were primarily responsible for reviewing sales reports and other information sent by the sales representatives, in order to record sales, assess employee performance, develop new sales strategies, and the like." [41]

How The FMLA Applies To Applicants And Former Employees.

Since the FMLA, on its face, only gives the right to sue to employees, virtually all FMLA lawsuits are brought by individuals who worked for an employer at the time they were allegedly denied rights protected by the FMLA.[42] In rare cases, however, even applicants for employment can bring an FMLA claim. This fairly unusual situation arises under a DOL regulation that prohibits employers from using FMLA leave as a negative factor "in employment actions such as hiring, promotions or disciplinary actions * * *" [43] Under these regulations, a prospective employee may have a claim if she can show that the employer refused to hire her because of her previous record of using FMLA leave, either with the same or a different employer.[44]

Otherwise, to be eligible under the FMLA, the employee's request for FMLA leave must occur during the individual's period of employment. For example, in one case a physician was terminated for falling asleep during surgical procedures. Since the surgeon did not seek medical treatment for his sleep apnea until after he was terminated, a court found him not to be covered by the FMLA.[45]

The FMLA Rights Of Federal Employees.

The Statute: 29 U.S.C. §2611(2).

(B) Exclusions

The term "eligible employee" does not include -

> (i) any Federal officer or employee covered under subchapter V of chapter 63 of title 5 . . .

Through the interaction of several statutes, most *federal* employees have fewer FMLA rights than other employees. Though the FMLA generally applies to federal employees, the law does not allow most federal employees to file a private lawsuit alleging a violation of the FMLA.[46] Because there is no independent cause of action available to a federal employee for asserting violations of the FMLA, a federal employee can only claim FMLA violations in connection with actions over which the Merit Systems Protection Board – the approximate equivalent of a civil service board – has authority. For example, when a federal employee is suspended for 20 days for abusing sick leave, the employee may contest the suspension if the use of sick leave is authorized under the FMLA.[47]

Federal employees who are fully covered by the FMLA include employees of the Postal Service, the Postal Rate Commission, part-time employees without a regular tour of duty, and temporary employees.[48]

Employees Versus Subcontractors.

Only "employees" are entitled to FMLA leave; subcontractors are not. In determining whether an individual is an employee as opposed to a subcontractor, most courts will apply an "economic realities" test developed under the Fair Labor Standards Act.[49] The "economic realities" test evaluates whether the individual is economically dependent upon the employer or is, instead, in business for herself.[50] Six factors are involved in determining whether an employment relationship exists:

- The permanency of the relationship (*the more permanent the relationship, the more likely the individual is an employee*);[51]

- The degree of skill required for the particular job (*the lower the skill level, the more likely the individual is an employee*);[52]

- The worker's capital investment (*the lack of a capital investment indicates an employment relationship*);[53]

- The opportunity for profit or loss (*the more this opportunity exists, the less likely the individual is to be an employee*);[54]

- The employer's right to control the individual (*the greater the right to control the work of the individual is, the more likely the individual will be an employee*); [55]

- Whether the worker was an integral part of the employer's business (*the more integral to the employer's business the worker is, the more likely the individual is an employee*).[56]

NOTES

[1] 29 C.F.R. §825.110(a).

[2] *Smith v. Hinkle Manufacturing, Inc.*, 6 WH Cas.2d 1429 (N.D.Ohio 2000); *Coleman v. Prudential Relocation*, 975 F.Supp. 234 (W.D.N.Y. 1997).

[3] *Stewart v. Intem, Inc.*, 141 Lab.Cas. ¶34,137 (D.Or. 2000).

[4] 29 C.F.R. §825.110(b).

[5] 29 C.F.R. §825.110(b).

[6] *Sewall v. Chicago Transit Authority*, 142 Lab.Cas. ¶34,200 (N.D.Ill. 2001); *Butler v. Owens-Brockaway Plastic Products, Inc.*, 199 F.3d 314 (6th Cir. 1999); *Nave v. Woolridge Construction*, 1997 WL 379174 (E.D.Pa. 1997); *Delgado v. Solopak Pharmaceuticals, Inc.*, 4 WH Cas.2d 1179 (N.D.Ill. 1997).

[7] 29 C.F.R. §825.110(d).

[8] *Walker v. Elmore County Board of Education*, 2002 WL 31162921 (M.D.Ala. 2002); *Meyer v. Imperial Trading Co., Inc.*, 153 F.Supp.2d 839 (E.D.La. 2001).

[9] *Bulmer v. Yellow Freight Systems, Inc.*, 213 F.3d 625 (2nd Cir. 2000); *Adams v. Honda of America Mfg., Inc.*, 2002 WL 31159307 (S.D.Ohio 2002); *Morehardt v. Spirit Airlines, Inc.*, 174 F.Supp.2d 1272 (M.D.Fla. 2001); *Pinegar v. Baptist Memorial Hospital – Desoto County*, 1997 WL 560872 (N.D.Miss. 1997); *Blidy v. Examination Management Services, Inc.*, 3 WH Cas.2d 989 (N.D.Ill. 1996); *Ilhardt v. Sara Lee Corporation*, 1996 WL 535236 (N.D.Ill. 1996).

[10] *Opinion Letter,* Wage and Hour Division, 1996 WL 1044775 (February 14, 1996).

[11] 29 U.S.C. §207(e)(2); *see Koontz v. USX Corporation*, 7 WH Cas.2d 425 (E.D.Pa. 2001); *Nelson v. City of Cranston*, 116 F.Supp.2d 260 (D.R.I. 2000); *Opinion Letter*, Wage and Hour Division, 1994 WL 1016754 (October 14, 1994).

[12] *Aldrich v. Greg*, 200 F.Supp.2d 784 (N.D.Ohio 2002); *Koontz v. USX Corporation*, 7 WH Cas.2d 425 (E.D.Pa. 2001); *McConnell v. State Farm Mutual Insurance Co.*, 61 F.Supp.2d 356 (D.N.J. 1999); *Clark v. Allegheny University Hospital*, 1998 WL 94803 (E.D.Pa. 1998); *Robbins v. Bureau of National Affairs*, 896 F.Supp. 18 (D.D.C. 1995). *See also Caruthers v. Proctor & Gamble Mfg. Co.*, 961 F.Supp. 1484 (D.Kan. 1997). *See generally* W. Aitchison, *The Fair Labor Standards Act – A User's Manual* (3rd Ed.)(Labor Relations Information System, 2002).

[13] *Ruder v. Maine General Medical Center,* 204 F.Supp.2d 16 (D.Me. 2002).

[14] *Plumley v. Southern Container, Inc.,* 303 F.3d 364 (1st Cir, 2002).

[15] *Opinion Letter,* Wage and Hour Division, 1995 WL 1036741 (August 23, 1995).

[16] *Kosakow v. New Rochelle Radiology Associates*, 274 F.3d 706 (2nd Cir. 2001); *MacSuga v. County of Spokane*, 983 P.2d 1167 (Wash.App. 1999).

[17] *Robinson-Scott v. Delta Air Lines*, 4 F.Supp.2d 1183 (N.D.Ga. 1998).

[18] 29 C.F.R. §825.110(d).

[19] 29 C.F.R. §825.110(d).

[20] 29 C.F.R. §825.110(d); *see Rockwell v. Mack Trucks*, 8 F.Supp.2d 499 (D.Md. 1998).

[21] *See generally Dorricott v. Fairhill Center for Aging*, 187 F.3d 635 (6th Cir. 1999); *Hansboro v. Clayton*, 172 F.3d 53 (7th Cir. 1999); *Simmons v. New York City Transit Authority*, 144 Lab.Cas. ¶984905 (E.D.N.Y. 2001); *Briody v. American General Finance Co.*, 5 WH Cas.2d 1146 (E.D.Pa. 1999); *Lambeth v. Edison Chouest Offshore, Inc.*, 1999 WL 679672 (E.D.La. 1999); *Brown v. Daimler Chrysler Corporation*, 1999 WL 766021 (N.D.Tex. 1999).

[22] *Opinion Letter*, Wage and Hour Division, 2000 WL 33157366 (September 11, 2000).

[23] 29 C.F.R. §825.110(d).

[24] *Woodford v. Community Action of Greene County*, 268 F.3d 51 (2nd Cir. 2001); *Evanoff v. Minneapolis Public Schools, Special School District No. 1*, 2001 WL 379017 (8th Cir. 2001); *Brungart v. BellSouth Telecomm., Inc.*, 231 F.3d 791 (11th Cir. 2000); *Dormeyer v. Comerica Bank-Illinois*, 223 F.3d 579 (7th Cir. 2000); *Caraballo v. Puerto Rico Telephone, Inc.*, 178 F.Supp.2d 60 (D.P.R. 2001); *Alexander v. Ford Motor Company*, 204 F.R.D. 314 (E.D.Mich. 2001); *Scheidecker v. Arvig Enterprises, Inc.*, 122 F.Supp.2d 1031 (D.Minn. 2000); *McQuain v. Ebner Furnaces, Inc.*, 55 F.Supp.2d 763 (N.D.Ohio 1999); *Wolke v. Dreadnought Marine, Inc.*, 954 F.Supp. 1133 (E.D.Va. 1997); *Seaman v. Downtown Partnership of Baltimore, Inc.*, 991 F.Supp. 751 (D.Md. 1998); *see Schlett v. Avco Financial Services, Inc.*, 950 F.Supp. 823 (N.D.Ohio 1996). *But see Miller v. Defiance Metal Prods., Inc.*, 989 F.Supp. 945 (N.D.Ohio 1997). Several courts, without considering the retroactivity of Section §825.110(d), refused to apply the regulation retroactively. *Thoele v. United States Postal Service*, 996 F.Supp. 818 (N.D.Ill. 1998); *Bauer v. Varity Dayton-Walther Corp.*, 118 F.3d 1109 (6th Cir.1997); *Schlett v. Avco Fin. Serv., Inc.*, 950 F.Supp. 823 (N.D.Ohio 1996); *Robbins v. Bureau of Nat'l Affairs, Inc.*, 896 F.Supp. 18 (D.D.C. 1995).

[25] *Woodford v. Community Action of Greene County, Inc.*, 2001 WL 1191393 (2nd Cir. 2001).

[26] *Bakery and Confectionery Union v. Ralph's Grocery Co.*, 118 F.3d 1018 (4th Cir. 1997).

[27] *Heckler v. Community Health Serv.*, 467 U.S. 51 (1984).

[28] *Rocha v. Sauder Woodworking Co.*, 2002 WL 31084620 (N.D.Ohio 2002).

[29] *Lissmann v. Hartford Fire Ins. Co.*, 848 F.2d 50 (4th Cir. 1988).

[30] *E.g., Clark v. Resistoflex Co.*, 854 F.2d 762 (5th Cir. 1988).

[31] *E.g., Richardson v. Frank*, 975 F.2d 1433 (10th Cir. 1991).

[32] *Blankenship v. Buchanan General Hosp.*, 999 F.Supp. 832 (W.D.Va. 1998); *see Dirham v. Van Wert County Hospital*, 6 WH Cas.2d 1526 (N.D.Ohio 2000); *Kruse v. LaGuardia Hospital*, 1996 WL 1057147 (E.D.N.Y. 1996); *cf. Marsdem v. Review*

Board of the Indiana Department of Workforce Development, 654 N.E.2d 907 (Ind.App. 1995)(no proof that employer actually approved leave, so no estoppel).

33 *Woodford v. Community Action of Greene County, Inc.*, 2001 WL 1191393 (2nd Cir. 2001). *See Kosakow v. New Rochelle Radiology Associates*, 274 F.3d 706 (2nd Cir. 2001); *Dormeyer v. Comerica Bank-Illinois,* 223 F.3d 579 (7th Cir. 2000).

34 *Paleologos v. Rehab Consultants, Inc.*, 990 F.Supp. 1460 (N.D.Ga. 1998); *see Opinion Letter*, Wage and Hour Division, 1994 WL 1016758 (November 23, 1994); Note, *The Family And Medical Leave Act Of 1993: A Progress Report*, Brandeis Journal of Family Law (Winter 1997-1998).

35 *Coen v. Sybron Dental Specialties*, 2001 WL 45478 (6th Cir. 2001); *Douglas v. E.G. Baldwin & Associates, Inc.*, 150 F.3d 604 (6th Cir. 1998); *Gazda v. Pioneer Chlor Alkali Co., Inc.*, 10 F.Supp.2d 656 (S.D.Tex. 1997); *Muller v. Hotsy Corporation*, 917 F.Supp. 1389 (N.D.Iowa 1996).

36 29 C.F.R. §825.110(f); 29 C.F.R. §825.111(c).

37 29 C.F.R. §825.111(b).

38 29 C.F.R. §825.111(a)(3).

39 29 C.F.R. §825.110(f).

40 29 C.F.R. §825.111(a)(2).

41 *Cialini v. Nilfisk-Advance America, Inc.*, 2000 WL 230215 (E.D.Pa. 2000), *quoting Ciarlante v. Brown & Williamson Tobacco Corp.*, 143 F.3d 139 (3rd Cir. 1998); *see Harvell v. North Carolina Association of Educators, Inc.*, 510 S.E.2d 403 (N.C.App. 1999); *Opinion Letter*, Wage and Hour Division 1993 WL 939399 (October 27, 1993).

42 *Wenzlaff v. Nationsbank*, 940 F.Supp. 889 (D.Md. 1996).

43 29 C.F.R. §825.220(c).

44 *Smith v. Bellsouth Telecommunications, Inc.*, 273 F.3d 1303 (11th Cir. 2001); *Duckworth v. Pratt & Whitney, Inc.*, 152 F.3d 1 (1st Cir. 1998); *see Passer v. Am. Chem. Society,* 935 F.2d 322 (D.C.Cir. 1991)(decided under ADEA); *Dunlop v. Carriage Carpet Co.*, 548 F.2d 139 (6th Cir. 1977)(decided under FLSA); *NLRB v. George D. Auchter Co.,* 209 F.2d 273 (5th Cir. 1954)(decided under NLRA).

45 *Brohm v. JH Properties, Inc.*, 149 F.3d 517 (6th Cir. 1998); *see Klaus v. Builders Concrete Co.,* 7 WH Cas.2d 1089 (N.D.Ill. 2002).

46 5 U.S.C. §§6381-6387; *see Mann v. Haigh,* 120 F.3d 34 (4th Cir. 1997); *Bogumill v. Office of Personnel Management*, 168 F.3d 1320 (Fed. Cir. 1998); *Weesner v. Glickman*, 59 F.Supp.2d 783 (N.D.Ind. 1999); *Keen v. Brown*, 958 F.Supp. 70 (D.Conn. 1997); *Sutherland v. Bowles*, 2 WH Cas.2d 1336 (E.D.Mich. 1995).

47 *See Fairley v. United States Postal Service*, 82 M.S.P.R. 588 (MSPB 1999); *Gardner v. United States Postal Service*, 79 M.S.P.R. 9 (MSPB 1998); *Gross v. Department of Justice,* 77 M.S.P.R. 83 (MSPB 1997).

48 29 C.F.R. § 825.109; *Baber v. Runyon*, 5 WH Cas.2d 111 (S.D.N.Y. 1998).

[49] *Bonnetts v. Arctic Express, Inc.*, 7 F.Supp.2d 977 (S.D.Ohio 1998); *see Opinion Letter*, Wage and Hour Division, 1994 WL 1016749 (August 8, 1994).

[50] *Lilley v. BTM Corp.*, 958 F.2d 746 (6th Cir. 1992).

[51] *Bonnetts v. Arctic Express, Inc.*, 7 F.Supp.2d 977 (S.D.Ohio 1998).

[52] *Dole v. Snell*, 875 F.2d 802 (10th Cir. 1989).

[53] *Sec'y of Labor, United States Dept. of Labor v. Lauritzen*, 835 F.2d 1529 (7th Cir. 1987).

[54] *Rutherford Food Corp. v. McComb*, 331 U.S. 722 (1947).

[55] *Sec'y of Labor, United States Dept. of Labor v. Lauritzen*, 835 F.2d 1529 (7th Cir. 1987).

[56] *Martin v. Selker Brothers, Inc.*, 949 F.2d 1286 (3rd Cir. 1991); *Donovan v. Brandel*, 736 F.2d 1114 (6th Cir. 1984).

CHAPTER 4

BIRTH, ADOPTION, AND FOSTER CARE

In A Nutshell . . .

An employee is entitled to 12 weeks of leave in conjunction with the birth or adoption of a child. If the mother and father work for the same employer, the combination of the mother and father is entitled to 12 weeks of FMLA rather than each receiving the full allotment of leave.

The Birth Of A Child Or The Placement Of A Child With The Employee For Adoption Or Foster Care.

The Statute: 29 U.S.C. §2612(a).

(a) In general

(1) Entitlement to leave

Subject to section 2613 of this title, an eligible employee shall be entitled to a total of 12 workweeks of leave during any 12-month period for one or more of the following:

(A) Because of the birth of a son or daughter of the employee and in order to care for such son or daughter.

(B) Because of the placement of a son or daughter with the employee for adoption or foster care.

(2) Expiration of entitlement

The entitlement to leave under subparagraphs (A) and (B) of paragraph (1) for a birth or placement of a son or daughter shall expire at the end of the 12-month period beginning on the date of such birth or placement.

Section 2612(a) of the FMLA allows an employee to use all or part of his or her FMLA leave allotment to care for the birth of a child or because of the placement of a child with the employee for adoption or foster care. A father as well as a mother is entitled to take leave for such purposes.[1] Multiple births, either at the same time or within the same 12-month period, do not gain an employee additional FMLA eligibility.[2]

While the DOL's regulations mercifully refrain from defining "birth" or "adoption," they do indicate "foster care is 24-hour care for children in substitution for, and away from, their parents or guardian. Such placement is made by or with the agreement of the State as a result of a voluntary agreement between the parent or guardian that the child be removed from the home, or pursuant to a judicial determination of the necessity for foster care, and involves agreement between the State and foster family that the foster family will take care of the child."[3]

In some cases, the FMLA leave can begin before the birth of a child or the placement for adoption or foster care. For example, an expectant mother could take leave prior to the birth of her child either for prenatal care or if her condition made her unable to work.[4] Similarly, if an employee seeking adoption or foster care is required to attend counseling sessions, appear in court, meet with her attorneys, submit to a physical examination, or attend to similar requirements before the placement of the child occurs, she would be entitled to FMLA leave.[5] However, if an employee simply wants to work a part-day schedule prior to giving birth in the absence of a medical reason compelling the schedule, the FMLA does not grant her the right to the modified schedule.[6]

The entitlement to FMLA leave for a birth or placement for adoption or foster care expires at the end of the 12-month period beginning on the date of the birth or placement. FMLA leave for such purposes must be concluded within the one-year period.[7] These time frames are rigid. In one example, in 1992 an employee adopted his brother's children who lived in the Philippines. Almost three years later, the employee petitioned for FMLA leave to travel to the Philippines to bring the children to the United States. A court upheld the denial of the leave, observing: "While we recognize the importance of child-parent bonding and of a parent's presence in early child rearing, we cannot read the Act to extend 'placement for adoption' to encompass [the employee's] situation."[8] Additionally, if a baby is still-born, FMLA leave must end shortly after the birth unless the employee also qualifies as having a serious health condition.[9]

Some employees accept responsibility for the care of multiple foster children. In such cases, the placement of each new child with the employee for foster care is a separate FMLA-qualifying event.[10]

In an unusual case, a court ruled that it would be possible for an employee to take FMLA leave in conjunction with the adoption of his own child. The employee had learned that a child welfare agency was preparing to take an eleven-year-old girl into custody who was born to another couple. The employee had reason to believe that he was the father of the girl, however, and missed four days of work while attending to the matter. Though the court was chary of turning FMLA into a tool that could be used in routine child-custody disputes, it nevertheless found that FMLA rights could apply in such a situation:

> "It will indeed be unusual to encounter a situation in which a biological parent takes a leave from work in order to adopt or take into foster care his own child. This situation may be rare, but [the employee] has proven that it is not entirely impossible. In a case such as this in which a biological parent has no custodial rights over a child and is not listed as the child's parent as a matter of record, it may be possible for that parent to adopt his own child. Thus, regardless of whether he was the biological father, Kelley could state a claim under the FMLA."[11]

Leave Standards Where A Husband And Wife Work For The Same Employer.

The Statute: 29 U.S.C. §2612(f)

In any case in which a husband and wife entitled to leave under subsection (a) of this section are employed by the same employer, the aggregate number of workweeks of leave to which both may be entitled may be limited to 12 workweeks during any 12-month period, if such leave is taken -

(1) under subparagraph (A) or (B) of subsection (a)(1) of this section * * *.

(2) to care for a sick parent under subparagraph (C) of such subsection.

Husbands and wives working for the same employer are each entitled to the full 12-week allotment of leave for their own health condition or because of the serious health condition of their spouse, son, or daughter. However, if the leave is used for the birth of a child or to care for a sick parent, the combination of husband and wife is entitled to 12 weeks of leave.

Section 2612(f) of the FMLA treats husbands and wives working for the same employer differently, depending upon the type of FMLA leave used. If a wife and husband use FMLA leave because of their own serious health condition, or because of the serious health condition of their spouse, son, or daughter, *each* spouse is entitled to the full 12-week allotment.[12] However, if the FMLA leave is used because of the birth or adoption of a child or to care for a sick parent, the *combination* of husband and wife are entitled to 12 weeks of leave rather than *each* being entitled to 12 weeks of leave. This limitation applies even if the spouses work at different worksites or at two different operating divisions of the same company.[13] When the wife and husband both use a portion of the total FMLA leave entitlement for these purposes, each are entitled to the difference between the amount each has taken individually and the weeks for FMLA leave eligibility remaining for other FMLA purposes. For example, a husband took two weeks of FMLA leave to care for a healthy, newborn child; he could use another ten weeks due to his own serious health condition.[14] These rules apply only to spouses, and not to siblings working for the same employer who are required to care for a seriously ill parent.[15]

The FMLA does not forbid a husband and wife from using FMLA simultaneously. In some states, however, family leave laws contain such prohibitions that would only apply to leave not covered by the FMLA.[16]

Intermittent Leave In Connection With Birth, Adoption, Or Foster Care.

The Statute: 29 U.S.C. §2612(b).

(b) Leave taken intermittently or on reduced leave schedule

(1) In general

Leave under subparagraph (A) or (B) of subsection (a)(1) of this section shall not be taken by an employee intermittently or on a reduced leave schedule unless the employee and the employer of the employee agree otherwise...The taking of leave intermittently or on a reduced leave schedule pursuant to this paragraph shall not result in a reduction in the total amount of leave to which the employee is entitled under subsection (a) of this section beyond the amount of leave actually taken...

As discussed in Chapter 8, in some circumstances FMLA leave need not be taken as a single block of time, but instead can be taken on an "intermittent" or a "reduced leave" basis. An exception to the FMLA's rules on intermittent leave exists with respect to leave taken for the birth of a child or for the placement of a child with the employee for adoption or foster care. In such cases, the FMLA requires the employer's agreement before the employee can use intermittent leave.[17] The employer's agreement is not required, however, if the mother has a serious health condition associated with the birth of her child or if the newborn child has a serious health condition.[18]

NOTES

1 29 C.F.R. §825.112(b).

2 *Opinion Letter*, Wage and Hour Division, 1994 WL 1016753 (October 14, 1994).

3 29 C.F.R. §825.112(e).

4 29 C.F.R. §825.112(c).

5 29 C.F.R. §825.112(d).

6 *Gudenkauf v. Stauffer Communications, Inc.*, 922 F.Supp. 465 (D.Kan. 1996); *see Burnette v. Vanguard Plastics*, 3 WH Cas.2d 1487 (D.Kan. 1996).

7 29 C.F.R. §825.201.

8 *Bocalbos v. National Western Life Insurance Co.*, 162 F.3d 379 (5th Cir. 1998).

9 *Szabo v. Trustees of Boston University*, 181 F.3d 80 (1st Cir. 1998).

10 *Opinion Letter*, Wage and Hour Division, 1996 WL 1044781 (October 25, 1996).

11 *Kelley v. Crosfield Catalysts*, 135 F.3d 1202 (7th Cir. 1998).

12 *Opinion Letter*, Wage and Hour Division, 1994 WL 1016750 (August 23, 1994).

13 29 C.F.R. §825.202(b); *Opinion Letter*, Wage and Hour Division, 1994 WL 1016751 (August 24, 1994).

14 29 C.F.R. §825.202(c).

15 *Opinion Letter*, Wage and Hour Division, 1999 WL 1002429 (January 12, 1999).

16 Alaska Statutes 23.10.500.

17 29 U.S.C. §2612(b).

18 29 C.F.R. §825.203(b).

CHAPTER 5

SERIOUS HEALTH CONDITION

In A Nutshell . . .

A serious health condition is one requiring inpatient treatment or one involving:

(1) Periods of incapacity of more than three consecutive calendar days,

(2) Any period of incapacity due to pregnancy or for prenatal care,

(3) Any period of incapacity or treatment for such incapacity that is due to a "chronic serious health condition,"

(4) A permanent or long-term period of incapacity due to a condition for which treatment may not be effective, or any period of absence to receive multiple treatments either for restorative surgery after an accident or for a condition that would likely result in a period of incapacity of more than three consecutive calendar days if medical treatment were not received. There is a significant debate as to when minor conditions such as influenza qualify under these standards.

What Is A Serious Health Condition?

The Statute: 29 U.S.C. §2611(11)

The term "serious health condition" means an illness, injury, impairment, or physical or mental condition that involves -

(A) inpatient care in a hospital, hospice, or residential medical care facility; or

(B) continuing treatment by a health care provider.

The FMLA grants employees the right to take leave for "serious health conditions." Congress intended there to be a broad definition of the term "serious health condition."[1] Under the FMLA, for a condition to qualify for protection it must be an illness, injury, impairment, or physical or mental condition that involves <u>either</u> (1) inpatient care in a hospital, hospice, or residential medical care facility, <u>or</u> (2) continuing treatment by a health care provider.[2] Beyond these simple definitions, the FMLA itself is silent about what constitutes a serious health condition.

When the FMLA was being considered in Congress, there was a good deal of discussion about what constituted a "serious health condition." It is clear that Congress did not intend the phrase to include minor illness, which it believed was more appropriately addressed through an employer's sick leave policies.[3] Congress gave the following examples of what it did consider to be serious health conditions:

> "Examples of serious health conditions include but are not limited to heart attacks, heart conditions requiring heart bypass of valve operations, most cancers, back conditions requiring extensive therapy or surgical procedures, strokes, severe respiratory conditions, spinal injuries, appendicitis, pneumonia, emphysema, severe arthritis, severe nervous disorders, injuries caused by serious accidents on or off the job, ongoing pregnancy, miscarriages, complications or illnesses related to pregnancy, such as severe morning sickness, the need for prenatal care, childbirth and recovery from childbirth. All of these conditions meet the general test that either the underlying health condition or the treatment for it requires that the employee be absent from work on a recurring basis or for more than a few days for treatment or recovery. They also involve either inpatient care or continuing treatment or supervision by a health care provider, and frequently involve both."[4]

The sparseness of the FMLA and questions raised by many Congressional examples as to what qualified as a "serious health condition" left much work for DOL in the writing of its regulations. The DOL's regulations concerning the first type of serious health condition – one requiring inpatient treatment – do indeed furnish a good deal of guidance. The regulations indicate that for a condition to qualify under the "inpatient care" provision of the FMLA, an overnight stay is required in a hospital, hospice, or residential medical care facility.[5] The DOL has defined "inpatient care" as including any period of incapacity or any subsequent treatment associated with the actual inpatient care. The DOL has defined "incapacity" as the inability to work, attend school or perform other regular daily activities due to a serious health condition.[6]

One kind of serious health condition involves inpatient treatment, and any incapacity or treatment in connection with inpatient treatment.

The more complicated question of what constitutes a serious health condition under the "continuing treatment" portion of the law led to the DOL writing lengthy regulations on the issue. A fair amount of the regulations deal with the definition of the term "health care provider." This is a significant definition since the portion of FMLA that deals with "continuing treatment" requires treatment by a health care provider. When DOL issued its draft regulations in advance of finalizing them, there was considerable debate about the DOL's proposed definition of "health care provider." Many employers commenting on the DOL's proposed definition of "health care provider" reflected a belief that the DOL's proposed definition was too broad. On the other hand, many purveyors of health care services objected to the proposed definition, finding it too narrow because it excluded their particular service.[7]

In the end, the DOL's regulations took a fairly conservative stance — under the final regulations, a "health care provider" is a person falling in one of the following six categories:

- A **doctor of medicine or osteopathy** who is authorized to practice medicine or surgery by the State in which he/she practices;
- **Podiatrists, dentists, clinical psychologists, optometrists, and chiropractors** authorized to practice in the State and performing within the scope of their practice as defined under State law;[8]
- **Nurse practitioners, nurse-midwives, and clinical social workers** who are authorized to practice under State law and who are performing within the scope of their practice as defined under State law;
- **Christian Science practitioners** listed with the First Church of Christ, Scientist in Boston, Massachusetts;
- Any health care provider from whom an employer or a group health plan's benefits manager **will accept certification** of the existence of a serious health condition to substantiate a claim for benefits;[9]
- A health care provider as defined above who practices **in a country other than the United States**, who is licensed to practice in accordance with the laws and regulations of that country.[10]

The DOL's regulations envision another type of health care professional – a "provider of health care services." Though the phrase "provider of health care services" is not defined in the DOL's regulations, the context in which the term is used in the regulations suggests that it includes individuals such as nurses, physician assistants, and physical therapists. So long as the treatment furnished by a "provider of health care services" is done at the direction or referral of a "health care provider," the services would fall under the "continuing treatment" portion of the law.

With these definitions fixed firmly in mind, the regulations describe five possible categories of serious health conditions involving continuing treatment:

The first kind of serious health condition involves incapacity for more than three consecutive days and includes treatment by a health care provider.

1. **Periods of incapacity of more than three consecutive calendar days** – where "incapacity" is defined again as the inability to work, attend school, or perform other daily activities. Such periods, as well as subsequent treatment relating to the same condition, include either (A) treatment two or more times by a "health care provider" or by "providers of health care services" under the orders of or by referral of a health care provider; or (B) treatment by a health care provider on at least one occasion which results in a "regimen of continuing treatment" under the supervision of the health care provider.[11]

The same health care provider need not provide all of the treatment for the minimum treatment requirements to be met, but some health care provider must be involved.[12] An employee's own assessment of his/her condition will not satisfy FMLA requirements.[13] The requirement that the incapacity be for more than three days has been mistakenly construed by one court to mean that the incapacity must last at least four days;[14] a better reading would allow part-day absences to qualify, so that three days of incapacity plus a partial fourth day for treatment would qualify for FMLA protection.[15]

A regimen of continuing treatment may include a course of prescription medicine or therapy requiring "special equipment" to alleviate the health condition. Simply taking over-the-counter medications, bed rest, drinking fluids, exercise, and similar activities that can be undertaken without the supervision of a health care provider do not, in and of themselves, constitute a regimen of continuing treatment for the purposes of the FMLA.[16] Excluded from the definition are routine physical examinations, eye exams or dental exams.[17] Cosmetic treatments are ordinarily not considered serious health conditions unless inpatient hospital care is required or complications develop.

A second type of serious health condition involves incapacity resulting from pregnancy or prenatal care, regardless of duration, and regardless of whether treatment is involved.

2. Any period of incapacity due to **pregnancy or for prenatal care**.[18] Absences from work in this category qualify for FMLA leave even though the individual does not receive treatment from a health care provider during the absence, and even if the absence does not last more than three days.[19] As one court has observed, "pregnancy is recognized as a special case that is treated differently from other serious health conditions throughout the DOL's regulations."[20]

A third type of serious health condition is a chronic condition continuing over an extended period of time featuring recurring episodes that requires periodic visits by a health care provider.

3. Any period of incapacity or treatment for such incapacity that is due to a "**chronic serious health condition**." A chronic serious health condition is one that meets two requirements: (A) It must require periodic visits by a health care provider or a nurse or physician's assistant under the direct supervision of a health care provider;[21] and (B) it must continue over an extended period of time, including recurring episodes associated with a single underlying condition. A chronic serious health condition may involve episodic rather than continuing incapacity,

e.g., asthma attacks.[22] Absences from work falling into this category qualify for FMLA leave even though the individual does not receive treatment from a health care provider during the absence and even though the absence does not last more than three days.[23]

4. A permanent or long-term period of incapacity due to **a condition for which treatment may not be effective**. In such cases, the individual must be under the continuing supervision of a health care provider but need not be receiving active treatment. The DOL's examples of such conditions include Alzheimer's disease, a severe stroke, or the terminal stages of a disease.[24]

The fourth type of serious health condition involves permanent or long-term incapacity due to a condition for which treatment may not be effective.

5. Any period of absence to receive **multiple treatments** either for restorative surgery after an accident or for a condition that would likely result in a period of incapacity of more than three consecutive calendar days if medical treatment were not received. The DOL's examples of treatments falling into the latter category include dialysis for kidney disease, various treatments such as chemotherapy for cancer, and physical therapy for arthritis.[25]

Applying these regulations, courts have developed what they refer to as a "bright line" test for determining what illnesses qualify as a serious health condition. Under the test, "if an employee is (1) incapacitated for more than three days, (2) seen once by a doctor, and (3) prescribed a course of medication, such as an antibiotic, he/she has a serious health condition worthy of FMLA protection."[26]

The fifth type of serious health condition involves the need for multiple treatments, either for restorative surgery after an accident or for a condition that would result in incapacity of three or more days if treatment were not received.

The DOL's regulations also contain specific inclusions in and exclusions from the definition of treatment for a serious health condition.[27] Included are examinations to determine if a serious health condition exists and evaluations of the condition.[28] Allergies, restorative dental or plastic surgery after an injury or removal of cancerous growths, and mental illness resulting from stress can be serious health conditions if they otherwise qualify under one of the five sections of the definition.[29] Substance abuse may be a serious health condition. However, FMLA leave may only be taken for treatment for substance abuse; absence because of the employee's use of the substance, rather than for treatment, does not qualify for FMLA leave.[30]

Incapacity – The Heart Of An FMLA Claim For A Serious Health Condition.

At the core of any claim for FMLA leave for a serious health condition is evidence of incapacity.[31] Where the claimed incapacity relates to the job, the incapacity requirement usually means that the employee must be unable to perform the essential functions of the job – in the words of one court, the employee must show that her "health condition was so serious that she was unable to perform the functions of her position."[32] Thus, where an employee's medical certification indicates an incapacity to perform work over a specific period of time, *but* where the employee actually reports for work and performs the essential functions of the job for one or more days during that period, in all likelihood the employee's claim that she was incapacitated during the period will be denied (absent evidence of an intermittent, chronic condition).[33] It is also possible, however, that an inability to perform the job, and thus the employee's incapacity, may be attributable to the need to obtain medical treatment or diagnosis.[34]

However, it is also possible that when the employee is claiming FMLA leave because of his own serious health condition, the employee need not necessarily prove that he is unable to perform the essential functions of the job. The DOL's regulations, which define incapacity as the "inability to work, attend school, <u>or</u> perform other regular daily activities," seems to clearly indicate that the inability to perform the job is <u>one</u> indicator of incapacity, but not the <u>only</u> indicator.[35] Thus, a court found that an employee who suffered a miscarriage and attendant emotional shock could still claim she was incapacitated by the impact of her condition on the remainder of her life despite the fact that she could perform the essential functions of the job.

Some courts appear to be wrongly requiring employees to show an even greater degree of debility than simply being unable to perform the essential functions of the job. In the words of one court, an employee must prove an "inability to perform routine daily activities on those days he was absent or unable to work" to prove that he was incapacitated.[36] Courts taking this approach require employees to demonstrate an inability to perform such basic functions as caring for themselves, eating, drinking, engaging in sexual relations, and the like.[37] Such courts have not considered that this more restrictive view seems to be clearly contradictory to the DOL's regulations.

Serious Health Conditions – What Qualifies And What Does Not?

The first of the two following tables summarizes the findings of courts that certain conditions either qualify or potentially qualify for FMLA leave. The second table summarizes the findings of courts that certain conditions *do not* qualify for FMLA leave. In some cases, the same medical conditions appear in both tables, with the different results in the cases generally attributable to the impact of the condition on the employee's ability to perform the essential functions of the job with the condition.

CONDITIONS QUALIFYING AS SERIOUS HEALTH CONDITIONS

Condition	Citation	Description
Anxiety	*Beckendorff v. Schwegmann Giant Super Markets, Inc.*, 4 WH Cas.2d 315 (E.D.La. 1997).	Condition was coupled with hypertension.
Asthma	*Oleson v. K-Mart Corporation*, 1996 WL 772604 (D.Kan. 1996).	Employee passed out from effects of bronchitic asthma.
Back Condition	*Kaylor v. Fannin Reg'l Hosp.*, 946 F.Supp. 988 (N.D.Ga. 1996).	Degenerative back condition.
Back Condition	*Mann v. Mass. Correa Electric, J.V.*, 7 WH Cas.2d 1045 (S.D.N.Y. 2002).	Lumbosacral strain which required bed rest.
Back Condition	*Slaughter v. American Building Maintenance Co. of New York*, 64 F.Supp.2d 319 (S.D.N.Y. 1999).[38]	Back injury with lumbar strain.
Cancer	*Sharpe v. MCI Telecommunications Corp.*, 83 F.Supp.2d 754 (E.D.N.C. 1998).	Employee's mother was diagnosed with terminal cancer.
Chicken Pox	*Reich v. Midwest Plastic Engineering, Inc.*, 66 Empl. Prac. Dec. ¶43,701 (W.D.Mich. 1995).	Employee was treated by a physician on three separate occasions; on one occasion, employee was admitted for an overnight hospital stay.

Condition	Citation	Description
Chicken Pox	*George v. Associated Stationers,* 932 F.Supp. 1012 (N.D.Ohio 1996).	Employee's doctor instructed him not to work for a week. Court comments "it is difficult . . . to understand why [the employer] would have wanted someone with chicken pox to report for work and expose his fellow employees to such a contagious disease."
Cold and Fever	*Brannon v. Oshkosh B'Gosh, Inc.,* 897 F.Supp. 1028 (M.D.Tenn. 1995).	A child's cold and fever, which resulted in a doctor advising that she remain out of day care for more than three consecutive days.
Colectomy	*Smallberger v. Federal Realty Investment Trust,* 5 WH Cas.2d 989 (E.D.Pa. 1999).	Surgery followed by several weeks of recuperation.
Cytomegalovirus	*Goodwin-Haulmark v. Menninger Clinic, Inc.,* 76 F.Supp.2d 1235 (D.Kan. 1999).	Condition is similar to mononucleosis and is caused by stress.
Depression	*Cooper v. Olin Corporation, Winchester Division,* 246 F.3d 1083 (8th Cir. 2001).	Employee was a locomotive driver.
Depression, Migraine Headaches & Alcoholism	*Routes v. Henderson,* 58 F.Supp.2d 959 (S.D.Ind. 1999).	Conditions required inpatient hospital treatment.
Depression	*Young v. United States Postal Service,* 79 M.S.P.R. 25 (MSPB 1998).[39]	Condition caused incapacity and was accompanied by treatment and prescription medicine.

Condition	Citation	Description
Ear Infection	*Caldwell v. Holland of Texas, Inc.*, 208 F.3d 671 (8th Cir. 2000).	Condition incapacitated three-year-old child; whether day care center would allow child with similar condition to attend relevant in determining incapacity.
Emotional Condition	*Vasconcellos v. Cybex Intern, Inc.*, 962 F.Supp. 701 (D.Md. 1997).	Shock, tremors, panic attacks, rapid heartbeat and heart palpitations, severe chest pain, inability to breathe, fright, nervousness, hypervigilence, jumpiness, crying spells, fatigue, gastrointestinal distress, stomach upset, nausea, insomnia, and flashbacks.
Epilepsy	*Moreno v. American Ingredients Co.*, 6 WH Cas.2d 62 (D.Kan. 2000).	Employee lost consciousness, became dizzy, disoriented, and weak for several hours after epileptic episodes.
Fainting Spell	*D'Amico v. Compass Group USA, Inc.,* 198 F.Supp.2d 18 (D.Mass. 2002).	Employee was left unconscious for four hours and was prescribed medication by a doctor.
Fibromyalgia	*Fields v. St. Charles School Board*, 2000 WL 943220 (E.D.La. 2000).	Pain in muscles, tendons, and ligaments that was intermittently disabling.
Heart Attack	*Barrilleaux v. Thayer Lodging Group, Inc.*, 5 WH Cas.2d 601 (E.D.La. 1999).	Recovery from heart attack and double coronary bypass surgery.

Condition	Citation	Description
Hepatitis	*Uema v. Nippon Express Hawaii, Inc.*, 26 F.Supp.2d 1241 (D.Haw. 1998).	Chronic hepatitis and intestinal bleeding.
Hernia	*Sarno v. Douglas Elliman-Gibbons & Ives, Inc.*, 183 F.3d 155 (2nd Cir. 1999).	Hernia with sprained rectus muscle.
Hernia	*Thorson v. Gemini, Inc.*, 205 F.3d 370 (8th Cir. 2001).	Employee's condition, caused by stress, could be treated with antacid.
High Blood Pressure	*Navarro v. Pfizer Corp.*, 261 F.3d 90 (1st Cir. 2001).	Condition associated with pregnancy and required bed rest.
Hypertension	*Oswalt v. Sara Lee Corp.*, 74 F.3d 91 (5th Cir. 1996).	Employee missed work because of side effects of hypertension medicine.
Injuries From Accident	*Ozolins v. Northwood-Kensett Community School District*, 40 F.Supp.2d 1055 (N.D.Iowa 1999).	Employee's elderly mother fell. Though fall resulted in no broken bones, injuries in conjunction with pre-existing condition resulted in period of incapacity.
Keloids	*Sheppard v. Diversified Foods & Seasonings, Inc.*, 1996 WL 54440 (E.D.La. 1996).	Congenital skin condition which eventually required outpatient surgery; condition did not impair performance of essential job functions.
Kidney Failure	*Bryant v. Delbar Products, Inc.*, 18 F.Supp.2d 799 (M.D.Tenn. 1998).	Hospitalization was required for condition.
Knee Injury	*Cormier v. Littlefield*, 13 F.Supp.2d 127 (D.Mass. 1998).	Injury required reconstructive knee surgery.

Condition	Citation	Description
Lumbar Strain	*Williamson v. Mississippi Department of Human Services*, 4 WH Cas.2d 262 (N.D.Miss. 1997).	Employee was briefly hospitalized and provided with an ongoing course of treatment afterwards.
Migraine Headaches	*Hendry v. GTE North, Inc.*, 896 F.Supp. 816 (N.D.Ind. 1995).	Employee received continuing treatment from her doctor for her migraines, and was unable to perform her job when a migraine struck.
Migraine Headaches	*Henderson v. Whirlpool Corp.*, 17 F.Supp.2d 1238 (N.D.Okla. 1998).[40]	No description in opinion of extent or frequency of condition.
Misalignment of Spine	*Legrand v. Village of McCook*, 1998 WL 182462 (N.D.Ill. 1998).	Injuries were treated by chiropractor.
Pharyngitis	*Corcino v. Banco Popular De Puerto Rico*, 200 F.Supp.2d 507 (D.V.I. 2002).	Acute inflammation of the pharynx which caused employee to miss six days of work.
Respiratory Condition	*Meyer v. Imperial Trading Co., Inc.*, 153 F.Supp.2d 839 (E.D.La. 2001).	Condition aggravated by smoke-filled work environment.
Sickle Cell Anemia	*Vincent v. Wells Fargo Guard Services, Inc. of Florida*, 3 F.Supp.2d 1405 (S.D.Fla. 1998).	Condition is chronic and incurable; employee had received ongoing treatment from physicians.
Strep Throat	*Schober v. SMC Pneumatics*, 2000 WL 1231557 (S.D.Ind. 2000).	Care for son after son's hospitalization for severe strep throat.
Ulcer	*Victorelli v. Shadyside Hospital*, 128 F.3d 184 (3rd Cir. 1997).	Employee was under the treatment of a doctor at the time of and after termination.

Condition	Citation	Description
Viral Illness (unspecified)	*Rankin v. Seagate Technologies, Inc.*, 246 F.3d 1145 (8th Cir. 2001).	Employee's affidavit stated that she was "too sick to work"; additionally, employee consulted with nurse practitioner who prescribed medication.

There are a variety of reasons why certain conditions would not qualify as "serious health conditions" under the FMLA. As noted above, the conditions might not be sufficiently incapacitating (for the employee or qualifying relative), though the same condition might incapacitate another individual. In other cases, employees have sought to extend FMLA for conditions that were once incapacitating but have resolved to the point where the employee can perform the essential functions of the job. In yet other circumstances, employees have sought FMLA leave for truly minor conditions never intended to be within the scope of the FMLA.

CONDITIONS NOT QUALIFYING AS SERIOUS HEALTH CONDITIONS		
Condition	**Citation**	**Description**
Alcoholism	*Gilbert v. Star Building Systems*, 1996 WL 931315 (W.D.Okla. 1996).	Employee's husband was a recovering alcoholic who, though he suffered from tremors, was able to care for himself.
Asthma	*Johnson v. Primerica*, 67 Empl. Prac. Dec. ¶43,934 (S.D.N.Y. 1996).	No dispute that an employee's son suffered from acute asthma that had required his hospitalization in the past. However, no showing that during the time period requested for FMLA leave, the boy was acutely ill, undergoing complex therapy, or was unable to attend school.
Back Condition	*Beal v. Rubbermaid Commercial Prods., Inc.*, 972 F.Supp. 1216 (S.D.Iowa 1997).	Back injury; employee could engage in normal activities with only minimal restrictions.

Condition	Citation	Description
Back Condition	*Delaney v. Alamo Workforce Development Council, Inc.*, 2000 WL 294831 (Tex.App. 2000).[41]	Employee did not seek treatment until more than two weeks after his injury; physician immediately released employee for full duty.
Bronchitis	*Beal v. Rubbermaid Commercial Products Inc.*, 972 F.Supp. 1216 (S.D.Iowa 1997).	No period of incapacity.
Bronchitis[42]	*Hott v. VDO Yazaki Corporation*, 922 F.Supp. 1114 (W.D.Va. 1996).	Employee was able to perform essential functions of the job.
Bronchitis	*Cabrera v. Enesco*, 4 WH Cas.2d 1592 (N.D.Ill. 1998).	Note from employee's doctor, submitted after employee was terminated, indicated that employee was not incapacitated.
Carpal Tunnel Syndrome	*Price v. Marathon Cheese Corp.*, 119 F.3d 330 (5th Cir. 1997).	While court acknowledged that condition could be incapacitating, it found employee's "unverified story had all the hallmarks of a post-hoc attempt to make a silk purse out of a sow's ear."
Chipped Tooth	*Flanagan v. Keller Products, Inc.*, 2002 WL 313138 (D.N.H. 2002).	Employee's condition never caused her to miss consecutive days of work.
Colds	*Brannon v. Oshkosh B'Gosh, Inc.*, 897 F.Supp. 1028 (M.D.Tenn. 1995).	A child's recurring but intermittent respiratory infections and sore throats.
Colds	*Gibbs v. American Airlines*, 87 Cal.Rptr.2d 554 (Cal.App. 1999).	Decided under state law equivalent of the FMLA.

Condition	Citation	Description
Ear Infection	*Seidle v. Provident Mutual Life Insurance Company*, 871 F.Supp. 238 (E.D.Pa. 1994).	Child's fever lasted less than 24 hours, treatment consisted of one 20-minute examination by a pediatrician, and child was not absent from day care for more than three days.
Emotional Condition	*Sharpe v. MCI Telecommunications Corp.*, 19 F.Supp.2d 483 (E.D.N.C. 1998).[43]	Employee remained off work after death of mother from cancer.
Emotional Condition	*Martyszenko v. Safeway, Inc.*, 120 F.3d 120 (8th Cir. 1997).	Alleged molestation of child where child showed no apparent psychological disorders.
Eczema	*Beal v. Rubbermaid Commercial Products, Inc.*, 972 F.Supp. 1216 (S.D.Iowa 1997).	Employee never missed more than one day of work with condition.
Fibromyalgia	*Mincey v. Dow Chemical Company*, 217 F.Supp.2d 737 (M.D.La. 2002).	Employee's doctor gave opinion that condition would not prevent her from performing the job.
Flu	*Raymond v. Albertson's Inc.*, 38 F.Supp.2d 866 (D.Nev. 1999).[44]	Employee's daughter had normal vital signs and was treated with over-the-counter medication.
Gastroesophageal Reflux Disease	*Levine v. Children's Museum of Indianapolis*, 2002 WL 1800254 (S.D.Ind. 2002).	No showing of continued treatment by health care provider.
Hematochezia	*Bauer v. Varity Dayton-Walther Corporation*, 118 F.3d 1109 (6th Cir. 1997).	Condition, which involved bloody stools, did not require hospitalization.
Hernia	*Hankins v. Adecco Services of Ohio*, 7 WH Cas.2d 1017 (OhioApp. 2001).	Employee saw doctor only once and was released to full duty the same day.

Condition	Citation	Description
Hypertension	*Austin v. Shelby County Government*, 5 WH Cas.2d 375 (Tenn.App. 1999).	No showing that employee's hypertension prevented the performance of essential functions of the job.
Metatarsalgia	*Reich v. The Standard Register Company*, 1997 WL 375744 (W.D.Va. 1997).	Condition involves arthritis of the feet and legs. Employee was capable of working a 40-hour week.
Miscarriage	*Stifle v. Allied Domecq Spirits & Wine U.S.A., Inc.*, 2002 WL 229896 (W.D.Ark. 2002).	Employee sought leave several months after miscarriage; no medical evidence supported employee's subjective assessment of medical condition.
Nosebleed	*Nowak v. EGW Home Care, Inc.*, 82 F.Supp.2d 101 (W.D.N.Y. 2000).	Employee failed to allege that any incapacity resulted from the condition.
Poison Ivy	*Godwin v. Rheem Manufacturing Company*, 15 F.Supp.2d 1197 (M.D.Ala. 1998).	Employee only received treatment on one occasion and no medication was prescribed.
Respiratory Infection	*Murray v. Red Kap Industries, Inc.*, 124 F.3d 695 (5th Cir. 1997).	Employee's condition was incapacitating at earlier point in time, but employee failed to establish that it remained incapacitating on days in question.
Shortness of Breath	*Joyce v. New York City Mission Society*, 963 F.Supp. 290 (S.D.N.Y. 1997).	Condition accompanied by chest pains; no indication that employee was incapacitated.
Shoulder Injury	*Frazier v. Iowa Beef Processors, Inc.*, 200 F.3d 1190 (8th Cir. 2000).	Rotator cuff strain did not impair employee's ability to perform his job.

Condition	Citation	Description
Trancelike, Non-Epileptic Spells	*Keys v. Joseph Beth Booksellers, Inc.*, 173 F.3d 429 (6th Cir. 1999).	Twitching, loss of concentration, and inability to speak; employee attended Elton John concert while on FMLA leave.
Upper Respiratory Infection	*Brannon v. Oshkosh B'Gosh, Inc.*, 897 F.Supp. 1028 (M.D.Tenn. 1995).	Condition lasted only a few days; medical evidence of extent of condition was sparse.
Urinary Tract Infection	*Bell v. Jewel Food Store*, 83 F.Supp.2d 951 (N.D.Ill. 2000).	Employee sought care of doctor only once and received no continuing treatment.
Vaginal Bleeding	*Roberts v. Human Development Association*, 4 F.Supp.2d 154 (E.D.N.Y. 1998).	Post-menopausal vaginal bleeding; employee did not prove that she was incapacitated for more than three consecutive days.

Potentially, multiple conditions, none of which alone amount to a serious health condition, could constitute a serious health condition in the aggregate. In one case, an employee received a thyroid ultrasound, a thyroid scan, an excision of a benign infected cyst, a needle biopsy of her thyroid, and a CT scan of her brain over a two-month period. Finding that the employee had a potential claim under the FMLA, a court ruled:

> "Can several diagnoses, if temporally linked, no one of which rises alone to the level of a serious health condition, if taken together, constitute a serious health condition? The FMLA was enacted to help working men and women balance the conflicting demands of work and personal life. It does so by recognizing that there will be times in a person's life when that person is incapable of performing her work duties for medical reasons. Whether these medical reasons take the form of one discrete illness, such as cancer, or the form of several different and seemingly unrelated illnesses all afflicting a single individual at the same time * * * is of no moment to the purposes of the FMLA. Thus we answer the question 'yes.' After all, it is not the disease that receives leave from work; it is the person. And how can one's ability to perform at work be seriously impaired by a single serious illness but not by multiple illnesses having a serious impact?

The answer, of course, is that it cannot; the disability is related to the cumulative impacts of illness on one's body and mind." [45]

It is possible for an individual to have a serious health condition even though the individual's condition is ultimately not successfully diagnosed by a doctor. As one court observed, "it seems unlikely that Congress intended to punish people who are unlucky enough to develop new diseases, or to suffer serious symptoms for some period of time before the medical profession is able to diagnose the cause of the problem." [46]

Colds, The Flu, Minor Ulcers, And Similar Conditions.

A good deal of debate has erupted over the provisions in the DOL's regulations that "ordinarily, unless complications arise," the common cold, the flu, earaches, upset stomach, minor ulcers, headaches other than migraine, routine dental or orthodontia problems, and periodontal disease are excluded from the definition of a serious health condition. As written, the regulations appear to exclude illnesses such as the flu and minor ulcers from the definition of a serious health condition unless complications arise. Indeed, in an opinion letter issued in 1995, the DOL took precisely that position. [47]

The problem, of course, is that conditions such as colds, the flu, and the like can, under some conditions and even absent complications, meet the tests for being a serious health condition under the FMLA – they can involve periods of incapacity, ongoing treatment by a doctor, and an inability to perform the essential functions of a job. Recognizing this conundrum, the DOL issued an almost impenetrable opinion letter in 1996 recanting its 1995 letter, explaining that "complications, *per se*, need not be present to qualify as a serious health condition if the regulatory * * * tests are otherwise met. The regulations reflect the view that, ordinarily, conditions like the common cold and flu would not be expected to meet the regulatory tests, not that such conditions could not routinely qualify under FMLA where the tests are, in fact, met in particular cases." [48] Current court decisions generally follow the DOL's 1996 opinion letter, concluding "although conditions like the common cold or the flu will not routinely satisfy the requirements of a serious health condition, absences resulting from such illnesses are protected under the FMLA when the regulatory tests are met." [49]

CASE IN POINT

Question: 2002 was a bad year for the flu for Donita Weaver. In January, she contracted the illness and missed ten days of work intermittently over the next two months as she was attempting to recover. Finally, because of the persistence of a fever, constant headaches, and vomiting, the doctor who had been treating her during her illness recommended that she be confined to bed rest for a week. Her employer, upset about Weaver's absences from work, terminated her employment when Weaver asked for the week off work. Is Weaver protected by the FMLA?

Answer: Weaver is probably protected by the FMLA. While in most cases minor illnesses such as colds and the flu will not qualify as serious medical conditions entitled to FMLA coverage, such illnesses can qualify for protection if their symptoms are serious enough. Weaver's flu resulted in a period of incapacity of more than three consecutive days (the period of bed rest), and was treated on more than one occasion by her health care provider.

The Family Members Covered By The FMLA.

The Statute – 29 U.S.C. §2612.

(a) In general

(1) Entitlement to leave

Subject to section 2613 of this title, an eligible employee shall be entitled to a total of 12 workweeks of leave during any 12-month period for one or more of the following:

* * *

(C) In order to care for the spouse, or a son, daughter, or parent, of the employee, if such spouse, son, daughter, or parent has a serious health condition.

The FMLA allows leave to be taken for a serious medical condition in the employee's family. The list of family members included within the FMLA is a short one: Spouses, sons, daughters, and parents. Other family members such as siblings, aunts, uncles, grandparents, and grandchildren are not covered by the FMLA.[50] Though the meaning of these terms might seem self-evident, the FMLA, with true federal-regulatory panache, furnishes definitions of each.

- **Parents.**

The FMLA defines a "parent" as "the biological parent of an employee or as an individual who stood *in loco parentis* to an employee when the employee was a son or daughter."[51] *In loco parentis*, a Latin phrase generally meaning "crazy parent" or "in the place of a parent," has been defined by the DOL as follows: "Persons who are '*in loco parentis*' include those with day-to-day responsibilities to care for and financially support a child or, in the case of an employee, who had such responsibility for the employee when the employee was a child. A biological or legal relationship is not necessary."[52] Relatives such as grandparents are potentially covered by the FMLA *only* if they have acted *in loco parentis* to the employee.[53] Similarly, parents-in-law do not qualify as "parents" under the FMLA.[54]

- **Sons and Daughters.**

The FMLA defines "son or daughter" as "a biological, adopted, or foster child, a stepchild, a legal ward, or a child of a person standing *in loco parentis*, who is (A) under 18 years of age or (B) 18 years of age or older and incapable of self-care because of a mental or physical disability."[55] This definition draws a distinction based on age: FMLA leave is appropriate to care for any son or daughter under the age of 18 who suffers from a serious health condition. However, FMLA leave care for a son or daughter 18 years of age or older with a serious health condition is only appropriate *if* the son or daughter (1) has a serious health condition, (2) is incapable of self-care, and (3) is so incapacitated because of a mental or physical disability.[56]

The DOL's regulations define "incapable of self-care" as follows:

> "Incapable of self-care means that the individual requires active assistance or supervision to provide daily self-care in three or more of the 'activities of daily living' (ADLs) or 'instrumental activities of daily living' (IADLs). Activities of daily living include adaptive activities such as caring appropriately for one's grooming and hygiene, bathing, dressing and eating. Instrumental activities of daily living include cooking, cleaning, shopping, taking public transportation, paying bills, maintaining a residence, using telephones and directories, using a post office, etc."[57]

To be incapable of self care means the need for active assistance or supervision in the performance of everyday activities such as cooking and cleaning.

There are few cases addressing what the phrase "incapable of self-care" means. One court made the rather easy determination that an employee's son, hospitalized for kidney failure, was incapable of self-care during the hospitalization – concluding that "it is only logical to conclude that [the son] could not cook, clean, shop, or take public transportation while he was in the hospital."[58] A second court found that a doctor prescribing that an employee's adult daughter be confined to bed rest for the duration of her pregnancy (due to high blood pressure) meant the daughter could be incapable of self-care. The Court reasoned that "at a bare minimum, such a prescription would appear to signal the patient's need for active assistance or supervision in the performance of everyday activities such as cooking, cleaning, shopping, and doing housework."[59] A third court held that an employee's own claim that her daughter needed to stay in bed was not sufficient evidence, in the absence of any medical support, for a jury to infer that her daughter was incapable of self-care.[60]

The DOL's answer to defining a "disability" in the context of its "adult son or daughter" regulations borrows from a three-part definition of disability in the Americans With Disabilities Act (ADA) – an **impairment** that **substantially limits** one or more **major life activities**.[61] Under the regulations of the Equal Employment Opportunities Commission (EEOC), the federal agency that administers the ADA, an **impairment** can be "any physiological disorder, or condition, cosmetic disfigurement, or anatomical loss affecting one or more of the following body systems: neurological, musculoskeletal, special sense organs, respiratory (including speech organs), cardiovascular, reproductive, digestive, genito-urinary, hemic and lymphatic, skin, and endocrine." [62] The EEOC has defined **major life activities** as "functions such as caring for oneself, performing manual tasks, walking, hearing, seeing, speaking, breathing, learning, and working."[63] **"Substantially limits"** means that an individual is: "(i) Unable to perform a major life activity that the average person in the general population can perform; or (ii) Significantly restricted as to the condition, manner or duration under which an individual can perform a particular major life activity as compared to the condition, manner, or duration under which the average person in the general population can perform that same major life activity." [64] For ADA purposes, the factors for assessing whether an individual is **substantially limited** in a major life activity include (1) the nature and severity of the impairment; (2) the duration or expected duration of the impairment; and (3) the permanent or long-term impact or the expected permanent or long-term impact of or resulting from the impairment.[65]

There is one notable departure the FMLA makes from using the ADA's definition of disability in its treatment of adult sons and daughters. Under the ADA, temporary or non-chronic conditions are generally excluded from the definition of disability. In a sweeping opinion, a federal appeals court has found that the FMLA should have no similar exclusion. In reaching its decision, the Court drew upon the distinct functions of the two laws in a passage, that though lengthy, bears repeating:

> "[T]he concept of disability serves a much different function in the ADA than in the FMLA. Where the ADA is concerned, a finding of disability is the key that unlocks the storehouse of statutory protections. Title I of the ADA provides that a covered employer may not discriminate against a qualified individual with a disability because of that disability. This means that the employer must, *inter alia*, make 'reasonable accommodations to the known physical or mental limitations of an otherwise qualified individual with a disability' as long as that disability persists, unless and until those accommodations impose an undue hardship on the employer. Such accommodations can take various forms, and the duty to accommodate is an ongoing responsibility that is not exhausted by a single effort on the employer's part. Given the centrality of a finding of disability under the ADA and the panoply of rights and responsibilities that such a finding triggers, it makes sense to insist that, in most cases, an impairment have an extended duration before it will be deemed so limiting as to constitute a disability.

* * *

"A worker who seeks to take FMLA leave to care for a child often does so in response to a crisis situation. In many instances, the emergency will have abated by the time that the duration of the child's impairment can be ascertained. If a hard-and-fast durational requirement is enforced, an employee will be effectively prevented from taking family leave to care for an adult child until it can be established that the child's problem will have an adequate duration. By then, the crisis may well have passed. Such a scenario would place an employee with a sick adult child between a rock and a hard place, forcing him or her to choose between employment demands and family needs. This would run at cross purposes with the FMLA's goal of reassuring workers that when a family emergency arises they will not be asked to choose between continuing their employment, and meeting their personal and family obligations. We do not believe that Congress intended to create so illusory a benefit." [66]

- **Spouses.**

Section 2611(13) of the FMLA defines "spouse" as a "husband or wife, as the case may be." The DOL's regulations do not elaborate much on this definition, indicating only that a spouse means a "husband or wife as defined or recognized under State law for purpose of marriage in the State where the employee resides, including common law marriage in States where it is recognized." [67] This definition excludes non-married domestic partners (though leave for domestic partners may be provided by some state or local laws) [68] but includes common-law spouses.[69]

In all cases where an employee is using FMLA leave to care for a family member, the employer has the right to request the employee to produce reasonable documentation of the family relationship. The documentation can be in a variety of forms, including a simple statement from the employee, a birth certificate or a court document.[70]

What Does It Mean To "Care For" A Seriously Ill Family Member?

The language of the FMLA is meager indeed on the issue of when leave can be used because of the illness of a spouse, child, or parent, stating only that leave can be used to "care for" the ill family member. The DOL's regulations shed a good deal more light on the matter, indicating that to "care for" a family member includes the following:

- To provide either physical or psychological care; and

- To provide psychological comfort and reassurance that would be beneficial to a family member receiving inpatient or home care.

An employee may also "care for" a family member:

- When the family member is unable to care for his/her own basic medical, hygienic, or nutritional needs or safety;

- When the family member is unable to transport himself to the doctor; or

- When the employee may be needed to fill in for others who are caring for the family member, or to make arrangements for changes in the family member's care.[71]

Indications are that courts are likely to broadly interpret the phrase "care for." In one case, for example, an employer tried to dismiss an FMLA claim, contending that the employee merely "hung out" with his sick father in his father's hospital room. Though a court rejected the employee's FMLA claim for other reasons, it still held that providing "comfort and reassurance" to the employee's father would have been within the scope of the FMLA.[72] In another case, a court observed that the DOL's regulations "clearly contemplate not only the physical but, just as important, also the psychological care that seriously ill parents often require from their care-giving children."[73]

Several cases have involved somewhat unusual claims for FMLA leave associated with a change in living arrangements for a family member. In one case, the employee was the mother of a troubled teenager who had a history of emotional and behavioral problems, including drug use. When the boy was beaten by some acquaintances, the mother sought leave under the FMLA to move her son to the Philippines to live with his uncle. The idea was to keep the boy safe from further beatings, not to seek medical or psychological treatment. In upholding the denial of FMLA leave, a court found that although the mother was motivated by an understandable concern for her son's safety, the FMLA demanded some level of participation in ongoing treatment for that condition. The Court subsequently concluded that she was not caring for him under the FMLA.[74] In a similar case under a state law that incorporated FMLA standards, a court upheld denying leave to help an employee's elderly mother move from a two-story house to a one-story apartment, concluding that the employee "was not there to directly, or even indirectly, provide or participate in medical care for her mother. Instead, she was there to help pack her mother's belongings and tell the movers where to place her mother's furniture. While [the employee's] presence may have provided her mother some degree of psychological comfort, this was merely a collateral benefit of activities not encompassed by the * * * regulations."[75]

There are no "bereavement leave" provisions in the FMLA.[76]

Alcohol And Substance Abuse.

Assuming all of the preconditions have been met, alcohol or substance abuse qualifies as a serious health condition protected by the FMLA. However, leave

While absence from work for treatment for alcohol or substance abuse can be covered by the FMLA, absence because of the underlying abuse itself is not.

can only be taken in cases of alcohol or substance abuse treated by a health care provider or by a provider of health care services referred by a health care provider.[77] Consequently, absence from work because of alcohol or substance abuse, as opposed to absence from work for treatment, is not covered by the FMLA.[78] Applying these principles, one court rejected a claim that the time spent in jail for driving while intoxicated was covered by the FMLA.[79] Moreover, if disciplinary action is taken against an employee for substance abuse, the fact that the employee took FMLA leave to deal with the substance abuse problem immediately after the incident will not protect the employee under the FMLA.[80] Similarly, if an employee is initially granted FMLA leave for treatment for alcoholism but later relapses, the FMLA will not prohibit an employer from discharging the employee for resuming alcohol abuse in violation of any back-to-work agreement.[81]

Treatment By A Chiropractor.

As described above, the FMLA defines a serious health condition as, in part, one that requires the continuing treatment of a "health care provider." The FMLA brings "doctors of medicine and osteopathy" within the scope of "health care providers," as well as any other person determined by the DOL "to be capable of providing health care services." In turn, the DOL's regulations include chiropractors within the scope of those "capable of providing health care services," but in a way "limited to treatment consisting of manual manipulation of the spine to correct a subluxation as demonstrated by X-ray to exist," and provided that the chiropractor is performing within the scope of his or her practice as defined under state law.[82] For the uninitiated, a "subluxation" is a misalignment of spinal segments, such as where a vertebra is misaligned in relation to the vertebrae above and/or below it.[83]

In summary, for chiropractic treatment to qualify as health care services under the FMLA, an employee must prove the following:

- The chiropractor is authorized to practice in the state where treatment is performed;

- The treatment must be within the scope of the chiropractor's practice, as defined under the law in the state where the chiropractor is practicing;

- The treatment must consist of manual manipulation of the spine to correct a subluxation; and

- X-rays must demonstrate the existence of the subluxation.

In one case, a court applied these regulations to deny FMLA coverage to an employee in South Dakota who sought leave because of her adult daughter's seizure condition. The daughter was receiving treatment for the seizures from a chiropractor. The Court found "there was no showing that the chiropractor who treated [the employee's] daughter was authorized to practice in South Dakota.

Nor was there any showing that South Dakota law allowed the chiropractor to treat neurological disorders like seizures. The record contained no X-rays to show that [the employee's] daughter even suffered from a subluxation."[84]

If The Employer Initially Approves FMLA Leave For A Serious Health Condition, Can It Later Change Its Mind?

On occasion, an employer will initially approve an employee's request for FMLA leave, only to later reevaluate whether the employee actually suffered from a serious health condition. Nothing in the FMLA prohibits such a reevaluation. As one court observed: "Under [the employee's] reasoning, all an employee need do is request FMLA leave and he is then absolutely protected, even if he is actually ineligible for FMLA leave. This was not Congress' intent in enacting the FMLA."[85]

NOTES

1 *Brannon v. Oshkosh B'Gosh, Inc.*, 897 F.Supp. 1028 (M.D.Tenn. 1995).

2 *Laughlin v. Cardiovascular Institute of the South*, 78 Empl.Prac. ¶40,147 (E.D.La. 2000).

3 S.Rep. No. 3, 103d Cong., 1st Sess.1993, 1993 U.S.C.C.A.N. 3, at pp. 30-31.

4 S.Rep. No. 3, 103d Cong., 1st Sess.1993, 1993 U.S.C.C.A.N. 3, at pp. 30-31.

5 29 C.F.R. §825.114(a)(1).

6 29 C.F.R. §825.114(a)(1).

7 *See Opinion Letter,* Wage and Hour Division, 1995 WL 1036743 (September 20, 1995).

8 *Opinion Letter,* Wage and Hour Division, 1995 WL 1036734 (June 19, 1995).

9 *See Washington v. Bosch Braking Systems Corp.*, 6 WH Cas.2d 1724 (W.D.Mich. 1999).

10 29 C.F.R. §825.800.

11 29 C.F.R. §825.114(a)(2)(i); *see Thorson v. Gemini, Inc.*, 205 F.3d 370 (8th Cir. 2001); *Haefling v. United Parcel Service, Inc.*, 169 F.3d 494 (7th Cir. 1999); *Beahm v. Line Management, Inc. T/A*, 1998 WL 526585 (W.D.Va. 1998).

12 *Sims v. Alameda-Contra Costa Transit Dist.*, 2 F.Supp.2d 1253 (N.D.Cal. 1998). *See generally Magiera v. Ford Motor Company*, 1998 WL 704061 (N.D.Ill. 1998).

13 *Joslin v. Rockwell International Corporation*, 8 F.Supp.2d 1158 (N.D.Iowa 1998).

14 *Murray v. Red Kap Indus., Inc.,* 124 F.3d 695 (5th Cir.1997).

15 *Roberts v. Human Development Association*, 4 F.Supp.2d 154 (E.D.N.Y. 1998).

16 29 C.F.R. §825.114(b).

17 *Baung v. Entergy Corp.*, 1999 WL 397403 (E.D.La. 1999); 29 C.F.R. §825.114(b).

18 29 C.F.R. §825.114(a)(2)(ii).

19 29 C.F.R. §825.114(e); *see Pendarvis v. Xerox Corporation*, 3 F.Supp.2d 53 (D.D.C. 1998); *Divizio v. Elmwood Care, Inc.*, 1998 WL 292982 (N.D.Ill. 1998).

20 *Pendarvis v. Xerox Corporation*, 3 F.Supp.2d 53 (D.D.C. 1998).

21 *Northern v. National Bank of Detroit*, 2000 WL 33521014 (Mich.App. 2000).

22 29 C.F.R. §825.114(a)(2)(iii).

23 29 C.F.R. §825.114(e).

24 29 C.F.R. §825.114(a)(2)(iv).

25 29 C.F.R. §825.114(a)(2)(v).

[26] *Bond v. Abbott Laboratories*, 188 F.3d 506 (6th Cir. 1999); *Price v. Marathon Cheese Corp.*, 119 F.3d 330 (5th Cir. 1997); *Brannon v. Oshkosh B'Gosh, Inc.*, 897 F.Supp. 1028 (M.D.Tenn. 1995); *see Mell v. Weyburn-Bartel, Inc.*, 4 WH Cas.2d 274 (W.D.Mich. 1997). *See generally* Comment, *The Family And Medical Leave Act: What Is A Serious Health Condition?*, University of Kansas Law Review (November, 1997).

[27] *Miller v. AT&T Corporation*, 250 F.3d 820 (4th Cir. 2001).

[28] 29 C.F.R. §825.114(b).

[29] 29 C.F.R. §825.114(c).

[30] 29 C.F.R. §825.114(d).

[31] *Martyszenko v. Safeway, Inc.*, 120 F.3d 120 (8th Cir. 1997); *Beal v. Rubbermaid Commercial Products Inc.*, 972 F.Supp. 1216 (S.D.Iowa 1997); *Boyce v. New York City Mission Society*, 963 F.Supp. 290 (S.D.N.Y. 1997). *See generally* Comment, *Evaluating The Current Judicial Interpretation Of "Serious Health Condition" Under The FMLA*, Boston University Public Interest Law Journal (Spring, 1997).

[32] *Barnhill v. Farmland Foods, Inc.*, 2001 WL 487939 (D.Kan. 2001), *quoting Gudenkauf v. Stauffer Communications, Inc.*, 922 F.Supp. 465 (D.Kan. 1996); *see Hodgens v. Gen. Dynamics Corp.*, 963 F.Supp. 102 (D.R.I. 1997); *Hott v. VDO Yazaki Corp.*, 922 F.Supp. 1114 (W.D.Va. 1996); *Guo v. Maricopa County Medical Center*, 992 P.2d 11 (Ariz.App. 1999); *Austin v. Shelby County Government*, 5 WH Cas.2d 375 (Tenn.App. 1999).

[33] *Barnhill v. Farmland Foods, Inc.*, 2001 WL 487939 (D.Kan. 2001).

[34] *Hodgens v. General Dynamics Corporation*, 144 F.3d 151 (1st Cir. 1998).

[35] 29 C.F.R. §825.114(a)(2); *see Dawson v. Leewood Nursing Home, Inc.*, 14 F.Supp.2d 828 (E.D.Va. 1998)(fact that employee able to travel to Hawaii did not mean she was not incapacitated).

[36] *Bell v. Jewel Food Store*, 83 F.Supp.2d 951 (N.D.Ill. 2000).

[37] *Haefling v. United Parcel Service, Inc.*, 169 F.3d 494 (7th Cir. 1999).

[38] *See Moore v. United States Postal Service*, 83 M.S.P.R. 533 (MSPB 1999).

[39] *See Kamtaprassad v. Chase Manhattan Corp.*, 2001 WL 1662071 (S.D.N.Y. 2001); *Guiliani v. Minnesota Vikings Football Club*, 2001 WL 667797 (D.Minn. 2001); *Haffner v. Bryan Cave LLP*, 6 WH Cas.2d 639 (S.D.N.Y. 2000); *Sieger v. Wisconsin Personnel Commission*, 512 N.W.2d 220 (Wis.App. 1994)(decided under state law).

[40] *See Ware v. Stahl Specialty Company*, 4 WH Cas.2d 974 (W.D.Mo. 1998); *Vargo-Adams v. United States Postal Service*, 992 F.Supp. 939 (N.D.Ohio 1998).

[41] *Rogers v. Bell Helicopter Textron Inc.*, 6 WH Cas.2d 1534 (N.D.Tex. 2000).

[42] *Hott v. VDO Yazaki Corporation*, 922 F.Supp. 1114 (W.D.Va. 1996); *see MPI Wisconsin Machining Division v. Department of Industry, Labor & Human Relations, Equal Rights Division*, 464 N.W.2d 79 (Wis.App. 1990)(decided under state law).

43 *See Cole v. Sisters of Charity of the Incarnate Word*, 79 F.Supp.2d 668 (E.D.Tex. 1999).

44 *Henderson v. Central Progressive Bank,* 147 Lab. Cases ¶34,601 (E.D.La. 2002); *Procopio v. Castrol Industrial North America, Inc.*, 3 WH Cas.2d 1130 (E.D.Pa. 1996); *Gibbs v. American Airlines, Inc.*, 87 Cal.Rptr.2d 554 (Cal.App. 1999)(decided under state law).

45 *Price v. City of Fort Wayne*, 117 F.3d 1022 (7th Cir. 1997).

46 *Hodgens v. General Dynamics Corporation*, 144 F.3d 151 (1st Cir. 1998).

47 *Opinion Letter,* Wage and Hour Division, 1995 WL 1051446 (April 7, 1995).

48 *Opinion Letter*, Wage and Hour Division, 1996 WL 1044783 (Dec. 12, 1996); *Opinion Letter,* Wage and Hour Division, 1996 WL 1044784 (December 12, 1996).

49 *Thorson v. Gemini, Inc.,* 205 F.3d 370 (8th Cir. 2000); *see Miller v. AT&T Corporation*, 250 F.3d 820 (4th Cir. 2001).

50 *Opinion Letter,* Wage and Hour Division, 1995 WL 1036744 (October 26, 1995).

51 29 U.S.C. §2611(7).

52 29 C.F.R. §825.113(c)(3).

53 *Krohn v. Forsting*, 11 F.Supp.2d 1082 (E.D.Mo. 1998).

54 *Opinion Letter*, Wage and Hour Division, 1998 WL 1147749 (June 4, 1998).

55 29 U.S.C. §2611(12).

56 *See Navarro v. Pfizer Corp.*, 261 F.3d 90 (1st Cir. 2001); *Opinion Letter*, Wage and Hour Division, 1994 WL 1016759 (November 28, 1994); *see Opinion Letter,* Wage and Hour Division, 1995 WL 1036738 (July 21, 1995).

57 29 C.F.R. §113(c)(1).

58 *Bryant v. Delbar Products, Inc.*, 18 F.Supp.2d 799 (M.D.Tenn. 1998).

59 *Navarro v. Pfizer Corp.*, 261 F.3d 90 (1st Cir. 2001).

60 *Sakellarion v. Judge & Dolph, Ltd.*, 893 F.Supp. 800 (N.D.Ill. 1995).

61 *See Bragdon v. Abbott*, 524 U.S. 624 (1998). For a thorough discussion of these issues, see D. Snyder, *The Americans With Disabilities Act (Second Edition)*, (LRIS 1998).

62 29 C.F.R. §1630.2(h)(1).

63 29 C.F.R. §1630.2(i).

64 29 C.F.R.§1630.2(j)(1)

65 29 C.F.R.§1630.2(j)(2)

66 *Navarro v. Pfizer Corp.*, 261 F.3d 90 (1st Cir. 2001).

67 29 C.F.R. §825.113(a).

[68] *Opinion Letter,* Wage & Hour Division, 1998 WL 1147747 (November 18, 1998); *Opinion Letter,* Wage and Hour Division, 1995 WL 1036737 (July 19, 1995).

[69] *Willard v. Ingram Construction Company, Inc.,* 194 F.3d 1315 (6th Cir. 1999).

[70] 29 C.F.R. §825.113(d).

[71] 29 C.F.R. §825.116(a)(b).

[72] *Plumley v. Southern Container, Inc.,* 145 Lab.Cas. ¶11,187 (D.Me. 2001); *see Opinion Letter,* Wage and Hour Division, 1998 WL 1147752 (February 6, 1998); *Opinion Letter,* Wage and Hour Division, 1998 WL 1147751 (February 27, 1998).

[73] *Scamihorn v. General Truck Drivers,* 282 F.3d 1078 (9th Cir. 2002).

[74] *Marchisheck v. San Mateo County,* 199 F.3d 1068 (9th Cir. 1999).

[75] *Pang v. Beverly Hospital, Inc.,* 94 Cal.Rptr.2d 643 (Cal.App. 2000).

[76] *Lange v. Showbiz Pizza Time, Inc.,* 12 F.Supp.2d 1150 (D.Kan. 1998).

[77] 29 C.F.R. §825.114(d).

[78] *Jeremy v. Northwest Ohio Development Center,* 210 F.3d 372 (6th Cir. 2000); *Sloop v. Abtco, Inc.,* 178 F.3d 1285 (4th Cir. 1999); *Opinion Letter,* Wage and Hour Division, 1995 WL 1036740 (July 21, 1995).

[79] *Jeremy v. Northwest Ohio Development Center,* 33 F.Supp.2d 635 (N.D.Ohio 1999).

[80] *Renaud v. Wyoming Dep't of Family Serv.,* 203 F.3d 723 (10th Cir. 2000); *Opinion Letter,* Wage and Hour Division, 1995 WL 1036730 (April 28, 1995).

[81] *Lottinger v. Shell Oil Company,* 143 F.Supp. 743 (S.D.Tex. 2001).

[82] 29 C.F.R. §825.118(b).

[83] Roscoe N. Gray, M.D. & Louise J. Gordy, M.D., *Attorney's Textbook of Medicine* paras. 12.41, 12.41(1), at 12-20 (3d ed.1998).

[84] *Sievers v. Iowa Mutual Insurance Co.,* 581 N.W.2d 633 (Iowa 1998); *see Olsen v. Ohio Edison Company,* 979 F.Supp. 1159 (N.D.Ohio 1997).

[85] *Fisher v. State Farm Mutual Automobile Insurance Co.,* 999 F.Supp. 866 (E.D.Tex. 1998).

CHAPTER 6

THE REQUIRED EXCHANGE OF INFORMATION ONCE FMLA LEAVE IS REQUESTED – THE NOTICES REQUIRED OF EMPLOYEES AND EMPLOYER

In A Nutshell . . .

The FMLA envisions a good deal of communication between and employer and employee about the need to use FMLA leave. The employee must notify the employer of the need for the leave, and the employer must then specifically advise the employee of rights under the FMLA.

The FMLA's Notice Requirements, Part 1 – The Notice An Employee Is Required To Give.

The Statute: 29 U.S.C. § 2612(e)(1) & (2)

Duties of employee

(1) Requirement of notice

In any case in which the necessity for leave under subparagraph (A) or (B) of subsection (a)(1) of this section is foreseeable based on an expected birth or placement, the employee shall provide the employer with not less than 30 days' notice, before the date the leave is to begin, of the employee's intention to take leave under such subparagraph, except that if the date of the birth or placement requires leave to begin in less than 30 days, the employee shall provide such notice as is practicable.

(2) In any case in which the necessity for leave under subparagraph (C) or (D) of subsection (a)(1) of this section is foreseeable based on planned medical treatment, the employee -

(A) shall make a reasonable effort to schedule the treatment so as not to disrupt unduly the operations of the employer, subject to the approval of the health care provider of the employee or the health care provider of the son, daughter, spouse, or parent of the employee, as appropriate; and (B) shall provide the employer with not less than 30 days' notice, before the date the leave is to begin, of the employee's intention to take leave under such subparagraph, except that if the date of the treatment requires leave to begin in less than 30 days, the employee shall provide such notice as is practicable.

The FMLA requires an employee to give 30 days' notice of the need for FMLA leave because of medical treatments for the employee or a qualifying family member, except where it is impractical to do so.

An employee desiring to use FMLA leave must provide the employer with notice of the intention to use FMLA leave.[1] In the words of one court, the right to FMLA leave is not "self-executing." While the precise <u>amount</u> of information to be provided to the employer is fairly minimal, there is no question that *the right to FMLA leave depends upon the employee submitting some form of request for the leave to the employer.*[2]

If the leave is desired in connection with an expected birth or placement of a child, the employee must provide 30 days' notice if possible. If the "date of the birth or placement requires leave to begin in less than 30 days," then the employee is required to provide notice of the intention to use FMLA leave "as is practicable."

The FMLA imposes similar notice requirements if the FMLA leave is to care for a qualifying family member with a serious health condition or because the employee is suffering from a serious health condition. If the need for the FMLA leave is "foreseeable based on planned medical treatment," then the employee must provide 30 days' notice of the intent to use FMLA leave.[3] If the employee fails to give the requisite 30-day notice, the employer may delay the onset of the leave until 30 days after receiving notice from the employee of the need for the leave.[4] When the necessity for leave is foreseeable based on planned medical treatment, the FMLA requires that the employee make a reasonable effort to schedule the treatment so as not to unduly disrupt the operations of the employer, subject to the approval of the health care provider.

The 30-day notice requirement only applies where the need for the leave is foreseeable.[5] Many times an employee will not know until the last minute of the need for FMLA leave, particularly when the leave is needed because of a serious health condition. Where the need for leave is unforeseeable, the ability to take FMLA leave will not be prohibited by an inability to given advance notice to the employer.[6] In such cases, notice of the need for leave must be given as soon as practicable.[7]

Several questions have arisen concerning the employee notice provisions of the FMLA.

When would the giving of 30 days' notice not be practicable? The DOL's regulations indicate 30 days' notice of the intent to use leave might not be practicable because the employee does not know approximately when the leave will need to begin, circumstances have changed, or there has been a medical emergency.[8] The DOL's rules give examples where 30 days' notice would be impractical, listing situations where an employee's health condition may require leave to begin sooner than anticipated, such as before the birth of a child or where little opportunity for notice may be given before placement for adoption.[9] One court has found that a change in insurance coverage impacting whether a surgical procedure was covered by insurance could be a change in circumstances allowing less than 30 days' notice.[10] However, an employee giving four days' notice of treatment for a long-standing back injury that required regular treatment would not be reasonable since it would be practicable to give greater advance notice.[11]

What does it mean to give notice as soon "as is practicable" when 30 days' notice cannot be given? The DOL's regulations indicate only that "as soon as practicable" means "as soon as both possible and practical, taking into account all of the facts and circumstances in the individual case."[12] Indeed, an employee sometimes may not be able to give notice in advance because of the rapid onset of a medical condition, a medical emergency, or immediate childbirth.[13] The employee can instead give notice after an absence from work, *provided* it is given as soon as practicable. Normally, this would require the employee to give notice to the employer within one or two working days of learning of the need for leave.[14]

What information, and in what form, does the FMLA require an employee to provide the employer when giving notice of the intent to use FMLA leave? The DOL specifies that an employee's request for leave can be verbal or in writing. The employee does not need to provide medical information at the time of the leave request; it is only the employer's subsequent request for certification of

> The giving of 30 days' notice of the intent to use FMLA leave would not be "practicable" in emergencies or where the employee does not know when the leave will begin.

> An employee is not required to provide medical documentation at the time of the FMLA leave request.

the medical condition that triggers the employee's obligation to furnish such information.[15] However, the employee clearly must ask to use some form of leave.[16]

Though the DOL's regulations also allow an employer to require an employee to comply with its usual and customary rules concerning leave requests (including requiring leave requests to be in writing or submitted using certain forms), they also indicate that an employee's failure to comply with such rules will not enable an employer to disallow FMLA leave if the employee has made an appropriate verbal request for leave.[17] Examples of reporting rules held to be reasonable by the courts include the need to verify a request for leave by filling out a leave form[18] and requiring an employee to notify the employer of plans concerning a return to work by the third consecutive day of absence.[19] If an employee does not comply with the employer's rules concerning leave requests, the employee may be disciplined for the failure to comply (though, again, the employee may not be denied the FMLA leave).[20]

The DOL's regulations assume there will be some degree of information exchange at the time the employee has made a leave request and after. Once the employee provides at least verbal notice sufficient to make the employer aware that the employee needs FMLA-qualifying leave and the anticipated timing and duration of the leave, the employer may "inquire further of the employee if it is necessary to have more information about whether FMLA leave is being sought by the employee, and obtain the necessary details of the leave to be taken."[21] In the case of medical conditions, the employer may require certification of the underlying medical condition, as discussed in Chapter 7. Moreover, when planning medical treatment, the employee must consult with the employer (ordinarily in advance of the taking of leave) and make a reasonable effort to schedule the leave so as not to unduly disrupt employer operations, subject to the approval of the health care provider. If the employee fails to consult with the employer in a reasonable attempt to arrange the schedule of treatments, the employer may initiate the discussions and require the employee to attempt to make such arrangements.[22]

Does the employee specifically have to request leave using words such as "FMLA" or "FMLA leave," or is it enough to make a general request for leave accompanied by information that might make the leave subject to the FMLA? The DOL's regulations indicate that an employee need only state that leave is needed for purposes that might fall within the scope of the Act to trigger FMLA rights.[23] The courts have approved of the DOL's view that employees need not necessarily mention the FMLA in order to invoke their FMLA rights. While one court observed succinctly, "these are workers, not lawyers,"[24] another court gave a more detailed rationale for imposing the obligation of determining whether a leave request falls within the parameters of the FMLA on the employer:

> "If [the need for the employee to expressly invoke the FMLA] constituted the test for whether an absence caused by a serious health condition qualified for FMLA protection, that protection could be reduced by actions of the employer who would have an incentive to keep employees ignorant of their rights and to refrain from designating

There are no magic buzzwords to invoke the FMLA. In fact, an employee does not even need to mention the FMLA to be entitled to FMLA leave.

a qualifying absence as FMLA leave. The Court does not accept these facts as the measure of whether the leave was FMLA-qualified. The statute does not contemplate allowing employers to benefit from their employee's lack of knowledge about their FMLA rights. Instead, when an employee who is eligible for FMLA leave notifies his or her employer of the need to take leave for a qualifying reason, the FMLA places the risk of ignorance on the employer. If the employee is eligible for FMLA leave and provides notification to the employer, it is the employer's duty to investigate to see whether the FMLA applies, and to notify the employee of its application. If the employer fails to notify the employee of applicability of the FMLA to the employee's medical leave, the employee is left without important information by which to structure the leave."[25]

Examples of statements made by employees that have been held to be **sufficient** notice of the intent to use FMLA leave include the following:

- An employee called to say she could not return to work due to complications from treatment of an ingrown toenail.[26]

- An employee called requesting that he be put in the "sick book."[27]

- An employee told her employer that she was needed to care for her mother, who was having "medical problems."[28]

- A doctor's note provided by the employee indicated that the employee was "unable to work."[29]

- An employee told the employer: "My son is in the hospital and I need to work things out."[30]

- A physician's statement diagnosing an employee with fibromyalgia was filed with the employer at about the time the employee began a lengthy absence from work.[31]

- An employee informed her employer in advance that her three-year-old daughter was ill and that she might have to miss work if her daughter's condition did not improve, notified her supervisor by phone each workday that she was at home caring for her ill daughter, and submitted a medical note to her employer requesting that her absences from work be excused on the basis of her daughter's illness.[32]

- An employee notified her supervisor that she was needed to care for her son with strep throat.[33]

- An employee called in sick due to swelling and tightness in her legs.[34]

- An employee notified her supervisor that she was absent from work because of a migraine headache.[35]

- An employee was unable to work because of the effects of chronic hepatitis.[36]

- An employee's request for leave was admittedly vague, but the employer's response to the request mentioned the FMLA.[37]

- A request for leave without pay because of medical conditions.[38]

- An employee told her supervisor she was not of "sound mind" and needed leave.[39]

- An employee told her employer that her doctor had advised her to stay home from work without specifying what illness was involved.[40]

In general, the employee must give some affirmative explanation of the reason leave is needed and why, not putting an employer in the position of "divining unspoken requests for leave." [41] Courts are split over whether the simple statement that an employee is ill constitutes sufficient notice under the FMLA. As shown by the descriptions set forth above, many courts require only a bare-bones statement of illness from an employee to shift the obligation to the employer who must then inquire as to the nature and extent of the illness. Other courts find that more information is needed from an employee to trigger the FMLA, reasoning that "requiring an employer to undertake to investigate whether FMLA leave is appropriate each time an employee * * * informs the employer that she will not be at work 'that day' because she is 'having a lot of pain in her side' or is 'sick,' is quite inconsistent with the purposes of the FMLA." [42]

Courts are also divided on whether an employer's knowledge that the employee or family member suffered from a serious health condition, coupled with an employee's unexplained request for leave, places the employer on enough notice that leave is needed for FMLA purposes.[43] For example, one court found that an employer potentially received adequate notice from the employee when it knew the employee's wife had a serious health condition and that the only reason the employee would be reporting an absence to a particular fellow employee would be to care for his wife.[44]

Examples of statements made by employees that have been held to provide **inadequate notice** to employers of the need to use FMLA have included the following:

- The employee stated that he required "personal leave."[45]

- The employee asked for vacation time to "look after his father's estate,"[46] and the employer knew the employee suffered from bipolar disorder.

- The employee's leave slip said that leave was needed for "personal problems and child care issues" [47] or the employee said she was absent because she would be "going to counseling."[48]

- The employee's husband, motivated by the desire to conceal the employee's nervous breakdown, only told supervisor that the employee needed time off to "have some tests run."[49]

- A statement by the employee that he was "in pain from his tailbone."[50]

- Where an employee called in on a daily basis indicating she had an adverse reaction from medication, and would not be able to work "that day," giving no indication that the condition would be of extended duration. [51]

- The employee said she had a lot of pain in her side and would be unable to work for one day.[52]

- The employee told a supervisor he would be out sick and, when queried as to the reason, said it was "personal."[53]

- The employee indicated only that he wished to visit his father, as his mother had recently died.[54]

- The employee provided no information about the reasons for an absence beyond leaving a message on an automated "sick leave" line.[55]

- Statements that a family member was ill or that an employee was going to counseling.[56]

- An "intimation" that leave was needed so a father could tend to his asthmatic son. (A court found that "oblique statements" made by the father without any direct references to his son's illness did not require the employer to be clairvoyant.)[57]

All things considered, courts are likely to find that any statements by an employee that even arguably place an employer on notice as to the reason for leave triggers an employee's FMLA rights. The best approach, courts reason, is for employers to inquire about the reasons for leave if they are having any doubts about those reasons. In addition, the employer should use the ability to demand certification as the basis for the leave to ensure that FMLA leave is being appropriately taken. With this bias, it is not surprising to find a court concluding that an employee stating repeatedly that she "could not work" created a legitimate factual question as to whether the employee gave proper notice under the FMLA.[58]

The FMLA's Notice Requirements, Part 2 – The Notice An Employer Is Required To Give In Addition To Posting.

In essence, the FMLA and the DOL's regulations require employers to issue three forms of notice to employees: (1) A job-site posting containing general information as to the FMLA's basic requirements; (2) an inclusion of some document outlining employee rights and obligations under the FMLA, to the extent that an employer has an employee handbook or other written policies describing leave benefits; and (3) a customized notice of FMLA rights, obligations, and procedures issued to an employee who asks to take leave for an FMLA-qualifying purpose. According to one court, the FMLA imposes a "significant burden" on employers to both inform itself as to the FMLA and to notify employees of their rights under the FMLA.[59]

If an employer has written policies or a manual, it must include in the materials an explanation of the FMLA rights and responsibilities of employees.

Written Policies and Manuals. If the employer has any written policies (such as an employee handbook) that informs employees about their leave and other benefits, information concerning the FMLA rights of employees must be included in the materials.[60] For this requirement to apply, the employer's written materials must provide some "written guidance to employees concerning employee benefits or leave rights"; a simple absenteeism policy alone will not constitute "written policies" and the employer remains obligated to include with such materials a full statement of FMLA rights and responsibilities.[61]

If an employer has written policies, manuals, or handbook provisions describing leave benefits, those materials must adequately describe an employee's FMLA rights and must not omit significant provisions of the FMLA, nor contain any provisions inconsistent with the FMLA. For example, in one case a court found an employer's manual was inadequate because it failed to describe either the FMLA's intermittent leave rights or the interaction between conflicting employer leave benefits and the FMLA. The Court's reasoning was as follows: "To hold otherwise renders such rights provided by FMLA meaningless. * * * [Under the regulations], for employers who do not have written policies, manuals or handbooks, they 'shall provide written guidance to an employee concerning all the employee's rights and obligations under the FMLA whenever an employee requests leave under the FMLA.' Clearly, the Secretary of Labor did not intend that employees who work for employers with handbooks should receive less information about their rights than employees who work for employers that do not have written materials or handbooks." [62]

Customized or Individualized Notice To Employees Requesting Leave. Even the most thorough employee handbook, standing alone, will not eliminate the requirement for the third type of notice – the customized written notice triggered by an employee's request for leave for FMLA-qualifying purposes.[63] This customized notice must be given regardless of whether the employer has written materials describing employee benefits and leave provisions.[64] The notice must contain at least the following elements:

- When the employee requests FMLA leave, the employer must notify employees of "the specific expectations and obligations of the employee" and explain "any consequences of a failure to meet these obligations."[65] A simple "come see me and talk about this" response to a request to use FMLA leave will not suffice.[66]

- When appropriate for the circumstances surrounding the leave taken, the notice <u>must</u> include the following provisions:

  ✓ That the leave will be counted against the employee's annual FMLA leave entitlement.

  ✓ Information about the employer's requirements that the employee furnish medical certification of a serious health condition and the consequences of failing to do so.

✓ That the employee has the right to substitute any accrued paid leave for unpaid FMLA leave, whether the employer will require the substitution of paid leave and the conditions under which such substitution can occur. The notice that the employer will require the substitution of paid leave for unpaid leave must be "unambiguous."[67]

  ✓ Whether the employee will be required to make premium payments to maintain health benefits, the arrangements for making such payments, and the possible consequences of not making such payments.

  ✓ Whether any requirement exists for the employee to present a fitness-for-duty certificate at the end of the FMLA leave.

  ✓ Whether the employee is a "key employee" who may be denied restoration to his or her former job at the conclusion of FMLA leave, and the conditions that may cause such a denial.

  ✓ That the employee has the right to the same or an equivalent job upon return from FMLA leave.

  ✓ Whether the employee will be liable for the payment of health insurance premiums paid by the employer during unpaid FMLA leave, *if* the employee fails to return to work after taking FMLA leave.[68]

- The notice to employees can <u>optionally</u> include other information – for example, whether the employer will require periodic reports on the employee's intention to return to work, but is not required to do so.[69]

The customized notice must be provided to employees within one to two business days after the employee has requested leave. If the employer initially gives verbal notice of the employee's FMLA rights, that notice must be confirmed in writing no later than the following payday.[70] Even if the employee is a management employee who could be expected to know of the employer's FMLA policies, the employer is still required to provide the notice.[71]

Employers need not give individual notice to an employee of the employee's FMLA rights until the employee actually requests leave.

This bent towards requiring employers to explain the FMLA to employees has only one significant exception. Unless the employee actually requests leave for purposes covered by the FMLA, there is no unilateral obligation on the part of the employer to provide customized notice about the FMLA to an employee who could benefit from the information. For example, if the employee is performing at a substandard level, and even if the employer is contemplating discharging the employee because the employee's physical limitations prevent the employee from performing his job, the employer still has no obligation to notify the employee of his FMLA rights *unless and until the employee requests leave.*[72]

Whenever the employer is giving customized notice to an employee of FMLA rights, the notice must initially be given at least in each six-month period that the employee gives notice of the need for and actually takes FMLA leave. Such customized notice must be given within a "reasonable time" after notice of the need for FMLA leave is received. If the initial information provided in the employer's notice changes during the six-month period – for example, if the initial leave period was paid leave and a subsequent leave period will be unpaid leave – then the employer must provide additional notice of any elements of the FMLA that are newly-impacted by the changed situation.

The DOL's regulations also mandate that employers "responsively answer questions from employees" about FMLA rights,[73] that they furnish FMLA-required notices to sensory-impaired individuals in a manner consistent with "all applicable requirements under Federal or State law,"[74] and that employers provide notices in languages other than English for employees who are not literate in English.[75] At least one court has strongly implied that these notice requirements mandate that supervisors be trained in the FMLA's requirements.[76]

To assist employers, the DOL has published a "prototype notice" as an appendix to its regulations. The DOL has indicated that "this option use form may be used to satisfy mandatory employer requirements to provide employees taking FMLA leave with written notice detailing specific expectations and obligations of the employee, and explaining any consequence of a failure to meet these requirements":

Employer Response to Employee
Request for Family or Medical Leave
(Optional *Use Form - See 29* CFR § 825.301)

U.S. Department of Labor
Employment Standards Administration
Wage and Hour Division

(Family and Medical Leave Act of 1993)

OMB No: 1215-0181
Expires: 06-30-02

Date:

To: _____
(*Employee's Name*)

From: _____
(*Name of Appropriate Employer Representative*)

Subject: REQUEST FOR FAMILY/MEDICAL LEAVE

On _____ , you notified us of your need to take family/medical leave due to:
(*Date*)

☐ The birth of a child, or the placement of a child with you for adoption or foster care; or

☐ A serious health condition that makes you unable to perform the essential functions for your job; or

☐ A serious health condition affecting your ☐ spouse, ☐ child, ☐ parent, for which you are needed to provide care.

You notified us that you need this leave beginning on _____ and that you expect
(*Date*)

leave to continue until on or about _____.
(*Date*)

Except as explained below, you have a right under the FMLA for up to 12 weeks of unpaid leave in a 12-month period for the reasons listed above. Also, your health benefits must be maintained during any period of unpaid leave under the same conditions as if you continued to work, and you must be reinstated to the same or an equivalent job with the same pay, benefits, and terms and conditions of employment on your return from leave. If you do not return to work following FMLA leave for a reason other than: (1) the continuation, recurrence, or onset of a serious health condition which would entitle you to FMLA leave; or (2) other circumstances beyond your control, you may be required to reimburse us for our share of health insurance premiums paid on your behalf during your FMLA leave.

This is to inform you that: (*Check appropriate boxes; explain where indicated*)

1.   You are ☐ eligible ☐ not eligible   for leave under the FMLA.

2.   The requested leave ☐ will ☐ will not   be counted against your annual FMLA leave entitlement.

3.   You ☐ will ☐ will not   be required to furnish medical certification of a serious health condition. If required, you must furnish certification by _____ (*insert date*) (must be at least 15 days after you are notified of this requirement), or we may delay the commencement of your leave until the certification is submitted.

4.   You may elect to substitute accrued paid leave for unpaid FMLA leave, We ☐ will ☐ will not   require that you substitute accrued paid leave for unpaid FMLA leave, If paid leave will be used, the following conditions will apply: (*Explain*)

Form WH-381
Rev. June 1997

5. (a) If you normally pay a portion of the premiums for your health insurance, these payments will continue during the period of FMLA leave. Arrangements for payment have been discussed with you, and it is agreed that you will make premium payments as follows: *(Set forth dates, e.g., the 10th of each month, or pay periods, etc. that specifically cover the agreement with the employee.)*

(b) You have a minimum 30-day *(or, indicate longer period, if applicable)* grace period in which to make premium payments. If payment is not made timely, your group health insurance may be cancelled, *provided* we notify you in writing at least 15 days before the date that your health coverage will lapse, or, at our option, we may pay your share of the premiums during FMLA leave, and recover these payments from you upon your return to work. We ☐ will ☐ will not   pay your share of health insurance premiums while you are on leave.

(c) We ☐ will ☐ will not   do the same with other benefits *(e.g., life insurance, disability insurance, etc.)* while you are on FMLA leave. If we do pay your premiums for other benefits, when you return from leave you ☐ will ☐ will not   be expected to reimburse us for the payments made on your behalf.

6.   You ☐ will ☐ will not   be required to present a fitness-for-duty certificate prior to being restored to employment. If such certification is required but not received, your return to work may be delayed until certification is provided.

7. (a) You ☐ are ☐ are not   a "key employee" as described in § 825.217 of the FMLA regulations. If you are a "key employee," restoration to employment may be denied following FMLA leave on the grounds that such restoration will cause substantial and grievous economic injury to us as discussed in § 825.218.

(b) We ☐ have ☐ have not   determined that restoring you to employment at the conclusion of FMLA leave will cause substantial and grievous economic harm to us. *(Explain (a) and/or (b) below See § 825.219 of the FMLA regulations*

8.   While on leave, you ☐ will ☐ will not   be required to furnish us with periodic reports every_____ _____ *(indicate interval of periodic reports, as appropriate for the particular leave situation)* of your status and intent to return to work *(see § 825.309 of the FMLA regulations).* If the circumstances of your leave change and you are able to return to work earlier than the date indicated on the reverse side of this form, you ☐ will ☐ will not   be required to notify us at least two work days prior to the date you intend to report to work.

9.   You ☐ will ☐ will not   be required to furnish recertification relating to a serious health condition. *(Explain below, if necessary, including the interval between certifications as prescribed in § 825.308 of the FMLA regulations.)*

This optional use form may be used to satisfy mandatory employer requirements to provide employees taking FMLA leave with written notice detailing specific expectations and obligations of the employee and explaining any consequences of a failure to meet these obligations. (29 CFR 825.301(b).)

Note: Persons are not required to respond to this collection of information unless it displays a currently valid OMB control number.

Public Burden Statement

We estimate that it will take an average of 5 minutes to complete this collection of information, Including the time for reviewing instructions, searching existing data sources, gathering and maintaining the data needed, and completing and reviewing the collection of Information. If you have any comments regarding this burden estimate or any other aspect of this collection of information, Including suggestions for reducing this burden, send them to the Administrator, Wage and Hour Division, Department of Labor, Room S-35O2, 200 Constitution Avenue, N.W., Washington, D.C. 20210.

DO *NOT* SEND THE COMPLETED FORM TO THE OFFICE SHOWN ABOVE.   Form WH-381
Rev. June 1997

What Is The Significance Of An Employer Failing To Give Appropriate Notice Under The FMLA?

The DOL's regulations take the position that failure to give appropriate notice bars the employer from counting the leave as FMLA leave. In a split decision in its first FMLA case, the Supreme Court held that the DOL exceeded its authority in enacting such regulations. The gist of the Court's decision was that the regulations impermissibly expanded and extended an employee's entitlement of 12 weeks of FMLA leave, since the consequence of an employer failing to give such notice could result in an employee receiving more than 12 weeks of leave.[77]

Simply because the Supreme Court held that the DOL's regulations are invalid does not mean an employer failing to give proper customized notice does not have consequences. Courts apply the general rule that an employer's failure to provide adequate notice of FMLA procedures interferes with FMLA rights *if* the employee can show that the failure of notice denied the employee FMLA protections.[78] In other words, if there is "some adverse consequence due to the lack of knowledge"[79] – some way in which the employer's failure to give appropriate notice resulted in an employee's loss of FMLA rights or opportunities – the employer's failure to give the appropriate customized notice still constitutes a violation of the FMLA.

A good example of how an employer's failure to give appropriate notice adversely impacted an employee's FMLA rights can be found in one case where an employee was using FMLA leave to care for his terminally ill father. He asked for and was granted five weeks of leave but was not informed by his employer that he must return to work immediately if his father died before the five-week period expired. When the employee, three weeks into the FMLA leave, did not immediately return to work after his father died, the employer demoted him. A court found that because the employer failed to notify the employee of his responsibility to return to work immediately after the death of his father, it could not claim that the employee's failure to do so forfeited his FMLA rights.[80]

NOTES

[1] *Neide v. Grand Court Lifestyles, Inc.*, 38 F.Supp.2d 938 (D.Kan. 1999). *See generally* Aalberts & Seidman, *Employee Notice Requirements Under The Family And Medical Leave Act: Are They Manageable?*, Pepperdine Law Review (1997).

[2] *Allen v. Boeing Company*, 23 Fed. Appx. 839 (9th Cir. 2001); *Oracle Corporation v. Curtis*, 2001 WL 1230895 (D.Or. 2001); *Sampson v. Citibank, F.S.B.*, 53 F.Supp.2d 13 (D.D.C. 1999); *Giles v. Christian Care Centers, Inc.*, 1997 WL 786256 (N.D.Tex. 1997); *Bethel v. City of Garland*, 1997 WL 325983 (N.D.Tex. 1997); *Cummings v. Circus Circus Mississippi, Inc.*, 1997 WL 560870 (N.D.Miss. 1997).

[3] 29 U.S.C. §2612(e)(2).

[4] 29 C.F.R. §825.312(a); *see Toro v. Mastex Industries*, 32 F.Supp.2d 25 (D.Mass. 1999).

[5] *Williams v. Schuller International, Inc.*, 2002 WL 193929 (6th Cir. 2002); *Fields v. St. Charles School Board*, 78 Empl.Prac. ¶40,178 (E.D.La. 2000).

[6] *Cole v. Uni-Marts, Inc.*, 88 F.Supp.2d 67 (W.D.N.Y. 2000); *see* S. Rep. No. 3, 103rd Cong., 1st Sess. 25 (1993), reprinted in 1993 U.S.C.C.A.N. 3, 27, *and* H.R. Rep. No. 8, 103rd Cong., 1st Sess., pt. 1, at 38 (1993).

[7] 29 U.S.C. §2612(e)(2); 29 C.F.R. §825.303(a); *see Cole v. Uni-Marts*, 88 F.Supp.2d 67 (W.D.N.Y. 2000); *Weeden v. Sears Roebuck & Company*, 1999 WL 970538 (D.N.H. 1999).

[8] 29 C.F.R. §825.302(a); *see Hopson v. Quitman County Hospital and Nursing Home, Inc.*, 126 F.3d 635 (5th Cir. 1997).

[9] *See Cooper v. Harbour Inns of Baltimore, Inc.*, 5 WH Cas.2d 1804 (D.Md. 2000).

[10] *Hopson v. Quitman County Hospital and Nursing Home, Inc.*, 119 F.3d 363 (5th Cir. 1997).

[11] *Kaylor v. Fannin Regional Hospital, Inc.*, 946 F.Supp. 988 (N.D.Ga. 1996).

[12] 29 C.F.R. §825.302(b).

[13] *Mora v. Chem-Tronics, Inc.*, 16 F.Supp.2d 1192 (S.D.Cal. 1998).

[14] 29 C.F.R. §825.302(b); *see Holmes v. The Boeing Company*, 166 F.3d 1221 (10th Cir. 1999); *Latella v. National Passenger Railroad Corporation*, 94 F.Supp.2d 186 (D.Conn. 1999); *Brannon v. Oshkosh B'Gosh, Inc.*, 897 F.Supp. 1028 (M.D.Tenn. 1995).

[15] *Shivakumar v. Abbot Laboratories*, 7 WH Cas.2d 173 (N.D.Ill. 2001).

[16] *Dey v. County of Hennepin*, 1997 WL 10878 (Minn.App. 1997).

[17] 29 C.F.R. §825.302(d); *see Ozolins v. Northwood-Kensett Community School District*, 40 F.Supp.2d 1055 (N.D.Iowa 1999); *Gross v. Department of Justice*, 77 M.S.P.R. 83 (MSPB 1997); *Opinion Letter*, Wage & Hour Division, 1999 WL 1002427 (January 15, 1999).

[18] *Niesse v. General Electric Appliances*, 6 WH Cas.2d 1578 (S.D.Ind. 2001).

[19] *Gilliam v. United Parcel Service,* 233 F.3d 969 (7th Cir. 2000).

[20] *Lewis v. Holsom of Fort Wayne, Inc.,* 278 F.3d 706 (7th Cir. 2002); *Delong v. Trujillo,* 25 P.3d 1194 (Colo. 2001).

[21] 29 C.F.R. §825.302(c).

[22] 29 C.F.R. §825.302(e).

[23] 29 C.F.R. §825.302(b), §825.303. *See generally* Timothy Bland, *The Required Content Of Employees' Notice To Employers Of The Need For Leave Under The FMLA,* Labor Lawyer (Summer/Fall, 1996).

[24] *Tate v. Farmland Industries, Inc.,* 268 F.3d 989 (10th Cir. 2001); *Manual v. Westlake Polymers Corp.,* 66 F.3d 758 (5th Cir. 1995); *see Price v. City of Fort Wayne,* 117 F.3d 1022 (7th Cir. 1997); *Slaughter v. American Building Maintenance Co. of New York,* 64 F.Supp.2d 319 (S.D.N.Y. 1999); *Stubl v. T.A. Systems, Inc.,* 984 F.Supp. 1075 (E.D.Mich. 1997); *Williamson v. Mississippi Department of Human Services,* 4 WH Cas.2d 262 (N.D.Miss. 1997); *Paasch v. City of Safety Harbor,* 915 F.Supp. 315 (M.D.Fla. 1995); *Robbins v. Bureau of National Affairs,* 896 F.Supp. 18 (D.D.C. 1995); *Ellshoff v. Department of the Interior,* 76 M.S.P.R. 54 (MSPB 1997); *see D'Alia v. Allied-Signal Corp.* 614 A.2d 1355 (App.Div. 1992)(decided under state law).

[25] *Routes v. Henderson,* 58 F.Supp.2d 959 (S.D.Ind. 1999); *see Hammond v. Interstate Brands Corporation,* 2002 WL 31093603 (S.D.Ind. 2002).

[26] *Manuel v. Westlake Polymers Corp.,* 66 F.3d 758 (5th Cir. 1995); *see Spangler v. Federal Home Loan Bank of Des Moines,* 278 F.3d 847 (8th Cir. 2002).

[27] *Sims v. Alameda-Contra Costa Transit Dist.,* 2 F.Supp.2d 1253 (N.D.Cal. 1998).

[28] *Ozolins v. Northwood-Kensett Community School District,* 40 F.Supp.2d 1055 (N.D.Iowa 1999).

[29] *Covucci v. Service Merchandise Co., Inc.,* 189 F.3d 1294 (6th Cir. 1999).

[30] *Rollins v. Wilson County Government,* 154 F.3d 626 (6th Cir. 1998); *see Gross v. Department of Justice,* 77 M.S.P.R. 83 (MSPB 1997).

[31] *Fields v. St. Charles School Board,* 78 Empl.Prac. ¶40,178 (E.D.La. 2000).

[32] *Brannon v. Oshkosh B'Gosh, Inc.,* 897 F. Supp. 1028 (D.Tenn 1995). *See generally* Aalberts & Seidman, *The Family And Medical Leave Act: Does It Make Unreasonable Demands On Employers?,* Marquette Law Review (Fall 1996).

[33] *Schober v. SMC Pneumatics,* 2000 WL 1231557 (S.D.Ind. 2000).

[34] *Barr v. New York City Transit Authority,* 2002 WL 257823 (E.D.N.Y. 2002).

[35] *Hendry v. GTE North, Inc.,* 896 F.Supp. 816 (N.D.Ind. 1995).

[36] *Uema v. Nippon Express Hawaii, Inc.,* 26 F.Supp.2d 1241 (D.Haw. 1998).

[37] *O'Hara v. Mt. Vernon Board of Education,* 16 F.Supp.2d 868 (S.D.Ohio 1998).

[38] *Burge v. Department of the Air Force,* 82 M.S.P.R. 75 (MSPB 1999).

39 *Owens v. Farmers Insurance Exchange*, 137 Lab. Cas. ¶33,832 (Wash.App. 1999).

40 *Wilson v. Lemington Home For The Aged*, 2001 WL 1079030 (W.D.Pa. 2001).

41 *Paasch v. City of Safety Harbor*, 915 F.Supp. 315 (M.D.Fla. 1995); *see Nelson v. Arkansas Pediatric Facility*, 1 Fed. Appx. 561 (8th Cir. 2001); *Woodard v. Union Pacific Railroad Company, Inc.*, 2002 WL 192993 (S.D.Tex. 2002); *Rineheimer v. Cemcolift, Inc.*, 6 WH Cas.2d 1324 (E.D.Pa. 2001); *Fry v. First Fidelity Bancorporation*, 1996 WL 36910 (E.D.Pa. 1996).

42 *Satterfield v. Wal-Mart Stores, Inc.*, 135 F.3d 973 (5th Cir. 1998); *see Collins v. NTN-Bower Corporation*, 272 F.3d 1006 (7th Cir. 2001).

43 *Johnson v. Primerica*, 67 Empl.Prac. ¶33,346 (S.D.N.Y. 1996).

44 *Zawadowicz v. CVS Corp.*, 99 F.Supp.2d 518 (D.N.J. 2000).

45 *Russell v. First Health Services*, 2001 WL 568037 (4th Cir. 2001).

46 *Seaman v. C.S.P.H., Inc.*, 1997 WL 538751 (N.D.Tex. 1997).

47 *Niesse v. General Electric Appliances*, 6 WH Cas.2d 1578 (S.D.Ind. 2001).

48 *McGraw v. Sears, Roebuck & Co.*, 21 F.Supp.2d 1017 (D.Minn. 1998).

49 *Gay v. Gilman Paper Company*, 125 F.3d 1432 (11th Cir. 1997).

50 *Haugie v., Equistar Chemical Company*, 8 WH Cas.2d 1968390 (N.D.Ill. 2002).

51 *Kramarski v. Village of Orland Park*, 2002 WL 1827637 (N.D.Ill. 2002).

52 *Satterfield v. Wal-Mart Stores, Inc.*, 135 F.3d 973 (5th Cir. 1998).

53 *Carter v.. Ford Motor Co.*, 121 F.3d 1146 (8th Cir. 1997).

54 *Sanghvi v. Frendel*, 242 F.3d 367 (2nd Cir. 2000).

55 *Slaughter v. American Building Maintenance Co. of New York*, 64 F.Supp.2d 319 (S.D.N.Y. 1999).

56 *McGraw v. Sears, Roebuck & Co.*, 21 F.Supp.2d 1017 (D.Minn. 1998); *see Browning v. Liberty Mutual Insurance Company*, 178 F.3d 1043 (8th Cir. 1999).

57 *Johnson v. Primerica*, 67 Empl.Prac. ¶33,346 (S.D.N.Y. 1996).

58 *Shivakumar v. Abbot Laboratories*, 7 WH Cas.2d 173 (N.D.Ill. 2001).

59 *Slaughter v. American Building Maintenance Co. of New York*, 64 F.Supp.2d 319 (S.D.N.Y. 1999); *see DeLong v. Trujillo*, 1 P.3d 195 (Colo.App. 1999).

60 29 C.F.R. §825.301(a)(1); *see Wilson v. Lemington Home For The Aged*, 2001 WL 1079030 (W.D.Pa. 2001); *Zawadowicz v. CVS Corp.*, 99 F.Supp.2d 518 (D.N.J. 2000).

61 *Bond v. Abbott Laboratories*, 188 F.3d 506 (6th Cir. 1999).

62 *Mora v. Chem-Tronics*, 16 F.Supp.2d 1192 (S.D.Cal. 1998).

[63] *Wilson v. Lemington Home For The Aged*, 2001 WL 1079030 (W.D.Pa. 2001); *Chan v. Loyola University Medical Center*, 6 WH Cas.2d 328 (N.D.Ill. 1999).

[64] 29 C.F.R. §825.301(a)(2).

[65] 29 C.F.R. §825.301(b)(1).

[66] *Sims v. Alameda-Contra Costa Transit Dist.*, 2 F.Supp.2d 1253 (N.D.Cal. 1998); *Reich v. Midwest Plastic Engineering, Inc.*, 66 Empl.Prac. ¶43701 (W.D.Mich. 1995).

[67] *Chan v. Loyola University Medical Center*, 5 WH Cas.2d 584 (N.D.Ill. 1999).

[68] 29 C.F.R. §825.301(b)(1)(i)-(viii); *see Howell v. Standard Motor Products, Inc.*, 144 Lab. Cas. ¶34,349 (N.D.Tex. 2001).

[69] 29 C.F.R. §825.301(b)(2).

[70] *Chan v. Loyola University Medical Center*, 6 WH Cas.2d 328 (N.D.Ill. 1999).

[71] *Wilson v. Lemington Home For The Aged*, 2001 WL 1079030 (W.D.Pa. 2001); *see Voorhees v. Time Warner Cable National Division*, 6 WH Cas.2d 598 (E.D.Pa. 1999). In *Delong v. Trujillo*, 25 P.3d 1194 (Colo. 2001), decided under the DOL's interim regulations that did not explicitly require written notice of FMLA rights and obligations, a state court found that an employee's experience with the FMLA sufficed to relieve the employer of the obligation to provide written notice.

[72] *Reynolds v. Phillips & Temro Indus., Inc.*, 195 F.3d 411 (8th Cir. 1999); *Rinehimer v. Cemcolift, Inc.*, 6 WH Cas.2d 1324 (E.D.Pa. 2001).

[73] 29 C.F.R. §825.301(d).

[74] 29 C.F.R. §825.301(e).

[75] 29 C.F.R. §825.301(g); *see Chan v. Loyola University Medical Center*, 5 WH Cas.2d 584 (N.D.Ill. 1999).

[76] *Mora v. Chem-Tronics*, 16 F.Supp.2d 1192 (S.D.Cal. 1998).

[77] *Ragsdale v. Wolverine Worldwide, Inc.*, 531 U.S. 991 (2002). Prior to the Supreme Court's decision, the majority of courts had upheld the validity of the DOL's regulations. *Compare McGregor v. Autozone, Inc.*, 180 F.3d 1305 (11th Cir. 1999)(regulations invalid); *Daley v. Wellpoint Health Networks, Inc.*, 2001 WL 539463 (D.Mass. 2001); *Nolan v. Hypercom Mfg. Resources*, 2001 WL 378235 (D.Ariz. 2001)(same); *Twyman v. Dilks*, 6 WH Cas.2d 550 (E.D.Pa. 2000); *Neal v. Children's Habilitation Center*, 1999 WL 706117 (N.D.Ill. 1999) *with Chan v. Loyola University Medical Center*, 6 WH Cas.2d 328 (N.D.Ill. 1999)(regulations valid); *Plant v. Morton Int'l, Inc.*, 212 F.3d 929 (6th Cir. 2000); *Nusbaum v. CB Richard Ellis, Inc.*, 171 F.Supp.2d 377 (D.N.J. 2001); *Ritchie v. Grand Casinos of Mississippi, Inc.*, 49 F.Supp.2d 878 (S.D.Miss. 1999); *Longstreth v. Copple*, 1999 WL 979451 (N.D.Iowa 1999); *cf. Cline v. Wal-Mart, Inc.*, 144 F.3d 294 (4th Cir. 1998); *Holmes v. e.spire Communications*, 135 F.Supp.2d 657 (D.Md. 2001); *Barone v. Leukemia Society of America*, 42 F.Supp.2d 452 (D.N.J. 1998); *Blankenship v. Buchanan General Hosp.*, 999 F.Supp. 832 (W.D.Va. 1998); *Drew v. Waffle House, Inc.*, 534 S.E.2d 282 (S.C.App. 2000). *See generally Steller v. Crystal Cruises, Inc.*, 188 F.3d 515 (9th Cir. 1999).

78 *See Lacoparra v. Pergament Home Centers, Inc.*, 982 F.Supp. 213 (S.D.N.Y. 1997); *Fry v. First Fidelity Bankcorp.*, 1996 WL 36910 (E.D.Pa. 1996).

79 *Gunderson v. Neiman-Marcus Group, Inc.*, 982 F.Supp. 1231 (N.D.Tex. 1997).

80 *Sherry v. Protection, Inc.*, 981 F.Supp. 1133 (N.D.Ill. 1997).

CHAPTER 7

CERTIFICATION OF SERIOUS HEALTH CONDITION AND SECOND OPINIONS

In A Nutshell . . .

If an employer has reason to suspect the validity of a request for FMLA leave, it can request certification of the underlying reason. The certification process, which can involve second and third medical opinions, is part of the FMLA's bias towards open communications between employers and employees about the need for FMLA leave.

An Employer's Right To Certification Of A Serious Health Condition.

The Statute: 29 U.S.C. §2613.

(a) In general

An employer may require that a request for leave under subparagraph (C) or (D) of section 2612(a)(1) of this title be supported by a certification issued by the health care provider of the eligible employee or of the son, daughter, spouse, or parent of the employee, as appropriate. The employee shall provide, in a timely manner, a copy of such certification to the employer.

(b) Sufficient certification provided under subsection (a) of this section shall be if it states -

(1) the date on which the serious health condition commenced;

(2) the probable duration of the condition;

(3) the appropriate medical facts within the knowledge of the health care provider regarding the condition;

(4)(A) for purposes of leave under section 2612(a)(1)(C) of this title, a statement that the eligible employee is needed to care for the son, daughter, spouse, or parent and an estimate of the amount of time that such employee is needed to care for the son, daughter, spouse, or parent; and (B) for purposes of leave under section 2612(a)(1)(D) of this title, a statement that the employee is unable to perform the functions of the position of the employee.

An employer receiving a request for FMLA leave accompanied by a doctor's note has three choices: (1) Inquire further of the employee of the need for leave; (2) Request certification; or (3) Grant the leave.

The FMLA grants employers the right to request that an employee provide "certification" of the need to use leave because of a serious health condition. At the time the employer asks for certification, it must also advise the employee what will happen if he/she fails to comply.[1] The certification must be furnished by the health care provider and must indicate at least four things to be valid, including:

(1) The date on which the serious health condition started;

(2) How long the condition is likely to last;

(3) Medical facts about the condition; and,

(4) A statement that the employee is unable to perform the functions of his job or that the employee is needed to care for an eligible family member.[2]

The rationale behind requiring certification is firmly rooted in the FMLA's bias towards an interaction between the employer and the employee about the need for FMLA leave. Congress, the DOL, and the courts clearly share the view that questions about the need for FMLA leave related to serious health conditions should be addressed at the employer-employee level rather than in the courts. The employer has the brunt of responsibility for initiating the discussion about the need for FMLA leave. According to one court, when an employee requests FMLA leave because of a serious health condition, the employer has three choices: (1) Inquire further about the employee's condition; (2) Request certification; or (3) Grant the leave.[3] Courts expect employers to approach the whole issue of certification in good faith, not as a way to use technical arguments about why an employee's certification may be inadequate. In the words of one court, "an employer cannot play games with the certification requirement by taking adverse action as soon as an incomplete certificate is supplied." [4]

The FMLA's certification requirements pose the following questions.

What is the appropriate form for a request for medical certification? The DOL's regulations suggest a medical certification request should be in writing and should advise the employee of what will happen if he/she fails to provide the certification.[5] Though the matter is not completely settled, it appears a certification request must be individualized and that a blanket request for certification in an employer's manual will not adequately inform the employee of the employer's request for certification.[6] The DOL's regulations are designed to give the employee information about the employer's certification rules and to give the employee the chance to alleviate any deficiency that might exist in a certification. For these reasons, an employer that fails to make a written request for certification cannot later complain of an insufficiency in the certification.[7]

The DOL has developed the following form to use in obtaining medical certification. The form is designed to elicit the information allowed under the FMLA and still be consistent with the privacy provisions of the Americans With Disabilities Act.[8]

Certification of Health Care Provider
(Family and Medical Leave Act of 1993)

U.S. Department of Labor
Employment Standards Administration
Wage and Hour Division

(When completed, this form goes to the employee, __not to the Department of Labor__.)	OMB No.: 1215-0181 Expires: 07/31/03

1. Employee's Name	2. Patient's Name *(If different from employee)*

3. Page 4 describes what is meant by a **"serious health condition"** under the Family and Medical Leave Act. Does the patient's condition[1] qualify under any of the categories described? If so, please check the applicable category.

   (1) _____ (2) _____ (3) _____ (4) _____ (5) _____ (6) _____ , or None of the above _____

4. Describe the **medical facts** which support your certification, including a brief statement as to how the medical facts meet the criteria of one of these categories:

5. a. State the approximate **date** the condition commenced, and the probable duration of the condition (and also the probable duration of the patient's present **incapacity**[2] if different):

   b. Will it be necessary for the employee to take work only **intermittently or to work on a less than full schedule** as a result of the condition (including for treatment described in Item 6 below)?

   If yes, give the probable duration:

   c. If the condition is a **chronic condition** (condition #4) or **pregnancy**, state whether the patient is presently incapacitated[2] and the likely duration and frequency of **episodes of incapacity**[2]:

---

[1] Here and elsewhere on this form, the information sought relates **only** to the condition for which the employee is taking FMLA leave.

[2] "Incapacity," for purposes of FMLA, is defined to mean inability to work, attend school or perform other regular daily activities due to the serious health condition, treatment therefor, or recovery therefrom.

Form WH-380
Revised December 1999

6. a. If additional **treatments** will be required for the condition, provide an estimate of the probable number of such treatments.

If the patient will be absent from work or other daily activities because of **treatment** on an **intermittent** or **part-time** basis, also provide an estimate of the probable number of and interval between such treatments, actual or estimated dates of treatment if known, and period required for recovery if any:

b. If any of these treatments will be provided by **another provider of health services** (e.g., physical therapist), please state the nature of the treatments:

c. **If a regimen of continuing treatment** by the patient is required under your supervision, provide a general description of such regimen (*e.g.*, prescription drugs, physical therapy requiring special equipment):

7. a. If medical leave is required for the employee's **absence from work** because of the **employee's own condition** (including absences due to pregnancy or a chronic condition), is the employee **unable to perform work** of any kind?

b. If able to perform some work, is the employee **unable to perform any one or more of the essential functions of the employee's job** (the employee or the employer should supply you with information about the essential job functions)? If yes, please list the essential functions the employee is unable to perform:

c. If neither a. nor b. applies, is it necessary for the employee to be **absent from work for treatment**?

8. a. If leave is required to **care for a family member** of the employee with a serious health condition, **does the patient require assistance** for basic medical or personal needs or safety, or for transportation?

   b. If no, would the employee's presence to provide **psychological comfort** be beneficial to the patient or assist in the patient's recovery?

   c. If the patient will need care only **intermittently** or on a part-time basis, please indicate the probable **duration** of this need:

Signature of Health Care Provider

Type of Practice

Address

Telephone Number

Date

To be completed by the employee needing family leave to care for a family member:

State the care you will provide and an estimate of the period during which care will be provided, including a schedule if leave is to be taken intermittently or if it will be necessary for you to work less than a full schedule:

Employee Signature

Date

A **"Serious Health Condition"** means an illness, injury impairment, or physical or mental condition that involves one of the following:

1. Hospital Care

   Inpatient care (*i.e.*, an overnight stay) in a hospital, hospice, or residential medical care facility, including any period of incapacity[2] or subsequent treatment in connection with or consequent to such inpatient care.

2. Absence Plus Treatment

   (a) A period of incapacity[2] of **more than three consecutive calendar days** (including any subsequent treatment or period of incapacity[2] relating to the same condition), that also involves:

   (1) **Treatment**[3] **two or more times** by a health care provider, by a nurse or physician's assistant under direct supervision of a health care provider, or by a provider of health care services (*e.g.*, physical therapist) under orders of, or on referral by, a health care provider; or

   (2) **Treatment** by a health care provider on **at least one occasion** which results in a **regimen of continuing treatment**[4] under the supervision of the health care provider.

3. Pregnancy

   Any period of incapacity due to **pregnancy**, or for **prenatal care**.

4. Chronic Conditions Requiring Treatments

   A **chronic condition** which:

   (1) Requires **periodic visits** for treatment by a health care provider, or by a nurse or physician's assistant under direct supervision of a health care provider;

   (2) Continues over an **extended period of time** (including recurring episodes of a single underlying condition); and

   (3) May cause **episodic** rather than a continuing period of incapacity[2] (*e.g.*, asthma, diabetes, epilepsy, etc.).

5. Permanent/Long-term Conditions Requiring Supervision

   A period of **Incapacity**[2] which is **permanent or long-term** due to a condition for which treatment may not be effective. The employee or family member must be **under the continuing supervision of, but need not be receiving active treatment by, a health care provider**. Examples include Alzheimer's, a severe stroke, or the terminal stages of a disease.

6. Multiple Treatments (Non-Chronic Conditions)

   Any period of absence to receive **multiple treatments** (including any period of recovery therefrom) by a health care provider or by a provider of health care services under orders of, or on referral by, a health care provider, either for **restorative surgery** after an accident or other injury, **or** for a condition that **would likely result in a period of Incapacity**[2] **of more than three consecutive calendar days in the absence of medical intervention or treatment**, such as cancer (chemotherapy, radiation, etc.), severe arthritis (physical therapy), and kidney disease (dialysis).

This optional form may be used by employees to satisfy a mandatory requirement to furnish a medical certification (when requested) from a health care provider, including second or third opinions and recertification (29 CFR 825.306).

Note: Persons are not required to respond to this collection of information unless it displays a currently valid OMB control number.

[3] Treatment includes examinations to determine if a serious health condition exists and evaluations of the condition. Treatment does not include routine physical examinations, eye examinations, or dental examinations.

[4] A regimen of continuing treatment includes, for example, a course of prescription medication (*e.g.*, an antibiotic) or therapy requiring special equipment to resolve or alleviate the health condition. A regimen of treatment does not include the taking of over-the-counter medications such as aspirin, antihistamines, or salves; or bed-rest, drinking fluids, exercise, and other similar activities that can be initiated without a visit to a health care provider.

Public Burden Statement

We estimate that it will take an average of 10 minutes to complete this collection of information, including the time for reviewing instructions, searching existing data sources, gathering and maintaining the data needed, and completing and reviewing the collection of information. If you have any comments regarding this burden estimate or any other aspect of this collection of information, including suggestions for reducing this burden, send them to the Administrator, Wage and Hour Division, Department of Labor, Room S-3502, 200 Constitution Avenue, N.W., Washington, D.C. 20210.

DO NOT SEND THE COMPLETED FORM TO THIS OFFICE; IT GOES TO THE EMPLOYEE.

What happens when the employer fails to advise the employee of the anticipated consequences of a failure to comply with a request for certification? Though the DOL's regulations require employers to notify employees of the likely consequences of failing to provide certification, they are silent on the consequences of an employer's failure to do so. Some employees have argued that an employer's failure to warn them of these consequences means they no longer need to provide certification. Courts have rejected this argument, finding that "to read such a penalty into the regulation could effectively nullify section 2613 of the FMLA, which authorizes an employer to require an employee with a serious health condition to supply the appropriate medical certification."[9]

What happens if the certification by the health care provider fails to answer the four certification questions or answers them in a manner that suggests that FMLA leave is not appropriate? As described above, the FMLA requires that the health care provider's certification include four things to be valid: (1) The date the serious health condition started; (2) how long the condition is likely to last; (3) medical facts about the condition; and (4) a statement that the employee is unable to perform the functions of her job or is needed to care for an eligible family member.[10] If the certification fails to provide this information, the employee is not entitled to FMLA leave or to remain on FMLA leave (if already on leave).[11] The employer may rely on that certification until the employee produces medical information to the contrary.[12] If an employee, claiming to suffer from a serious health condition, fails to return to work after a doctor's certification indicates they can perform the essential functions of the job, the employee may be terminated.[13]

What type of certification is appropriate when the FMLA leave is used for a serious illness in the employee's family? If the employee is using FMLA leave to care for a member of the employee's family, certification must generally do more than merely recite the family member's medical condition. The best form of certification is a doctor's statement not only of the family member's condition, but stating that the employee is needed to care for the family member.[14]

If requested, an employee must provide certification before taking FMLA leave. If the need for the leave is unforeseeable, the certification must be provided within 15 days of the request if "practicable."

How much time does the employee have to respond to a request for certification? If the need for FMLA leave is foreseeable, and at least 30 days' notice of the need for certification has been given by the employer, the employee must provide the medical certification before the FMLA leave begins.[15] If the leave is unforeseeable, the employer must allow at least 15 calendar days for the employee to comply with the request for certification, unless it is not practicable despite the employee's diligent, good faith efforts.[16] If the employee cannot provide certification within the required time period, the employee must contact the employer to explain why the certification is not being provided.[17] In one case, an employee furnished the results of a doctor's complete evaluation in addition to an earlier doctor's note; the court found that providing the information 12 days *after* the employer's request for information was "as soon as practicable."[18] If the employee simply does not respond to a request for certification, the employer may deny the request for FMLA leave.[19]

Sometimes dealings between the employer and the employee will define when certification must be provided. In one case, an employee who used intermittent FMLA leave to care for his seriously-ill wife often submitted certification to document past absences, sometimes providing them weeks after the absences occurred. A court found it an open question whether this practice rendered the employer's general request for contemporaneous certification for each absence unenforceable.[20]

Can the employer make an ongoing request for certification every time an employee uses FMLA leave without renewing the request when the employee subsequently requests leave? For an employee with a chronic condition, an employer may find it easier to make a blanket request for certification for *all future use* of FMLA leave rather than request certification on each occasion of leave requested. However, the DOL's regulations do not appear to allow blanket requests, providing instead that "an employer must give notice of a requirement for medical certification each time a certification is required."[21] Applying this regulation, one court has held that an employer handbook requiring certification for each use of FMLA leave did not satisfy the employer's obligation to notify the employee as to the need for certification when she required FMLA leave. In the words of the Court, "the regulations clearly contemplate that the employer may not need certification for every FMLA absence and any additional requirement for providing notice of absences should be conducted, in the first instance, through informal means."[22]

Is an employer required to request certification? Nothing in the FMLA or the DOL's regulations *require* an employer to request certification; rather, certification is merely an option open to employers. An employer is free to dispense with the certification requirement or to allow certification with more generous deadlines than the FMLA's.[23]

Certification When Leave Is Intermittent Or On A Reduced Leave Schedule.

The Statute: 29 U.S.C. §2613.

(5) in the case of certification for intermittent leave, or leave on a reduced leave schedule, for planned medical treatment, the dates on which such treatment is expected to be given and the duration of such treatment;

(6) in the case of certification for intermittent leave, or leave on a reduced leave schedule, under section 2612(a)(1)(D) of this title, a statement of the medical necessity for the intermittent leave or leave on a reduced leave schedule, and the expected duration of the intermittent leave or reduced leave schedule; and

(7) in the case of certification for intermittent leave, or leave on

> a reduced leave schedule, under section 2612(a)(1)(C) of this title, a statement that the employee's intermittent leave or leave on a reduced leave schedule is necessary for the care of the son, daughter, parent, or spouse who has a serious health condition, or will assist in their recovery, and the expected duration and schedule of the intermittent leave or reduced leave schedule.

The type of certification needed when leave is intermittent or reduced differs slightly, depending on why the leave is being used. When the employee is using intermittent or reduced FMLA leave *and* the leave is needed for **planned medical treatment**, certification should include the dates that treatment is expected and for how long. When the intermittent FMLA leave is being used because of the **employee's own serious health condition** (but not for treatment), certification must explain the medical necessity of the intermittent or reduced leave and the expected duration of the leave. When the intermittent FMLA leave is being used because of the **serious health condition of a qualifying family member** (but not for treatment), certification must include a statement that the leave is necessary to care for the family member or will assist in their recovery, and must indicate the anticipated duration and schedule of the leave. An employer requesting certification of intermittent leave should also notify the employee of the consequences of failing to provide certification.[24]

An Employer's Questions About The Adequacy Of Certification And The Employer's Right To A Second Opinion.

> ### The Statute: 29 U.S.C. §2613.
>
> (c) Second opinion
>
> (1) In general
>
> In any case in which the employer has reason to doubt the validity of the certification provided under subsection (a) of this section for leave under subparagraph (C) or (D) of section 2612(a)(1) of this title, the employer may require, at the expense of the employer, that the eligible employee obtain the opinion of a second health care provider designated or approved by the employer concerning any information certified under subsection (b) of this section for such leave.
>
> (2) Limitation

A health care provider designated or approved under paragraph (1) shall not be employed on a regular basis by the employer.

Once an employer receives medical certification, it may have questions about the validity of the certification. The FMLA does not allow an employer to reject a certification out-of-hand; rather, it creates a verification process an employer can use.[25] Because of privacy concerns, the DOL's rules forbid an employer from directly requesting additional information from the employee's health care provider.[26] However, the DOL's rules do allow the employer's health care provider to contact the employee's health care provider (with the employee's permission) for purposes of clarifying any questions about medical certification.[27] And, if the employee's condition is covered by workers' compensation, the DOL's rules allow direct contact with the employee's workers' compensation health care provider, provided such direct contact is allowed by state law.[28]

The FMLA allows an employer with questions about the adequacy of an employee's certification to require that the employee get the opinion of a second health care provider designated or approved by the employer. If the employer elects to ask for a second opinion, it must pay all associated expenses, including travel expenses.[29] Until the second opinion is received, the employee is provisionally entitled to FMLA benefits.[30] The employee is entitled to a copy of the second opinion.[31] The health care provider may not be regularly employed by the employer except in locations where access to health care is extremely limited.[32] However, if the health care provider indicates that the employee should be granted FMLA leave, the employee will not be harmed by the fact that the health care provider is employed on a regular basis by the employer.[33]

An employer is only required to use the second opinion process if it has doubts as to the employee's (or family member's) underlying medical condition. If, after reviewing the employee's initial medical certification, the employer has no questions about the underlying medical condition but believes that the condition does not justify FMLA leave, it is under no obligation to request a second opinion.[34]

Breaking The Tie Between Dueling Doctors – Resolving Conflicting Medical Opinions.

The Statute: 29 U.S.C. §2613.

(d) Resolution of conflicting opinions

(1) In general

In any case in which the second opinion described in subsection (c) of this section differs from the opinion in the original certification provided under subsection (a) of this section, the employer may require, at the expense of the employer, that the employee obtain the opinion of a third health care provider designated or approved jointly by the employer and the employee concerning the information certified under subsection (b) of this section.

(2) Finality

The opinion of the third health care provider concerning the information certified under subsection (b) of this section shall be considered to be final and shall be binding on the employer and the employee.

The FMLA envisions that occasionally the opinions of the employee's doctor may not be in accord with that of the doctor rendering the second opinion. The FJMLA allows an employer to compel a third medical examination at its own expense. The health care provider rendering the third opinion must be approved by the employer and the employee, who are required to act in "good faith" in selecting an individual to render the opinion.[35] If either side does not put forth the requisite "good faith" effort, the medical issue is considered resolved against that party's position. The opinion of the third health care provider is "final and shall be binding on the employer and the employee."[36] The employee is entitled to a copy of the third opinion within two business days unless extenuating circumstances prevail.[37]

The Rationale Behind The Certification Requirement.

The whole idea behind the certification, second opinion, and third opinion provisions of the FMLA is to have medical decisions made by doctors, not by the courts or employers.[38] In issuing its final regulations, the DOL commented that once an employee provides certification, "the only recourse available to an employer that doubts the validity of the certification is to request a second medical opinion at the employer's expense. Employers may not substitute their personal judgments for the test in the regulations or the medical opinions of the health care providers of employees * * * to determine whether an employee is entitled to FMLA leave for a serious health condition."[39]

Perhaps somewhat surprisingly, the courts are split over whether an employer's failing to ask for certification precludes its asserting later that no serious health condition existed. Some courts find that since the right to request certification is optional, the failure to request certification does not impact the employer's later ability to argue that no serious health condition existed.[40] Other courts find that unless an employer that failed to request certification is later barred from contesting the existence of a serious health condition, an employee is put in the difficult position of having to guess about whether or not an employer will challenge at a later date the employee's claim of a serious health condition.[41]

What if the employee provides certification, as requested by the employer, and the employer fails to use the second and third-opinion process? Courts seem to agree that the employer will be bound by the *medical* conclusions in the certification.[42] However, an employer may later argue that the medical conclusions do not amount to an FMLA-qualifying serious health condition.[43]

Even in courts adhering to the notion that an employer not requesting certification may later contest the existence of a serious health condition, an employer faces potential pitfalls in later litigation if it does not request certification. For example, in one case an employer failing to request certification was required to rely on a physician's examination made months after the employee was terminated. An appeals court upheld the judgment against the employer, finding that the employee's evidence (contemporaneous notes from her physician that she was not to work) could not be rebutted by the employer.[44]

Recertification Of Health Conditions.

The Statute: 29 U.S.C. §2613.

(e) Subsequent recertification

The employer may require that the eligible employee obtain subsequent recertifications on a reasonable basis.

The FMLA is particularly brief in only requiring that an employer may ask an eligible employee to obtain subsequent recertifications on a "reasonable basis." The DOL has fleshed out this provision a bit, indicating that for pregnancy, chronic conditions, or permanent or long-term conditions under the continued supervision of a health care provider, an employer may request recertification no more often than every 30 days.[45] Two exceptions to this 30-day rule exist: (1) If circumstances, such as the severity of the condition or complications described by the previous certification, have changed significantly; or (2) if the employer receives information that casts doubt on the stated reasons for the absence.[46]

If the period of incapacity specified on a certification exceeds 30 days, then the employer may not request recertification until that time has passed. Similarly, if FMLA leave is taken intermittently or on a reduced leave schedule, the employer may not request recertification before the minimum period specified.[47] Exceptions to these two rules are (1) if the employee requests an extension of leave; (2) if the circumstances described by the previous certification have changed significantly; or (3) if the employer receives information that casts doubt upon the continuing validity of the certification.[48]

Three special rules on recertification exist. First, any recertification requested by the employer is at the employee's expense, unless the employer provides otherwise (through insurance coverage, for example).[49] Second, an employer is not allowed to ask for a second or third opinion on recertification.[50] Third, the employer must give the employee at least 15 calendar days, or such longer time as may be reasonable, to provide recertification.[51]

When is an employer's request a request for recertification and when is it a request for "new certification?" Since the employer can only request recertification every 30 days, and since no second or third opinion is available with recertification, the distinction may be significant. In one case, an employee began using FMLA leave because of her son's Attention Deficit Hyperactivity Disorder (ADHD), providing medical certification to the employer of the son's condition. Later, the employee's son's behavior improved, and the employee returned to work. Then the son's school recommended a number of measures to deal with his ADHD, and the employee requested a modified work schedule that included intermittent FMLA leave. The employer responded to this request with a demand for certification. A court found the employer's demand was a request for new certification, reasoning that the employee's return to work ended the "recertification" process. [52]

Certification As A Condition Of Restoration To The Employee's Former Job.

The Statute: 29 U.S.C. §2614.

(a) Restoration to position

(1) In general

Except as provided in subsection (b) of this section, any eligible employee who takes leave under section 2612 of this title for the intended purpose of the leave shall be entitled, on return from such leave -

(A) to be restored by the employer to the position of employment held by the employee when the leave commenced; or

(B) to be restored to an equivalent position with equivalent employment benefits, pay, and other terms and conditions of employment. . . .

(4) Certification

As a condition of restoration under paragraph (1) for an employee who has taken leave under section 2612(a)(1)(D) of this title, the employer may have a uniformly applied practice or policy that requires each such employee to receive certification from the health care provider of the employee that the employee is able to resume work, except that nothing in this paragraph shall supersede a valid State or local law or a collective bargaining agreement that governs the return to work of such employees.

The FMLA allows the employer to have a "uniformly applied practice or policy" requiring certification from the employee's health care provider that an employee who has taken FMLA leave is able to return to work. The DOL has interpreted "uniformly applied" to mean that the employer requires all similarly-situated employees (those who hold the same occupation or who have the same health condition) who take leave for such conditions to obtain certification before returning to work.[53] The employer may require that the employee pay for the certification, which need only be "a simple statement of [the employee's] ability to return to work," and the employer's requirement should be announced to the employee in advance of the employee's actual request for job restoration.[54] The employer may delay restoring the employee to his former job pending certification results.[55] These return-to-work procedures can be changed if state or local law or a collective bargaining agreement governs the terms of an employee's return to work. In such a case, the employer is required to follow the procedures set forth in the collective bargaining agreement or law.[56]

Assuming an employer has a "uniformly applied practice" of requiring certification as a precondition to job restoration, the employer may seek fitness-for-duty certification only for the health condition underlying the FMLA leave.[57] If the employee produces certification that the employee is fit for duty, the employer must honor the certification and restore the employee to her job.[58] While the employer has the right to get "clarification" of the certification, the employee is entitled to be reinstated pending the clarification.[59]

CASE IN POINT

Question: Advanced Information Technologies, a rapidly growing company with 750 employees, believes some of its employees may be abusing FMLA leave. In particular, the Company is concerned about a spate of requests for FMLA leave from employees claiming back injuries. To address the issue, the Company issues a new directive requiring that in the future all employees seeking FMLA leave because of their back conditions must obtain medical certification of their condition. Under the directive, employees are required to pay for the certification and must present it to the Company before returning to work. Is the directive valid?

Answer: Because the directive does not apply retroactively and because it will apply uniformly to all employees with particular kinds of conditions, the directive is permissible under the FMLA. An employer may have difficulties demanding certification under the FMLA, however, if the employer's practice is not uniformly applied or if the employer attempts to change its practices and apply the new rules retroactively.

Certification When An Employee Is Unable To Return To Work.

The Statute: 29 U.S.C. §2614(c).

(3) Certification

(A) An employer may require that a claim that an employee is unable to return to work because of the continuation, recurrence, or onset of the serious health condition described in paragraph (2)(B)(i) be supported by -

(i) a certification issued by the health care provider of the son, daughter, spouse, or parent of the employee, as appropriate, in the case of an employee unable to return to work because of a condition specified in section 2612(a)(1)(C) of this title; or

(ii) a certification issued by the health care provider of the eligible employee, in the case of an employee unable to return to work because of a condition specified in section 2612(a)(1)(D) of this title.

(B) The employee shall provide, in a timely manner, a copy of such certification to the employer.

(C)(i) Leave due to serious health condition of employee

The certification described in subparagraph (A)(ii) shall be sufficient if the certification states that a serious health condition prevented the employee from being able to perform the functions of the position of the employee on the date that the leave of the employee expired.

(ii) Leave due to serious health condition of family member

The certification described in subparagraph (A)(i) shall be sufficient if the certification states that the employee is needed to care for the son, daughter, spouse, or parent who has a serious health condition on the date that the leave of the employee expired.

If an employee fails to return to work at the end of unpaid FMLA leave, the employer may have the right to recover health insurance premiums paid by the employer during the leave. However, if the reason the employee fails to return to work is due to the continuation of the health condition, or other reasons beyond the employee's control, the employer may not recover the premium costs.

Section 2614(c)(3) of the FMLA states that when the employee indicates that he or she is unable to return to work, the employer may demand, at the employee's expense, a certification of the underlying medical condition by the health care provider.[60] If the leave was used because of the employee's serious health condition, the certification must state that the condition prevented the employee from being able to perform the employee's job functions on the date that the leave expired. In the case of leave for a family member, the certification must state that the employee is needed to care for the family member on the date that the leave of the employee expired.

NOTES

1 29 C.F.R. §825.305(d).

2 *Henthorn v. Olsten Corp.*, 5 WH Cas.2d 539 (N.D.Ill. 1999); *Kinchelow v. Robinson Property Group, L.P.*, 4 WH Cas.2d 987 (N.D.Miss. 1998).

3 *Goodwin-Haulmark v. Menninger Clinic, Inc.*, 76 F.Supp.2d 1235 (D.Kan. 1999); *Williams v. Shenango, Inc.*, 986 F.Supp. 309 (W.D.Pa. 1997); *see Barnett v. Revere Smelting & Refining Corp.*, 67 F.Supp.2d 378 (S.D.N.Y. 1999).

4 *Morris v. VCW, Inc.*, 3 WH Cas.2d 763 (W.D.Mo. 1996).

5 29 C.F.R. §825.301(b)(ii). It is unclear whether an employer can make a blanket request for certification insisting that each instance of an employee's future use of FMLA leave be certified. *See Pagan v. U.S. Postal Service*, 230 F.3d 1374 (Fed. Cir. 1999).

6 *Henderson v. Whirlpool Corp.*, 17 F.Supp.2d 1238 (N.D.Okla. 1998).

7 *Fantasia v. Ethan Allen, Inc.*, 1999 WL 22735 (Conn.Super. 1999).

8 *Opinion Letter,* Wage and Hour Division, 1995 WL 1036742 (September 14, 1995).

9 *Henthorn v. Olsten Corp.*, 5 WH Cas.2d 539 (N.D.Ill. 1999).

10 *Henthorn v. Olsten Corp.*, 5 WH Cas.2d 539 (N.D.Ill. 1999).

11 *Bailey v. Southwest Gas Co.*, 275 F.3d 1181 (9th Cir. 2002); *Curry v. Neumann,* 142 Lab. Cas. ¶34,209 (S.D.Fla. 2000); *Michele v. Eyelets for Indus., Inc.*, 1999 WL 703170 (Conn.Super. 1999).

12 *See, e.g., Stoops v. One Call Communications, Inc.*, 141 F.3d 309 (7th Cir. 1998); *Sicoli v. Nabisco Biscuit Co.*, 1998 WL 614840 (E.D.Pa. 1998).

13 *Harrington v. Boysville of Mich., Inc.*, 145 F.3d 1331 (6th Cir. 1998); *Collins v. Merck-Medco RX Servs. of Tex., LLC*, 2001 WL 1142794 (N.D.Tex. 2001).

14 *Jefferies v. Dep't of the Navy*, 78 M.S.P.R. 255 (MSPB 1998).

15 29 C.F.R. §825.305(b).

16 29 C.F.R. §825.305(b); *see Rager v. Dad Behring, Inc.*, 210 F.3d 776 (7th Cir. 2000); *Guiliani v. Minn. Vikings Football Club*, 144 Lab. Cases ¶34,399 (D.Minn. 2001); *Schober v. SMC Pneumatics*, 2000 WL 1231557 (S.D.Ind. 2000).

17 *Washington v. Fort James Operating Co.*, 142 Lab. Cases ¶34,180 (D.Or. 2000).

18 *Koontz v. USX Corp.*, 7 WH Cas.2d 425 (E.D.Pa. 2001).

19 *Robinson v. Franklin County Bd. of Comm'rs*, 144 Lab. Cases ¶34,363 (S.D.Ohio 2002).

20 *Zawadowicz v. CVS Corp.*, 99 F.Supp.2d 518 (D.N.J. 2000).

21 29 C.F.R. §825.305(a).

[22] *Henderson v. Whirlpool Corp.*, 17 F.Supp.2d 1238 (N.D.Okla. 1998); *see LeGrand v. Village of McCook*, 1998 WL 182462 (N.D.III. 1998).

[23] *Rager v. Dade Behring, Inc.*, 210 F.3d 776 (7th Cir. 2000).

[24] 29 C.F.R. §825.301(b)(1)(ii); §825.305; *see Price v. Multnomah County*, 132 F.Supp.2d 1290 (D.Or. 2001).

[25] *Opinion Letter,* Wage and Hour Division, 1996 WL 1044774 (January 30, 1996).

[26] *Opinion Letter,* Wage and Hour Division, 1995 WL 1036746 (November 14, 1995).

[27] 29 C.F.R. §825.307(a).

[28] 29 C.F.R. §825.307(a)(1).

[29] 29 C.F.R. §825.307(e).

[30] 29 C.F.R. §825.307(a)(2); 29 C.F.R. §825.307(b).

[31] 29 C.F.R. §825.307(d).

[32] *Price v. City of Fort Wayne*, 117 F.3d 1022 (7th Cir. 1997); *Opinion Letter,* Wage and Hour Division, 1994 WL 1016756 (October 19, 1994).

[33] *Pollard v. City of Northwood*, 161 F.Supp.2d 782 (N.D.Ohio 2001).

[34] *Curry v. Neumann*, 142 Lab. Cas. ¶34,209 (S.D.Fla. 2000).

[35] 29 C.F.R. §825.307(c).

[36] 29 U.S.C. §2613(d)(2).

[37] 29 C.F.R. §825.307(d).

[38] *See Reich v. The Standard Register Co.,* 1997 WL 375744 (W.D.Va. 1997).

[39] 60 Fed.Reg. 2180, 2235 (1995); *see Williams v. Rubicon, Inc.,* 754 So.2d 1081 (La.App. 1999).

[40] *Rhoads v. FDIC*, 257 F.3d 373 (4th Cir. 2001); *Stekloff v. St. John's Mercy Health Sys.,* 218 F.3d 858 (8th Cir. 2000); *Barnhill v. Farmland Foods, Inc.,* 143 Lab. Cases ¶34,254 (D.Kan. 2001).

[41] *Miller v. AT&T*, 60 F.Supp.2d 574 (S.D.W.Va. 1999); *Sims v. Alameda-Contra Costa Transit Dist.,* 2 F.Supp.2d 1253 (N.D.Cal. 1998); *Williams v. Rubicon, Inc.,* 754 So.2d 1081 (La.App. 1999).

[42] *Sims v. Alameda-Contra Costa Transit Dist.,* 2 F.Supp.2d 1253 (N.D.Cal. 1998).

[43] *Marchisheck v. San Mateo County*, 199 F.3d 1068 (9th Cir. 1999).

[44] *Thorson v. Gemini, Inc.,* 205 F.3d 370 (8th Cir. 2001).

[45] *See Williams v. Boeing Co.,* 166 F.3d 1219 (9th Cir. 1999). *See also Hibbler v. Regional Medical Center at Memphis*, 2001 WL 700829 (6th Cir. 2001).

[46] 29 C.F.R. §825.308(a).

[47] 29 C.F.R. §825.308(b).

[48] 29 C.F.R. §825.308(c).

[49] 29 C.F.R. §825.308(e).

[50] 29 C.F.R. §825.308(e).

[51] *Lara v. Central Grocers Cooperative, Inc.,* 2002 WL 31006132 (N.D. Ohio 2002); 29 C.F.R. §825.308(d).

[52] *Dillon v. Carlton,* 977 F.Supp. 1155 (M.D.Fla. 1997).

[53] 29 C.F.R. §825.310(a).

[54] *Opinion Letter,* Wage and Hour Division, 1995 WL 1036729 (April 28, 1995).

[55] 29 C.F.R. §825.310(c)(f).

[56] 29 C.F.R. §825.310(b); *see Opinion Letter,* Wage and Hour Division, 2000 WL 33157367 (September 11, 2000).

[57] 29 C.F.R. §825.310(c); *Opinion Letter,* Wage and Hour Division, 1995 WL 1036729 (April 28, 1995); *see Fantasia v. Ethan Allen, Inc.,* 1999 WL 22735 (Conn.Super. 1999).

[58] *Underhill v. Willamina Lumber Co.,* 1999 WL 421596 (D.Or. 1999); *see Albert v. Runyon,* 6 F.Supp.2d 57 (D.Mass. 1998).

[59] *Albert v. Runyon,* 6 F.Supp.2d 57 (D.Mass. 1998); *see Opinion Letter,* Wage and Hour Division, 1995 WL 1036729 (April 28, 1995).

[60] 29 C.F.R. §825.310(h).

CHAPTER 8

DURATION OF FMLA LEAVE

In A Nutshell . . .

Employees are entitled to 12 weeks of FMLA leave per year. Though an employer can choose between four ways of measuring a "year," it must do so uniformly for all employees. Unless FMLA leave is taken intermittently or on a reduced leave schedule, FMLA leave is counted in full-week blocks so that any part of a week missed counts as a full week toward the 12-week entitlement.

The Entitlement To 12 Weeks Of FMLA Leave.

The Statute: 29 U.S.C. §2612.

(a) In general

(1) Entitlement to leave

Subject to section 2613 of this title, an eligible employee shall be entitled to a total of 12 workweeks of leave during any 12-month period for one or more of the following:

(A) Because of the birth of a son or daughter of the employee and in order to care for such son or daughter.

(B) Because of the placement of a son or daughter with the employee for adoption or foster care.

(C) In order to care for the spouse, or a son, daughter, or parent, of the employee, if such spouse, son, daughter, or parent has a serious health condition.

(D) Because of a serious health condition that makes the employee unable to perform the functions of the position of such employee.

(2) Expiration of entitlement

The entitlement to leave under subparagraphs (A) and (B) of paragraph (1) for a birth or placement of a son or daughter shall expire at the end of the 12-month period beginning on the date of such birth or placement.

Employees are entitled to 12 weeks of FMLA leave over the course of any 12-month period for all FMLA purposes, and no more. If an employee uses eight weeks of leave due to a serious health condition, the employee only has a balance of four weeks of FMLA leave remaining for all FMLA purposes, no matter whether the reason for the leave is for the employee's health condition, a qualifying relative's serious health condition, or the birth or adoption of a child.[1] An employer's leave plan might be more generous than the FMLA, but the FMLA's benefits are capped at 12 weeks. Even if the employer's conduct somehow causes the underlying condition (as with some on-the-job/workers' compensation injuries), the maximum of 12 weeks of FMLA leave stands.[2]

The matter of counting weeks under the FMLA is usually a straightforward proposition, with the FMLA's basic presumption being that FMLA leave will be taken in full-week increments. The fact that a holiday occurs within a week taken as FMLA leave has no impact; the employee is not entitled to a "makeup day" for the holiday.[3] However, if the employer's business has closed for one or more weeks

– for example, schools closing for vacation, or an employer closing a mill for two weeks because of a business slowdown – the days the employer's activities have ceased do not count against the employee's FMLA leave entitlement.[4]

What if intermittent FMLA leave involves only a part of the workday, but the employee's job is such that even a short absence from the work requires the employee to miss the entire day? Under the DOL's regulations, only the amount of leave actually taken can be counted toward the 12 weeks of leave to which an employee is entitled.[5] While there is no limit in the FMLA to the size of the leave increments that can be used on an intermittent leave basis, the employer *can* limit leave increments to the smallest period of time (one hour or less) that the employer's payroll system uses to account for leave.[6] In an opinion letter, the DOL described a situation where a flight attendant who, if she missed part of the day to care for her sick mother, was unable to work any part of her schedule. The DOL indicated that the portion of the day needed to tend to the mother (three hours) could be charged against the employee's FMLA allotment, and the remainder of the workday would have to come out of some other bank of paid or unpaid leave.

In some cases, an employer may allow an employee who needs to use FMLA leave to care for a qualifying relative to work at the employee's residence. At times, the employee will be working while at home; at other times, the employee will be caring for the relative. In such circumstances, the time spent working while at home cannot be counted against the employee's FMLA allotment.[7]

Calculating an employee's FMLA entitlement is more difficult when the employee's regular work schedule varies. In such cases, the DOL requires that the employer average the employee's work hours over the 12 weeks prior to the beginning of the leave period for the purposes of calculating the employee's FMLA entitlement. For example, if an employee averages a 20-hour workweek in a 12-week period prior to requesting FMLA leave, each day of FMLA leave would count as a half week of the employee's FMLA entitlement.[8]

In some cases, an employee may have taken leave that would ordinarily qualify as FMLA leave before the one-year eligibility period for FMLA benefits had been completed. In such cases, the leave taken will not count against the employee's 12-week FMLA benefit once the employee becomes eligible.[9]

In What 12-Month Period Is An Employee Entitled To 12 Workweeks Of Leave?

The FMLA offers little guidance in terms of how to count the 12-month period that is the basis for the 12 workweeks of FMLA leave entitlement. In setting forth its FMLA regulations, the DOL made clear that employers would enjoy a good deal of flexibility in calculating the 12-month period. As stated by the DOL, "the choice of options was intended to give maximum flexibility for ease in administering FMLA in conjunction with other ongoing employer leave plans, given that some employers establish a 'leave year' and because of state laws that may require a particular result."[10] Consistent with that approach, the DOL's regulations provide

An employer has four choices in calculating the year in which employees are entitled to 12 weeks of FMLA leave: (1) The calendar year, (2) A "leave year," and (3) A 12-month period from the date FMLA leave begins, and (4) A "rolling year."

employers with the following choices for how to determine the "12-month period" during which an employee is entitled to 12 weeks of FMLA-protected leave:

"An employer is permitted to choose any one of the following methods for determining the '12-month period' in which the 12 weeks of leave entitlement occurs:

"(1) The calendar year;

"(2) Any fixed 12-month 'leave year,' such as a fiscal year, a year required by State law, or a year starting on an employee's 'anniversary' date;

"(3) The 12-month period measured forward from the date an employee's first FMLA leave begins; or,

"(4) A 'rolling' 12-month period measured backward from the date an employee uses any FMLA leave."[11]

As the DOL has explained, the method selected by the employer for calculating the 12-month period can produce different results as to the eligibility of employees for FMLA leave.

"Under methods in paragraphs (b)(1) and (b)(2) of this section an employee would be entitled to up to 12 weeks of FMLA leave at any time in the fixed 12-month period selected. An employee could, therefore, take 12 weeks of leave at the end of the year and 12 weeks at the beginning of the following year. Under the method in paragraph (b)(3) of this section, an employee would be entitled to 12 weeks of leave during the year beginning on the first date FMLA leave is taken; the next 12-month period would begin the first time FMLA leave is taken after completion of any previous 12-month period. Under the method in paragraph (b)(4) of this section, the 'rolling' 12-month period, each time an employee takes FMLA leave the remaining leave entitlement would be any balance of the 12 weeks which has not been used during the immediately preceding 12 months. For example, if an employee has taken eight weeks of leave during the past 12 months, an additional four weeks of leave could be taken. If an employee used four weeks beginning February 1, 1994, four weeks beginning June 1, 1994, and four weeks beginning December 1, 1994, the employee would not be entitled to any additional leave until February 1, 1995. However, beginning on February 1, 1995, the employee would be entitled to four weeks of leave, on June 1 the employee would be entitled to an additional four weeks, etc."[12]

For example, assume an employer operates on a fiscal year starting October 1, and an employee wants to use three-week blocks of FMLA leave starting on the following dates:

July 1, 2002
September 1, 2002
January 1, 2003
February 1, 2003
June 1, 2003

If the employer selects the first option – calculating the 12-month period on the basis of the calendar year – the employee would be entitled to all of the FMLA leave requested since no more than 12 weeks of FMLA leave is used in any **calendar year.**

If the employer selects the second option – calculating the 12-month period on the basis of its fiscal year – the employee would again be entitled to all the FMLA leave requested since no more than 12 weeks of the FMLA leave would have been taken in either of the employer's two **leave years** (as measured by the fiscal year beginning October 1).

However, if the employer selects the third option – calculating the 12-month period from the date marking the onset of the employee's first FMLA leave request – the employee would not be entitled to the June 1, 2003 request for leave since that would mean 15 weeks of FMLA leave would be taken in a 12-month period using the date of the **onset of the employee's first FMLA leave.**

Similarly, if the employer selects the fourth option – calculating the 12-month period on a "rolling" basis measured backward from the date an employee uses any FMLA leave – the employee would not be entitled to the June 1, 2003 request for FMLA leave since more than 12 weeks of FMLA leave would have been used in any **rolling 12-month period**.

These optional methods of calculating the 12-month period are nothing if not confusing. This was apparent in a case where an employee was on FMLA-qualifying leave from December 16 to May 19, a total of 22 weeks. When the employer denied the employee's request for intermittent leave after May 19, the employee sued under the FMLA. Without even analyzing which method of calculating the 12-month period was used by the employer, a court dismissed the lawsuit on the grounds that the employee had "exhausted his eligibility for leave" and could not make a claim under the FMLA under any set of facts.[13] The Court's decision was wrong, of course. Depending upon the method of calculation used, the employee could have had a significant amount of eligibility for FMLA leave remaining as of May 19. For example, if the employer used a **leave year** system (with the leave year beginning May 1), the employee could have had almost ten weeks of FMLA eligibility remaining as of May 19.[14]

Whichever option an employer chooses, calculations must be applied consistently and uniformly to all employees,[15] and the employer must notify employees of the calculation method selected.[16] If an employer does not choose one of the four options, the option most beneficial to the employee will be applied.[17] If an employer wishes to change to one of the other permitted calculation options, it may do so provided it gives at least 60 days' notice to all employees, and the transition to the new method allows employees to retain the full benefit of 12 weeks

Whichever option the employer chooses for calculating a "year," it must use that option with all employees.

of leave under the more generous of the two methods used by the employer.[18] A change in the calculation method cannot be made to avoid the FMLA's requirements.[19]

The DOL's regulations allow a modest exception to these rules for multi-state employers. Since some state family leave laws require a single method of determining the period during which use of the family leave entitlement is measured, an employer will not violate the DOL's "uniformity" rule by complying with the laws of such states for its employees in those states, and yet have a different method for calculating the 12-month period for the remainder of its employees. [20]

By preventing employers from calculating FMLA leave eligibility in their favor on an employee-by-employee basis, the DOL's regulations encourage employers to choose the calculation method prospectively. As one court has observed, the regulation "not only prevents unfairness to employees through retroactive manipulation of the 'leave year,' but also encourages a system under which both employees and employers can plan for future leaves in an orderly fashion."[21]

Intermittent Leave And Leave On A Reduced-Leave Schedule.

The Statute: 29 U.S.C. §2612(b)

(1) In general

* * * Subject to paragraph (2), subsection (e)(2) of this section, and section 2613(b)(5) of this title, leave under subparagraph (C) or (D) of subsection (a)(1) of this section may be taken intermittently or on a reduced leave schedule when medically necessary. The taking of leave intermittently or on a reduced leave schedule pursuant to this paragraph shall not result in a reduction in the total amount of leave to which the employee is entitled under subsection (a) of this section beyond the amount of leave actually taken.

Section 2612(b) of the FMLA provides for intermittent leave or leave on a reduced leave schedule when it is medically necessary to do so. The idea of "medical necessity" under the FMLA is a bit different from how the words are commonly used. "Medical necessity" in common parlance means something that is necessary for health. "Medical necessity," in the context of the FMLA, implies a certain urgency, a need for a particular procedure to be done by a certain time, or that the need for the leave is time-sensitive in some other way.[22]

Intermittent leave is leave taken in increments due to a single illness or injury, rather than in one continuous period of time. Intermittent leave may include leave periods of anywhere from an hour or more to several weeks. Leave on a **reduced leave schedule** means a leave schedule that reduces the usual number of hours worked per workweek, or hours per workday of an employee.[23] The leave must be medically necessary because of a serious health condition before FMLA leave may be used on an intermittent or at a reduced leave basis.[24] Intermittent leave or a reduced leave schedule can be used by an employee to attend appointments with a health care provider for necessary treatment of a serious health condition, either for the employee or for a qualifying family member.[25] If the employee uses the leave in less than full-day increments, and if the employee elects to use paid leave to account for absences from work, the employee would continue to receive full pay even though working a reduced schedule.[26]

Where intermittent leave or a reduced leave schedule is foreseeable, based on planned medical treatment, the employee must "provide the employer with not less than 30 days' notice, before the leave is to begin, of the employee's intention to take leave" under the FMLA.[27] In the words of one court, "an employer is entitled to expect that the employee will be cognizant of her own job responsibilities as well as the operation of the employer and will give notice as soon as practicable."[28]

Where the approximate timing of the need for leave is not foreseeable – for example, where the employee suffers from migraine headaches that have an unpredictable onset – the employee must give notice of the need for leave as soon as practicable.[29] In such circumstances, the employer cannot insist on a precise leave schedule before granting the leave.[30] The expectation is that "an employee will give notice to the employer within no more than one or two working days of learning of the need for leave, except in extraordinary circumstances where such notice is not feasible."[31] The required notice can be given in person, by telephone, fax, or other electronic means. Exercising hyperbolic caution, the DOL even envisions the notice of the need for intermittent leave being provided "by telegraph."[32]

If the need for leave is too intermittent, the employee may lose the protections of the FMLA. For example, one case involved an employee who requested repeated intermittent leave for her depression flare-ups. The Court cautioned the employee that the FMLA "does not give an employee suffering from depression the right to unscheduled, unpredictable, but cumulatively substantial, absences or a right to take unscheduled leave at a moment's notice for the rest of her career. On the contrary, such a situation implies she is not qualified for a position where reliable attendance is a bona fide requirement."[33]

An unusual feature of intermittent leave or a reduced leave schedule is that the health condition need not be presently incapacitating for FMLA coverage. For example, an employee in the early stages of cancer may be required to undertake periodic treatments. While the cancer might not be disabling, the use of leave for the treatments would be covered.[34]

Employees needing intermittent leave or a reduced leave schedule "must attempt to schedule their leave so as not to disrupt the employer's operations."[35] And, as detailed in Chapter 10, an employer may temporarily reassign or transfer an employee using intermittent leave or a reduced leave schedule to a job (with equivalent pay and benefits) that better fits the schedule.

CASE IN POINT

Question: Painton Printing, while a large company, is organized into many small divisions. The absence of even one employee from some divisions can put a severe crimp in the production schedule. In addition to the usual run of absences, the Company is now facing two requests from employees who want to take partial days off.

The first request, from Daryl Turner, has been made more than 45 days in advance. Turner will be undergoing back surgery and has been told by his doctor that he will need to undergo physical therapy three days a week, for two hours each session. The second request is an ongoing one from Roberta King, who suffers from continuing migraine headaches that occur randomly. When King suffers a migraine, she calls the Company right away and generally requires three to four hours away from work until the headache subsides. King is undergoing treatment for her migraines, and her doctor is optimistic that they will be controllable within six months. Must the Company grant the requests for time off?

Answer: Yes. The two requests are classic examples of where the use of intermittent leave is allowed under the FMLA. The first example deals with "predictable" intermittent leave – where the employee has advance notice of the need for the leave. The DOL's rules allow the use of intermittent leave in such circumstances if the employee has given 30 days' notice (if practicable).

The second request deals with unpredictable leave resulting from a serious health condition. In such circumstances, the employee must give notice of the leave as soon as it is practicable (in this case, when the headaches start), and the notice can be given by telephone. Only if the employee's use of intermittent leave is so frequent that she is unable to perform the essential functions of the job may the employer take action against the employee.

When Does FMLA Leave End?

Though employees are entitled to a maximum of 12 weeks of FMLA leave, when the leave actually ends depends upon why the leave is being used. If FMLA leave is being used for a serious medical condition, the leave ends when the condition has improved to the point that it is no longer a "serious medical condition." This normally means that leave expires when an employee is able to perform the essential functions of the job,[36] subject, of course, to the need for intermittent leave for medical treatments. FMLA leave taken for the birth of a child or the placement of a child for adoption or foster care must be used within the 12-month period after the birth or placement.[37]

What Happens When FMLA Leave Ends And The Employee Does Not Return To Work?

At the conclusion of FMLA leave, the employee has an obligation to return to work. If the employee fails to do so, the employer can terminate the employee for failing to return to work and/or post the employee's job to be filled without violating the FMLA.[38] Of course, there may be other restrictions on an employer's ability to terminate the employee. For example, there may be a collective bargaining agreement restricting the employer's ability to discipline employees to circumstances where "just cause" exists, or the employer may be required to reasonably accommodate the employee under the Americans With Disabilities Act. However, the FMLA itself will not prevent an employee's termination, even if the employee's inability to return to work is due to the same serious health condition that occasioned the need for FMLA leave in the first place.[39] Similarly, if an employee fails to return to work because he is emotionally distraught over the death of the terminally ill family member and originally sought FMLA leave to care for the member, the FMLA provides no protections.[40]

A slightly different situation is presented when the employer wrongly terminates an employee before the end of FMLA leave, and it later develops that the employee would not have been physically capable of returning to work at the end of her FMLA allotment. In one case, an employer terminated an employee who had six days of her FMLA allotment left. When the employee's doctor testified at a trial that the employee would not have been able to return to work for another four weeks, the employer argued that the termination could not possibly have violated the FMLA. A court rejected the argument, however, observing that the argument was based on evidence developed after the employee's termination and noting that there was evidence that the termination itself aggravated the employee's mental condition.[41]

> *If the employee's FMLA leave runs out and the employee does not return to work, the employee is subject to discharge even if still suffering from the condition that required the FMLA leave in the first place.*

Intermittent Leave For Educational Employees.

The Statute – 29 U.S.C. §2618(c).

(c) Intermittent leave or leave on reduced schedule for instructional employees

(1) In general

Subject to paragraph (2), in any case in which an eligible employee employed principally in an instructional capacity by any such educational agency or school requests leave under subparagraph (C) or (D) of section 2612(a)(1) of this title that is foreseeable based on planned medical treatment and the employee would be on leave for greater than 20 percent of the total number of working days in the period during which the leave would extend, the agency or school may require that such employee elect either -

(A) to take leave for periods of a particular duration, not to exceed the duration of the planned medical treatment; or

(B) to transfer temporarily to an available alternative position offered by the employer for which the employee is qualified, and that -

(i) has equivalent pay and benefits; and (ii) better accommodates recurring periods of leave than the regular employment position of the employee.

(2) Application

The elections described in subparagraphs (A) and (B) of paragraph (1) shall apply only with respect to an eligible employee who complies with section 2612(e)(2) of this title.

Among the special rules for educational employees (see Chapter 2) are rules for intermittent leave for employees working principally "in an instructional capacity." The DOL has indicated that these rules apply to "those whose principal function is to teach and instruct students in a class, a small group, or an individual setting." [42] Accordingly, the special rules apply to teachers, athletic coaches, driving instructors, and special education assistants, such as signers for the hearing impaired. The special rules do not apply to teaching assistants or aides because their principal job is not actual teaching or instructing, or to counselors, psychologists, curriculum specialists, cafeteria workers, maintenance workers, or bus drivers.[43]

If an instructional employee wishes to take intermittent leave or a reduced leave schedule, *and* if the leave is because of the employee's own serious health condition or that of a qualifying family member, *and* if the leave is foreseeable because of planned medical treatment, *and* if the employee would be on leave for more than 20 percent of the total number of working days within the total leave period, then the employer may offer the employee two options:

(1) The employee can elect to take leave for a period (or periods) "of a particular duration," not greater than the duration of the planned treatment; or;

(2) The employee can temporarily transfer to another available position (for which the employee is qualified), which has equivalent pay and benefits, and which better accommodates recurring periods of leave than does the employee's regular position.

These rules introduce a new concept known as "periods of a particular duration" into the FMLA. The phrase refers to blocks of time beginning no earlier than the first day that leave is needed and ending no later than the last day that leave is needed.[44] Essentially, the rules allow an employer to force an instructional employee to take off on leave up to the entire block of days involving the planned treatment, even though the treatment itself might only involve intermittent days or partial days. If the employee elects to take leave for a "period of particular duration," the entire period of leave taken counts against the employee's FMLA allotment.[45]

If an instructional employee uses FMLA leave for a period that ends with the school year and begins again the next semester, the leave is considered consecutive rather than intermittent. Summer vacation (or an equivalent break), when the employee does not have to report for duty is not counted against the employee's FMLA leave entitlement. An instructional employee on FMLA leave at the end of the school year must be provided with any benefits over the summer vacation that employees would normally receive if they had been working at the end of the school year.[46]

Instructional Employees And End-Of-School-Year Leave.

The Statute – 29 U.S.C. §2618(d).

(d) Rules applicable to periods near conclusion of academic term

The following rules shall apply with respect to periods of leave near the conclusion of an academic term in the case of any eligible employee employed principally in an instructional capacity by any such educational agency or school:

(1) Leave more than 5 weeks prior to end of term

If the eligible employee begins leave under section 2612 of this title more than 5 weeks prior to the end of the academic term, the agency or school may require the employee to continue taking leave until the end of such term, if -

(A) the leave is of at least 3 weeks duration; and (B) the return to employment would occur during the 3-week period before the end of such term.

(2) Leave less than 5 weeks prior to end of term

If the eligible employee begins leave under subparagraph (A), that commences 5 weeks prior to the end of the academic term, the agency or school may require the employee to continue taking leave until the end of such term, if -

(A) the leave is of greater than 2 weeks duration; and (B) the return to employment would occur during the 2-week period before the end of such term.

(3) Leave less than 3 weeks prior to end of term

If the eligible employee begins leave under subparagraph (A), that commences 3 weeks prior to the end of the academic term and the duration of the leave is greater than 5 working days, the agency or school may require the employee to continue to take leave until the end of such term.

Different rules also apply to instructional employees when they want to take leave near the end of a school term. If an instructional employee begins leave **more than five weeks before the end of a term**, the employer may require the employee to continue taking leave until the end of the term *if* two conditions are met: (1) The intended leave must last at least three weeks; and (2) the employee would return to work at the end of her intended leave during the three-week period before the end of the term.[47] If the instructional employee begins leave for a purpose other than the employee's own serious health condition **during the five-week period before the end of a term**, the employer may require the employee to continue taking leave until the end of the term *if* (1) the intended leave will last more than two weeks; and (2) the employee would return to work at the end of her intended leave during the two-week period before the end of the term.[48] If the instructional employee begins leave for a purpose other than the employee's own serious health condition **during the three-week period before the end of a term**, and the leave will last more than five working days, the employer may require that the leave last until the end of the term.[49]

The DOL's rules indicate "in no case may a school have more than two academic terms or semesters each year for purposes of FMLA."[50] If the employee must take leave that lasts until the end of an academic term under these rules, only the period of leave that lasts until the employee is ready and able to return to work is counted against the employee's FMLA allotment.[51]

NOTES

1 *Opinion Letter*, Wage and Hour Division, 1994 WL 1016740 (March 24, 1994); *see Haas v. Dept. of Indus., Labor & Human Relations, Equal Rights Div.*, 479 N.W.2d 229 (Wis.App. 1991)(decided under state law).

2 *Stopka v. Alliance of Am. Insurers*, 3 WH Cas.2d 1298 (N.D.Ill. 1996).

3 29 C.F.R. §825.200(f).

4 29 C.F.R. §825.200(f).

5 *Green v. New Balance Athletic Shoe, Inc.*, 182 F.Supp.2d 128 (D.Me. 2002).

6 29 C.F.R. §825.205(a); 29 C.F.R. §825.203(d).

7 *Opinion Letter*, Wage and Hour Division, 1995 WL 1036738 (July 21, 1995).

8 29 C.F.R. §825.205(b)(d).

9 *Opinion Letter*, Wage and Hour Division, 1997 WL 1169956 (December 9, 1997).

10 Family and Medical Leave Act of 1993, 60 Fed.Reg. 2180, 2199 (Jan. 6, 1995).

11 29 C.F.R. §825.200(b).

12 29 C.F.R. §825.200(c).

13 *Barnett v. Southern Foods Groups, L.P.*, 1997 WL 369413 (N.D.Tex. 1997); *see Voskuil v. Environmental Health Ctr. – Dallas*, 1997 WL 527309 (N.D.Tex. 1997).

14 *Opinion Letter,* Wage and Hour Division, 1995 WL 1036745 (October 30, 1995).

15 29 C.F.R. §825.200(d)(1); *see Opinion Letter,* Wage & Hour Division, 1999 WL 1002423 (June 16, 1999).

16 *Bachelder v. America West Airlines, Inc.*, 259 F.3d 1112 (9th Cir. 2001); *Contra Kelso v. Corning-Cable Systems International Corp.*, 2002 WL 31175138 (W.D.N.C. 2002).

17 29 C.F.R. §825.200(e); *see McKeirnan v. Smith-Edwards-Dunlap Co.*, 180 Lab. Cases ¶33,296 (E.D.Pa. 1995).

18 29 C.F.R. §825.200(d)(1); *Opinion Letter,* Wage and Hour Division, 1996 WL 1044785 (December 13, 1996).

19 29 C.F.R. §825.200(d)(1).

20 29 C.F.R. §825.200(d)(2).

21 *Bachelder v. America West Airlines, Inc.*, 259 F.3d 1112 (9th Cir. 2001).

22 *Palazzolo v. Galen Hosps. of Tex., Inc.*, 4 WH Cas.2d 532 (N.D.Ga. 1997); *Kaylor v. Fannin Reg'l Hosp., Inc.*, 946 F.Supp. 988 (N.D.Ga. 1996).

23 29 C.F.R. §825.800; *see Opinion Letter*, Wage and Hour Division, 1994 WL 1016761 (December 29, 1994).

[24] *Haggard v. Levi Strauss & Co.*, 2001 WL 527504 (8th Cir. 2001).

[25] 29 C.F.R. §825.116; *Beal v. Rubbermaid Commercial Prods., Inc.*, 972 F.Supp. 1216 (S.D.Iowa 1997).

[26] *Opinion Letter*, Wage and Hour Division, 1998 WL 1147748 (July 10, 1998).

[27] 29 U.S.C. §2612(e)(2)(B).

[28] *Gay v. Gilman Paper Co.*, 125 F.3d 1432 (11th Cir. 1997); *see Godwin v. Rheem Mfg. Co.*, 15 F.Supp.2d 1197 (M.D.Ala. 1998).

[29] *Ware v. Stahl Specialty Co.*, 4 WH Cas.2d 974 (W.D.Mo. 1998); *Opinion Letter*, Wage and Hour Division, 1994 WL 1016737 (February 7, 1994).

[30] *McGinnis v. Wonder Chem. Co.*, 3 WH Cas.2d 71 (E.D.Pa. 1995); *Opinion Letter*, Wage and Hour Division, 1997 WL 1039255 (July 3, 1997).

[31] 29 C.F.R. §825.303 (1997).

[32] 29 C.F.R. §825.303 (1997).

[33] *Spangler v. Fed. Home Loan Bank of Des Moines*, 278 F.3d 847 (8th Cir. 2002), quoting *Collins v. NTN-Bower Corp.*, 272 F.3d 1006 (7th Cir. 2001).

[34] *Opinion Letter,* Wage and Hour Division, 1995 WL 1036731 (May 2, 1995).

[35] 29 C.F.R. §825.117; *see Kaylor v. Fannin Reg'l Hosp., Inc.*, 946 F.Supp. 988 (N.D.Ga. 1996).

[36] *Dean v. Methodist Hospitals of Dallas*, 1998 WL 826882 (N.D.Tex. 1998).

[37] 29 U.S.C. §2612(a)(2).

[38] *Nunes v. Wal-Mart Stores, Inc.*, 164 F.3d 1243 (9th Cir. 1999); *Cehrs v. Northeast Ohio Alzheimer's Research Center*, 155 F.3d 775 (6th Cir. 1998); *Holmes v. e.spire Communications*, 135 F.Supp.2d 657 (D.Md. 2001); *Gray v. Sears, Roebuck & Co., Inc.*, 131 F.Supp.2d 895 (S.D.Tex. 2001); *Rosales v. City of San Antonio*, 2001 WL 1168797 (W.D.Tex. 2001); *Warren v. Aetna Life Ins. Co.*, 1999 WL 615095 (N.D.Tex. 1999); *Baker v. SPL Polyols, Inc.*, 1998 WL 109945 (Del.Super. 1998); *Garofalo v. Tonti Realty Corp.*, 5 WH Cas.2d 860 (E.D.La. 1997); *Parker v. Bank One, N.A.*, 2001 WL 303284 (OhioApp. 2001); *Smith v. Guard Publishing, Inc.*, 963 P.2d 115 (Or.App. 1998); *Young v. Dept. of Veterans Affairs*, 83 M.S.P.R. 187 (MSPB 1999).

[39] *Alifano v. Merck & Co., Inc.*, 175 F.Supp.2d 792 (E.D.Pa. 2001); *Barry v. Wing Memorial Hosp.*, 142 F.Supp.2d 161 (D.Mass. 2001); *see Green v. Alcan Aluminum Corporation*, 198 F.3d 245 (6th Cir. 1999); *Reynolds v. Phillips & Temro Indus., Inc.*, 195 F.3d 411 (8th Cir. 1999); *Soodman v. Wildman, Harrold, Allen & Dixon*, 4 WH Cas.2d 1043 (N.D.Ill. 1997); *Urbano v. Continental Airlines*, 3 WH Cas.2d 1032 (S.D.Tex. 1996).

[40] *Brown v. J.C. Penney Corp.*, 924 F.Supp. 1158 (S.D.Fla. 1996).

[41] *Shepherd v. Honda of Am. Mfg., Inc.*, 2001 WL 909257 (S.D.Ohio 2001).

[42] 29 C.F.R. §825.600(c).

[43] 29 C.F.R. §825.600(c).

[44] 29 C.F.R. §825.601(a)(2).

[45] 29 C.F.R. §825.603(a).

[46] 29 C.F.R. §825.601(a).

[47] 29 C.F.R. §825.602(a)(1).

[48] 29 C.F.R. §825.602(a)(2).

[49] 29 C.F.R. §825.602(a)(3).

[50] 29 C.F.R. §825.602(b).

[51] 29 C.F.R. §825.603(b).

CHAPTER 9

THE RELATIONSHIP OF FAMILY LEAVE TO OTHER FORMS OF PAID LEAVE AND OTHER FAMILY LEAVE LAWS

In A Nutshell . . .

The FMLA is the baseline below which family leave benefits may not go. Employer practices, state and local laws, and collective bargaining agreements can (and frequently do) provide more generous benefits than those in the FMLA. In cases of conflict, the employer must observe the most generous grant of rights to employees. Though the "default condition" for FMLA leave is the granting of unpaid leave, either the employer or the employee can substitute paid leave such as vacation time for the unpaid leave.

In General - The Relationship Of The FMLA To Other Leave Plans.

The Statute: 29 U.S.C. §2652.

(a) More protective

Nothing in this Act or any amendment made by this Act shall be construed to diminish the obligation of an employer to comply with any collective bargaining agreement or any employment benefit program or plan that provides greater family or medical leave rights to employees than the rights established under this Act or any amendment made by this Act.

(b) Less protective

The rights established for employees under this Act or any amendment made by this Act shall not be diminished by any collective bargaining agreement or any employment benefit program or plan.

When considering the relationship between the FMLA and other leave plans, it is important to remember the basic proposition that the FMLA specifies the *minimum* amount of family leave required by the law. Leave benefits may be more generous than FMLA's but cannot be less generous.[1] Moreover, Congress made it clear, in Section 2652 of the FMLA, that nothing in the FMLA diminished any obligation on the part of an employer to comply with more generous provisions of a collective bargaining agreement or the employer's own leave plan. The FMLA thus sets a baseline of leave benefits below which any qualifying employer may not go.[2]

The FMLA's Basic Requirement – 12 Weeks' Leave, Paid Or Unpaid.

The Statute: 29 U.S.C. §2612(d)

(1) Unpaid leave

If an employer provides paid leave for fewer than 12 workweeks, the additional weeks of leave necessary to attain the 12 workweeks of leave required under this subchapter may be provided without compensation.

(2) Substitution of paid leave

(A) In general

An eligible employee may elect, or an employer may require the employee, to substitute any of the accrued paid vacation leave, personal leave, or family leave of the employee for leave provided under subparagraph (A), (B), or (C) of subsection (a)(1) of this section for any part of the 12-week period of such leave under such subsection.

(B) Serious health condition

An eligible employee may elect, or an employer may require the employee, to substitute any of the accrued paid vacation leave, personal leave, or medical or sick leave of the employee for leave provided under subparagraph (C) or (D) of subsection (a)(1) of this section for any part of the 12-week period of such leave under such subsection, except that nothing in this subchapter shall require an employer to provide paid sick leave or paid medical leave in any situation in which such employer would not normally provide any such paid leave.

The "default condition" for FMLA leave is that leave is unpaid. However, either an employee or employer may "substitute" accrued paid leave for unpaid FMLA leave.[3] To be substituted for unpaid FMLA leave, the paid leave must be "available" and "accrued." Leave is not "available" if, under the employer's policies, it is accrued in one year but cannot be used until the following year.[4] If the employee does not have enough accrued paid leave to cover an absence from work, the employer and employee may agree on an "advance" of paid leave to be paid back when the employee returns from FMLA leave.[5] If the employee's absence from work is covered by some other form of disability plan — paid disability leave, maternity leave either under a state law or under an employer's plan, and the like — the employer cannot require under the FMLA that paid leave be used for absences covered by the other disability plan.[6]

If the employer requires paid leave to be substituted for unpaid leave, it must decide to do so within two business days of the time the employee gives notice of the need for leave.[7] If the employer only later learns that the purpose of the leave was FMLA qualifying, it must require the substitution of paid leave for unpaid leave within two days of gaining such information.[8]

Thus, nothing in the FMLA requires an employer to furnish paid leave for FMLA purposes. Rather, all the FMLA requires is that if the employer does provide certain forms of paid leave, it must allow employees to use that leave for FMLA purposes. Consistent with these basic principles, an employer is free to amend or even eliminate paid leave programs in spite of their incidental impact on the ability of employees to use FMLA leave.[9]

There are essentially four types of paid leave that may be substituted for unpaid FMLA leave — vacation time, personal time off, compensatory time off, and sick leave. With vacation time and personal time off, the employee or the employer have the unilateral right to substitute the particular form of paid leave for unpaid FMLA leave.[10] If the employer's leave program is a "combined leave" or "paid day off" program without the traditional breakdown between vacation time and sick leave, the employer or the employee retain this unilateral right to substitute the paid leave for unpaid FMLA leave.

With compensatory time off, the rules are different. Compensatory time off is allowed under the Fair Labor Standards Act as a substitute for cash compensation for overtime hours worked, but *only for public sector employers*, and only under strict conditions.[11] Because compensatory time off is really just a form of overtime compensation, the DOL treats it differently than other forms of paid leave. Though the DOL has not spoken at length on the issue, it appears that while an employee could choose to use compensatory time off for FMLA leave, an employer could not compel an employee to do so. If the employee uses compensatory time off to account for an FMLA-qualifying absence, the compensatory time off used is not deducted from the employee's FMLA allotment.[12]

The fourth type of paid leave – sick leave – is treated differently as well. Where paid vacation time is generally considered an unconditional benefit – all the employee needs to do is to schedule vacation time in accordance with the employer's policies – sick leave is a conditional benefit in that certain conditions must exist to use sick leave. Depending upon the sick leave program, those conditions may include the employee's own illness, an illness in the employee's immediate family as defined by the FMLA (child, spouse, or parent), and/or an illness on the part of a member of the employee's family not covered by the FMLA. The DOL's rules specify that paid sick leave can only be substituted for unpaid FMLA leave "to the extent the circumstances meet the employer's usual requirements for the use of sick/medical leave."[13] Put another way, the FMLA is not designed to replace or augment an employer's sick leave policies.[14] Thus, if the employer's paid sick leave policy does not allow the use of sick leave because a family member is ill, or to recover from childbirth (where the mother is not incapacitated), neither the employer nor the employee may substitute paid sick leave for unpaid FMLA leave.[15]

Another wrinkle in the DOL's sick leave regulations emerges when an employer's paid sick leave policy allows the use of sick leave for circumstances which are <u>not</u> FMLA qualifying. For example, the employer's sick leave policy could allow employees to use sick leave for less than "serious health conditions" or to provide care to family members such as brothers or cousins. When sick leave is used for purposes not covered by the FMLA, the employer cannot count it as FMLA leave.[16]

If the employer's procedural requirements for using paid leave are less stringent than the FMLA's, the employer can only impose the *less-stringent* requirements. For example, if an employer does not require employees to provide medical certification in the manner specified by the FMLA, the employer can only impose the standards found in its rules, not the FMLA's certification requirements.[17]

Designating FMLA Leave.

The DOL has lengthy regulations on how leave is designated as FMLA leave. Those regulations clearly state that "in all circumstances," it is the employer's obligation to designate leave as FMLA-qualifying and to give prompt notice of such designation.[18] The employer may designate leave as FMLA leave even though the employee does not request or even desire it.[19]

The main reason for the requirement that the employer give notice of the designation of leave as FMLA leave is so the employee will know whether his or her 12-week FMLA allotment will be reduced by the leave being taken. As such, if the employer is <u>not</u> designating leave as FMLA leave, there is no obligation on the employer's part to inform the employee of that fact.[20] Moreover, if leave qualifies for FMLA protections, an employer cannot choose not to designate the leave as FMLA-qualifying and, in so doing, remove the FMLA's protections from the leave.[21]

The regulations envision dialogue between the employer and the employee (or the employee's "spokesperson" if the employee is incapacitated) that identifies the underlying need for the leave and whether it qualifies as FMLA leave, and oblige an employer to inquire as to why leave is being taken.[22] If an employee refuses to provide pertinent information about the need for leave, the leave can be denied.[23] If, after leave is denied, the employee provides more information that identifies the leave to be for FMLA-qualifying purposes, the employee regains the right to the FMLA leave, and the employer retains the right to designate the leave as FMLA leave.

Once an employer learns that leave is being taken for an FMLA-qualifying purpose, the employer must "promptly" notify the employee that the leave is being so designated and will be counted as FMLA leave. "Promptly" means within two business days, unless extenuating circumstances exist.[24] Though notice that leave has been designated as FMLA leave can be verbal or written, verbal notice must be confirmed in writing no later than the following payday.[25] No particular form is required for the employer's notice that leave has been designated as FMLA leave; a simple notation on a paycheck will suffice.[26] The regulations optimistically suggest that if there is a dispute as to whether paid leave qualifies as FMLA leave, it should be "resolved through discussions between the employee and the employer" that are documented.[27]

If an employer learns that paid leave is for an FMLA purpose after leave has begun, some or all of the paid leave may be retroactively counted as FMLA leave. The DOL's regulations give the example of an employee who planned to take two weeks of paid vacation for a skiing trip. In mid-week of the second week, the employee suffers a skiing accident requiring hospitalization. The regulation provides that "the employer may notify the employee that both the extension and the second week of paid vacation leave (from the date of the injury) is designated as FMLA leave."[28] Employers are given a bit more latitude when a health condition changes from not serious to serious (for example, when a cold turns into pneumonia). In such cases, the regulations appear to allow the employer to designate the entire period of leave as FMLA leave.[29]

In some circumstances, an employer's rules may allow the employer to force disabled employees to use leave, whether paid or unpaid. In such cases, the employer is allowed by the FMLA to designate the compelled leave as FMLA leave, though there remains some debate as to the legality of such a designation.[30]

Certainly the most controversial of the DOL's "designation" regulations is Section 825.208(c), which provides that if an employer has enough information to designate leave as FMLA leave but fails to do so in a timely manner, "the employer may not designate leave as FMLA leave retroactively, and may designate only prospectively as of the date of notification to the employee of the designation." Some courts have found this regulation beyond the DOL's authority to enact, concluding that it impermissibly expands and extends the entitlement to 12 weeks of FMLA leave. These courts reason that since an employer is prohibited from retroactively designating leave as FMLA leave, the regulation might result in an employee receiving more than 12 weeks of FMLA leave (the original leave plus the 12-week unused balance of FMLA leave), a result beyond the scope of the FMLA.[31] Other courts have rejected challenges to the regulation, concluding that the regulation reflects a "reasonable accommodation of conflicting policies" and that the DOL appropriately determined "that employers should bear some modest burden of informing employees about certain aspects of FMLA leave as to which the statute gives the employer choices."[32]

Assuming that Section 825.208(c) of the regulations is enforceable, the DOL's regulations contemplate only two situations where an employer may designate leave as FMLA leave after the employee has returned to work. First, if the employer only learned of the FMLA-qualifying reason for the leave when the employee returned to work, the employer can retroactively designate the leave as FMLA leave, provided it does so within two business days and gives prompt notice to the employee. If the employee wants that leave to be counted retroactively as FMLA leave (perhaps as a shield against disciplinary action), the employee must notify the employer within two business days of returning to work of the reason for the leave.[33] Second, if the employer has been unable to confirm through reasonable efforts that the leave qualified as FMLA leave, it may designate the leave as FMLA leave after the employee returns to work.

Counting Leave That Qualifies Both As FMLA Leave And As Leave Under An Employer's Leave Plan.

The same absence from work can count both as FMLA leave and as leave under an employer's paid leave program.

In counting leave under the FMLA, an employer may also count any other time off granted under an employer's leave program as FMLA leave, provided the leave is used for FMLA-qualifying purposes. Put another way, an employer can insist that FMLA leave run concurrently with paid leave without regard to the employee's wishes.[34] For example, assume that an employer's leave plan allows employees to accrue sick leave at the rate of one day a month, to a maximum of 1,000 hours. If an employee suffers from a serious health condition that requires her to miss 20 weeks of work, the employer could both deduct 800 hours of sick leave from leave banks (40 hours of sick leave for each of the 20 weeks) *and* count the first 12 weeks of sick leave as FMLA leave. In such a case, the employee's FMLA eligibility for the year would expire after the first 12 weeks of sick leave.[35]

Similarly, if an employer learns that an employee suffers from a serious medical condition that impairs her ability to perform essential job functions, nothing in the FMLA forbids the employer from placing the employee on leave and designating the leave as FMLA leave. As one court reasoned, "nowhere in the Act does it provide that FMLA leave must be granted only when the employee wishes it to be granted. On the contrary, the FMLA only provides that leave must be given when certain conditions are present. In the instant case, [the employer] was informed that [the employee] was pregnant, patently a 'serious health condition' under the Act, and that as a result, she could not work with or be exposed to chemicals. [The employer] was under no obligation under the FMLA to provide alternative employment within the company to accommodate [the employee] as it had been able to do in the past."[36]

As described previously in this chapter, there is one form of leave an employer cannot insist be run concurrently with FMLA leave – compensatory time off. Since compensatory time off is just another form of overtime and is not true "leave," an employer cannot deplete an employee's compensatory time off at the same time with the employee's FMLA allotment.[37]

The Applicability Of The FMLA To Leave Benefits Provided By An Employer That Are More Generous Than The FMLA.

The Statute: 29 U.S.C. §2653.

Nothing in this Act or any amendment made by this Act shall be construed to discourage employers from adopting or retaining leave policies more generous than any policies that comply with the requirements under this Act or any amendment made by this Act.

The FMLA does not apply to that portion of an employer's leave polices that is more generous than the FMLA.

Section 2653 of the FMLA itself clearly assumes that employers may have leave plans more generous than the FMLA. A question that occasionally arises is whether the FMLA applies to protect leave benefits that are more generous than the FMLA. For example, if an employer provides for 24 weeks of leave for a serious medical condition, and the employer is alleged to have committed an FMLA violation in the 23rd week of an employee's leave, does the FMLA apply at all?

All courts directly addressing the issue have held that the FMLA does not apply to leave benefits more generous than those required by the FMLA, at least to that part of the leave plans that is more generous than the FMLA. As one federal court of appeals put it, "where an employer exceeds the baseline 12 weeks by providing not only more leave than the FMLA requires but also paid leave, the employer should not find itself sued for violating the FMLA."[38]

Would that it were that simple, however. Section 825.700 of the DOL's regulations state that "an employer *must observe* any employment benefit program or plan that provides greater family or medical leave rights to employee than the rights established by the FMLA" (emphasis supplied).[39] The regulations also allow an employer to amend a more generous leave plan, provided the ultimate plan complies with the FMLA.[40] The clear implication is that the DOL believes it has the authority under the FMLA to enforce more generous leave plans than the FMLA.[41]

To say that the DOL's approach has not been well received by the courts is an understatement. All courts considering the issue have found that the FMLA does not legitimately extend the DOL's regulatory authority over leave plans more generous than the FMLA and that Section 825.700 exceeded the DOL's power to enact, at least to the extent that the regulation could be seen as extending the DOL's authority over more generous leave plans. In addition, seemingly contrary to the plain terms of the regulations, courts have suggested that the DOL may not have even intended the regulation to cover more generous leave plans. As one court concluded, Section 825.700 "does not, and could not, create a federal cause of action under the FMLA to enforce the voluntary employer policies of providing benefits that exceed those required by the FMLA. The Department of Labor has no regulatory power to rewrite, and clearly did not rewrite, the FMLA in such a manner."[42] At best, one is left with the conclusion that Section 825.700 may help the employee argue that a more generous leave plan is a private contract between the employer and the employee which the employer must observe, even if the leave plan is not necessarily enforceable under the FMLA.[43]

The Integration Of The FMLA With Collective Bargaining Agreements.

As noted at the beginning of this chapter, the FMLA, like many other federal labor laws, represents the minimum benefits an employer may legally provide to employees. While collective bargaining agreements can establish family leave benefits more generous than the FMLA, less generous provisions in a collective bargaining agreement are not enforceable. As put in the DOL's regulations, "employees cannot waive, nor may employers induce employees to waive, their rights under the FMLA. For example, employees (or their collective bargaining representatives) cannot 'trade off' the right to take FMLA leave against some other benefit offered by the employer." [44]

There are many ways for collective bargaining agreements to improve on the minimum benefits of the FMLA. For example, a collective bargaining agreement can freely allow the substitution of sick leave for FMLA leave, limit or take away an employer's option to substitute paid leave for FMLA leave, provide for paid "maternity leave" benefits over and above sick leave or vacation time, or allow more than the FMLA's 12 weeks for family leave purposes.[45]

Questions have quickly come up about whether employees can be forced to arbitrate FMLA claims under a collective bargaining agreement in lieu of bringing a private lawsuit for those claims. A good deal of uncertainty exists in the area, owing largely to seemingly inconsistent Supreme Court decisions nibbling around the edge of a fundamental question – under what circumstances can a labor organization waive its members' rights to private lawsuits for violations of federal law?[46] In 1998, the Supreme Court skirted the question in a lawsuit under the Americans With Disabilities Act, but did hold in the case that even assuming such a waiver clause could be enforceable, it would have to "explicitly waive" the federal court cause of action in a "clear and unmistakable" way.[47]

Thus far, courts have been very reluctant to find waivers of the right to bring FMLA lawsuits in collective bargaining agreements. In a typical case, a federal appeals court, while acknowledging that a collective bargaining agreement contained both a non-discrimination clause forbidding gender discrimination and compulsory arbitration, declined to find a waiver of employees' ability to bring FMLA lawsuits. The Court concluded that "while the agreement provides for arbitration of disputes between the Union, employee, and the Company growing out of the interpretation or application of any of the terms of the agreement, the agreement does not purport to submit any noncontract-based dispute or any statutory dispute to arbitration." [48] In another case, a court found that incorporation of the FMLA into contract language "in no way replaced, reduced, or changed any articles in the collective bargaining agreement" and did not constitute an effective waiver of the ability to bring an FMLA lawsuit.[49] In another case, a court simply held that a clear waiver was unenforceable under the FMLA.[50]

A different question has arisen about whether arbitration hearing results held under a collective bargaining agreement will later bind a federal court considering an FMLA case dealing with the same set of facts. The area is a legally complicated one, involving such topics as "fact-preclusion" (sometimes referred to as "collateral estoppel") and "issue-preclusion" (also known as "*res judicata*"). Federal courts are deeply divided over when to consider a prior arbitration decision, and, if the decision is to be considered at all, how much credit to give it. For several reasons, though, most courts are very reluctant to attach much weight to prior arbitration decisions. Why? Because in the first place, as observed by the Supreme Court, the expertise an arbitrator brings to the resolution of claims "concerns itself primarily with the law of the shop, not the law of the land." [51] In the second place, in labor arbitrations, the union, not the employee, has exclusive control over the way in

Courts have been reluctant to find that a collective bargaining agreement waives the rights of union members to bring lawsuits under the FMLA.

which an individual grievance is presented and may make strategy decisions the employee would not have made.[52] Thirdly, courts consider "arbitral factfinding generally not equivalent to judicial factfinding," leading to the belief that giving more credence to arbitration awards might undermine the protection of federal rights. [53] Applying these principles, the courts to thus far address the issue under the FMLA have decided that they are not bound by labor arbitrators' decisions.[54]

The Integration Of The FMLA With Disciplinary Systems.

Some employers have disciplinary or sick leave policies that call for discipline if an employee uses more than a specified amount of sick leave. The FMLA makes clear that such disciplinary policies must yield to the requirements of FMLA leave.[55] In addition, the DOL's regulations specify that FMLA leave cannot "be counted under 'no-fault' attendance policies."[56] In the words of one court, "an employer's policy as to calculation of occurrences [of absences] and disciplinary actions flowing from such calculations cannot be applied to decrease an employee's rights under the FMLA."[57]

For example, in one case the federal Merit Systems Protection Board considered the discharge of a Postal Service employee for violating its policies on unscheduled leave. Though the employer's leave policies had long since been upheld as valid,[58] the Board nonetheless found that "when an employee has an unscheduled absence meeting the requirements of FMLA leave, [a] charge of unscheduled absence must be scrutinized in light of the employee's rights and requirements under the FMLA. The FMLA therefore may be a relevant and material defense to a charge that requires proof of failure to follow leave procedures."[59]

State Family And Medical Leave Laws.

The Statute: 29 U.S.C. §2651(b).

(b) State and local laws

Nothing in this Act or any amendment made by this Act shall be construed to supersede any provision of any State or local law that provides greater family or medical leave rights than the rights established under this Act or any amendment made by this Act.

At the time the FMLA was passed, many states and local governmental bodies already had enacted family and/or medical leave laws, many of which provide greater benefits than the FMLA. Section 2651(b) of the FMLA makes clear that such laws, to the extent they provide greater benefits than the FMLA, are still enforceable.[60]

The following table provides a brief description of the laws in those states that, as of September, 2002, had some provisions similar to those provided in the FMLA. Thirty-two states have no equivalent to the FMLA; 18 states and the District of Columbia do have analogous state statutory provisions. Some of the state family leave laws include significantly more generous benefits than the FMLA. For example, in 2002, California modified its family leave laws to allow paid leave for the first six weeks of family leave.[61] Oregon's family leave law allows for the recovery of damages for emotional distress.[62] Alaska's law allows for up to 18 workweeks of leave over a 12-month period of time.

State	Statute Reference	Leave For Birth/ Adoption	Leave For Employee's Illness	Leave For Illness In Family	Definition Of Family
Alaska	Alaska Stat. §23.10.500 (2000)	18 work weeks over 12-month period.	18 work weeks	18 work weeks	Child (biological, adopted, foster child, stepchild, legal ward), spouse, parent
California	Cal. Gov't. Code §12945.2 (2001)	12 work weeks over 12 months[63]	12 work weeks	12 work weeks	Child (biological, adopted, foster child, stepchild, legal ward), spouse, parent
	SB 1661 Amending §§984, 2116, 2601, 2613, 2708, 3254 and to add Ch. 7 to California Unemploy-ment Code (Effective January 1, 2004)	6 weeks paid leave over 12 motnhs	6 weeks paid leave over 12 months	6 weeks paid leave over 12 months	Child, spouse, parent, domestice partner

State	Statute Reference	Leave For Birth/ Adoption	Leave For Employee's Illness	Leave For Illness In Family	Definition Of Family
Colorado	Colo. Rev. Stat. §19-5-211 (2002)	Employer must allow time off for adopting parents if employer allows time off for birth parents.			
Connecticut	Conn. Gen. Stat. §31-51ll (2001) State Employees Conn. Gen. Stat. §5-248a (2001)	16 work weeks over 24 months 24 work weeks over 24 months	16 work weeks 24 work weeks	16 work weeks 24 work weeks	Child, spouse, parent of employee Child, spouse, parent of employee
District of Columbia	D.C. Code Ann. §35-502 (2000)	16 work weeks over 24 months		16 work weeks	Family member
Florida	State Employees Fla. Rev. Stat. §110.221 (2000)	6 months	6 months	6 months	Child, parent, spouse
Hawaii	Haw. Rev. Stat. §398 (2000)	4 work weeks over 12 months	Employer policy	4 work weeks	Child (biological, adopted, foster child, stepchild, legal ward), spouse, parent
Iowa	Iowa Code Annotated §70A.1 (2002)	Employee allowed to use sick and vacation leave.			
Maine	26 Me. Rev. Stat. Ann. §843-848 (1999)	10 work weeks over 24 months	10 work weeks	10 work weeks	Child, parent, spouse

State	Statute Reference	Leave For Birth/ Adoption	Leave For Employee's Illness	Leave For Illness In Family	Definition Of Family
Maryland	State Employees Md. Code. Ann. State Pers. & Pens. §9-505 (2000)	30 days			
Massachusetts	Mass. Gen. Laws 149 §105D (2002)	8 weeks			
Minnesota	Minn. Stat. §181.941 (2000)	6 work weeks			
Montana	State Employee Mont. Code Ann. §2-18-606 (2001)	6 work weeks, 15 days for father			
Nevada	Nev. Rev. Stat §613.335 (2001)	Maternity leave treated as medical condition authorizing use of sick leave.			
New Jersey	N.J. Stat. Ann. §34: 11B-4 (2001)	12 work weeks over 24 months	12 work weeks	12 work weeks	Child (biological, adopted, foster child, stepchild, legal ward), parent, spouse
North Dakota	State Employees N.D. Cent.Code §54-52.4-02 (2001)	16 work weeks		16 work weeks	Child, spouse, parent

State	Statute Reference	Leave For Birth/ Adoption	Leave For Employee's Illness	Leave For Illness In Family	Definition Of Family
Ohio	State Employees Ohio Rev. Code Ann. §124.136 (2001)	6 work weeks			
Oregon	Or. Rev. Stat. §659A.150 186 (2001)	12 work weeks over one year	12 work weeks	12 work weeks	Spouse, biological, adoptive or foster parent or child, parent-in-law, person with whom the employee was or is in a relationship of *in loco parentis.*
Rhode Island	R.I Gen. Laws §28.48.1 (2000)	13 work weeks over 24 months	13 work weeks	13 work weeks	Parent, spouse, child, mother-in-law, father-in-law, employee him/herself
Vermont	Vt. Stat. Ann. Tit. 21, §470-474 (1999)	12 work weeks over 12 months	12 work weeks	12 work weeks	Child, foster child, stepchild, legal ward, spouse, parent, parent of the employee's spouse
Washington	Wash. Rev. Code §49.78.020 030 (2000)	12 work weeks over 24 months		12 weeks to care for child with terminal health condition	Child (biological, adopted, step)

State	Statute Reference	Leave For Birth/ Adoption	Leave For Employee's Illness	Leave For Illness In Family	Definition Of Family
West Virginia	W. Va. Code §21-5D-1-9 (2000)	12 work weeks over 12 months		12 work weeks	Son, daughter, spouse, parent or dependant
Wisconsin	Wis. Stat. Ann. §103.10 (2001)	6 work weeks over 12 months, beginning within 16 weeks of birth[64] Or up to 8 weeks by combining 6 weeks for birth and 2 weeks for illness	2 weeks	2 weeks	Child, spouse, parent

The Integration Of The FMLA With Workers' Compensation Laws.

In the legislative history of the FMLA, Congress indicated that a serious health condition covered by the FMLA could result from an injury to the employee "on or off" the job.[65] Accordingly, if an employee's condition merits workers' compensation *and* meets the test for a serious health condition under the FMLA, the employer may designate the workers' compensation leave as running concurrently with the employee's FMLA leave.[66] This results in the anomalous situation that an employee whose workers' compensation injury is not severe enough to qualify as a serious health condition under the FMLA will preserve his or her FMLA benefits while on workers' compensation leave, while an employee suffering from a truly severe condition may find his or her FMLA leave exhausted. If the employer designates workers' compensation leave as running concurrently with FMLA leave, it must provide contemporaneous notice to the employee of that designation.[67]

Some difficult questions surround the job restoration rights of an employee with a workers' compensation-eligible illness or injury who is designated by the employer as concurrently being on FMLA leave. As noted in Chapter 10, the FMLA does not have any "reasonable accommodation" provisions, and an employee is entitled to remain on FMLA leave for up to 12 weeks so long as the underlying purpose for the FMLA leave remains present. However, many workers' compensation laws require or allow an employer to assign an employee to light-duty work consistent with the employee's medical condition. As a result, while the employee has the right under the FMLA to refuse a light-duty job and remain off work on FMLA leave, she may no longer be eligible for workers' compensation benefits.[68]

Another job-restoration issue arising from the meshing of the FMLA with workers' compensation systems is when the employee's workers' compensation injury lasts longer than 12 weeks. In this case, if the employer has concurrently designated the workers' compensation leave as FMLA leave, the employee loses his job-restoration rights under the FMLA at the conclusion of the 12 weeks of FMLA leave. After that, the employee's job restoration rights will exist, if at all, under the workers' compensation system (and virtually all workers' compensation systems have comprehensive job restoration benefits), the Americans With Disabilities Act, or a collective bargaining agreement.[69]

CASE IN POINT

Question: Tom Mumgaard and Nancy Henderson work for Office, Inc., a wholesale office-supply company. Each has the full allotment of 12 weeks of FMLA leave remaining for the year. One day, a large pile of boxes collapses, injuring both Mumgaard and Henderson. Mumgaard receives outpatient treatment for his condition and misses only three days of work. Henderson also suffers from a back injury but a much more serious one. Henderson is hospitalized for three weeks and misses another three weeks of work while recuperating. During the periods they are off work, Mumgaard and Henderson receive workers' compensation benefits. Assuming Office, Inc. takes full advantage of its rights under the FMLA, how much FMLA leave may it subtract from the accounts of Mumgaard and Henderson?

Answer: Since Mumgaard did not suffer from a serious health condition (he did not receive inpatient treatment and did not miss more than three consecutive days of work), Office, Inc. can make no deduction from his FMLA account. Since Henderson did suffer from a serious health condition, Office, Inc. can reduce her FMLA account by the six weeks she missed from work.

The Relationship Of The FMLA To The FLSA.

The DOL recognized that the FMLA could impact whether an employee is exempt from overtime under the Fair Labor Standards Act. Under the FLSA, employees who perform duties that are executive, administrative, or professional in nature are exempt from overtime if they are "salaried." Under the DOL's regulations, an employee is "salaried" only if they receive a fixed amount of compensation over a given period of time *without* regard to how many hours they actually work.[70] Consequently, if an employer reduces an employee's salary to account for unpaid FMLA leave, the potential exists for the employee to be considered no longer "salaried" since their salary *depends* on the actual hours worked; and, if an employee is no longer salaried, they are no longer exempt from the overtime provisions of the FLSA.

The DOL's FMLA regulations solve this problem by expressly indicating that granting unpaid FMLA-qualifying leave to an FLSA-exempt employee will not cause the employee to lose the FLSA exemption.[71] In the words of the DOL, "this means that under regulations currently in effect, where an employee meets the specified duties test, is paid on a salary basis, and is paid a salary of at least the amount specified in the regulations, the employer may make deductions from the employee's salary for any hours taken as intermittent or reduced FMLA leave within a workweek, without affecting the exempt status of the employee. The fact that an employer provides FMLA leave, whether paid or unpaid, and maintains records required by this part regarding FMLA leave, will not be relevant to the determination whether an employee is exempt..." [72] In addition, an employer does not necessarily have to designate leave as qualifying for the FMLA to later claim that the leave should be treated as FMLA leave for purposes of the FLSA.[73]

The FLSA also allows an employer to use a "fluctuating workweek" method of calculating overtime for certain employees.[74] The idea behind it is that both the employer and the employee have reached an understanding that a salary payment to the employee is intended to compensate the employee for all hours worked, and that the hours of work are expected to fluctuate from workweek to workweek. The use of a fluctuating workweek impacts the employee's overtime rate of pay.[75] The DOL's FMLA regulations allow employers using a fluctuating workweek to pay an employee *only* for the hours worked in the week in which FMLA leave is taken, provided the employer pays the employee time and one-half for any overtime worked.[76] This new rate of payment, which essentially converts what would be a salaried employee to an hourly employee, can apply for the entire time an employee is on intermittent leave, including weeks in which no leave is taken. The employee's hourly rate is then determined by dividing the employee's weekly salary by the normal or average hours worked during weeks in which FMLA leave is not taken. If the employer does not elect to convert the employee's compensation to an hourly basis, no deduction may be taken for FMLA leave absences.

The Relationship Of The FMLA To The Americans With Disabilities Act.

There is only a slight overlap between the Americans With Disabilities Act (ADA) and the FMLA. One of the DOL's regulations, for example, adopts the ADA's standards for the "essential functions of the job" in defining when an employee is eligible for job restoration after using FMLA leave.[77] Another rule defines "physical or mental disability" by borrowing from the ADA's definition of an impairment as substantially limiting one or more major life activities.[78] For the most part, though, the FMLA and the ADA stand as independent obligations, each of which must be complied with by the employer. An individual can have a "serious health condition" under the FMLA and not qualify for ADA protections, and vice-versa.[79]

In the case of an employee with a serious health condition under FMLA who is also qualified as disabled under the ADA, an employer must comply with both laws in a manner that assures the most beneficial rights and protection for the employee.[80] For example, nothing in the FMLA requires an employer to make "reasonable accommodation" for an employee who wants to return to work but suffers from a serious health condition.[81] Since such an obligation does, however, exist under the ADA, the employer must proceed through the reasonable accommodation process with the employee.[82] Conversely, nothing in the FMLA requires an employee using FMLA leave to accept a light-duty job if the employee remains eligible for FMLA leave.[83]

Along the same lines, the FMLA does not allow an employer to require a full fitness-for-duty examination as a condition to returning from FMLA leave (*see* Chapter 7). Since the ADA allows an employer, under some circumstances, to require a medical examination to determine if the employee can perform essential job functions, the FMLA does not prohibit an employer from requiring an ADA physical examination.[84]

The Relationship Of The FMLA To The Civil Rights Act.

Section 1983 of the Civil Rights Act is the normal vehicle used to address a wide variety of civil rights claims brought against states and their political subdivisions such as cities and counties, including questions relating to on-the-job discrimination. In part, Section 1983 offers the possibility of greater remedies than does the FMLA. Almost immediately after the enactment of the FMLA, there were questions about whether an individual could maintain both a Section 1983 and an FMLA claim for the same underlying conduct.

The Supreme Court has used a three-part test to determine whether Congress intended to "foreclose" Section 1983 claims by enacting a specific statutory scheme. For such foreclosure to exist: (1) Congress must have intended that the statute vest a right that is both potentially within the scope of the statute itself *and* Section 1983; (2) Congress must have intended that the specific statute foreclose Section 1983 claims; *and* (3) the statute must unambiguously impose a binding obligation on the states.[85] Since to date the Supreme Court has only found two statutory schemes (the Federal Pollution Control Act and the Education of the Handicapped Act) sufficiently comprehensive to foreclose Section 1983 lawsuits,[86] it is surprising that decisions have fairly evenly split on the issue of whether the FMLA forecloses a Section 1983 lawsuit for the same claim.[87]

The Relationship Of The FMLA To Common-Law Civil Lawsuits.

The underlying claims in an FMLA lawsuit sometimes give rise to claims under a private cause of action under the common law of a state. The most frequently lodged claim of this type is for "wrongful discharge," a claim that an employer's decision to fire an employee violates an important public policy of the state. A majority of those cases addressing the issue have ruled that the FMLA preempts wrongful discharge claims, thereby prohibiting wrongful discharge lawsuits for the same underlying facts. Courts holding to this view believe Congress has spoken on the issue of family medical leave in the workplace, eliminating the possibility of common-law claims in the area.[88] This result is perhaps a bit surprising, given the statement in the FMLA that the FMLA is not intended to curtail any rights established under state and local law.[89]

Another claim occasionally brought by employees is that the employer's decision amounts to the common-law claim of "intentional infliction of emotional distress," sometimes called the tort of "outrage." To make a claim for intentional infliction of emotional distress, an employee must prove that the employer's conduct goes so beyond the bounds of what is socially acceptable as to be "outrageous." Thus far, courts have found that the failure to grant FMLA leave is not outrageous enough to amount to common-law intentional infliction of emotional distress.[90]

NOTES

1 *Rich v. Delta Air Lines, Inc.*, 921 F.Supp. 767 (N.D.Ga. 1996).

2 *Diaz v. Fort Wayne Foundry Corp.,* 131 F.3d 711 (7th Cir. 1997); *McConaughy v. Boswell Oil Co.*, 711 N.E.2d 719 (OhioApp. 1998); *Austin v. Shelby County Gov't*, 3 S.W.3d 474 (Tenn.App. 1999).

3 29 C.F.R. §825.207(a); *see Strickland v. Water Works and Sewer Bd. of the City of Birmingham*, 239 F.3d 1199 (11th Cir. 2001); *Lau v. Behr Heat Transfer Sys., Inc.*, 150 F.Supp.2d 1017 (D.S.D. 2001).

4 *Opinion Letter,* Wage and Hour Division, 1996 WL 1044778 (June 18, 1996); *see Haggard v. Farmers Insurance Exchange*, 3 WH Cas.2d 339 (D.Or. 1996).

5 *Opinion Letter,* Wage and Hour Division, 1995 WL 1036732 (May 12, 1995).

6 *Opinion Letter*, Wage and Hour Division, 1994 WL 1016760 (December 28, 1994).

7 29 C.F.R. §825.208(c).

8 29 C.F.R. §825.208(c).

9 *Funkhouser v. Wells Fargo Bank, N.A.*, 289 F.3d 1137 (9th Cir. 2002).

10 *Paniagua v. Texas Dept. of Criminal Justice*, 2001 WL 540908 (N.D.Tex. 2001); *McKnight v. Dormitory Auth. of the State of New York*, 699 N.Y.S.2d 524 (A.D. 1999); 11 C.F.R. §825.207(e)(i); *see Richland School Dist. v. Dept. of Industry, Labor, and Human Relations, Equal Rights Div.*, 498 N.W.2d 826 (Wis. 1993)(decided under state law).

11 *See* 29 U.S.C. §207(o).

12 *Opinion Letter,* Wage and Hour Division, 1996 WL 1044780 (August 7, 1996); *Opinion Letter*, Wage and Hour Division, 1994 WL 1016742 (April 12, 1994).

13 29 C.F.R. §825.207(c).

14 *Kenyon v. Western Extrusions Corp.*, 2000 WL 12902 (N.D.Tex. 2000).

15 *Opinion Letter,* Wage and Hour Division, 1996 WL 1044782 (November 18, 1996).

16 29 C.F.R. §825.207(g).

17 29 C.F.R. §825.207(h).

18 29 C.F.R. §825.208(a).

19 *Opinion Letter*, Wage and Hour Division, 1994 WL 1016750 (August 23, 1994).

20 *Thornton v. BASF*, 217 F.3d 840 (4th Cir. 2000).

21 *Williamson v. Mississippi Dept. of Human Services*, 4 WH Cas.2d 262 (N.D.Miss. 1997).

22 29 C.F.R. §825.208(a).

[23] 29 C.F.R. §825.208(a)(1).

[24] 29 C.F.R. §825.208(b).

[25] 29 C.F.R. §825.208(b)(2).

[26] 29 C.F.R. §825.208(b)(2); *see Bala v. Jacobson Stores, Inc.*, 2001 WL 1543503 (E.D.Mich. 2001); *Chan v. Loyola Univ. Med. Ctr.*, 5 WH Cas.2d 584 (N.D.Ill. 1999).

[27] 29 C.F.R. §825.208(b)(1).

[28] 29 C.F.R. §825.208(d).

[29] 29 C.F.R. §825.208(d).

[30] *Moss v. Formosa Plastics Corp.*, 99 F.Supp.2d 737 (M.D.La. 2000); *Harvender v. Norton Co.*, 1997 WL 793085 (N.D.N.Y. 1997); *Love v. City of Dallas*, 1997 WL 278126 (N.D.Tex. 1997); *see* Note, *A Shield, Not A Sword: Involuntary Leave Under the Family and Medical Leave Act*, Washington Law Review (April, 2001).

[31] *Ragsdale v. Wolverine Worldwide, Inc.*, 218 F.3d 933 (8th Cir. 2000); *McGregor v. Autozone, Inc.*, 180 F.3d 1305 (11th Cir. 1999); *Fulham v. HSBC Bank USA*, 7 WH Cas.2d 474 (S.D.N.Y. 2001); *Daley v. Wellpoint Health Networks, Inc.*, 146 F.Supp.2d 92 (D.Mass. 2001); *Nolan v. Hypercom Mfg. Resources*, 2001 WL 378235 (D.Ariz. 2001); *Twyman v. Dilks*, 2000 WL 1277917 (E.D.Pa. 2000); *Neal v. Children's Habilitation Ctr.*, 1999 WL 706117 (N.D.Ill. 1999); *cf. Covucci v. Serv. Merchandise Co., Inc.*, 178 F.3d 1294 (6th Cir. 1999); *see Donnellan v. New York City Transit Auth.*, 5 WH Cas.2d 942 (S.D.N.Y. 1999).

[32] *Chan v. Loyola Univ. Med. Ctr.*, 6 WH Cas.2d 328 (N.D.Ill. 1999); *see Plant v. Morton Int'l*, 212 F.3d 929 (6th Cir. 2000); *Cline v. Wal-Mart Stores, Inc.*, 144 F.3d 294 (4th Cir. 1998); *Nott v. Woodstock Care Ctr., Inc.*, 2001 WL 1135057 (S.D.Ohio 2001); *Ritchie v. Grand Casinos of Mississippi, Inc.*, 49 F.Supp.2d 878 (S.D.Miss. 1999); *Longstreth v. Copple*, 189 F.R.D. 401 (N.D.Iowa 1999); *cf. Barone v. Leukemia Society of America*, 42 F.Supp.2d 452 (D.N.J. 1998)(similar result under New Jersey state law). *See generally Price v. City of Fort Wayne*, 117 F.3d 1022 (7th Cir. 1997).

[33] 29 C.F.R. §825.208(e)(1).

[34] *Hicks v. Leroy's Jewelers, Inc.*, 225 F.3d 659 (6th Cir. 2000); *Opinion Letter,* Wage and Hour Division, 1995 WL 1036739 (July 21, 1995); *see Harrison v. Children's Nat'l Med. Ctr.*, 678 A.2d 562 (D.C.App. 1996)(decided under District of Columbia law).

[35] *Opinion Letter*, Wage and Hour Division, 1997 WL 1169956 (December 9, 1997); *see Kramer v. Hickey-Freeman, Inc.*, 142 F.Supp.2d 555 (S.D.N.Y. 2001); *McKnight v. Dormitory Auth. of the State of New York*, 699 N.Y.S.2d 524 (A.D. 1999).

[36] *Harvender v. Norton Co.*, 4 WH Cas.2d 560 (N.D.N.Y. 1997).

[37] *Opinion Letter*, Wage and Hour Division, 1996 WL 1044780 (August 7, 1996).

[38] *McGregor v. Autozone, Inc.*, 180 F.3d 1305 (11th Cir. 1999). *See Ragsdale v. Wolverine Worldwide, Inc.*, 218 F.3d 933 (8th Cir. 2000); *Dolese v. Office Depot, Inc.*, 231 F.3d 202 (5th Cir. 2000); *Hite v. Biomet, Inc.*, 53 F.Supp.2d 1013 (N.D.Ind. 1999); *Santos v. Shields Health Group*, 996 F.Supp. 87 (D.Mass. 1998); *Rich v. Delta Air*

Lines, Inc., 921 F.Supp. 767 (N.D.Ga. 1996); *Pert v. Value RX*, 1996 WL 1089866 (E.D.Mich. 1996); *Szpryngel v. Waterbury Extended Care Facility, Inc.*, 29 Conn. L. Rptr. 401, 2001 WL 490776 (Conn.Super. 2001). *But see Plant v. Morton Int'l, Inc.*, 212 F.3d 929 (6th Cir. 2000)(disagrees with *McGregor*, but remanded to determine whether plaintiff pled elements of FMLA).

[39] 29 C.F.R. §825.700(a).

[40] 29 C.F.R. §825.700(b).

[41] *Opinion Letter*, Wage and Hour Division, 1997 WL 1169956 (December 9, 1997).

[42] *Rich v. Delta Air Lines, Inc.*, 921 F.Supp. 767 (N.D.Ga. 1996); *see Dolese v. Office Depot, Inc.*, 231 F.3d 202 (5th Cir. 2000); *Fulham v. HSBC Bank USA*, 2001 WL 1029051 (S.D.N.Y. 2001); *Holmes v. e.spire Communications*, 135 F.Supp.2d 657 (D.Md. 2001); *Covey v. Methodist Hosp. of Dyersburg, Inc.*, 56 F.Supp.2d 965 (W.D.Tenn. 1999); *Hite v. Biomet, Inc.*, 53 F.Supp.2d 1013 (N.D.Ind. 1999); *Cantrell v. Delta Air Lines, Inc.*, 2 F.Supp.2d 1460 (N.D.Ga. 1998); *Robinson-Scott v. Delta Air Lines*, 4 F.Supp.2d 1183 (N.D.Ga. 1998); *cf. Barron v. Runyon*, 11 F.Supp.2d 676 (E.D.Va. 1998).

[43] *Cf. Opinion Letter*, Wage & Hour Division, 1999 WL 1002425 (March 26, 1999).

[44] 29 C.F.R. §825.702(d); *see Marrero v. Camden County Board of Soc. Servs.*, 164 F.Supp.2d 455 (D.N.J. 2001); *Bluitt v. Eval Co. of America, Inc.*, 3 F.Supp.2d 761 (S.D.Tex. 1998); *Opinion Letter*, Wage and Hour Division, 1994 WL 1016757 (October 27, 1994).

[45] *See Opinion Letter*, Wage and Hour Division, 1994 WL 1016741 (March 29, 1994).

[46] *Compare Alexander v. Gardner-Denver Co.*, 415 U.S. 36 (1974)(disfavoring arbitration as the exclusive remedy) *and Barrentine v. Arkansas-Best Freight Sys. Inc.*, 450 U.S. 728 (1981)(same) *and McDonald v. City of West Branch*, 466 U.S. 284 (1984)(same) *with Gilmer v. Interstate/Johnson Lane Corp.*, 500 U.S. 20 (1991)(appears to favor arbitration) *and Circuit City Stores, Inc. v. Adams*, 121 S.Ct. 1302 (2001)(same).

[47] *Wright v. Universal Maritime Serv. Corp.*, 525 U.S. 70 (1998).

[48] *Brown v. Trans World Airlines*, 127 F.3d 337 (4th Cir. 1997); *see Rogers v. New York Univ.*, 220 F.3d 73 (2nd Cir. 2000)(waiver was not "clear and unmistakable"); *Bonilla v. Small Assemblies Company*, 143 Lab. Cas. ¶34,276 (N.D.Ill. 2001)(same); *Ozolins v. Northwood-Kensett Community Sch. Dist.*, 40 F.Supp.2d 1055 (N.D.Iowa 1999)(same); *O'Hara v. Mt. Vernon Bd. of Education*, 16 F.Supp.2d 868 (S.D.Ohio 1998)(same); *McGinnis v. Wonder Chem. Co.*, 1995 WL 756590 (E.D.Pa. 1995)(same). *See also Wikle v. CAN Holdings, Inc.*, 2001 WL 474692 (4th Cir. 2001); *Bonilla v. Small Assemblies Co.*, 143 Lab. Cas. ¶34,276 (N.D.Ill. 2001). *Contra Smith v. CPC Foodservice*, 955 F.Supp. 84 (N.D.Ill. 1997).

[49] *Ozolins v. Northwood-Kensett Community Sch. Dist.*, 40 F.Supp.2d 1055 (N.D.Iowa 1999).

[50] *Hess v. Anheuser-Busch Companies, Inc.*, 2002 WL 483564 (S.D.Ohio 2002).

[51] *McDonald v. City of West Branch*, 466 U.S. 284 (1984).

[52] *Alexander v. Gardner-Denver Co.*, 415 U.S. 36 (1974).

[53] *McDonald v. City of West Branch*, 466 U.S. 284 (1984).

[54] *Shtab v. Greate Bay Hotel and Casino, Inc.*, 173 F.Supp.2d 255 (D.N.J. 2001); *Slaughter v. American Bldg. Maintenance Co.*, 64 F.Supp.2d 319 (S.D.N.Y. 1999); *Contra Trivisonno v. Metropolitan Life Insurance Company*, 39 Fed.Appx. 236 (6th Cir. 2002).

[55] *Hendry v. GTE North, Inc.*, 896 F.Supp. 816 (N.D.Ind. 1995).

[56] *Jones v. Adm'r, Ohio Bureau of Employment Servs.*, 2000 WL 1670681 (OhioApp. 2000); 29 C.F.R. §825.220(c). *See generally Austin v. Haaker*, 76 F.Supp.2d 1213 (D.Kan. 1999); *Opinion Letter*, Wage and Hour Division, 1999 WL 1002426 (March 26, 1999); *Opinion Letter*, Wage & Hour Division, 1999 WL 1002428 (January 12, 1999); *Opinion Letter*, Wage & Hour Division, 1999 WL 1002428 (January 12, 1999).

[57] *Jones v. Adm'r, Ohio Bureau of Employment Servs.*, 2000 WL 1670681 (OhioApp. 2000). *See also Saladin v. Packerware Corp.*, 143 Lab. Cas. ¶34,264 (D.Kan. 2001). *See generally* Stacy A. Hickox, *Absenteeism Under The Family And Medical Leave Act And The Americans With Disabilities Act*, 50 DePaul Law Review 183 (2000); Gordon & Ekman, *Attendance Control Issues Under The ADA And FMLA*, Labor Lawyer (Fall, 1997).

[58] *Fleming v. U.S. Postal Srv.*, 30 M.S.P.R. 302 (MSPB 1986).

[59] *Ramey v. U.S. Postal Srv.*, 70 M.S.P.R. 463 (MSPB 1996).

[60] *Opinion Letter*, Wage and Hour Division, 1994 WL 1016744 (May 18, 1994).

[61] 2002 Cal. Stat. S.B. 1661.

[62] *See Centennial Sch. Dust No. 28J v. Oregon Bureau of Labor and Industries*, 10 P.3d 945 (Or.App. 2000).

[63] *See generally Nelson v. United Technologies*, 88 Cal.Rptr.2d 239 (Cal.App. 1999).

[64] *Schwedt v. Dept. of Industry, Labor and Human Relations*, 525 N.W.2d 130 (Wis.App. 1994).

[65] S.Rep. No. 3, 103d Cong., 1st Sess.1993, 1993 U.S.C.C.A.N. 3, at pp. 30-31.

[66] 29 C.F.R. §825.207(d); *see Opinion Letter*, Wage and Hour Division, 1994 WL 1016751 (August 24, 1994); *Opinion Letter*, Wage and Hour Division, 1994 WL 1016750 (August 23, 1994). *See generally* Walter E. Zink & Hukk Gradwohl Schroeder, *Evaluating The Interplay Among FMLA, ADA And Workers' Comp Statutes Isn't Child's Play*, 66 Def. Couns. J. 79 (1999).

[67] *Jacobsen v. New York State Dept. of Labor*, 711 N.Y.S.2d 61 (App.Div. 2000).

[68] 29 C.F.R. §825.702(d)(2).

[69] 29 C.F.R. §825.216(d).

[70] 29 C.F.R. §§541.118(a), (a)(2), (a)(3).

[71] 29 C.F.R. §825.206(a); *see Rowe v. Laidlaw Transp., Inc.*, 1 Fed. Appx. 386 (D.Or. 2000), *aff'd* 244 F.3d 1115 (9th Cir. 2001); *Opinion Letter*, Wage and Hour Division, 1997 WL 1039254 (July 3, 1997).

[72] 29 C.F.R. §825.206(a).

[73] *Rowe v. Laidlaw Transp., Inc.*, 244 F.3d 1115 (9th Cir. 2001); *see Furlong v. Johnson Controls World Srvs.*, 97 F.Supp.2d 1312 (S.D.Fla. 2000); *Cash v. Conn Appliances, Inc.*, 2 F.Supp.2d 884 (E.D.Tenn. 1995).

[74] *See* 29 C.F.R. §778.114.

[75] *See* W. Aitchison, *The FLSA – A User's Manual, Third Edition* (LRIS, 2002).

[76] 29 C.F.R. §825.206(b).

[77] 29 C.F.R. §825.115.

[78] 29 C.F.R. §825.113(c).

[79] *Vincent v. Wells Fargo Guard Srvs., Inc. of Fla.*, 3 F.Supp.2d 1405 (S.D.Fla. 1998). *See generally* Angres & Albrecht, *Accommodating Disabilities At Work And Giving Leave Under The Family And Medical Leave Act*, 4 Jul. Nev. Law. 19 (1996).

[80] *Opinion Letter,* Wage and Hour Division, 1995 WL 1036726 (March 10, 1995).

[81] *Williams v. Saad's Health Care*, 2000 WL 362038 (S.D.Ala. 2000).

[82] 29 C.F.R. §825.702(d)(1); *see* D. Snyder, *The Americans With Disabilities Act (Second Edition)*(LRIS, 1998).

[83] *Opinion Letter,* Wage and Hour Division, 1995 WL 1036746 (November 14, 1995); *Opinion Letter*, Wage and Hour Division, 1994 WL 1016743 (April 19, 1994).

[84] *Porter v. U.S. Alumoweld Co., Inc.*, 125 F.3d 243 (4th Cir. 1997).

[85] *Blessing v. Freestone,* 520 U.S. 329 (1997).

[86] *Smith v. Robinson,* 468 U.S. 992 (1984); *Middlesex County Sewerage Auth. v. National Sea Clammers Assn.,* 453 U.S. 1 (1981). The Supreme Court has found that several federal statutes do not foreclose Section 1983 suits. *Blessing v. Freestone,* 520 U.S. 329 (1997)(finding Title IV-D of the Social Security Act does not foreclose Section 1983 actions); *Wilder v. Virginia Hosp. Assn.,* 496 U.S. 498 (1990)(finding that despite oversight provisions in the Medicaid Act, Section 1983 suits are still available); *Golden State Transit Corp. v. Los Angeles,* 493 U.S. 103 (1989)(finding that the National Labor Relations Act does not foreclose Section 1983 suits); *Livadas v. Bradshaw,* 512 U.S. 107 (1994)(same); *Wright v. City of Roanoke Redev. & Housing Auth.,* 479 U.S. 418 (1987)(finding the Housing Act does not foreclose Section 1983 actions).

[87] *Compare O'Hara v. Mount Vernon Bd. of Educ.,* 16 F.Supp.2d 868 (S.D.Ohio 1998); *Jolliffe v. Mitchell,* 971 F.Supp. 1039 (W.D.Va. 1997); *Clay v. City of Chicago, Dept. of Health,* 1996 WL 613164 (N.D.Ill. 1996) *with Peterson v. Slidell Memorial Hosp. and Med. Ctr.,* 1996 WL 732840 (E.D.La. 1996); *Knussman v. State of Maryland,* 16 F.Supp.2d 601 (D.Md. 1998), *rev'd on other grounds,* 272 F.3d 625 (4th Cir. 2001).

[88] *Cavin v. Honda of American Mfg.*, 138 F.Supp.2d 987 (S.D.Ohio 2001). *See Johnson v. Honda of America Mfg., Inc.*, 2002 WL 31155793 (S.D.Ohio 2002); *Wiles v. Medina Auto Parts*, 773 N.E.2d 526 (Ohio 2002); *Cooper v. Harbour Inns of Baltimore, Inc.*, 2000 WL 351373 (D.Md. 2000); *Weeden v. Sears, Roebuck & Co.*, 1999 WL 1209494 (D.N.H. 1999); *Desrochers v. Hilton Hotels Corp.*, 28 F.Supp.2d 693 (D.Mass. 1998); *Gearhart v. Sears, Roebuck & Co., Inc.*, 27 F.Supp.2d 1263 (D.Kan. 1998), *aff'd*, 194 F.3d 1320 (10th Cir. 1999); *Phelan v. Town of Derry*, 1998 WL 1285898 (D.N.H. 1998); *Callozzo v. Office Depot, Inc.*, 1998 WL 111628 (N.D.Ill. 1998); *Parker v. Chestnut Hill Hosp.*, 1996 WL 334426 (E.D.Pa. 1996); *McClain v. Southwest Steel Co.*, 940 F.Supp. 295 (N.D.Okla. 1996); *McKiernan v. Smith-Edwards-Dunlap Co.*, 3 WH Cas.2d 272 (E.D.Pa. 1995); *Hamros v. Bethany Homes and Methodist Hosp.*, 894 F.Supp. 1176 (N.D.Ill. 1995); *Gall v. Quaker City Castings, Inc.*, 874 F.Supp. 161 (N.D.Ohio 1995). *But see Arthur v. Armco, Inc.*, 122 F.Supp.2d 876 (S.D.Ohio 2000); *Bellido-Sullivan v. American Int'l Group, Inc.*, 123 F.Supp.2d 161 (S.D.N.Y. 2000); *Wilson v. Tarr, Inc.*, 2000 WL 1292590 (D.Or. 2000); *Findlay v. PHE, Inc.*, 1999 WL 1939246 (M.D.N.C. 1999); *Danfelt v. Bd. of County Comm'rs of Washington County*, 998 F.Supp. 606 (D.Md. 1998); *Findlay v. PHE, Inc.*, 1999 WL 1939246 (M.D.N.C. 1999).

[89] 29 U.S.C. §2651(a)(b).

[90] *Neal v. Children's Habilitation Ctr.*, 4 WH Cas.2d 1779 (N.D.Ill. 1998); *see Atkins v. USF Dugan, Inc.*, 106 F.Supp.2d 799 (M.D.N.C. 1999).

CHAPTER 10

THE FMLA'S PROTECTIONS OF EMPLOYMENT AND BENEFITS

In A Nutshell . . .

The FMLA requires an employer to restore an employee to her former job or an equivalent job at the conclusion of FMLA leave, with no loss of wages and benefits. The right to job restoration can be modified only if the employer has restructured its operations for independent reasons during the FMLA leave, or if the employee is physically incapable of performing her former job. During FMLA leave, the employer must continue providing health insurance on the same terms and conditions as existed prior to the employee's beginning of FMLA leave.

The Right To Restoration To The Employee's Former Job.

The Statute: 29 U.S.C. §2614.

(a) Restoration to position

(1) In general

Except as provided in subsection (b) of this section, any eligible employee who takes leave under section 2612 of this title for the intended purpose of the leave shall be entitled, on return from such leave -

(A) to be restored by the employer to the position of employment held by the employee when the leave commenced; or

(B) to be restored to an equivalent position with equivalent employment benefits, pay, and other terms and conditions of employment.

(2) Loss of benefits

The taking of leave under section 2612 of this title shall not result in the loss of any employment benefit accrued prior to the date on which the leave commenced.

(3) Limitations

Nothing in this section shall be construed to entitle any restored employee to -

(A) the accrual of any seniority or employment benefits during any period of leave; or

(B) any right, benefit, or position of employment other than any right, benefit, or position to which the employee would have been entitled had the employee not taken the leave.

Section 2614(a) of the FMLA guarantees an employee the right to return to the same position she held before going on FMLA leave or to a position with equivalent employment benefits, pay, and other terms and conditions of employment.[1] The term "employment benefits," referenced in Section 2614(a), includes such tangible benefits as vacation and sick leave,[2] and probably even extends to more intangible benefits such as job security[3] and the authority and responsibility that goes along with a particular job.[4] However, this right to "restoration" does not include the *continued* accrual of benefits such as sick leave, vacation leave, and seniority while on FMLA leave.[5]

The right to reinstatement exists even if the employee has been replaced and even if the employee's job has been restructured to accommodate the employee's absence. [6] A permanent employee may not be placed on probation upon returning from FMLA leave, and a probationary employee who uses FMLA leave cannot be compelled to start the probationary period over again at the end of the FMLA leave.[7] However, if the employer has a policy of not counting leave days in determining when a probationary period is complete, the employer will not violate the FMLA by not counting FMLA leave time taken during the probationary period.[8]

The right to reinstatement is qualified by three conditions. First, the employee must be able to perform the essential job functions upon returning to work.[9] If the employee's physical or mental condition is such that the employee cannot perform the essential job functions, the employee has no right to restoration to her former job or to a comparable position. For example, an employee suffering from serious and ongoing epileptic seizures would have no right to restoration to a job as a control panel operator in a caustic chlorine plant.[10] The burden is on the employer to prove the employee's inability to perform the job.[11] If one of the job's essential functions requires the employee to work more than 40 hours a week, the employee must be able to work such hours upon returning from FMLA leave to be entitled to automatic restoration.[12] If an employee is no longer qualified for the position because of the employee's inability to attend a necessary course, renew a license, or maintain minimum qualifications needed for possession of a required certificate as a result of the leave, he/she must be given a reasonable opportunity to fulfill those conditions upon return to work.[13]

The second condition qualifying the right to job restoration is that the employee has no greater right to his former position than would have been the case had he been continuously employed during the FMLA leave period.[14] Thus, an employer would not violate the FMLA by laying off an employee on FMLA leave if business considerations would have resulted in the layoff of the employee in any case.[15] An employer need not place an employee returning from FMLA leave in a better position than would have been the case had the leave not been taken.[16] As put by one court quoting from a case unrelated to the FMLA:

> "A restored employee does not step back on the [employee benefit] escalator at the point she stepped off. Rather, she steps back on at the precise point she would have occupied had she kept her position continuously."[17]

The third condition qualifying the right to job restoration is a simple one – the employee must present herself to the employer as willing to work at the end of the FMLA leave. If at the end of FMLA leave, the employee fails to return to work and neglects to indicate a willingness to work, the employee will be considered to have forfeited job restoration rights.[18] The employee will forfeit job restoration rights even if the failure to return to work is because of the employee's mistaken belief that she has FMLA leave remaining.[19]

The right to reinstatement is qualified by only three conditions: (1) The employee must be able to perform the essential functions of the job; (2) the employee has no greater right to his former job than had he been continuously employed during the period while on FMLA leave; and (3) the employee must be willing to work at the end of FMLA leave.

If the employer restructures its workforce while an employee is on FMLA leave, the employee's right to job restoration may be impacted. The key consideration is whether the employee's job would have been restructured *if it were not for* the employee's use of FMLA leave. Depending on the circumstances, the employee may be assigned to a different job, transferred to another location, or conceivably even laid off upon returning to work.[20] If there is any evidence that the employee's use of FMLA leave influenced the employer's decision, it may still be liable to the employee under the FMLA even though the employee's job was impacted as part of a larger job restructuring.[21] The courts carefully scrutinize employer claims of a need to restructure, reasoning that "manipulating the workforce to avoid responsibilities under the FMLA violates the law."[22] Similarly, if an employee's shift has been legitimately eliminated, the employee has no right to restoration to the former shift.[23]

What Is An "Equivalent" Position?

If the employee's former position is unavailable upon the employee's return to work, or has been modified during the period of FMLA leave, the employee must be restored to an "equivalent" position. The employee's physical capabilities are considered in determining whether the position is equivalent.[24] The DOL has defined an equivalent position as one that is "virtually identical" to the employee's position in the following respects:

- Equivalent pay.

- Equivalent benefits.

- Equivalent terms and conditions of employment.[25]

If an employee cannot be restored to her job after FMLA leave, the employee must be placed in an equivalent position in terms of pay, benefits, and terms and conditions of employment.

"**Equivalent pay**" means that the employee is entitled to any pay increases that may have occurred while on FMLA leave.[26] "Equivalent pay" also includes premium pay such as shift differential and the right to work as much overtime as that worked prior to FMLA leave. However, an employee on FMLA leave need only be credited for time served for the purpose of calculating step increases or other pay based on seniority *if* the employer's normal practice is to grant such credit to employees on unpaid leave.[27] Many employers have some form of sick leave incentive or bonus plan granting some benefit to employees whose sick leave use falls below a certain level. For such plans, time spent on FMLA leave must be treated as if the employee was actually at work.[28]

"**Equivalent benefits**" means all benefits provided or made available to employees by an employer. Such benefits include insurance, sick leave, annual leave, educational benefits, and pensions.[29] An employer cannot require an employee to requalify for any benefits the employee received before FMLA leave began.[30] Along these lines, unpaid FMLA leave cannot be counted as a break in service for pension plan purposes.[31] However, if the employer's benefit structure for all employees changed while the employee was on FMLA leave, that structure will dictate what benefits the employee receives after returning from leave.[32]

"**Equivalent terms and conditions of employment**" means the new position must have substantially similar duties, conditions, responsibilities, privileges and status as the employee's original position.[33] This means that the restoration must be to the same or a geographically equivalent worksite, to the same shift or a shift with an equivalent work schedule, and that the employee must have the same or an equivalent opportunity for bonuses, profit sharing, and other discretionary and non-discretionary payments.[34] If the employer and employee agree, the employer can accommodate the employee's request for assignment to a different position so long as the employee is not "induced by the employer to accept a different position against the employee's wishes."[35]

Under these rules, assigning an employee to a job with greater or lesser responsibilities after an FMLA leave would probably violate the FMLA. For example, a secretary whose typing demands increase upon her return to work after FMLA leave has a claim based on the employer's failure to properly restore her to her former position.[36]

Periodic Reports During FMLA Leave As To The Employee's Status And Intention To Return To Work.

The Statute: 29 U.S.C. §2614.

(5) Construction

Nothing in this subsection shall be construed to prohibit an employer from requiring an employee on leave under section 2612 of this title to report periodically to the employer on the status and intention of the employee to return to work.

Section 2614 of the FMLA gives an employer the discretion to require an employee using FMLA leave to report to the employer periodically as to the employee's intention to return to work. Under the DOL's rules, the employer's policy regarding such reports "may not be discriminatory and must take into account all of the relevant facts and circumstances related to the individual employee's leave situation."[37]

Nothing in the FMLA or the DOL's regulations requires an employee to physically report for work to the employer at the end of the leave period. Though there is not much guidance in this area, it appears that all an employee is required to do is to give some affirmative indication to the employer of her desire to return to work to trigger the FMLA's job-restoration obligations.[38]

What Happens If The Employee Indicates She Will Not Be Returning To Work?

Under the DOL's regulations, if the employee gives "unequivocal" notice of the intent not to return to work, the employer's obligations under the FMLA to maintain health benefits cease,[39] subject, of course, to the employer's responsibility to offer continuing participation in health care coverage under COBRA.[40] In addition, when the employer receives an unequivocal notice of an intent not to return to work, the employer's obligation to restore the employee to his former job ceases.[41]

An employer must be careful in concluding that an employee has given unequivocal notice of the intent not to return to work. For example, if the employee merely communicates that the employee "may be unable to return to work" but expresses a desire to do so, the employee has not given unequivocal notice of the intent not to return to work.[42]

When Is An Employer Entitled To Refuse To Restore An Employee Or To Delay Restoration?

The reasons why an employer may refuse to restore an employee to his former job are detailed throughout this chapter. In summary, those reasons are as follows:

- The employee is no longer able to perform the essential functions of the job because of his or her physical condition.

- The employer has restructured its workforce while the employee was on FMLA leave in such a manner that the employee's job no longer exists. The restructuring cannot have been influenced by the employee's use of FMLA leave.

- The employee unequivocally indicated while taking FMLA leave that he does not intend to return to work. In such cases, the employment relationship is terminated and the right to restoration ends.[43]

- The employer has a legitimate fitness-for-duty certificate requirement (*see* Chapter 7), and the employee fails to provide a requested fitness-for-duty certification to return to work. In such cases, the employer may delay restoration until the employee submits the certificate.[44]

- The employee is a "key employee" and to restore the employee would cause substantial and grievous economic injury.

- The employee has fraudulently obtained FMLA leave.[45]

- The "wheels of termination" of the employee had already been set in motion before the employee used FMLA leave (*see* Chapter 11).

- Where the employee has returned to work after the conclusion of FMLA leave, has worked for a short period of time, but then has abandoned the job.[46]

The Transfer Of Employees Using Intermittent Leave.

The Statute: 29 U.S.C. §2612(b)

(2) Alternative position

If an employee requests intermittent leave, or leave on a reduced leave schedule, under subparagraph (C) or (D) of subsection (a)(1) of this section, that is foreseeable based on planned medical treatment, the employer may require such employee to transfer temporarily to an available alternative position offered by the employer for which the employee is qualified and that -

(A) has equivalent pay and benefits; and (B) better accommodates recurring periods of leave than the regular employment position of the employee.

Section 2612(b) of the FMLA allows an employer to transfer an employee using intermittent leave *provided certain conditions are met*. First, the transfer must usually be temporary. However, if the employee's need for intermittent leave is permanent, the transfer can be permanent.[47] Second, the position to which the employee is transferred must have equivalent pay and benefits. Even if the transfer is from a union position with higher benefits to a non-union position, the higher level of benefits must continue.[48] Third, the position to which the employee is transferred must better accommodate the intermittent leave than the employee's normal job.

What if the employer desires to transfer an employee using intermittent leave to a different location? The DOL's view is that an employee is entitled to refuse a transfer when it "adversely affects" the employee, taking into consideration commuting distance, time, and cost. The DOL has indicated "an example of a transfer that would adversely affect an employee would be the situation where the employee currently uses public transportation to commute to his/her job and such transportation is not available to the worksite the employer seeks to transfer the employee." [49]

The Exemption For Key Employees.

The Statute: 29 U.S.C. §2614.

(b) Exemption concerning certain highly compensated employees

(1) Denial of restoration

An employer may deny restoration under subsection (a) of this section to any eligible employee described in paragraph (2) if -

(A) such denial is necessary to prevent substantial and grievous economic injury to the operations of the employer;

(B) the employer notifies the employee of the intent of the employer to deny restoration on such basis at the time the employer determines that such injury would occur; and

(C) in any case in which the leave has commenced, the employee elects not to return to employment after receiving such notice.

(2) Affected employees

An eligible employee described in paragraph (1) is a salaried eligible employee who is among the highest paid 10 percent of the employees employed by the employer within 75 miles of the facility at which the employee is employed.

One class of employees, known as "key employees," has potentially no job restoration rights at the end of FMLA leave. A "key employee" must be salaried and among the highest paid ten percent of all employees employed by the employer within 75 miles of the employee's worksite. The term "salaried" has the same meaning as when the term is used in the FLSA.[50]

An employer may deny a "key employee" job restoration rights if to restore the employee to her job would cause "substantial and grievous economic injury" to the operations of the employer. In making this judgment, the employer may take into account how easily it may replace the employee on a temporary basis or whether a permanent replacement is needed.[51] The DOL has provided little useful guidance in defining "substantial and grievous economic injury," indicating only that (1) if the restoration of the employee would threaten the economic viability of a company, the individual may qualify for "key employee" status; but that (2) "minor inconveniences and costs that the employer would experience in the normal course of doing business would certainly not constitute substantial and grievous economic injury."[52] As to the vast gulf between these two examples, the DOL has said little, specifying only that the "substantial and grievous economic injury" test is more difficult to prove than it would be to show an "undue hardship" eliminating an employer's obligation to reasonably accommodate a disability under the Americans With Disabilities Act.[53]

If an employer believes that restoration may be denied to a "key employee," it must give detailed notice to the employee at the time the employee requests FMLA leave. If the employer cannot give immediate notice because it needs to determine whether the employee is a "key employee," the notice must be given as soon as practicable. An employer failing to provide the required notice will lose its right to deny restoration even if substantial and grievous economic injury results from reinstatement.[54] The notice must indicate the following:

- That the employer regards the employee as a "key employee."

- The potential consequences with respect to restoration in the event the employer determines that substantial and grievous economic injury to the employer's operations would result from the employee's reinstatement.

- The impact of being a key employee on the maintenance of health benefits during FMLA leave.[55]

The DOL's regulations require a second notice once the employer actually determines that operations will suffer substantial and grievous harm if the "key employee" is restored. Since the purpose of the second notice is, in part, to allow the "key employee" a chance to change her mind about whether to use FMLA leave, the second notice is expected to be served in person or by certified mail before the employee begins FMLA leave and must contain the following elements:

- That the employer regards the employee as a "key employee."

- That the employer has determined that substantial and grievous economic injury to its operations will occur upon reinstating the employee and the basis of that determination.

- That the employer cannot deny FMLA leave.

- If leave has commenced, the second notice must give the employee a reasonable time to return to work, taking into account all of the circumstances.[56]

If the employee still elects to use FMLA leave, the employee remains in the employment of the employer and is entitled to request restoration at the end of the leave period.[57] At that point, the employer must again determine whether substantial and grievous economic injury would result from the employee's reinstatement. If so, the employer must notify the employee in writing, again served in person or by certified mail, of the denial of restoration.[58] Key employees do receive one benefit not received by all other employees on FMLA leave – if the employee does not return to work in response to the employer's notification of its intent to deny restoration, the employer must maintain the employee's health insurance benefits until the employee either gives notice of her intent not to return to work or the employer actually denies restoration, and may not recover the premiums paid on behalf of the employee.[59]

In any litigation over whether an employer has appropriately treated an employee as a "key employee," the employer must prove all elements of the key employee status, including whether substantial and grievous economic injury would result from reinstatement.[60] In such a case, the injury must flow from the employee's <u>restoration</u> to her former job, not merely from her <u>absence</u>. [61]

The Special Case Of Certain Educational Employers.

The Statute – 29 U.S.C. §2618(e)

(e) Restoration to equivalent employment position

For purposes of determinations under section 2614(a)(1)(B) of this title (relating to the restoration of an eligible employee to an equivalent position), in the case of a local educational agency or a private elementary or secondary school, such determination shall be made on the basis of established school board policies and practices, private school policies and practices, and collective bargaining agreements.

(f) Reduction of amount of liability

If a local educational agency or a private elementary or secondary school that has violated this subchapter proves to the satisfaction of the court that the agency, school, or department had reasonable grounds for believing that the underlying act or omission was not a violation of this subchapter, such court may, in the discretion of the court, reduce the amount of the liability provided for under section 2617(a)(1)(A) of this title to the amount and interest determined under clauses (i) and (ii), respectively, of such section.

Special restoration rules exist for educational employees, who are treated differently with respect to several portions of the FMLA. Under Section 2618(e) of the FMLA, the determination of how an employee is to be restored to his position at the conclusion of FMLA leave should be made on the basis of "established school board policies and practices, private school policies and practices, and collective bargaining agreements." Whichever of these is used must be in writing, must be made known to the employee before FMLA leave begins, and must clearly explain job restoration rights.[62] Such policies must provide "substantially the same protections" as the FMLA for reinstated employees. As explained by the DOL, "the policy or collective bargaining agreement must provide for restoration to an 'equivalent position' with equivalent employment benefits, pay, and other terms and conditions of employment. For example, an employee may not be restored to a position requiring additional licensure or certification." [63]

Maintenance Of Health Benefits During Leave.

The Statute: 29 U.S.C. §2614.

(c) Maintenance of health benefits

(1) Coverage

Except as provided in paragraph (2), during any period that an eligible employee takes leave under section 2612 of this title, the employer shall maintain coverage under any "group health plan" (as defined in section 5000(b)(1) of title 26) for the duration of such leave at the level and under the conditions coverage would have been provided if the employee had continued in employment continuously for the duration of such leave.

When an employee takes FMLA leave, the employer must maintain coverage under a "group health plan" for the employee during the duration of the leave. Under the DOL's regulations, a "group health plan" includes not only a plan purchased from a health insurance company, but also an employer's self-insured benefit plan.[64]

Coverage must be maintained at a level and under the conditions that would have been provided if the employee had remained in employment. If the employer changes health benefits or plans while the employee is on FMLA leave, the employee is entitled to the changed benefits as if the employee had been continuously employed.[65] If the coverage allows an employee to change plans or benefits – either through an open enrollment period or because of a change in the employee's status – employees on FMLA leave must be given the same opportunity to change plans or benefits.[66] A set of special rules applies if the employer participates in a multi-employer health insurance group.[67]

The obligation to maintain coverage "at the level and under the conditions" in place before FMLA leave began includes the employer's obligation to continue the same premium-payment arrangements. As such, any share of health insurance premiums paid by the employee before FMLA leave must be paid during the FMLA leave. If a change in the employer's plan causes premiums to be raised or lowered, employees on FMLA leave must pay the new premium rates as if their employment was continuous.[68]

The employer must give the employee advance notice of the terms under which any health care premiums are to be paid.[69] If the employee is using paid

Health care coverage during FMLA leave must be maintained on the same basis as if the employee remained continuously employed.

FMLA leave, the employee's share of the premiums must be paid through payroll deduction (or whatever method is normally used during any paid leave).[70] If the employee is using unpaid FMLA leave, the employer may ask that the employee's premium be paid to the employer or to the insurance carrier, but no additional charge may be added to the employee's premium as an administrative expense. The DOL's rules give an employer five options for requiring premium payments from employees on unpaid FMLA leave:

> (1) Requiring payment at the same time it would be made if by payroll deduction;

> (2) Requiring payment on the same schedule as payments made under COBRA;

> (3) Requiring payment to be prepaid according to a cafeteria plan at the employee's option;

> (4) Requiring the employee to follow the employer's existing rules for payment by employees on leave without pay, provided that such rules do not require premium payment prior to the beginning of the leave; or

> (5) Another system voluntarily agreed to between the employer and the employee, which may include prepayment of premiums (e.g., through increased payroll deductions when the need for the FMLA leave is foreseeable).[71]

If the employer paid nothing toward health insurance premiums prior to the taking of FMLA leave, the employer does not have to pay any premiums during an employee's FMLA leave.[72] Nothing in the FMLA prohibits an employer from making pro-rated deductions from the employee's vacation bank to cover health insurance premiums.[73] If the employee chooses not to retain group coverage during FMLA leave, the employee is still entitled to be reinstated to coverage upon return from FMLA leave, and to be reinstated on the same terms as prior to taking the leave.[74]

Some employers may elect to pay the full health insurance premiums for employees on FMLA leave to ensure it can provide equivalent group health insurance coverage once the employees return to work (so there is no lapse of coverage). If the employer elects to maintain such benefits during the leave, the employer is entitled to recover the costs incurred when paying the employee's share of any premiums at the end of leave.[75] In such cases, the employer is able to recover what was paid on the employee's behalf but on the same schedule that was used to originally pay the premiums – no faster.[76]

The employer's obligation to allow employees on FMLA leave to continue to participate in group health coverage ceases under four conditions. First, if the employee's premium payment is more than 30 days late, the employer is allowed to terminate the coverage.[77] Second, if the employment relationship would have been terminated had the employee not taken FMLA leave – for example, if there were layoffs that would have included the employee – the employer may terminate the coverage. Third, if the employee informs the employer of the intent not to return from leave, coverage may be terminated once notice from the employee has been received. Lastly, coverage may be terminated if the employee fails to return from FMLA at the end of the leave or continues after the FMLA entitlement is used up.[78]

The Recovery Of Health Insurance Premiums From Employees Who Do Not Return To Work At The End Of FMLA Leave.

If the employee does not return to work when paid FMLA leave ends, the employer cannot recover health insurance premiums paid on the employee's behalf during the leave.[79] There are two significant exceptions to this having to do with the employee's failure to return to work after the employee's FMLA entitlement has been exhausted. In this context, "returns to work" means the employee works for at least 30 calendar days after the FMLA leave ends.[80]

The first of the two exceptions to this rule is "the continuation, recurrence, or onset of a serious health condition of the employee or the employee's family member which would otherwise entitle the employee to leave under the FMLA.[81] In such a case, the employer is allowed to require certification of the health condition.[82] The second exception is the broadly stated "other circumstances beyond the employee's control." The DOL's regulations give the following examples of what might constitute "other circumstances beyond the employee's control":

- When a parent chooses to stay home with a newborn child who has a serious health condition (but not with a healthy child);

- When an employee's spouse is unexpectedly transferred to a job location more than 75 miles from the employee's worksite;

- When a relative or individual, other than an immediate family member, has a serious health condition and the employee is needed to provide care;

- When the employee is laid off while on leave; and

- When the employee is a "key employee" who decides not to return to work after being notified of the employer's intention to deny restoration due to the substantial and grievous economic injury there would be to operations and is not reinstated.[83]

The Accrual Of Other Benefits While On FMLA Leave.

An employer may, but is not required to allow an employee to accrue additional benefits such as sick leave and pension credits while on FMLA leave.[84] However, if the employer has an established policy of providing certain benefits to employees on other forms of leave, whether paid or unpaid, the employer must provide similar benefits to employees on FMLA leave.[85]

NOTES

[1] 29 C.F.R. §214(a); *see* Note, *The Federal Courts' Struggle With Burden Allocation For Reinstatement Claims Under The Family And Medical Leave Act: Breakdown Of The Rigid Duel*, Catholic University Law Review (Summer, 2001).

[2] *Lloyd v. Wyoming Valley Health Care System, Inc.*, 994 F.Supp. 288 (M.D.Pa. 1998).

[3] *Lloyd v. Wyoming Valley Health Care System, Inc.*, 994 F.Supp. 288 (M.D.Pa. 1998).

[4] *Noyer v. Viacom, Inc.*, 4 WH Cas.2d 1229 (S.D.N.Y. 1998); *see Kelley Company, Inc. v. Marquardt*, 493 N.W.2d 68 (Wis. 1992)(decided under state law).

[5] *Opinion Letter*, Wage & Hour Division, 1999 WL 1002426 (March 26, 1999); *Opinion Letter,* Wage and Hour Division, 1996 WL 1044776 (February 23, 1996); *Opinion Letter*, Wage and Hour Division, 1994 WL 1016732 (January 6, 1994).

[6] 29 C.F.R. §825.214(a).

[7] *See Blackwell v. Harris Chem. N. Am., Inc.*, 11 F.Supp.2d 1302 (D.Kan. 1998); *Opinion Letter,* Wage and Hour Division, 1996 WL 1044777 (April 24, 1996).

[8] *Cf. Sawyer v. Ball Corp.*, 151 F.3d 1030 (4th Cir. 1998).

[9] 29 C.F.R. §214(b); *see Sarno v. Douglas Elliman-Gibbons & Ives, Inc.*, 183 F.3d 155 (2nd Cir. 1999); *Tardie v. Rehabilitation Hosp. of Rhode Island*, 168 F.3d 538 (1st Cir. 1999); *Ariza v Vallicorp, Inc.*, 141 F.3d 1173 (9th Cir. 1998); *Rinehimer v. Cemcolift, Inc.*, 6 WH Cas.2d 1324 (E.D.Pa. 2001); *Santos v. Shields Health Group*, 996 F.Supp. 87 (D.Mass. 1998).

[10] *Jewell v. Reid's Confectionary Co.*, 172 F.Supp.2d 212 (D.Me. 2001); *see Oatman v. Fuji Photo Film U.S.A., Inc.*, 2002 WL 245972 (N.D.Tex. 2002); *Moss v. Formosa Plastics Corp.*, 99 F.Supp.2d 737 (M.D.La. 2000).

[11] *Routes v. Henderson*, 58 F.Supp.2d 959 (S.D.Ind. 1999).

[12] *Tardie v. Rehabilitation Hosp. of Rhode Island*, 168 F.3d 538 (1st Cir. 1999).

[13] 29 C.F.R. §825.215(b).

[14] 29 C.F.R. §825.216(a); 29 C.F.R. §825.312(d); *see Voorhees v. Time Warner Cable Nat'l Div.*, 6 WH Cas.2d 598 (E.D.Pa. 1999); *Lempres v. CBS Inc.*, 916 F.Supp. 15 (D.D.C. 1996).

[15] *Gventer v. Theraphysics Partners of Western Pennsylvania, Inc.*, 41 Fed.Appx. 552 (3rd Cir. 2002).

[16] *Vargas v. Globetrotters Engineering Corporation*, 4 F.Supp.2d 780 (N.D.Ill. 1998).

[17] *Peters v. Community Action Comm., Inc.*, 977 F.Supp. 1428 (M.D.Ala. 1997), quoting *Fishgold v. Sullivan Drydock & Repair Corp.*, 328 U.S. 275 (1946).

[18] *Carpenter v. Northwest Airlines, Inc.*, 7 WH Cas.2d 1107 (D.Minn. 2002).

[19] *Johnson v. Morehouse College, Inc.*, 199 F.Supp.2d 1345 (N.D.Ga. 2002).

[20] *O'Connor v. PCA Family Health Plan, Inc.*, 200 F.3d 1349 (11th Cir. 2000); *Hodgens v. Gen. Dynamics Corp.*, 144 F.3d 151 (1st Cir. 1998); *Ilhardt v. Sara Lee Corp.*, 118 F.3d 1151 (7th Cir. 1997); *Weston-Smith v. Cooley Dickinson Hosp., Inc.*, 282 F.3d 60 (1st Cir. 2002); *Worcester v. Ansewn Shoe Co. Ltd. Partnership*, 1999 WL 1957774 (D.Me. 1999); *Hopkins v. Electronic Data Systems Corp.*, 196 F.3d 655 (6th Cir. 1999); *Sieger v. Wisconsin Personnel Comm'n*, 573 N.W.2d 901 (Wis.App. 1997); *Day v. Excel Corp.*, 3 WH Cas.2d 1335 (D.Kan. 1996); *Opinion Letter*, Wage and Hour Division, 1994 WL 1016750 (August 23, 1994). *See also Marzano v. Computer Science Corp.*, 91 F.3d 497 (3rd Cir. 1996)(discusses New Jersey state law); *Smith v. Goodwill Industries of West Michigan, Inc.*, 622 N.W.2d 337 (Mich.App. 2000)(discusses Michigan law).

[21] *Cross v. Southwest Recreational Industries, Inc.*, 17 F.Supp.2d 1362 (N.D.Ga. 1998).

[22] *Dodgens v. Kent Mfg. Co.*, 955 F.Supp. 560 (D.S.C. 1997).

[23] 29 C.F.R. §825.216(a)(2); *see Roshetko v. Beverly Enterprises, Inc.*, 137 Lab.Cas. ¶33,841 (S.D.Ala. 1999).

[24] *Watkins v. J & S Oil Co., Inc.*, 164 F.3d 55 (1st Cir. 1998).

[25] 29 C.F.R. §825.215(a).

[26] 29 C.F.R. §825.215(c).

[27] 29 C.F.R. §825.215(a)(1).

[28] 29 C.F.R. §825.215(a)(1); *Opinion Letter*, Wage and Hour Division, 2000 WL 33157364 (September 11, 2000); *see Opinion Letter,* Wage and Hour Division, 1995 WL 1036727 (March 28, 1995); *Opinion Letter*, Wage and Hour Division, 1994 WL 1016739 (March 21, 1994).

[29] 29 C.F.R. §825.215(d).

[30] 29 C.F.R. §825.215(d)(1); *Opinion Letter*, Wage and Hour Division, 1994 WL 1016733 (January 10, 1994).

[31] 29 C.F.R. §825.215(d)(4); *Opinion Letter*, Wage and Hour Division, 1995 WL 1036725 (February 22, 1995).

[32] 29 C.F.R. §825.215(d)(1).

[33] 29 C.F.R. §825.215(e); *see Taylor v. Cameron Coca-Cola Bottling Company, Inc.*, 3 WH Cas.2d 1749 (W.D.Pa. 1997).

[34] 29 C.F.R. §825.215(e)(1)-(3).

[35] 29 C.F.R. §825.215(e)(4).

[36] *Peterson v. Slidell Memorial Hospital and Medical Center*, 3 WH Cas.2d 1131 (E.D.La. 1996).

37 29 C.F.R. §825.309(a); *see Gilliam v. United Parcel Service, Inc.*, 233 F.3d 969 (7th Cir. 2000); *Garcia v. Fulbright & Jaworski, L.L.P.*, 3 WH Cas.2d 742 (S.D.Tex. 1996); *Delong v. Trujillo*, 25 P.3d 1194 (Colo. 2001).

38 *Watkins v. J & S Oil Co., Inc.*, 164 F.3d 55 (1st Cir. 1998).

39 29 C.F.R. §825.309; *see Santrizos v. Aramark Corp.*, 1998 WL 704114 (N.D.Ill. 1998).

40 The Consolidated Omnibus Budget Reconciliation Act of 1986, 29 U.S.C. §1161, *et seq.*, requires employers to provide continuation health insurance coverage for terminated employees under certain circumstances. *Local 217, Hotel & Restaurant Employees Union v. MHM. Inc.*, 976 F.2d 805 (2nd Cir. 1992).

41 29 C.F.R. §825.309(b); *see Harper v. Hosp. Srv. Dist. No. 1 of Tangipahoa Parish*, 5 WH Cas. 167 (E.D.La. 1999).

42 29 C.F.R. §825.309(b).

43 29 C.F.R. §825.312(e).

44 29 C.F.R. §825.312(c).

45 29 C.F.R. §825.312(g); *Mosley v. Hedges*, 1998 WL 182479 (N.D.Ill. 1998).

46 *Shelvin v. Dillard University*, 137 Lab.Cas. ¶33,843 (E.D.La. 1999).

47 *Covey v. Methodist Hosp. Of Dyersburg, Inc.*, 56 F.Supp.2d 965 (W.D.Tenn. 1999).

48 *Opinion Letter*, Wage and Hour Division, 1994 WL 1016750 (August 23, 1994).

49 *Opinion Letter*, Wage and Hour Division, 1994 WL 1016750 (August 23, 1994).

50 *See O'Grady v. Catholic Health Partners Servs.*, 2002 WL 221583 (N.D.Ill. 2002). For a discussion of the meaning of "salary" under the FLSA, see Chapter 10.51 29 C.F.R. §825.818; *see* Note, Neil S. Levinbook, *The Family And Medical Leave Act: Unlocking The Door To The "Key Employee" Exemption*, 15 Hofstra Labor & Employment Law Journal 513 (1998).

52 29 C.F.R. §825.218(c).

53 29 C.F.R. §825.218(d); *see Opinion Letter,* Wage & Hour Division, 1998 WL 1147750 (June 3, 1998).

54 *Panza v. The Grappone Companies*, 6 WH Cas.2d 843 (D.N.Y. 2000).

55 29 C.F.R. §825.219(a).

56 29 C.F.R. §825.219(b).

57 *Kelly v. Decisionone Corp.*, 6 WH Cas.2d 1459 (E.D.Pa. 2000).

58 29 C.F.R. §825.219(d).

59 29 C.F.R. §825.219(c); 29 C.F.R. §825.209(f)(g).

60 *See Cross v. Southwest Recreational Indus., Inc.*, 17 F.Supp.2d 1362 (N.D.Ga. 1998).

61 *Kephart v. Cherokee County*, 229 F.3d 1142 (4th Cir. 2000).

62 29 C.F.R. §825.604.

63 29 C.F.R. §825.604; *see O'Hara v. Mt. Vernon Bd. of Educ.*, 16 F.Supp.2d 868 (S.D.Ohio 1998).

64 29 C.F.R. §825.800; *see Opinion Letter*, Wage and Hour Division, 1994 WL 1016734 (January 14, 1994).

65 29 C.F.R. §825.209(b).

66 29 C.F.R. §825.209(d).

67 29 C.F.R. §825.211.

68 29 C.F.R. §825.210(a).

69 29 C.F.R. §825.210(d).

70 29 C.F.R. §825.210(b).

71 29 C.F.R. §825.210(c).

72 *LaCoparra v. Pergament Home Centers, Inc.*, 982 F.Supp. 213 (S.D.N.Y. 1997).

73 *Deily v. Waste Management of Allentown*, 118 F.Supp.2d 539 (E.D.Pa. 2000).

74 29 C.F.R. §825.209(e).

75 *Opinion Letter,* Wage and Hour Division, 1995 WL 103635 (June 21, 1995).

76 *Opinion Letter,* Wage and Hour Division, 1995 WL 1036736 (July 13, 1995).

77 *Opinion Letter*, Wage and Hour Division, 1994 WL 1016750 (August 23, 1994).

78 29 C.F.R. §825.209(f).

79 29 C.F.R. §825.213(d).

80 29 C.F.R. §825.213(c); *see Opinion Letter*, Wage and Hour Division, 1994 WL 1016750 (August 23, 1994).

81 29 C.F.R. §825.213(a)(1).

82 29 C.F.R. §825.213(a)(3).

83 29 C.F.R. §825.213(a)(2).

84 29 C.F.R. §825.215(d)(2).

85 29 C.F.R. §825.209(h); *Opinion Letter*, Wage and Hour Division, 1994 WL 1016750 (August 23, 1994).

CHAPTER 11

DISCRIMINATION, INTERFERENCE, AND RETALIATION

In A Nutshell . . .

The FMLA has powerful anti-discrimination and anti-retaliation provisions. The basic principles are (1) The FMLA grants employees certain basic rights and compels employers to observe those rights; (2) the FMLA prevents an employer from considering an employee's use of FMLA rights in making any employment decision.

The FMLA's Enforcement Provisions.

The Statute: 29 U.S.C. §2615.

(a) Interference with rights

(1) Exercise of rights

It shall be unlawful for any employer to interfere with, restrain, or deny the exercise of or the attempt to exercise, any right provided under this subchapter.

(2) Discrimination

It shall be unlawful for any employer to discharge or in any other manner discriminate against any individual for opposing any practice made unlawful by this subchapter.

(b) Interference with proceedings or inquiries

It shall be unlawful for any person to discharge or in any other manner discriminate against any individual because such individual -

(1) has filed any charge, or has instituted or caused to be instituted any proceeding, under or related to this subchapter;

(2) has given, or is about to give, any information in connection with any inquiry or proceeding relating to any right provided under this subchapter; or

(3) has testified, or is about to testify, in any inquiry or proceeding relating to any right provided under this subchapter.

Like most federal labor statutes, the FMLA contains broad provisions forbidding discrimination or retaliation against an employee for exercising his or her rights under the FMLA.[1] Unfortunately, the enforcement sections of the FMLA are badly worded, and have led to more than a little confusion as courts have tried to apply them.

There are three distinct portions of the enforcement section of the FMLA also known as Section 2615. The first prohibits an employer from interfering with, restraining, or denying an employee rights guaranteed under the FMLA and may be found in subsection (a)(1) of the statute.[2] This section is known as the **interference** provision of the FMLA.

The second prohibits an employer from discriminating against an employee for opposing any practice deemed illegal under the FMLA, and is found in subsection (a)(2) of the statute. The third prohibits an employer from discriminating against an employee for instituting or participating in FMLA proceedings or inquiries, and is located in subsection (b) of the statute.[3] The terms in the two latter sections, each dealing with different forms of **discrimination**, do not address the most likely type of discrimination – where an employer has taken adverse action against an employee simply for using FMLA leave.

This peculiar structure and unfortunate wording has created confusion in the courts about which subsection of Section 2615 applies in a given case. As Section 2615 is written, when an employer retaliates or discriminates in any way against an employee for using FMLA leave – as distinct from the employee opposing practices made illegal by the FMLA or participating in FMLA proceedings – such actions amount to **interference** with the exercise of an employee's FMLA rights, not **discrimination** in violation of the FMLA.[4] However, because of the way Section 2615 is written, several courts have clearly (and inappropriately) mixed standard discrimination analysis into the interference concepts of the FMLA.[5]

The more appropriate approach is a bit more subtle, but emerges clearly when one considers the whole of the FMLA. Moving away from the awkward wording of the enforcement sections of the FMLA, it can be readily seen that there are three fundamental principles behind the FMLA, and consequently, three types of FMLA cases. The principles are as follows: (1) The FMLA grants employees certain basic rights and compels employers to observe those rights; (2) the FMLA prevents an employer from considering an employee's use of FMLA rights in making employment decisions; and (3) the FMLA prohibits an employer from discriminating against employees in the two specific areas listed in Section 2615.

Enforcing The First Core Principle Of The FMLA – The Substantive Grant Of Rights To Employees Of Family Leave Benefits.

The first underlying or guiding principle of the FMLA is a substantive grant of rights to employees to be observed by employers – 12 weeks of leave, continuing health coverage, job restoration, and the like. Subsection (a)(1) of Section 2615, which makes it unlawful for "any employer to * * * deny the exercise of or the attempt to exercise any right" afforded by the FMLA, contains the enforcement vehicle for ensuring these rights. These rights not only create entitlements for employees, they also set "the floor" for acceptable conduct by an employer.

The first core principle of the FMLA – employees are guaranteed certain rights to family leave that an employer must observe.

If an employee claims an employer denied him any of these rights, the employer's intent or state of mind does not matter. All that matters, or should matter, is whether the employer granted the employee the right protected by the FMLA. As one court described succinctly:

> "Under the FMLA an employee need not show that other employees were treated less favorably. The question is not how the Foundry treats others, but whether it respected each employee's entitlements. This is the big difference between anti-discrimination statutes and laws such as the FMLA that set substantive floors."[6]

Like many labor laws, these portions of the FMLA impose a "strict liability" scheme. Under the FMLA and the DOL's regulations, the employer's good faith or lack of knowledge that its conduct violated the FMLA is irrelevant in "interference" cases to the question of whether the employer is liable for violating the FMLA – all that matters is whether the employer's actions in fact violated the law.[7] While an employer's motivations might play a part when liquidated damages are assessed, they have no impact on the finding of the employer's liability for whatever economic damages resulted from the employer's violation of the FMLA. For example, if an employer fails to notify employees of the method used to calculate the "leave year," it will still be liable to employees adversely impacted by the failure to notify even if the employer honestly believed the law did not impose a notification requirement.[8]

Under the DOL's regulations, an employer interferes with an employee's FMLA rights not just by denying FMLA leave, but also by "discouraging" an employee from using FMLA leave.[9] Applying this rule in a case where an employer allegedly told an employee that if she used FMLA leave to care for her ill husband, she would forfeit all of her vacation and sick leave, a court commented: "Informing an employee that she would be irrevocably deprived of all accrued sick leave and annual leave as a condition of taking leave under the FMLA would operate as a powerful disincentive to assertion of that employee's rights under the FMLA. This is true regardless of whether she actually applied for leave and subjected herself to the unwarranted consequences announced by the employer. We conclude that the actions alleged here fall within the definition of interference with an attempt to assert FMLA rights."[10]

The Standards For Enforcing The FMLA's Second Core Principle: An Employer May Not Take Into Account The Employee's Use Of FMLA Leave In Making Employment Decisions.

The FMLA's second core principle – an employee's use of FMLA must not be taken into account by an employer in making employment decisions.

The second important principle behind the FMLA prohibits an employer from taking into account an employee's use of FMLA leave when making other employment decisions that would impact that employee. The enforcement vehicle for this second principle is also derived from the "interference" prohibitions in Section 2615. These prohibitions state, in part, that "it shall be unlawful for any employer to interfere with [or] restrain * * * the exercise of or the attempt to exercise, any right provided under this subchapter." The language of Section 2615 is very similar to "interference" prohibitions found in Section 8(a)(1) of the National Labor Relations Act (NLRA), which also gives employees the right to engage in certain activities free from employer interference and restraint.[11] Because the FMLA's language so closely resembles that of the NLRA, courts have used the latter to assist them in the interpretation of the FMLA. One court cited an NLRA case, giving the underlying reasons behind the FMLA's prohibiting employers taking an employee's FMLA leave into account in making employment decisions: "The courts have long recognized that employers violate [the NLRA's] prohibition on interfering with or restraining employee rights by engaging in activity that tends to chill an employee's freedom to exercise his rights."[12] Along similar lines, the Supreme Court has noted "it is the tendency of those discharges to weaken or destroy the right that is controlling."[13]

An employee claiming her employer inappropriately took the use of FMLA leave into account in making an employment decision is only required to prove by a preponderance of evidence that she availed herself of an FMLA right, and that this fact was considered by her employer in making an employment decision about the employee.[14] These principles apply no matter whether the employer takes into consideration the FMLA leave after the employee has taken it, or whether it takes the employee's anticipated FMLA leave into account in making an employment decision.[15] As well, these principles apply no matter whether the employee's taking of FMLA leave is the entire basis for the employer's decision or simply was one of many factors taken into account.[16]

These principles extend not just to the types of employment decisions appearing most often in FMLA cases, such as disciplinary decisions where the employee has been allegedly fired for using FMLA leave, but also mandates that an employer's treatment of fringe benefits for employees on FMLA leave be equivalent to those associated with other forms of leave. For example, the DOL's regulations require that employees on FMLA leave be treated like all other employees on unpaid leave with respect to eligibility for benefits such as health insurance.[17]

An employee claiming that her employer retaliated against her for exercising FMLA rights has the burden of proving that the retaliation occurred.[18] On most occasions, this proof will have to be indirect. Only an incautious employer would publicly announce that certain employment decisions have been made because of an employee's exercise of a right protected by the FMLA. As one court observed:

> "'Smoking gun' evidence is, of course, not required in order to prove discrimination. Such evidence is rarely found in today's sophisticated employment world, [and there will seldom be 'eyewitness' testimony as to the employer's mental processes]. Discriminatory motive is more often demonstrated through indirect evidence * * * "[19]

Indirect proof can be found in, among other things, how employees who did not use FMLA leave were treated, statements by managers that are hostile to the principles of the FMLA (for example, using the term "babybonding" in a pejorative manner),[20] and by a repeated course of conduct.[21] Another way an employee may show indirect proof is to establish "such weaknesses, implausibilities, inconsistencies, incoherencies, or contradictions in the employer's proffered legitimate reasons for its action that a reasonable factfinder could rationally find them unworthy of credence and infer that the employer did not act for the asserted non-discriminatory reasons."[22] Similarly, proof that the employer treated more leniently employees not requesting FMLA leave who committed the same offense as the employee requesting FMLA leave gives rise to indirect proof of discrimination.[23]

The close proximity of a negative employment action to the use of FMLA leave can be most telling.[24] In the words of one court, "suspicious timing constitutes circumstantial evidence" upon which an FMLA claim can be made.[25] The closer in time between the use of FMLA leave and the negative employment action, the greater the inference to be drawn against the employer. Conversely, if disciplinary action occurs months after the use of FMLA leave, courts are hesitant to draw much, if any, of an inference of retaliation.[26] Usually, suspicious timing alone is not sufficient basis for a retaliation claim.[27]

Given such an analytical context, many courts find a three-part framework known as the *McDonnell Douglas* test (so named after the Supreme Court decision in which the test was announced) helpful for assessing the key issue – did the employer inappropriately take into account the employee's use of the FMLA rights in making an employment decision.[28] In this approach, the employee must first show that she was engaged in an activity that is protected by the FMLA. Then, the employee must establish that a negative employment action occurred, and that there was a causal connection between the protected activity and the employment decision. This initial burden of proof is usually referred to as the employee establishing a *prima facie* case of discrimination, and creates a presumption of discrimination.[29]

If the employee meets his initial burden of showing the *prima facie* case, then the employer bears the burden of articulating a legitimate, non-discriminatory reason for the employment action.[30] If the employer's evidence creates a genuine issue as to its reasons for taking the employment action, the presumption of discrimination drops from the case, and the plaintiff retains the ultimate burden of showing that the employer's stated reason for terminating him was in fact a pretext for retaliating against him for having taken protected FMLA leave.[31] When evaluating a contention of pretext, a court will examine the facts "as they appear to the person making the decision to terminate [the employee]."[32] If the employer has made a business judgment in terminating the employee, it will ordinarily not be "second guessed" by a court.[33] The critical question is instead whether the reason articulated by the employer was the real reason for the employee's discharge.

While a satisfactory explanation by the employer for its actions destroys the mandatory inference of discrimination arising from the employee's *prima facie* case, the evidence and inferences that *can be* drawn from the evidence presented during the employee's *prima facie* case may be considered in determining whether the employer's explanation is a pretext for discrimination. If the employee presents a *prima facie* case and the employer has a legitimate non-discriminatory reason for its actions, usually a jury will then decide which party to believe.

In some cases, an employee will take leave protected by the FMLA and then follow up with another leave period unprotected by the FMLA (either because of a change in the underlying condition or because the employee has exhausted her leave eligibility). In such circumstances, the FMLA does not prohibit an employer from disciplining or discharging the employee for the second absence, provided it does not take into account the FMLA-protected first absence in making its decision.[34]

Enforcing The Third Core Principle Of The FMLA – The Prohibition Against The Specific Types Of Discrimination.

The third core principle of the proterctions of the FMLA is the more standard anti-discrimination type of concept, prohibiting retaliating against an employee for opposing practices made unlawful by the FMLA, or for participating in FMLA investigations or proceedings. Because of the narrow prohibitions against discrimination contained in the FMLA, this third type of FMLA case is so rare as to be almost non-existent.[35] In such cases, the employer's knowledge that the employee engaged in the protected activity, whether that knowledge is shown through direct evidence or through inference, is critical to an employee's case.[36] An odd feature of the FMLA is that for illegal discrimination to exist, it is not even necessary that the employee have a valid FMLA claim. Because the mere act of filing an FMLA claim is protected by the FMLA, it is just as illegal to discriminate against an employee who has filed a valid FMLA claim as it is to discriminate against an employee who has filed an FMLA claim that has no validity whatsoever.[37]

The FMLA's third core principle – employees may not be discriminated against for opposing practices made illegal by the FMLA, or for participating in FMLA investigations or proceedings.

Disciplinary Action Concurrent With But Independent Of FMLA Leave.

It can happen, of course, that an employee's request to use FMLA leave is concurrent with or subsequent to the employer's taking disciplinary action against the employee for reasons entirely unrelated to an FMLA leave. In some cases, an employee facing termination – or, in the words of one court, who is on "thin ice" for reasons unrelated to the FMLA – may even ask for FMLA leave to postpone the employer's inevitable disciplinary decision.[38] Courts have found that if the "wheels of termination" have been set in motion for reasons independent of the FMLA, an employer's decision to terminate the employee for those reasons will not violate the FMLA *even* if the employee has made a subsequent request for family leave.[39] Thus, if the employer initiates disciplinary action before a request for FMLA-qualifying leave is made, or if it disciplines the employee for entirely independent reasons after FMLA leave has been taken, the FMLA will not be a bar to the disciplinary action.[40] As put by one court, "it is not unlawful to terminate an employee while they are on FMLA leave, provided the taking of FMLA leave was not the cause for termination." [41] Additionally, if the employer legitimately terminates an employee while on FMLA leave for reasons independent of the FMLA, the employee is not entitled under the FMLA to payment for any unused portion

If the "wheels of termination" have already been set in motion for independent reasons before the employee requested FMLA leave, the taking of FMLA leave will not gain the employee any additional job protections.

of accrued leave for the balance of the 12-week FMLA allotment not used before the termination.[42]

Along these lines, if an employee has a long-standing absenteeism problem and the employer terminates the employee for excessive absenteeism closely in conjunction to the employee taking FMLA leave, the employee will not necessarily be able to establish that he was discharged because of the use of FMLA leave. Usually in such cases, the employee's tenure will end with a number of absences, some of which are covered by the FMLA and some of which are not. If the employer shows a pattern of unexcused absences unrelated to the FMLA and submits proof that it would have terminated the employee for those absence regardless of whether the employee used FMLA leave, then the employee "must demonstrate that the basis for her termination was not her excessive absences, but requests for leave under the FMLA leave." [43] Similarly, an employer does not violate the FMLA by terminating an employee for failing to comply with its absence-notification policy by not notifying the employer of when he desires FMLA time off before simply taking the time off.[44]

However, simply because an employer contends that the "wheels of termination" were already in motion does not mean that such a claim will not be closely scrutinized. In one case, a court upheld a jury's verdict in favor of a plant manager who was terminated after his return from FMLA leave used for open-heart surgery. Though the employer argued that it had intended to terminate the manager *before* he used FMLA leave, an appeals court cited the positive performance evaluations given the manager before his FMLA leave as evidence from which a jury could conclude that the use of FMLA leave was the true reason for the termination.[45] Other courts have not always been as impressed by performance evaluations, finding that a good performance evaluation has "little significance in a case in which there is so dramatic a discrepancy between evaluation and performance." [46]

It can also occur that an employee's utilization of FMLA leave is, in and of itself, improper or fraudulent. If an employer has an "honest belief" that is "reasonably based on particularized facts" that an employee is abusing FMLA leave, the FMLA's anti-discrimination statutes will not prevent the employee's discharge.[47] In one case, an employer hired a private detective to follow an employee who claimed FMLA leave to tend to her mother who was seriously ill. When the employer was able to prove that the employee had spent only a few minutes a day at her mother's residence – even on days on which she took eight hours of FMLA leave – the employee lost both her job and her FMLA claim.[48]

Where an employer faces the greatest risk is in trying to terminate an employee for leave-related offenses, *e.g.*, taking too much leave or abusing leave, when the employee has legitimately used FMLA leave somewhere in the time span covered by the employer's disciplinary decision. In such cases, an employer will have to clearly establish that its reasons for terminating the employee were completely independent of the employee's use of FMLA leave – a difficult burden of proof when the employee has been terminated for any type of leave offense.[49]

In general, when an employee has voluntarily resigned, she cannot contend that she suffered a negative employment action because of her use of FMLA leave.[50] Certainly the most problematic cases involve situations where the employee has quit, but later claims that she was "constructively discharged." Though the rules vary somewhat across the country, a "constructive discharge" occurs when an employer deliberately makes an employee's working conditions intolerable, thereby forcing the employee to quit.[51] Under this standard, an employee claiming a constructive discharge must show two things: (1) That the employer's actions were deliberate, and (2) that the working conditions were intolerable.[52] Meeting this burden of proof is usually quite difficult.[53]

CASE IN POINT

Question: Lucien Vandegaart had an absenteeism problem from the date he started working for the Elise Arthur clothing manufacturing company. Most notable among his absenteeism issues was a distinct Friday-Monday pattern, in which 60% of his "illnesses" occurred on days abutting his weekends. After two years, the Company begins to progressively discipline Vandegaart, beginning with issuing written reprimands and moving to issuing short term unpaid suspensions from work. As he was receiving a five-day suspension notice, which came with the warning that further absenteeism difficulties would result in his termination, Vandegaart had a mild heart attack that required hospitalization and gradual recuperation. Though many of his subsequent absences were clearly related to his recuperation, some were simply unexplained, and demonstrated yet more of the Monday-Friday pattern. If the Company chooses to terminate Vandegaart for unacceptable absenteeism, will it be liable under the FMLA?

Answer: Probably not. If an employer can show that the "wheels of termination" were in motion before a request for FMLA leave was made, or if it can show a pattern of unacceptable absences from work unrelated to the FMLA, it will be able to terminate the employee even though the employee may be simultaneously exercising FMLA rights.

The Courts' Mistaken Use Of The Term "Adverse Employment Action."

A last word should be said about the confusing way courts have treated the FMLA's enforcement provisions. The phrase "adverse employment action" is a term of art in labor law – one that comes out of standard race and gender discrimination cases. Generally speaking, an "adverse employment action" is one that visits serious economic consequences upon an employee. The most frequently cited adverse employment actions are the trilogy of discharge, demotion, and most, but not all, transfers. A variety of low-level disciplinary actions are not considered "adverse employment actions" for discrimination law purposes, including:

- Some transfers.[54]

- Pending disciplinary charges.[55]

- Negative performance evaluations.[56]

- Reprimands.[57]

- Shift changes to an undesirable shift.[58]

- Withholding training from an employee.[59]

The phrase "adverse employment action" literally litters FMLA "interference" cases.[60] It should not. As described in this chapter, all that is required in an "interference" case is either that the employee show (1) he was denied a benefit guaranteed by the FMLA; or (2) that the employer took the employee's exercise of FMLA rights into consideration in making an employment decision. While determining whether an employer's actions amount to an "adverse employment action" might be relevant in an FMLA *discrimination* case, such an analysis has no business in an *interference* case.

NOTES

[1] *Nero v. Industrial Molding Corp.*, 167 F.3d 921 (5th Cir. 1999).

[2] *Diaz v. Fort Wayne Foundry Corp.*, 131 F.3d 711 (7th Cir. 1997).

[3] *Henthorn v. Olsten Corp.*, 5 WH Cas.2d 539 (N.D.Ill. 1999).

[4] *Bachelder v. America West Airlines, Inc.*, 259 F.3d 1112 (9th Cir. 2001); *Diaz v. Fort Wayne Foundry Corp.*, 131 F.3d 711 (7th Cir. 1997); *Rankin v. Seagate Techs., Inc.*, 246 F.3d 1145 (8th Cir. 2001); *see Morgan v. FBL Financial Services, Inc.*, 178 F.Supp.2d 1022 (S.D.Iowa 2001).

[5] *See Morgan v. Hilti, Inc.*, 108 F.3d 1319 (10th Cir. 1997); *Hodgens v. General Dynamics Corp.*, 144 F.3d 151 (1st Cir. 1998); *King v. Preferred Tech. Group*, 166 F.3d 887 (7th Cir. 1999); *Chaffin v. John H. Carter Co.*, 179 F.3d 316 (5th Cir. 1999); *Gleklen v. Democratic Congressional Campaign Comm.*, 199 F.3d 1365 (D.C.Cir. 2000); *Brungart v. BellSouth Telecommunications, Inc.*, 231 F.3d 791 (11th Cir. 2000); *Barnhill v. Farmland Foods, Inc.*, 2001 WL 487939 (D.Kan. 2001); *Hillman v. Hamilton College*, 4 WH Cas.2d 1035 (N.D.N.Y. 1998).

[6] *Diaz v. Fort Wayne Foundry Corp.*, 131 F.3d 711 (7th Cir. 1997).

[7] *Hodgens v. General Dynamics Corporation*, 144 F.3d 151 (1st Cir. 1998); *Peters v. Community Action Committee, Inc. of Chambers-Tallapoosa-Coosa*, 977 F.Supp. 1428 (M.D.Ala. 1997); *Kaylor v. Fannin Regional Hosp., Inc.*, 946 F.Supp. 988 (N.D.Ga. 1996).

[8] *Bachelder v. America West Airlines, Inc.*, 259 F.3d 1112 (9th Cir. 2001); *Hodgens v. General Dynamics Corp.*, 144 F.3d 151 (1st Cir. 1998); *Diaz v. Fort Wayne Foundry Corp.*, 131 F.3d 711 (7th Cir. 1997); *Price v. Multnomah County*, 132 F.Supp.2d 1290 (D.Or. 2001).

[9] 29 C.F.R. §825.220(b).

[10] *Mardis v. Central National Bank & Trust of Enid*, 173 F.3d 864 (10th Cir. 1999).

[11] *See* 29 U.S.C. §158(a)(1)(providing that it is an unfair labor practice for an employer "to interfere with, restrain, or coerce employees in the exercise of the rights guaranteed" by § 7 of the NLRA).

[12] *Bachelder v. America West Airlines, Inc.*, 259 F.3d 1112 (9th Cir. 2001), *quoting California Acrylic Indus. Inc. v. NLRB,* 150 F.3d 1095 (9th Cir. 1998).

[13] *NLRB v. Burnup & Sims, Inc.*, 379 U.S. 21 (1964).

[14] *Bachelder v. America West Airlines, Inc.*, 259 F.3d 1112 (9th Cir. 2001); *Watkins v. J & S Oil Co., Inc.*, 164 F.3d 55 (1st Cir. 1998); *Diaz v. Fort Wayne Foundry Corp.*, 131 F.3d 711 (7th Cir. 1997); *Price v. Multnomah County*, 132 F.Supp.2d 1290 (D.Or. 2001); *Wilson v. Lemington Home For The Aged*, 2001 WL 1079030 (W.D.Pa. 2001); *Jeremy v. Northwest Ohio Development Center*, 33 F.Supp.2d 635 (N.D.Ohio 1999); *Dormeyer v. Comerica Bank,* 1998 WL 729591 (N.D.Ill. 1998); *Voorhees v. Time Warner Cable National Division*, 6 WH Cas.2d 598 (E.D.Pa. 1999); *Viereck v. City of Gloucester City*, 961 F.Supp. 703 (D.N.J. 1997); *McClain v. Southwest Steel Co.,*

940 F.Supp. 295 (N.D.Okla. 1996); *Dudley v. Department of Transportation*, 108 Cal.Rptr.2d 739 (Cal.App. 2001); *see Medley v. Polk Company*, 260 F.3d 1202 (10th Cir. 2001).

[15] *Glunt v. GES Exposition Services, Inc.*, 123 F.Supp.2d 847 (D.Md. 2000); *Houben v. Telular Corporation*, 119 F.Supp.2d 792 (N.D.Ill. 1999).

[16] *Monica v. Nalco Chemical Company*, 1996 WL 736946 (E.D.La. 1996).

[17] 29 C.F.R. §825.220(c).

[18] *Snelling v. Clarian Health Partners, Inc.*, 184 F.Supp.2d 838 (S.D.Ind. 2002).

[19] *Hodgens v. General Dynamics Corporation*, 144 F.3d 151 (1st Cir. 1998); *see United States Postal Serv. Bd. of Gov. v. Aikens*, 460 U.S. 711 (1983); *Speen v. Crown Clothing Corp.*, 102 F.3d 625 (1st Cir. 1997).

[20] *Munizza v. State Farm Mutual Automobile Insurance Company*, 103 F.3d 139 (9th Cir. 1996); *Hillman v. Hamilton College*, 4 WH Cas.2d 1035 (N.D.N.Y. 1998).

[21] *EEOC v. G-K-G, Inc.*, 39 F.3d 740 (7th Cir. 1994).

[22] *Morgan v. Hilti, Inc.*, 108 F.3d 1319 (10th Cir. 1997); *Cross v. Southwest Recreational Industries, Inc.*, 17 F.Supp.2d 1362 (N.D.Ga. 1998).

[23] *Carter v. Enterprise Rent-A-Car Co.*, 7 WH Cas.2d 1816 (N.D.Ill. 2002).

[24] *McClendon v. Indiana Sugars, Inc.*, 108 F.3d 789 (7th Cir. 1997); *Doebele v. Sprint Corporation*, 157 F.Supp.2d 1191 (D.Kan. 2001); *Voorhees v. Time Warner Cable National Division*, 6 WH Cas.2d 598 (E.D.Pa. 1999); *Keiss v. St. Francis Hospital of Evanston*, 1997 WL 417524 (N.D.Ill. 1997).

[25] *Haschmann v. Time Warner Entertainment Company*, 151 F.3d 591 (7th Cir. 1998). *See generally Parris v. Miami Herald Publishing Company*, 216 F.3d 1298 (11th Cir. 2000); *King v. Preferred Technical Group*, 166 F.3d 887 (7th Cir. 1999); *Klausner v. Industrial Risk Insurers*, 1999 WL 476285 (S.D.N.Y. 1999).

[26] *Trujillo-Cummings v. Public Service Company of New Mexico*, 173 F.3d 864 (10th Cir. 1999); *Niemiec v. H & K Inc.*, 66 Empl. Prac. Dec. ¶43,587 (E.D.Wis. 1995).

[27] *Klaus v. Builders Concrete Co.*, 7 WH Cas.2d 1089 (N.D.Ill. 2002); *Dollar v. Shoney's, Inc.*, 981 F.Supp. 1417 (N.D.Ala. 1997).

[28] *See McDonnell Douglas Corp. v. Green*, 411 U.S. 792 (1973); *see Reeves v. Sanderson Plumbing Products*, 530 U.S. 133 (2000). Some courts eschew using the *McDonnell Douglas* test in any form of "interference" FMLA case. *See Rice v. Sunrise Express*, 209 F.3d 1008 (7th Cir. 2000).

[29] *Texas Dep't of Community Affairs v. Burdine*, 450 U.S. 248 (1981); *Chaffin v. John H. Carter Co., Inc.*, 179 F.3d 316 (5th Cir. 1999); *Cooper v. Thomson Newspapers, Inc.*, 6 F.Supp.2d 109 (D.N.H. 1998).

[30] *Fields v. St. Charles School Board*, 78 Empl. Prac. Dec. ¶40,178 (E.D.La. 2000); *Sharpe v. MCI Telecommunications Corp.*, 19 F.Supp.2d 483 (E.D.N.C. 1998).

[31] *St. Mary's Honor Ctr. v. Hicks*, 509 U.S. 502 (1993); *Smith v. Allen Health Systems, Inc.*, 302 F.3d 827 (8th Cir. 2002); *Street v. Kraft Foods, Inc.*, 221 F.3d

1344 (8th Cir. 2000); *Rocky v. Columbia Lawnwood Regional Medical Center*, 54 F.Supp.2d 1159 (S.D.Fla. 1999); *Vanderhoof v. Life Extension Institute*, 988 F.Supp. 507 (D.N.J. 1997); *Dodgens v. Kent Manufacturing Co.*, 955 F.Supp. 560 (D.S.C. 1997); *Petsche v. Home Federal Savings Bank, Northern Ohio*, 952 F.Supp. 536 (N.D.Ohio 1997); *Marks v. School District of Kansas City, Missouri,* 941 F.Supp. 886 (W.D.Mo. 1996).

[32] *Kendrick v. Penske Transp. Servs., Inc.*, 220 F.3d 1220 (10th Cir. 2000); *Shorter v. ICG Holdings, Inc.*, 188 F.3d 1204 (10th Cir. 1999); *see Skrjanc v. Great Lakes Power Service Company*, 272 F.3d 309 (6th Cir. 2001).

[33] *Simms v. Okla. ex rel. Dept. of Mental Health & Substance Abuse Servs.*, 165 F.3d 1321 (10th Cir. 1999); *see Leary v. Hobet Mining, Inc.*, 981 F.Supp. 452 (S.D.W.Va. 1997).

[34] *Kur v. Fox Valley Press, Inc.*, 3 WH Cas.2d 1882 (N.D.Ill. 1997).

[35] *See Frankel v. United States Postal Service*, 96 F.Supp.2d 19 (D.Mass. 2000).

[36] *Laird v. Chamber of Commerce*, 4 WH Cas.2d 1629 (E.D.La. 1998).

[37] *Jeremy v. Northwest Ohio Development Center*, 33 F.Supp.2d 635 (N.D.Ohio 1999).

[38] *Price v. Multnomah County*, 132 F.Supp.2d 1290 (D.Or. 2001).

[39] *Tuberville v. Personal Finance Corp.*, 132 Lab.Cas. ¶33,463 (N.D.Miss. 1996); *see Kohls v. Beverly Enterprises Wisconsin, Inc.*, 259 F.3d 799 (7th Cir. 2001); *Sepe v. McDonnell Douglas Corporation*, 176 F.3d 1113 (8th Cir. 1999); *Kennebrew v. New York City Housing Authority*, 2002 WL 265120 (S.D.N.Y. 2002); *Serio v. Jojo's Bakery Restaurant*, 102 F.Supp.2d 1044 (S.D.Ind. 2000); *Messick v. Sears, Roebuck & Company*, 89 F.Supp.2d 848 (W.D.Tex. 2000); *Baltuskonis v. U.S. Airways, Inc.*, 60 F.Supp.2d 445 (E.D.Pa. 1999); *Leung v. SHK Management, Inc.*, 5 WH Cas.2d 1614 (E.D.Pa. 1999); *Carrillo v. National Council of the Churches of Christ in the U.S.A.*, 976 F.Supp. 254 (S.D.N.Y. 1997); *Holmes v. Pizza Hut of America, Inc.*, 4 WH Cas.2d 1681 (E.D. Pa.1998); *Muska v. AT & T Corp.*, 4 WH Cas.2d 1672 (N.D.Ill. 1998); *Patterson v. Alltel Information Services, Inc.*, 919 F.Supp. 500 (D.Me. 1996).

[40] *Ogborn v. United Food & Commercial Workers Union, Local No. 881,* 305 F.3d 763 (7th Cir. 2002); *Earl v. Mervyns, Inc.*, 207 F.3d 1361 (11th Cir. 2000); *Richmond v. ONEOK*, 120 F.3d 205 (10th Cir. 1997); *Kenyon v. Western Extrusions Corporation*, 2000 WL 12902 (N.D.Tex. 2000); *Clark v. New York State Electric & Gas Corporation*, 67 F.Supp.2d 63 (N.D.N.Y. 1999); *Hubbard v. Blue Cross Blue Shield Ass'n*, 1 F.Supp.2d 867 (N.D.Ill. 1998); *Carrillo v. The National Council of Churches of Christ in the U.S.A.*, 976 F.Supp. 254 (S.D.N.Y. 1997); *Beal v. Rubbermaid Commercial Products, Inc.*, 972 F.Supp. 1216 (S.D.Iowa 1997); *Beno v. United Telephone Company of Florida*, 969 F.Supp. 723 (M.D.Fla. 1997); *Coleman v. Anne Arundel County Police Department*, 766 A.2d 169 (Md.App. 2001); *Guo v. Maricopa County Medical Center*, 992 P.2d 11 (Ariz.App. 1999).

[41] *Clark v. New York State Electric & Gas Corp.*, 67 F.Supp.2d 63 (N.D.N.Y. 1999); *see Doe v. King County*, 168 F.3d 498 (9th Cir. 1999); *Kariotis v. Navistar International Transportation Corp.*, 131 F.3d 672 (7th Cir. 1997); *Ilhardt v. Sara Lee Corp.*, 118 F.3d 1151 (7th Cir. 1997); *Hale v. Mann*, 219 F.3d 61 (2nd Cir. 2000); *O'Connor v. PCA Family Health Plan, Inc.*, 200 F.3d 1349 (11th Cir. 2000);

Serio v. Jojo's Bakery Restaurant, 102 F.Supp.2d 1044 (S.D.Ind. 2000); *Routes v. Henderson,* 58 F.Supp.2d 959 (S.D.Ind. 1999); *Mayo v. Trinity Marine Industries, Inc.,* 5 WH Cas.2d 443 (E.D.La. 1999); *Hubbard v. Blue Cross Blue Shield Association,* 1 F.Supp.2d 867 (N.D.Ill. 1998); *Sidaris v. Runyon,* 967 F.Supp. 1260 (M.D.Ala. 1997). *See generally Gunnell v. Utah State College,* 152 F.3d 1253 (10th Cir. 1998).

[42] *Santos v. Knitgoods Workers' Union, Local 155,* 252 F.3d 175 (2nd Cir. 2001).

[43] *Bailey v. Amsted Industries Inc.,* 172 F.3d 1041 (8th Cir. 1999); *see Ahern v. Department of the Treasury,* 230 F.3d 1373 (Fed.Cir. 1999); *Dormeyer v. Comerica Bank-Illinois,* 1998 WL 729591 (N.D.Ill. 1998), *aff'd* 223 F.3d 579 (7th Cir. 2000); *Polderman v. Northwest Airlines, Inc.,* 40 F.Supp.2d 456 (N.D.Ohio 1999); *Washington v. Bosch Braking Systems Corporation,* 6 WH Cas.2d 1724 (W.D.Mich. 1999); *Enright v. CGH Medical Center,* 1999 WL 24683 (N.D.Ill. 1999); *Hypes v. First Commerce Corporation,* 3 F.Supp.2d 712 (E.D.La. 1996), *aff'd,* 134 F.3d. 721 (6th Cir. 1998).

[44] *Bones v. Honeywell International, Inc.,* 2002 WL 31307852 (D.Kan. 2002).

[45] *Nero v. Industrial Molding Corp.,* 167 F.3d 921 (5th Cir. 1999); *see Dumoulin v. Formica,* 968 F.Supp. 68 (N.D.N.Y. 1997).

[46] *Clay v. City of Chicago Department of Health,* 143 F.3d 1092 (7th Cir. 1998).

[47] *Twilley v. Integris Baptist Medical Center, Inc.,* 2001 WL 901102 (10th Cir. 2001); *Smith v. Chrysler Corp.,* 155 F.3d 799 (6th Cir. 1998); *Pesterfield v. TVA,* 941 F.2d 437 (6th Cir. 1991); *Connel v. Hallmark Cards, Inc.,* 147 Lab. Cas. ¶34,599 (D.Kan. 2002); *Agee v. Northwest Airlines, Inc.,* 151 F.Supp.2d 890 (E.D.Mich. 2001); *Moughari v. Publix Super Markets, Inc.,* 1998 WL 307454 (N.D.Fla. 1998), *aff'd,* 170 F.3d 188 (11th Cir. 1999). *See generally* 29 C.F.R. §825.312(g).

[48] *Stonum v. U.S. Airways, Inc.,* 83 F.Supp.2d 894 (S.D.Ohio 1999); *see Kariotis v. Navistar International Transp. Corp.,* 131 F.3d 672 (7th Cir. 1997).

[49] *Sharpe v. MCI Telecommunications Corp.,* 19 F.Supp.2d 483 (E.D.N.C. 1998).

[50] *See Hammon v. DHL Airways, Inc.,* 165 F.3d 441 (6th Cir. 1999); *Lau v. Behr Heat Transfer System, Inc.,* 150 F.Supp.2d 1017 (D.S.D. 2001).

[51] *Bristow v. Daily Press, Inc.,* 770 F.2d 1251 (4th Cir. 1985); *cf. Wallace v. Comprehealth, Inc.,* 36 F.Supp.2d 892 (E.D.Mo. 1998).

[52] *Sharpe v. MCI Telecommunications Corp.,* 19 F.Supp.2d 483 (E.D.N.C. 1998).

[53] *Landahl v. Department of Commerce,* 2001 WL 619079 (Fed.Cir. 2001); *Tremblay v. Liberty Enterprises, Inc.,* 7 WH Cas.2d 818 (D.Minn. 2001); *Richio v. Miami-Dade County,* 163 F.Supp.2d 1352 (S.D.Fla. 2001); *Banuskevich v. City of Nashua, NH,* 143 Lab. Cas. ¶34,274 (D.N.H. 2001); *Paasch v. City of Safety Harbor,* 915 F.Supp. 315 (M.D.Fla. 1995); *Dey v. County of Hennepin,* 1997 WL 10878 (Minn.App. 1997).

[54] *Tyler v. Ispat Inland Inc.,* 245 F.3d 969 (7th Cir. 2001).

[55] *Williams v. NYC Department of Sanitation,* 2001 WL 1154627 (S.D.N.Y. 2001).

[56] *Breland-Starling v. Disney Publishing Worldwide,* 166 F.Supp.2d 826 (S.D.N.Y. 2001).

[57] *Benningfield v. City of Houston*, 157 F.3d 369 (5th Cir. 1998); *Nunez v. City of Los Angeles*, 147 F.3d 867 (9th Cir. 1998); *Mattern v. Eastman Kodak Co.*, 104 F.3d 702 (5th Cir. 1997); *Smiley v. Jekyll Island State Park Authority*, 12 F.Supp.2d 1377 (S.D.Ga. 1998).

[58] *Hunt v. Rapides Healthcare System, LLC*, 277 F.3d 757 (5th Cir. 2001); *Caples v. Media One Express of Illinois, Inc.*, 2001 WL 1188882 (N.D.Ill. 2001).

[59] *Veal v. AT & T Corporation*, 5 WH Cas.2d 1876 (E.D.La. 2000).

[60] *E.g. Harris v. Emergency Providers, Inc.*, 2002 WL 1972997 (8th Cir. 2002); *Fleming v. Boeing Co.*, 120 F.3d 242 (11th Cir. 1997); *Mistretta v. Volusia County Department of Corrections*, 61 F.Supp.2d 1255 (M.D.Fla. 1999).

CHAPTER 12

FMLA REMEDIES

In A Nutshell . . .

An employee successfully proving an FMLA violation is entitled to recover a variety of damages, including lost wages, "front pay" or the loss of future earnings, attorney fees, litigation costs, and liquidated damages. In addition, the FMLA gives courts the right to order employers to take such affirmative action as reinstating the employee to his former job.

Damages Under The FMLA.

The Statute: 29 U.S.C. § 2617(a)(1).

Any employer who violates section 2615 of this title shall be liable to any eligible employee affected -

(A) for damages equal to -

(i) the amount of -

(I) any wages, salary, employment benefits, or other compensation denied or lost to such employee by reason of the violation; or

(II) in a case in which wages, salary, employment benefits, or other compensation have not been denied or lost to the employee, any actual monetary losses sustained by the employee as a direct result of the violation, such as the cost of providing care, up to a sum equal to 12 weeks of wages or salary for the employee;

(ii) the interest on the amount described in clause (i) calculated at the prevailing rate; and

(iii) an additional amount as liquidated damages equal to the sum of the amount described in clause (i) and the interest described in clause (ii), except that if an employer who has violated section 2615 of this title proves to the satisfaction of the court that the act or omission which violated section 2615 of this title was in good faith and that the employer had reasonable grounds for believing that the act or omission was not a violation of section 2615 of this title, such court may, in the discretion of the court, reduce the amount of the liability to the amount and interest determined under clauses (i) and (ii), respectively; and

(B) for such equitable relief as may be appropriate, including employment, reinstatement, and promotion.

Central to a damage award under the FMLA is the notion that the employer's violation of the law caused the employee economic harm.[1] Employees are entitled to a jury trial on issues related to the employer's liability under the FMLA and to the amount of damages flowing from that liability.[2] There are five kinds of economic damages that can be recovered under the FMLA: (1) Lost wages or salary; (2) employment benefits or other compensation; (3) an award by the court compensating for actual monetary losses sustained by the employee (if no wages, employment benefits, or other compensation is awarded); (4) interest; and (5) liquidated damages. Each of these is discussed in greater detail below.

Wages and Salary.

Lost wages and salary, in the form of back pay, is the normal remedy when an employee has been disciplined or discharged for exercising FMLA rights ("front pay," or future wage losses, is discussed later in this chapter). If the employee is a salesperson, for example, lost commissions might serve as the equivalent of back pay.[3] Since the amount of back pay must be clearly ascertainable, lost overtime opportunities may not be recoverable if they are too speculative.[4] An employer might limit the amount of back pay awarded by making an unconditional offer to reinstate the employee at any point after the employer's violation of the FMLA, *if* it can show that the employee's rejection of the reinstatement offer was unreasonable.[5] In addition, in the unusual case where an employer has retaliated against an employee for using FMLA leave by discharging the employee but the employee's health condition would not have allowed the employee to return to work at the end of 12 weeks in any event, the employer's back pay liability will be limited to the unpaid balance of the 12 weeks of FMLA eligibility.[6]

In general, an employee who has been wrongly discharged is obliged to mitigate his damages by diligently seeking and accepting new employment substantially equivalent to that from which he was discharged.[7] Failure to do so may result in no back pay award for the time employment was not sought. However, as the Supreme Court has observed, the employee is not required to "go into another line of work, accept a demotion, or take a demeaning position."[8] Thus, an employee refusing to accept a part-time job without benefits would not be viewed as failing to mitigate her damages.[9] If the employee is unable to find equivalent work, the employee is entitled to enroll in a trade school or go to college for retraining without prejudicing an award of back pay.[10] In some cases, the employee's health condition may be such that mitigating damages by accepting a new job may not be an option.[11]

Some employers have argued that the back wages owed a wrongly-terminated employee should be limited by the length of FMLA leave, contending that it would make no sense to calculate damages for any period after the expiration of an FMLA leave since the employee could have been freely terminated after that time. Courts have rejected this idea, concluding that an employer is liable for the ongoing loss of wages and benefits caused by an FMLA violation until the employee is able to find other work at the same rate of pay, regardless of the length of the requested leave.[12]

What is the impact on damages under the FMLA if the employee engaged in conduct that would have warranted termination *after* the employer violated the FMLA? There are few cases on this issue, but early indications are that the employee's ability to claim lost wages may be limited from the time the employer violated the FMLA to the time it developed a legitimate non-discriminatory reason to terminate the employee.[13]

Back pay is the FMLA's basic remedy in cases where an employee has been improperly disciplined or discharged.

Employment Benefits or Other Compensation.

A second aspect of damages under the FMLA is payment for "employment benefits" or "other compensation" lost as a result of the employer's violation of the FMLA. At first glance, this seems expansive in terms of its affording at least the potential to recover a broad array of damages. However, most courts narrowly construe this element of FMLA damages, limiting recovery to "things which arise as a *quid pro quo* in the employment arrangement."[14] Such "other compensation" could potentially include lost leave benefits such as vacations, sick leave, and holidays. It does not include out-of-pocket expenses such as moving costs and relocating the employee's family,[15] nor does not include a loss of job security.[16]

Emotional Distress.

The FMLA clearly does not provide a remedy for emotional distress.[17] Similarly, damages as compensation for time lost with a newborn child for whom the FMLA leave was sought are not recoverable.[18] As well, punitive damages are not recoverable under the FMLA.[19] On occasion, an employee may bring several claims against an employer, including both an FMLA claim and a claim under a statute such as the Pregnancy Discrimination Act that allows punitive damages. In such a situation, the employee is entitled to claim both punitive damages under the other statute and liquidated damages under the FMLA.[20]

Actual Monetary Losses.

If there have been no lost wages, salary, employment benefits or other compensation, the employee is entitled to recover any actual monetary losses sustained as a direct result of the employer's violating the FMLA. Such damages may include the cost of providing care for a seriously ill family member for whom the employee sought leave. The amount of such monetary losses recoverable are capped by the FMLA at an amount equal to 12 weeks of wages or salary for the employee.[21]

Under the structure of the FMLA, the "actual monetary losses" component of FMLA damages is an alternative to the ability to recover wages, salary, employment benefits or other compensation.[22] Thus, an employee claiming lost wages cannot also claim child care expenses she incurred when her employer denied her request for FMLA leave to care for her seriously ill child.[23]

Thus far, courts have taken a conservative view of what constitutes actual monetary losses under the FMLA. In one case, an employee argued that her employer's refusal to allow her to return to work at her previous job made her so ill that she could not return to work; and, thus, she was entitled to recover future lost wages. A court rejected the employee's lawsuit, concluding that it could "find no legal authority within the FMLA upon which to allow her to recover for the injuries she sustained." In dismissing the case, the Court found that even if the employee could prove the employer violated the FMLA by refusing to allow her to return to work, the employee could "recover nothing but a symbolic victory."[24]

If (and only if) the employee lost no wages, salary, employment benefits or other compensation, the employee is entitled to recover "actual monetary losses" resulting from the employer's FMLA violation.

- **Interest.**

The FMLA requires that an award of interest be awarded on the amount of lost wages, salary, employment benefits or other compensation, and actual monetary losses.[25] Unlike other labor statutes, an award of interest is mandatory and does not reside with the discretion of the court.[26]

- **Liquidated Damages.**

Unless an employer can prove that it acted both reasonably and in good faith in taking the actions that violated the FMLA, the employee is also entitled to "liquidated damages" equivalent to back wages, lost benefits and other compensation, actual monetary losses, and interest.[27] An award of liquidated damages is generally expected in FMLA cases. One court has observed that "doubling of an award is the norm under the FMLA."[28] As of yet, there are few cases involving the circumstances under which an employer will be excused from paying liquidated damages under the FMLA. Thus far, most courts have been reluctant to award liquidated damages under the FMLA, citing as a reason the newness and complexity of the law.[29] In time, this reluctance will ultimately abate once the FMLA becomes an established part of the fabric of federal labor requirements.

However, there is a rich body of law under the liquidated damages provisions of the Fair Labor Standards Act, which also requires that liquidated damages be assessed unless the employer is acting reasonably and in good faith. Under the FLSA, liquidated damages "are considered compensatory rather than punitive in nature, and constitute compensation for the retention of a workman's pay which might result in damages too obscure and difficult of proof for estimate other than by liquidated damages."[30] In order to avoid liquidated damages, the employer must persuade the court by proving its actions were in subjective and objective good faith.[31] As the court noted in *Hayes v. Bill Haley & His Comets*, the granting of liquidated damages is mandatory unless the employer can show the requisite good faith.[32] Most cases turn on whether the employer was acting as a reasonable employer would under all of the circumstances.[33] Deliberate acts of malfeasance need not be proven to support a liquidated damages award; it is sufficient to establish unreasonable conduct on the part of the employer by simply showing that it did little or nothing to either find out what the law was or to bring its practices into compliance with the law.[34] As one court put it, good faith "requires more than ignorance of the prevailing law or uncertainty about its development. It requires that an employer first take active steps to ascertain the dictates of the FLSA and then move to comply with them."[35]

Factors leading to a conclusion that an employer acted in good faith include reliance on opinion letters issued by the DOL, and on a *bona-fide* effort on the part of the employer to evaluate the job duties and work hours for employees for whom an FLSA exemption is claimed.[36] Examples of good faith conduct by employers that resulted in the avoidance of liquidated damages have included the following:

Liquidated (or double) damages are the norm in FMLA cases, unless an employer can prove it acted both reasonably and in good faith.

- Reliance on DOL regulations or the regulations of other federal agencies;[37]

- Reliance on erroneous conclusions from "minor" officials of the DOL[38] or other governmental agencies;[39]

- Reliance on erroneous advice from attorneys;[40]

- Formation of a committee to review the proper way to calculate the overtime rate and contracting with outside counsel to review employment practices with FLSA compliance in mind;[41] and

- Adoption of a compensation plan after its attorneys and the DOL consult, only to have the compensation plan not be implemented by another employee.[42]

Examples of conduct that has been held insufficient to avoid the award of liquidated damages have included the following:

- An employer which "blindly" relied on unclear DOL regulations;[43]

- An employer that relied on the lack of employee complaints to conclude that it was not violating the FLSA;[44]

- An employer that was "well aware" of the FLSA's requirements;[45]

- An employer that made no changes in its practices after it had previously been involved in litigation under the FLSA;[46]

- An employer that simply "chose to remain ignorant of case law;"[47]

- An employer that processed the overtime claims of its employees in a "negligent" manner.[48]

- An employer that merely adhered to "industry practice" without trying to determine the legality of that practice;[49] and

- An employer whose supervisors instructed employees not to report the hours they had worked.[50]

There is some question about whether an employer may simply rely on the terms of a collective bargaining agreement in support of the argument that it should not be assessed liquidated damages. The better rule would seem to be that reliance on a collective bargaining agreement will not avoid FLSA and FMLA liability.[51] A minority of courts find to the contrary, though, holding that reliance on a collective bargaining agreement along with other factors can establish the requisite good faith and reasonableness needed to avoid liquidated damages.[52]

Question: When the FMLA was enacted, Pritiken County instructed its Human Resources Manager to make sure it was in compliance with the new law. The Manager went to a convention of other counties and learned what they were doing to comply with the law. She returned to the County, put in place several changes, and instituted the use of FMLA forms issued by the Department of Labor. The County did not receive any FMLA complaints for eight years. The Human Resources Manager retired; her successor reviewed the County's HR rules and concluded the rules complied with the FMLA.

Two years later, an employee of the County's Sheriff's Office filed an FMLA lawsuit, contending that the County violated her FMLA rights by denying her the right to take intermittent leave. A court rules for the employee, finding that the practice in the Sheriff's Office of denying requests for intermittent leave for off-the-job injuries violated the FMLA. Has the County taken enough steps to comply with the FMLA to escape an award of liquidated damages?

Answer: Probably not. An employer must do more than simply adopt industry practices, or rely on the lack of FMLA complaints. Instead, to avoid an award of liquidated damages, the employer must make an affirmative effort to learn what the law is, and then implement changes based upon that understanding. Such efforts should involve a review of the DOL's regulations, either by the employer itself or by its attorneys or other representatives.

Equitable Relief Under The FMLA.

The Statutes – 29 U.S.C. §2617(a)(1)(B) & 2617(d)

(a) Civil action by employees

(1) Liability

Any employer who violates section 2615 of this title shall be liable to any eligible employee affected—

(B) for such equitable relief as may be appropriate, including employment, reinstatement, and promotion.

(d) Action for injunction by Secretary

The district courts of the United States shall have jurisdiction, for cause shown, in an action brought by the Secretary -

(1) to restrain violations of section 2615 of this title, including the restraint of any withholding of payment of wages, salary, employment benefits, or other compensation, plus interest, found

by the court to be due to eligible employees; or

(2) to award such other equitable relief as may be appropriate, including employment, reinstatement, and promotion.

The FMLA gives an employee the ability to obtain "equitable relief" from FMLA violations. This grant includes the ability to obtain a court order, usually referred to as an injunction, either requiring an employer to take an action or forbidding an employer from continuing certain conduct.[53]

There are a wide variety of equitable relief options available under the FMLA. Common forms include reinstating the employee to his former job and prohibiting the employer from further discrimination. Ordering the promotion of an employee is also possible under the FMLA.[54]

One form of equitable relief that is often claimed is "front pay," or damages for wage losses expected to continue into the future. Though front pay is clearly recoverable under the FMLA,[55] the decision to award it rests with the court, and a jury's verdict of front pay is considered advisory only.[56] In general, front pay is recoverable when the employee shows that he lost or has been denied reinstatement to his job because of the exercise of his FMLA rights, and where, because of circumstances, the employee's future wage loss is reasonably predictable.[57] Because there is the potential for a windfall award to an employee who might be able to work in the future, some courts are cautious in making front pay awards.[58] Since front pay does not amount to back wages, liquidated damages are not awarded on front pay.[59] Under some circumstances, front pay can be extensive. For example, one court accepted the testimony of an employee that she would have worked for the employer until age 65 in awarding her 19 years of front pay totaling $304,845.[60]

Attorney Fees Under The FMLA.

The Statute: 29 U.S.C. §2617(a)(3)

The court in such an action shall, in addition to any judgment awarded to the plaintiff, allow a reasonable attorney's fee, reasonable expert witness fees, and other costs of the action to be paid by the defendant.

On occasion, an employer's greatest liability for an FMLA violation will be the payment of attorney fees to the employee's lawyer.

If an employee proves that the employer violated the FMLA, an award of attorney fees is mandatory.[61] The amount of attorney fees may well be the most significant part of a judgment against an employer. Several cases provide vivid examples of this exposure to liability. In one case, an employee's FMLA damages were limited to six days of pay (the employee brought ADA claims as well). In spite of this low recovery, the court awarded an additional $41,000 in attorney fees to the employee.[62] In another case, a jury award of $1,297 in the equivalent of back pay was augmented by an attorney fee award of $70,711.[63]

On occasion, the relationship between attorney fees and damages may be too attenuated for a court to accept. In one case, an employee won $1.00 in nominal damages for her FMLA claim. This amount was doubled to $2.00 by an award of liquidated damages, and another ten cents was added in interest for a total damage award of $2.10. In reversing a trial court's award of $19,698 in attorney fees, an appellate court sent the case back to the trial court to evaluate "the nature and extent of its discretion to adjust a mandatory attorneys' fee award to account for the limited success achieved by the plaintiff." [64]

The method of setting attorney fees in FMLA cases and lawsuits brought under similar federal statutes is now fairly routine. As a general rule, a successful employee is entitled to reimbursement for 100% of the hourly rate normally charged by the attorney for the hours worked on the case, so long as the hourly rate is in keeping with the normal rates charged for such services in the community. This amount – referred to by the courts as the "lodestar" amount – may be adjusted up or down, depending upon the circumstances.[65] If the employee fails to recover on a significant portion of the claims raised in the case, a court may reduce the fees;[66] however, simply because a plaintiff has "set high sights" in terms of claiming damages that are not completely recovered does not warrant a reduction in the amount of attorney fees.[67] If the case presents novel or difficult questions of law or fact, a court may increase the amount of attorney fees.[68] The fact that an employee may have retained a small or a large law firm to pursue the case is irrelevant in the amount of fees the employee is entitled to; what is most important is the overall market rate for the type of services provided by the attorney.[69]

Some employees bringing FMLA lawsuits are represented by attorneys on a contingent fee basis. This means the attorney is entitled to a percentage of the employee's total recovery. If the contingent fee is more than what the attorney fees would be if the attorney's normal hourly rate were used, the employer is only liable for the hourly equivalent of the attorney's time, not the full amount of the contingent fee.[70] Moreover, the fact that a contingent fee agreement was used weighs with the court in determining the amount of attorney fees.[71] A trial court's ruling on the matter of attorney fees is extremely unlikely to be overturned on appeal. Appellate courts will only review an attorney fees judgment if the trial court has somehow "abused its discretion" in awarding or calculating attorney fees.[72]

Class Actions Under The FMLA.

The Statute: 29 U.S.C. §2617(2)

An action to recover the damages or equitable relief prescribed in paragraph (1) may be maintained against any employer (including a public agency) in any Federal or State court of competent jurisdiction by any one or more employees for and in behalf of -

(A) the employees; or

(B) the employees and other employees similarly situated.

Perhaps mostly in name only, the FMLA authorizes the bringing of class actions on behalf of "the employees and other employees similarly situated." Since the passage of the FMLA, no reported court decision has discussed when such a class action might be appropriate. And, in fact, since FMLA violations are peculiarly individual in nature, depending upon the factual basis for each employee's request for FMLA leave, it is somewhat difficult to understand how there ever could be a class action lawsuit for FMLA violations – except, perhaps, in the event of an employer that was so outwardly hostile to the FMLA that a class action retaliation lawsuit might be brought. Since the FMLA's provisions authorizing lawsuits flow only to "employees" and the DOL, and since a union is not an "employee," a union has no right to bring an FMLA action on behalf of its members.[73]

Actions By The Secretary Of Labor.

The Statute: 29 U.S.C. §2617(b)

(1) Administrative action

The Secretary shall receive, investigate, and attempt to resolve complaints of violations of section 2615 of this title in the same manner that the Secretary receives, investigates, and attempts to resolve complaints of violations of sections 206 and 207 of this title.

(2) Civil action

The Secretary may bring an action in any court of competent jurisdiction to recover the damages described in subsection (a)(1)(A) of this section.

(3) Sums recovered

Any sums recovered by the Secretary pursuant to paragraph (2) shall be held in a special deposit account and shall be paid, on order of the Secretary, directly to each employee affected. Any such sums not paid to an employee because of inability to do so within a period of 3 years shall be deposited into the Treasury of the United States as miscellaneous receipts.

As with the Fair Labor Standards Act, the DOL has the ability to bring lawsuits on behalf of employees alleging violations of the FMLA. In addition, the FMLA gives the DOL the authority to "receive, investigate, and attempt to resolve complaints" of violations of the FMLA. The power to receive and investigate complaints is a significant one. In 2000, the DOL received 2833 complaints alleging violations of the FMLA, and recovered more than $2.9 million on behalf of employees. If the DOL brings an action on behalf of an employee, the DOL rather than the employee ultimately decides how the litigation should proceed or be settled. Any amounts recovered by the DOL on behalf of an employee are paid to the employee.

The Relationship Between Private Lawsuits And Suits By The Secretary Of Labor.

The Statute: 29 U.S.C. §2617(a)(4)

The right provided by paragraph (2) to bring an action by or on behalf of any employee shall terminate -

(A) on the filing of a complaint by the Secretary in an action under subsection (d) of this section in which restraint is sought of any further delay in the payment of the amount described in paragraph (1)(A) to such employee by an employer responsible under paragraph (1) for the payment; or

(B) on the filing of a complaint by the Secretary in an action under subsection (b) of this section in which a recovery is sought of the damages described in paragraph (1)(A) owing to an eligible employee by an employer liable under paragraph (1), unless the action described in subparagraph (A) or (B) is dismissed without prejudice on motion of the Secretary.

Section 2617(a)(4) of the FMLA contains a somewhat unusual restriction on an employee's ability to bring a lawsuit for a violation of the FMLA. Under the law, an employee's ability to bring or maintain a lawsuit is ended if the DOL elects to bring an action on the employee's behalf. In the words of one court, "an employee's cause of action brought under the FMLA is 'trumped' by the DOL's filing of a complaint."[74] In order for the DOL's actions to eliminate the employee's ability to file a lawsuit, the DOL must formally initiate a court case. If the employee merely files a complaint with the DOL, the employee will not be precluded from bringing a simultaneous lawsuit.[75]

The Statutes Of Limitations For FMLA Actions.

The Statute: 29 U.S.C. §2617(c)

(1) In general

Except as provided in paragraph (2), an action may be brought under this section not later than 2 years after the date of the last event constituting the alleged violation for which the action is brought.

(2) Willful violation

In the case of such action brought for a willful violation of section 2615 of this title, such action may be brought within 3 years of the date of the last event constituting the alleged violation for which such action is brought.

(3) Commencement

In determining when an action is commenced by the Secretary under this section for the purposes of this subsection, it shall be considered to be commenced on the date when the complaint is filed.

As with many of its other procedural provisions, the FMLA borrows from the FLSA's statutes of limitations to set time limits for the filing of lawsuits. The usual statute of limitations for FMLA actions is two years "after the date of the last event constituting the violation" – in other words, two years from the last action or inaction by the employer that violated the FMLA.[76] The statute of limitations clock begins to run when the violation occurs. In cases where the employee has been disciplined for using FMLA-qualifying leave, the clock begins to run when the employer provides notice of the disciplinary action to the employee.[77] Where the notice of disciplinary action is sent by mail, the statute of limitations begins to run when the employee receives the notice.[78]

Where the employer's violation is "willful," the statute of limitations is three years.[79] Though few FMLA cases define "willful violation" for purposes of the three-year statute of limitations,[80] there are any number of FLSA cases describing how the term should be applied under the FMLA.[81] Certainly the leading case is the decision of the United States Supreme Court in *McLaughlin v. Richland Shoe Co.*, where the Court ruled that the word "willful" is synonymous with such words as "voluntary," "deliberate" and "intentional," and refers to conduct which is not merely negligent.[82] In the case, the Supreme Court established that the standard for a willful violation of the FLSA is where the employer either knew or showed reckless disregard for whether its conduct was prohibited by statute. Under the FLSA, such willfulness can be established when the employer acknowledges that the employee is entitled to overtime compensation but refuses to pay the overtime because of a philosophical belief that "supervisors" should not be entitled to overtime.[83]

These standards have ready application to the FMLA. For example, in one case, a court considered a lawsuit claiming an employee was fired in retaliation for using FMLA leave. The lawsuit was filed more than two, but less than three years after the employee was fired. The court refused to allow the lawsuit to proceed, finding that, at most, the employee demonstrated mere negligence on the employer's part rather than a deliberate violation of the law.[84]

Where Can FMLA Lawsuits Be Filed?

The Statute – 29 U.S.C. §2617(d)

(2) Right of action

An action to recover the damages or equitable relief prescribed in paragraph (1) may be maintained against any employer (including a public agency) in any Federal or State court of competent jurisdiction by any one or more employees for and in behalf of -

(A) the employees; or

(B) the employees and other employees similarly situated.

Section 2617(d) of the FMLA explicitly allows an employee to bring an FMLA lawsuit in federal or state court. This provides for what the courts call "concurrent jurisdiction," with *either* federal or state courts having the authority to decide an FMLA case.[85] Since the FMLA is a federal law, if the employee first brings the claim in state court, the employer has the right to "remove" the action to a federal court.[86] In fact, the vast majority of FMLA cases are brought in the federal courts.

In some cases, it might be to an employee's advantage to bring the claim in state court. For example, in one case an employee argued that an arbitrator's award reversing his discharge and ordering that he be made whole for all lost wages and benefits required a finding that he had worked the requisite minimum 1,250 hours for FMLA coverage. Otherwise, the employee argued, the employer could benefit from its own wrongful decision to terminate the employee. A federal court refused to give the arbitrator's award full effect, noting that (1) state law in the area was unclear, (2) the employee chose not to bring the action in state court, and (3) the employee "cannot now expect this court to blaze new trails in state law in the absence of any well-plotted road map showing an avenue of relief that the state's highest court would likely follow."[87]

Need An Employee "Exhaust" Administrative Remedies Before Bringing An FMLA Lawsuit?

Occasionally employers will argue that employees need to "exhaust" their administrative remedies before bringing an FMLA lawsuit. The exhaustion requirement is based on the idea that requiring an employee to pursue all possible internal remedies may eliminate the need for the lawsuit, saving the court system time and money.

Where a federal statute specifically <u>requires</u> the exhaustion of administrative remedies, courts have not hesitated to require that an employee use those administrative procedures as a prerequisite to bringing a lawsuit.[88] The FMLA, however, does not contain a specific exhaustion requirement, leaving the matter to the courts' discretion.[89] Thus far, courts have not been inclined to require employees to exhaust administrative remedies as a prerequisite to bringing an FMLA lawsuit, reasoning that the FMLA grants "important rights" under federal law that permit an employee to bring an FMLA claim directly to court.[90]

Occasionally, the employer's conduct may potentially violate several federal statutes. For example, it is not difficult to imagine that an underlying action by an employer might violate the FMLA, the ADA, the Pregnancy Discrimination Act, and Title VII of the Civil Rights Act. Employees with multiple claims must remember that *other* federal statutes may require the exhaustion of administrative remedies while the FMLA does not. Since exhausting administrative remedies may take some time, an employee could conceivably need to file his FMLA lawsuit before the administrative remedies under the other statutes are exhausted. The pitfall to the employee doing so is that the results in the FMLA suit may be given "preclusive effect" when the other federal claims are eventually filed, and may either severely limit or eliminate the employee's ability to bring such claims.[91] In such cases, the employee is forced to evaluate the relative merits of each of the various claims and pursue only those with the greatest potential.

The Compulsory Arbitration Of FMLA Claims In Private Employment Contracts.

In recent years, the United States Supreme Court has shown a definite trend toward allowing private employment contracts to call for the mandatory arbitration of certain federal labor claims.[92] Given this trend, it is not surprising that a number of court decisions are testing the validity of private employment contracts compelling the arbitration of FMLA claims. Employers generally favor such contracts, since arbitrators are not as ready to award attorney fees and liquidated damages as courts, and because arbitrators lack some of the powers granted courts under the FMLA. Employees generally dislike such arbitration contracts for precisely the same reasons, although signing a contract calling for the mandatory arbitration of FMLA claims may be a precondition to obtaining a job.

As suggested in Chapter 9, courts are reluctant to find provisions in a collective bargaining agreement waiving an employee's right to bring a federal lawsuit for FMLA claims. Such reluctance extends only in part to private employment agreements, which some courts have been willing to uphold provided certain conditions are met.[93] In general, for a court to defer to arbitration, all parties must agree to arbitrate the dispute.[94] Additionally, the arbitration process in the employment contract must provide for an "effective and accessible alternative forum" to court proceedings.[95]

In one case a non-union employee was covered by a contract that required the arbitration of any issue arising out of the employer-employee relationship. The contract was implemented seven years after the employee began work and, under the state's rules of "at-will" employment, became part of the employment relationship between the employer and the employee. While a court upheld in principle such a contract to mandate arbitration of FMLA claims, it found the particular contract defective because it required the employee to pay half of the arbitrator's fees and any costs associated with the use of a court reporter and transcript should the employee desire either. In the view of the Court, "a former worker in [the employer's] shipping department cannot afford such a fee. Thus, while the Arbitration Policy prohibits Plaintiff from using the judicial forum, the prohibitive cost substantially limits the use of the arbitral forum." As a solution, the Court mandated arbitration but struck down the fee splitting and court reporter portions of the employment contract.[96]

The Special Case Of Certain Educational Employers.

The Statute – 29 U.S.C. §2618(e)

If a local educational agency or a private elementary or secondary school that has violated this subchapter proves to the satisfaction of the court that the agency, school, or department had reasonable grounds for believing that the underlying act or omission was not a violation of this subchapter, such court may, in the discretion of the court, reduce the amount of the liability provided for under section 2617(a)(1)(A) of this title to the amount and interest determined under clauses (i) and (ii), respectively, of such section.

Special liquidated damages rules apply to educational employers, who are treated differently in many parts of the FMLA (see Chapter 3). Section 2618(e) of the FMLA eliminates the liquidated damages liability for such employers *if* they have "reasonable grounds for believing that the underlying act or omission" did not violate the law. Looking at the legislative history behind the FMLA, Congress indicated that "reasonable grounds" could include such factors as advice of counsel, collective bargaining agreements, and compliance with valid state and local laws or the DOL's regulations.[97]

This partial exemption for liquidated damages applies only to violations of the special FMLA rules pertaining to educational employers and does not apply to violations of the remainder of the FMLA's provisions.

The Validity Of Agreements Releasing An Employer From Liability Under The FMLA.

Terminated employees have the ability to release an employer of FMLA liability, provided certain conditions are met.

An increasingly common practice is for an employer to ask that an employee sign an agreement releasing the employer from different kinds of potential liability prior to terminating his employment. On occasion, employees agree to sign these releases, usually for some benefit like severance pay, continued health insurance, and the like. Since a thoroughly written release will attempt to release the employer of virtually all forms of possible liability under federal statutes, questions have arisen as to whether an employee can validly release the employer of FMLA liability, or whether such releases are unenforceable.

The courts have viewed the validity of releases differently depending upon which federal statute is involved. Employees may waive claims arising under Title VII of the Civil Rights Act and the Age Discrimination in Employment Act.[98] However, the Supreme Court has held that an employee cannot waive claims under the Fair Labor Standards Act.[99] The cases addressing the issue have split on whether such waivers are legal under the FMLA. Some courts have found that the DOL's regulations that seemingly prohibit a waiver are consistent with the intent of Congress that FMLA rights be fully enforceable.[100] Other courts have concluded that an employee does have the power to release an employer from liability under the FMLA.[101]

For a release to be valid, the waiver of a federal right must be made "knowingly and willfully," considering the "totality of circumstances."[102] Under this test, courts consider a variety of factors, including:

- The clarity and specificity of the release language;

- The employee's education and business experience;

- The amount of time given the employee to consider the release before signing it;

- Whether the employee knew or should have known his rights upon execution of the release;

- Whether the employee was encouraged to seek or, in fact, received the benefit of advice from an attorney;

- Whether there was an opportunity for negotiation of the terms of the release; and

- Whether the consideration received in exchange for the release and by the employee exceeds the benefits to which the employee was already entitled by contract or law.[103]

Simply because the employer may have obtained the employee's release from FMLA liability does not necessarily mean the end of the issue, however. In 2001, the Supreme Court held that a private arbitration agreement requiring the arbitration of all federal statutory claims does not prevent the Equal Employment Opportunity Commission from filing a lawsuit for reinstatement, damages, and other relief on the employee's behalf.[104] The Court reasoned that the public policy issues behind federal anti-discrimination statutes vested with the federal government an enforcement authority that could not be waived by an employee. Though the matter is as yet unresolved, it would appear that the same logic would allow the EEOC to proceed with action against an employer even in the face of a release signed by the impacted employee.

Though the law in the area is unclear, the employee does not necessarily have to return the payments made to her as consideration for the signing of the release in order to challenge the voluntariness of the release.[105]

NOTES

[1] *Dawson v. Leewood Nursing Home, Inc.*, 14 F.Supp.2d 828 (E.D.Va. 1998); *Nordhoff v. Haverty's Furniture Companies, Inc.*, 1997 WL 667888 (N.D.Tex. 1997).

[2] *McNeela v. United Air Lines*, 1999 WL 987096 (N.D.Ill. 1999); *Frizzell v. Southwest Motor Freight*, 154 F.3d 641 (6th Cir. 1998); *Bryant v. Delbar Prods., Inc.*, 18 F.Supp.2d 799 (M.D.Tenn. 1998); *Helmly v. Stone Container Corporation*, 957 F.Supp. 1274 (S.D.Ga. 1997); *Souders v. Fleming Companies, Inc.*, 960 F.Supp. 218 (D.Neb. 1997). *Contra Hicks v. Maytag Corporation*, 3 WH Cas.2d 992 (E.D.Tenn. 1995).

[3] *Estes v. Meridian One Corporation*, 246 F.3d 664 (4th Cir. 2001).

[4] *Thorson v. Gemini, Inc.*, 205 F.3d 370 (8th Cir. 2001).

[5] *Barrileaux v. Thayer Lodging Group, Inc.*, 4 WH Cas.2d 1725 (E.D.La. 1998); *see Ford Motor Company v. EEOC*, 458 U.S. 219 (1982). *See generally Smith v. World Ins. Co.*,38 F.3d 1456 (8th Cir. 1994)(discussing when rejecting an offer of reinstatement would be unreasonable); *Pierce v. F.R. Tripler & Co.*, 955 F.2d 820 (2nd Cir. 1992)(same); *Graefenhain v. Pabst Brewing Co.*, 870 F.2d 1198 (7th Cir. 1989)(same).

[6] *Rogers v. AC Humko Corp.*, 56 F.Supp.2d 972 (W.D.Tenn. 1999).

[7] *Brady v. Thurston Motor Lines, Inc.*, 753 F.2d 1269 (4th Cir. 1985); *Williams v. Rubicon, Inc.*, 808 So.2d 852 (La.App. 2002).

[8] *Ford Motor Co. v. EEOC*, 458 U.S. 219 (1982).

[9] *Sherman v. AI/FOCS*, 113 F.Supp.2d 65 (D.Mass. 2000).

[10] *Miller v. AT & T Corporation*, 250 F.3d 820 (4th Cir. 2001).

[11] *Nichols v. Ashland Hosp. Corp.*, 251 F.3d 496 (4th Cir. 2001).

[12] *Mummert v. Vencor Inc.*, 21 Fed. Appx. 710 (9th Cir. 2001).

[13] *Hite v. Biomet, Inc.*, 53 F.Supp.2d 1013 (N.D.Ind. 1999).

[14] *Lloyd v. Wyoming Valley Healthcare System, Inc.*, 994 F.Supp. 288 (M.D.Pa. 1998); *McAnnally v. Wyn South Molded Prods., Inc.*, 912 F.Supp. 512 (N.D.Ala. 1996).

[15] *Nero v. Industrial Molding Corp.*, 167 F.3d 921 (5th Cir. 1999).

[16] *McAnally v. Wyn South Molded Products, Inc.*, 912 F.Supp. 512 (N.D.Ala. 1996).

[17] *Damon v. American Rail Car Industries, Inc.*, 2002 WL 340792 (E.D.Ark. 2002); *Scarborough v. Trans World Airlines*, 5 WH Cas.2d 1625 (E.D.Mo. 2000); *Biermann v. Aluminum Company of America*, 7 WH Cas.2d 1431 (S.D.Iowa 2000); *Findlay v. PHE, Inc.*, 1999 WL 1939245 (M.D.N.C. 1999); *Knussman v. Maryland,* 65 F.Supp.2d 353 (D.Md. 1999), *rev'd on other grounds*, 272 F.3d 625 (4th Cir. 2001); *Rogers v. AC Humko Corp.*, 56 F.Supp.2d 972 (W.D.Tenn. 1999). *See generally* Note, Kelly N.

Honohan, *Remedying The Liability Limitation Under The Family And Medical Leave Act*, 79 B.U. L. Rev. 1043 (1999).

[18] *Knussman v. Maryland,* 935 F.Supp. 659 (D.Md. 1996), *rev'd on other grounds,* 272 F.3d 625 (4th Cir. 2001).

[19] *Keene v. Rinaldi,* 127 F.Supp.2d 770 (M.D.N.C. 2000); *Johnson v. Runyon,* 138 Lab. Cas. ¶33,929 (W.D.Mich. 1999); *Vicioso v. Pisa Brothers,* 4 WH Cas.2d 1433 (S.D.N.Y. 1998); *McAnnally v. Wyn South Molded Products, Inc.,* 912 F.Supp. 512 (N.D.Ala. 1996); *see Hite v. Biomet, Inc.,* 53 F.Supp.2d 1013 (N.D.Ind. 1999).

[20] *Atchley v. Nordam Group, Inc.,* 180 F.3d 1143 (10th Cir. 1999).

[21] 29 U.S.C. §2917(A)(i)(II).

[22] *Cianci v. Pettibone Corp.,* 152 F.3d 723 (7th Cir. 1998).

[23] *Barrileaux v. Thayer Lodging Group, Inc.,* 4 WH Cas.2d 1725 (E.D.La. 1998).

[24] *Dawson v. Leewood Nursing Home, Inc.,* 14 F.Supp.2d 828 (E.D.Va. 1998); *see Graham v. State Farm Mutual Insurance Company,* 193 F.3d 1274 (11th Cir. 1999); *Lapham v. Vanguard Cellular Systems, Inc.,* 102 F.Supp.2d 266 (M.D.Pa. 2000); *Nordhoff v. Haverty's Furniture Companies, Inc.,* 1997 WL 667888 (N.D.Tex. 1997). *See generally* Kelly N. Honohan, Note, *Remedying the Liability Limitation under the Family and Medical Leave Act,* 73 B.U.L.Rev. 1043 (1999).

[25] 29 U.S.C. § 2917(A)(ii).

[26] *Brenlla v. LaSorsa Buick Pontiac Chevrolet, Inc.,* 7 WH Cas.2d 1688 (S.D.N.Y. 2002).

[27] 29 U.S.C. §2617(2); *see Reich v. Midwest Plastic Engineering, Inc.,* 66 Empl. Prac. Dec. ¶43,701 (W.D.Mich. 1995).

[28] *Nero v. Industrial Molding Corp.,* 167 F.3d 921 (5th Cir. 1999); *see Miller v. Julia Corporation,* 3 WH Cas.2d 913 (S.D.Ohio 1996).

[29] *Thorson v. Gemini, Inc.,* 205 F.3d 370 (8th Cir. 2000).

[30] *Roy v. County of Lexington,* 141 F.3d 533 (4th Cir. 1998).

[31] *Block v. City of Los Angeles,* 2001 WL 609818 (9th Cir. 2001); *Joiner v. City of Macon,* 814 F.2d 1537 (11th Cir. 1987). *See generally McClanahan v. Matthews,* 440 F.2d 320 (6th Cir. 1971), *quoting Rothman v. Publicker Industries, Inc.,* 201 F.2d 618 (3rd Cir. 1953).

[32] *Hayes v. Bill Haley & His Comets,* 274 F.Supp. 34 (E.D.Pa. 1967).

[33] *Dybach v. Florida Department of Corrections,* 942 F.2d 1562 (11th Cir. 1991); *Westfall v. District of Columbia,* 30 WH Cases 921 (D.D.C. 1991).

[34] *Thomas v. Howard University Hospital,* 39 F.3d 370 (D.C.Cir. 1994).

[35] *Lockwood v. Prince Georges County, Maryland,* 217 F.3d 839 (4th Cir. 2000).

[36] *Atlanta Professional Firefighters Union v. City of Atlanta,* 920 F.2d 800 (11th Cir. 1991).

[37] *Cross v. Arkansas Forestry Commission*, 938 F.2d 912 (8th Cir. 1991).

[38] *Bauler v. Pressed Steel Car Co.*, 81 F.Supp. 172 (N.D.Ill. 1948), *aff'd* 182 F.2d 357 (7th Cir. 1950).

[39] *Reed v. Murphy*, 232 F.2d 668 (5th Cir. 1956).

[40] *Coleman v. Jiffy June Farms, Inc.*, 458 F.2d 1139 (5th Cir. 1972). The Court only discussed whether the FLSA violation was willful so as to trigger the three-year statute of limitations; the lower court, 324 F.Supp. 664 (1970), denied plaintiff's request for liquidated damages without really discussing the reliance upon erroneous advice from the attorney.

[41] *Aaron v. City Of Wichita, Kansas*, 1 WH Cas.2d 550 (D.Kan. 1993).

[42] *Lee v. Coahoma County, Mississippi*, 937 F.2d 220 (5th Cir. 1991).

[43] *Adams v. Pittsburgh State Univ.*, 832 F.Supp. 318 (D.Kan. 1993).

[44] *Ackler v. Cowlitz County*, 248 F.3d 1169 (9th Cir. 2001).

[45] *Farmer v. Ottawa County Sheriff's Dept.*, 142 Lab.Cas. ¶34,182 (W.D.Mich. 2000).

[46] *Tripp v. May*, 189 F.2d 198 (7th Cir. 1951).

[47] *Williams v. Tri-County Growers, Inc.*, 747 F.2d 121 (3rd Cir. 1984); *Barcellona v. Tiffany English Pub., Inc.*, 597 F.2d 464 (5th Cir. 1979).

[48] *AFSCME, Council 17 v. State of Louisiana*, 142 Lab.Cas. ¶34,195 (E.D.La. 2001).

[49] *Renfro v. City of Emporia*, 948 F.2d 1529 (10th Cir. 1991).

[50] *Pearson v. Ross G. Stephenson Assoc.*, 1 WH Cas.2d 46 (D.Kan. 1992).

[51] *Ackler v. Cowlitz County*, 248 F.3d 1169 (9th Cir. 2001).

[52] *Foremost Dairies, Inc. v. Ivey*, 204 F.2d 186 (5th Cir. 1953).

[53] *Knussman v. Maryland*, 935 F.Supp. 659 (D.Md. 1996), *rev'd on other grounds*, 272 F.3d 625 (4th Cir. 2001).

[54] 29 U.S.C. §2617(a)(l)(B).

[55] *Cline v. Wal-Mart, Inc.*, 144 F.3d 294 (4th Cir. 1998); *Williams v. Rubicon, Inc.*, 808 So.2d 852 (La.App. 2002).

[56] *Hardin v. Caterpillar, Inc.*, 227 F.3d 268 (5th Cir. 2000); *Brenlla v. LaSorsa Buick Pontiac Chevrolet, Inc.*, 7 WH Cas.2d 1688 (S.D.N.Y. 2002).

[57] *Smith v. Diffee Ford-Lincoln-Mercury, Inc.*, 298 F.3d 955 (10th Cir. 2002).

[58] *Nichols v. Ashland Hosp. Corp.*, 251 F.3d 496 (4th Cir. 2001).

[59] *Drew v. Waffle House, Inc.*, 534 S.E.2d 282 (S.C.App. 2000), *aff'd in part, rev'd in part on other grounds.* 2002 WL 31235724 (S.C. 2002).

[60] *Drew v. Waffle House, Inc.*, 2002 WL 31235724 (S.C. 2002).

[61] *Bond v. Abbott Laboratories*, 188 F.3d 506 (6th Cir. 1999); *Dawson v. Leewood Nursing Home Inc.*, 14 F.Supp.2d 828 (E.D.Va. 1998); *Smith v. Berry Co.*, 1997 WL 736697 (E.D.La. 1997).

[62] *Shepherd v. Honda of America Mfg., Inc.*, 160 F.Supp.2d 860 (S.D.Ohio 2001); *see Anastacio v. Initial Contract Services, Inc.*, 1998 WL 310767 (S.D.N.Y. 1998).

[63] *Estes v. Meridian One Corporation*, 246 F.3d 664 (4th Cir. 2001).

[64] *McDonnell v. Miller Oil Co., Inc.*, 134 F.3d 638 (4th Cir. 1998); *see Cooper v. Harbour Inns of Baltimore, Inc.*, 5 WH Cas.2d 1804 (D.Md. 2000).

[65] *See Hensley v. Eckerhart*, 461 U.S. 424 (1983); *Blackman v. District of Columbia*, 59 F.Supp.2d 37 (D.D.C. 1999); *Cookston v. Miller Freeman, Inc.*, 1999 WL 714760 (N.D.Tex. 1999).

[66] *Burks v. Siemens Energy & Automation, Inc.*, 215 F.3d 880 (8th Cir. 2000); *George v. GTE Directories Corp.*, 114 F.Supp.2d 1281 (M.D.Fla. 2000); *Pearson v. Ross G. Stephenson Assoc.*, 1 WH Cas.2d 46 (D.Kan. 1992).

[67] *Bankston v. State of Illinois*, 60 F.3d 1249 (7th Cir. 1995).

[68] *Lyle v. Food Lion, Inc.*, 954 F.2d 984 (4th Cir. 1992).

[69] *Bankston v. State of Illinois*, 60 F.3d 1249 (7th Cir. 1995).

[70] *Lyle v. Food Lion, Inc.*, 954 F.2d 984 (4th Cir. 1992).

[71] *Jarrett v. ERC Properties, Inc.*, 211 F.3d 1078 (8th Cir. 2000).

[72] *Spegon v. Catholic Bishop of Chicago*, 175 F.3d 544 (7th Cir. 1999).

[73] *Local 100, Service Employees Intern. Union, AFL-CIO v. Integrated Health Services, Inc.*, 96 F.Supp.2d 537 (M.D.La. 2000).

[74] *O'Hara v. Mount Vernon Board of Education*, 16 F.Supp.2d 868 (S.D.Ohio 1998).

[75] *Wilson v. Dallas Independent School District*, 1998 WL 47635 (N.D.Tex. 1998).

[76] 29 U.S.C. §2617(c)(1); *see Garner v. Falcione*, 173 F.3d 855 (6th Cir. 1999); *Carter v. General Electric Co.*, 5 WH Cas.2d 1884 (N.D.Ill. 2000); *Shannon v. City of Philadelphia*, 5 WH Cas.2d 380 (E.D.Pa. 1999).

[77] *Biermann v. Aluminum Company of America*, 7 WH Cas.2d 1431 (S.D.Iowa 2000); *Burke v. Nalco Chemical Company*, 1996 WL 411456 (N.D.Ill. 1996).

[78] *Hammond v. Interstate Brands Corporation*, 2002 WL 31093603 (S.D.Ind. 2002).

[79] 29 U.S.C. §2617(c)(2); *see* 29 U.S.C. §2617(c)(1).

[80] *See Edwards v. Ford Motor Company*, 179 F.Supp.2d 714 (W.D.Ky. 2001); *Caucci v. Prison Health Services, Inc.*, 153 F.Supp.2d 605 (E.D.Pa. 2001); *Sampson v. Citibank, F.S.B.*, 53 F.Supp.2d 13 (D.D.C. 1999).

[81] *Settle v. S.W. Rodgers, Co., Inc.*, 998 F.Supp. 657 (E.D.Va. 1998), *aff'd*, 182 F.3d 909 (4th Cir. 1999).

[82] *McLaughlin v. Richland Shoe Co.*, 486 U.S. 128 (1988).

[83] *Harris v. District of Columbia*, 749 F.Supp. 301 (D.D.C. 1990). *See also Wyland v. District of Columbia*, 728 F.Supp. 35 (D.D.C. 1990).

[84] *Settle v. S.W. Rodgers Co., Inc.*, 182 F.3d 909 (4th Cir. 1999), *aff'd*, 182 F.3d 909 (4th Cir. 1999).

[85] *Tavares v. Barbour Threads, Inc.*, 1999 WL 1078056 (Conn.Super. 1999)

[86] *Eastus v. Blue Bell Creameries, L.P.*, 97 F.3d 100 (5th Cir. 1996); *Holden v. Goodyear Tire & Rubber Company*, 5 WH Cas.2d 1567 (D.Kan. 1999); *Henriquez v. Royal Sonesta, Inc.*, 1996 WL 169237 (E.D.La. 1996); *Ladner v. Alexander & Alexander, Inc.*, 879 F.Supp. 598 (W.D.La. 1995).

[87] *Plumley v. Southern Container, Inc.*, 145 Lab.Cas. ¶11,187 (D.Me. 2001).

[88] *Coit Independence Joint Venture v. FSLIC*, 489 U.S. 561 (1989).

[89] *Danfelt v. Board of County Commissioners of Washington Co.*, 998 F.Supp. 606 (D.Md. 1998); *Spurlock v. Nynex*, 949 F.Supp. 1022 (W.D.N.Y. 1996).

[90] *Ogborn v. United Food & Commercial Workers, Local No. 881*, 142 Lab.Cas. ¶34,152 (N.D.Ill. 2000); *Krohn v. Forsting*, 11 F.Supp.2d 1082 (E.D.Mo. 1998); *Danfelt v. Board of County Commissioners of Washington County*, 998 F.Supp. 606 (D.Md. 1998); *Simmons v. District of Columbia*, 977 F.Supp. 62 (D.D.C. 1997); *Spurlock v. NYNEX*, 949 F.Supp. 1022 (W.D.N.Y. 1996); *Ritz v. Wapello County Board of Supervisors*, 595 N.W.2d 786 (Iowa 1999).

[91] *Churchill v. Star Enterprises*, 183 F.3d 184 (3rd Cir. 1999).

[92] *Gilmer v. Interstate/Johnson Lane Corp.*, 500 U.S. 20 (1991)(upholds private employment contract calling for arbitration of Age Discrimination in Employment Act claim).

[93] *See O'Neil v. Hilton Head Hospital*, 115 F.3d 272 (4th Cir. 1997); *Reese v. Commercial Credit Corporation*, 955 F.Supp. 567 (D.S.C. 1997); *Shaw v. Walsh Services, Inc.*, 1997 WL 30907 (N.D.Tex. 1997); *Pilanski v. Metropolitan Life Insurance Co.*, 73 Fair Empl. Prac. Cas. 1506 (S.D.N.Y. 1996); *Satarino v. A.G. Edwards & Sons, Inc.*, 941 F.Supp. 609 (N.D.Tex. 1996); *Kindred v. Second Judicial District Court*, 996 P.2d 903 (Nev. 2000). *See generally Blocker v. Providian Life & Health*, 2001 WL 43644 (E.D.Pa. 2001).

[94] *Sherry v. Sisters of Charity Medical Center*, 1999 WL 287738 (E.D.N.Y. 1999); *Hoffman v. Aaron Kamhi, Inc.*, 927 F.Supp. 640 (S.D.N.Y. 1996).

[95] *Cole v. Burns Int'l Sec. Servs.*, 105 F.3d 1465 (D.C.Cir. 1997).

[96] *Jones v. Fujitsu Network Communications, Inc.*, 81 F.Supp.2d 688 (N.D.Tex. 1999); *see Shankle v. B-G Maintenance Mgmt. of Colo., Inc.*, 163 F.3d 1230 (10th Cir. 1999); *Cole v. Burns Int'l Sec. Servs.*, 105 F.3d 1465 (D.C.Cir. 1997).

[97] S.Rep. No. 3, 103d Cong., 1st Ses. 3-5 (1993), *reprinted in* 1993 U.S.C.C.A.N. 37.

[98] *Alexander v. Gardner-Denver Co.*, 415 U.S. 36 (1974); *Coventry v. United States Steel Corp.*, 856 F.2d 514 (3rd Cir. 1988).

[99] *Brooklyn Savings Bank v. O'Neil*, 324 U.S. 697 (1945).

[100] *Dierlam v. Wesley-Jessen Corporation,* 2002 WL 31118319 (N.D.III. 2002); *Bluitt v. Eval Co. of America, Inc.,* 3 F.Supp.2d 761 (S.D.Tex. 1998); *see* 29 C.F.R. §825.220(d).

[101] *Halvorson v. Boy Scouts of America,* 215 F.3d 1326 (6th Cir. 2000); *Poppelreiter v. Straub International, Inc.,* 2001 WL 1464788 (D.Kan. 2001); *Kujawski v. U.S. Filer Wastewater Group, Inc.,* 7 WH Cas.2d 400 (D.Minn. 2001); *Riddell v. Medical Inter-Insurance Exchange,* 18 F.Supp.2d 468 (D.N.J. 1998).

[102] *See Alexander v. Gardner-Denver Co.,* 415 U.S. 36 (1974); *Rivera-Flores v. Bristol-Myers Squibb Caribbean,* 112 F.3d 9 (1st Cir. 1997); *Bledsoe v. Palm Beach County Soil & Water Conservation Dist.,* 133 F.3d 816 (11th Cir. 1998); *Martinez v. NBC,* 877 F.Supp. 219 (D.N.J. 1994).

[103] *See Cirillo v. Arco Chemical Co.,* 862 F.2d 448 (3rd Cir. 1988); *EEOC v. Waffle House, Inc.,* 122 S.Ct. 754 (2002).

[104] *EEOC v. Waffle House, Inc.,* 534 U.S. 279 (2002).

[105] *Riddell v. Medical Inter-Insurance Exchange,* 18 F.Supp.2d 468 (D.N.J. 1998). *But see Schoenwald v. Arco Alaska, Inc.,* 191 F.3d 461 (9th Cir. 1999).

CHAPTER 13

POSTING AND RECORDKEEPING REQUIREMENTS UNDER THE FMLA

In A Nutshell . . .

The Department of Labor has developed an easily-accessible form for use by employers to comply with the FMLA's requirement that employers conspicuously post notices detailing the FMLA rights of employees. A failure to post the notice deprives the employer of the right to claim that an employee did not give appropriate advance warning of the need to use FMLA leave.

The FMLA's Posting Requirements.

The Statute: 29 U.S.C. §2619.

(a) In general

Each employer shall post and keep posted, in conspicuous places on the premises of the employer where notices to employees and applicants for employment are customarily posted, a notice, to be prepared or approved by the Secretary, setting forth excerpts from, or summaries of, the pertinent provisions of this subchapter and information pertaining to the filing of a charge.

(b) Penalty

Any employer that willfully violates this section may be assessed a civil money penalty not to exceed $100 for each separate offense.

The FMLA requires employers to post conspicuous notices to employees and applicants about the requirements of the FMLA, and imposes a fine not to exceed $100 on employers who willfully violate the posting requirement.[1] The FMLA itself furnishes few details about the content of such notices, indicating only that the notices must set forth "excerpts from, or summaries of, the pertinent provisions" of the law.[2] The DOL's regulations flesh out the language of the statute only a little, indicating that the notices must (1) specify whether the employer has any eligible employees, (2) set forth the "Act's provisions," and (3) provide information about how to contact the DOL to file complaints.[3] Moreover, the DOL's regulations state that an employer that has failed to post the required notice "cannot take any adverse action against an employee, including denying FMLA leave, for failing to furnish the employer with advance notice of a need to take FMLA leave."[4] As put by one court, an employer that fails to comply with the FMLA's posting requirements cannot turn around and claim that an employee "should have known of his FMLA rights and was required to properly apply for FMLA leave."[5]

A failure to comply with the FMLA's posting requirements eliminates only one obligation imposed by the FMLA on employees – that they give appropriate *advance* notice of the need to take FMLA leave. As discussed in Chapter 6, when the need for leave is unforeseeable, an employee does not need to give advance notice but must give notice of the need for leave "as soon as practicable." In such cases, the employee's failure to provide appropriate after-the-fact notice will not be excused by the employer's breach of the FMLA's posting requirements.[6]

The FMLA provides for only limited enforcement rights of the posting requirement beyond indicating that a failure to comply with the posting requirement may eliminate an employee's need to provide advance notice of the intent to use FMLA leave. Individual employees do not have the right to seek an injunction forcing an employer to comply with the posting requirement; instead, the FMLA only gives the DOL such ability.[7] Additionally, employees do not have the right to damages arising solely out of an employer's failure to comply with the posting requirements.[8]

Appendix C to the DOL's regulations contains helpful information on the issue of posting, furnishing a sample notice, and allowing employers to duplicate the text of that notice. While an employer need not copy the sample notice in its posting, the employer's posting must contain at least as much information as the sample notice.[9] The DOL's sample notice is as follows:

Your Rights
Under The
Family and Medical Leave Act of 1993

FMLA requires covered employers to provide up to 12 weeks of unpaid, job-protected leave to "eligible" employees for certain family and medical reasons.

Employees are eligible if they have worked for a covered employer for at least one year, and for 1,250 hours over the previous 12 months, and if there are at least 50 employees within 75 miles.

Reasons For Taking Leave:

Unpaid leave must be granted for *any* of the following reasons:

- to care for the employee's child after birth, or placement for adoption or foster care;
- to care for the employee's spouse, son or daughter, or parent, who has a serious health condition; or
- for a serious health condition that makes the employee unable to perform the employee's job.

At the employee's or employer's option, certain kinds of *paid* leave may be substituted for unpaid leave.

Advance Notice and Medical Certification:

The employee may be required to provide advance leave notice and medical certification. Taking of leave may be denied if requirements are not met.

- The employee ordinarily must provide 30 days advance notice when the leave is "foreseeable."
- An employer may require medical certification to support a request for leave because of a serious health condition, and may require second or third opinions (at the employer's expense) and a fitness for duty report to return to work.

Job Benefits and Protection:

- For the duration of FMLA leave, the employer must maintain the employee's health coverage under any "group health plan."

- Upon return from FMLA leave, most employees must be restored to their original or equivalent positions with equivalent pay, benefits, and other employment terms.
- The use of FMLA leave cannot result in the loss of any employment benefit that accrued prior to the start of an employee's leave.

Unlawful Acts By Employers:

FMLA makes it unlawful for any employer to:

- interfere with, restrain, or deny the exercise of any right provided under FMLA:
- discharge or discriminate against any person for opposing any practice made unlawful by FMLA or for involvement in any proceeding under or relating to FMLA.

Enforcement:

- The U.S. Department of Labor is authorized to investigate and resolve complaints of violations.
- An eligible employee may bring a civil action against an employer for violations.

FMLA does not affect any Federal or State law prohibiting discrimination, or supersede any State or local law or collective bargaining agreement which provides greater family or medical leave rights.

For Additional Information:

Contact the nearest office of the Wage and Hour Division, listed in most telephone directories under U.S. Government, Department of Labor.

U.S. Department of Labor
Employment Standards Administration
Wage and Hour Division
Washington, D.C. 20210

WH Publication 1420
June 1993

U.S. GOVERNMENT PRINTING OFFICE:1996 171-169

An unusual situation exists for small public employers under the FMLA. Public agencies are covered by the FMLA regardless of whether they have fewer than 50 employees.[10] However, public employees are not exempt from the FMLA's requirement that to be covered, they must work for an employer that has 50 employees in a 75-mile area.[11] Thus, while employees of public agencies with less than 50 employees may have no right to sue under the FMLA, their employers – included by definition under the FMLA – must still comply with the FMLA's posting requirements.[12]

The FMLA's Recordkeeping Requirements.

The Statute: 29 U .S.C. §2616

(b) Obligation to keep and preserve records

Any employer shall make, keep, and preserve records pertaining to compliance with this subchapter in accordance with section 211(c) of this title and in accordance with regulations issued by the Secretary.

(c) Required submissions generally limited to annual basis

The Secretary shall not under the authority of this section require any employer or any plan, fund, or program to submit to the Secretary any books or records more than once during any 12-month period, unless the Secretary has reasonable cause to believe there may exist a violation of this subchapter or any regulation or order issued pursuant to this subchapter, or is investigating a charge pursuant to section 2617(b) of this title.

As with most federal labor laws, the FMLA's description of the records an employer is required to maintain is sparse at best, providing only that employers must maintain records in accordance with the DOL's regulations. The DOL's regulations, found at Section 825.500 of the Code of Federal Regulations, specify that no particular "order or form" of records is required, and allow for records to be maintained in electronic form. The DOL's regulations also mandate a minimum three-year retention period for records, and require that employers make the records available for inspection and copying by the DOL.[13]

Under Section 825.500(c) of the DOL's regulations, employers must maintain records of the following:

1. Basic payroll and identifying employee data, including name, address, and occupation; rate or basis of pay and terms of compensation; daily and weekly hours worked per pay period; additions to or deductions from wages; and total compensation paid.

2. The dates FMLA leave is taken by FMLA-eligible employees. Leave must be designated in records as FMLA leave; leave so designated may not include leave required under state law or an employer plan which is not also covered by FMLA.

3. If FMLA leave is taken by eligible employees in increments of less than one full day, the hours of the leave.

4. Copies of employee notices of leave furnished to the employer under the FMLA, if in writing, and copies of all general and specific written notices given to employees as required under the FMLA and the DOL's regulations. Copies of these notices may be maintained in employee personnel files.

5. Any documents (including written and electronic records) describing employee benefits or employer policies and practices regarding the taking of paid and unpaid leaves.

6. Premium payments of employee benefits.

7. Records of any dispute between the employer and an eligible employee regarding designation of leave as FMLA leave, including any written statement from the employer or employee of the reasons for the designation and for the disagreement.

The DOL's regulations even require employers with no eligible employees to maintain the records described in Paragraph 1, immediately above. Records and documents relating to medical certifications, recertifications or medical histories of employees or family members created for purposes of FMLA must be maintained as confidential medical records in separate files from the usual personnel files. Moreover, if the ADA applies to the same medical condition, records must be maintained in compliance with the ADA.[14]

To date, only one court has dealt with these recordkeeping requirements. In the case, a court was confronted with only fragmentary records kept by an employer. Noting that the employer's practice of keeping "absentee calendar" forms failed to distinguish between FMLA leave and sick leave, the Court observed that "if such forms are the only records kept by [the employer] of its employees' leave, and [the employer] does not distinguish between normal sick days and FMLA absences, then [the employer] would at the very least be in violation of the regulations governing an employer's maintenance of records in compliance with the FMLA."[15]

NOTES

1 *Lacoparra v. Pergament Home Centers, Inc.*, 982 F.Supp. 213 (S.D.N.Y. 1997); *see In-Sink-Erator, Division of Emerson Electric Co. v. Department of Industry, Labor and Human Relations*, 547 N.W.2d 792 (Wis.App. 1996)(discusses posting requirement under state law).

2 29 U.S.C. §2619(a).

3 29 C.F.R. §825.300(a).

4 29 C.F.R. §825.300(b); *see Satterfield v. Wal-Mart Stores*, 135 F.3d 973 (5th Cir. 1998).

5 *Knussman v. State of Maryland*, 16 F.Supp.2d 601 (D.Md. 1998), *rev'd on other grounds*, 272 F.3d 625 (4th Cir. 2001); *see Hendry v. GTE North, Inc.*, 896 F.Supp. 816 (N.D.Ind. 1995).

6 *Satterfield v. Wal-Mart Stores*, 135 F.3d 973 (5th Cir. 1998); *Gay v. Gilman Paper Co.*, 125 F.3d 1432 (11th Cir. 1997); *Mora v. Chem-Tronics*, 16 F.Supp.2d 1192 (S.D.Cal. 1998); *Knussman v. State of Maryland*, 16 F.Supp.2d 601 (D.Md. 1998), *rev'd on other grounds*, 272 F.3d 625 (4th Cir. 2001); *Reich v. Midwest Plastic Engineering*, Inc., 66 Empl. Prac. Dec. ¶ 43,701 (W.D.Mich. 1995).

7 See *Blumenthal v. Murray*, 946 F.Supp. 623 (N.D.Ill. 1996).

8 *Deily v. Waste Management of Allentown*, 118 F.Supp.2d 539 (E.D.Pa. 2000); *Antoine-Tubbs v. Local 513, Air Transport Division, Transport Workers Union of America*, 50 F.Supp.2d 601 (N.D.Tex. 1998); *Mora v. Chem-Tronics*, 16 F.Supp.2d 1192 (S.D.Cal. 1998); *Knussman v. Maryland*, 16 F.Supp.2d 601 (D.Md. 1998), *rev'd on other grounds*, 272 F.3d 625 (4th Cir. 2001); *Jessie v. Carter Healthcare Center, Inc.*, 926 F.Supp. 613 (E.D.Ky. 1996); *Hendry v. GTE North, Inc.*, 896 F.Supp. 816 (N.D.Ind. 1995).

9 *Mora v. Chem-Tronics*, 16 F.Supp.2d 1192 (S.D.Cal. 1998).

10 29 C.F.R. §825.104(b).

11 29 C.F.R. §825.108(d).

12 *Opinion Letter,* Wage and Hour Division, 1995 WL 1036733 (May 17, 1995)

13 29 C.F.R. §825.500(b).

14 29 C.F.R. §825.500(g).

15 *Slaughter v. American Building Maintenance Co. of New York*, 64 F.Supp.2d 319 (S.D.N.Y. 1999).

APPENDIX A

A GLOSSARY OF TERMS AND WHERE TO FIND FMLA RESOURCES

Though a reasonable, good faith effort was made to minimize the use of acronyms, jargon, and other occasionally unintelligible mnemonic devices in this book, it was impossible (at least for this author) to avoid it entirely. To assist the reader, the following table describes some of the more commonly used terms in this book:

Term	Description	Source
ADA	The Americans With Disabilities Act, the federal law prohibiting discrimination against qualified individuals with a disability.	42 U.S.C. §§12112
ADEA	The Age Discrimination in Employment Act, the federal law prohibiting age discrimination.	29 U.S.C. §621
C.F.R.	The Code of Federal Regulations, which contains the regulations issued by all federal agencies.	
ERISA	The Employee Retirement Income Security Act	29 U.S.C. §1002(16)(A)
FLSA	The Fair Labor Standards Act, the federal law that sets the minimum wage and requires the payment of overtime under certain conditions.	29 U.S.C. §207
PDA	The Pregnancy Discrimination Act, the federal statute prohibiting discrimination on the basis of pregnancy.	42 U.S.C. §2000e(k)
Title VII	Title VII of the Civil Rights Act of 1964, the basic federal anti-discrimination statute.	2 U.S.C. §2000e
U.S.C.	The United States Code, which contains all federal statutes.	

Where To Find The Court Decisions Cited In This Book.

For those unfamiliar with legal citation form, court decisions are cited in fairly typical volume/page format, and lead to the legal "reporters" (collections of decisions) where the case can be found. For example, one of the most important FMLA cases is the decision of the federal First Circuit Court of Appeals cited as *Hodgens v. General Dynamics Corporation*, 144 F.3d 151 (1st Cir. 1998). This citation tells the reader that the case involved a lawsuit by an individual named *Hodgens* (in FMLA cases, the employee is usually listed first in citations) against *General Dynamics Corporation*. The decision, issued by the *First Circuit* in *1998*, can be found on page *151* of volume *144* of the third series of the *Federal Reporter*. A trip to any law library or to many on-line legal research services will quickly take one to the Federal Reporter, allowing the reader to find the case. The following table lists the abbreviations used in the footnotes in this book.

LEGAL SOURCES USED IN THIS BOOK		
Abbreviation	Full Name	Publisher
A.2d	Atlantic Reporter, 2nd Series	West Group
A.L.R.	American Law Reporter	West Group
Cal.Rptr.	California Reporter	West Group
Cal.Rptr.2d	California Reporter, 2nd Series	West Group
C.F.R.	Code of Federal Regulations	Office of the Federal Register
F.2d	Federal Reporter, 2nd Series	West Group
F.3d	Federal Reporter, 3rd Series	West Group
F.Supp.	Federal Supplement	West Group
F.Supp.2d	Federal Supplement, 2nd Series	West Group
Fed. Reg.	Federal Register	Office of the Federal Register
FEP Cases	Fair Employment Practices Cases	Bureau of National Affairs (BNA)
F.R.D.	Federal Rules Decisions	West Group
GERR	Government Employee Relations Reporter	BNA
IER Cases	Individual Employee Rights Cases	BNA
LEXIS	Lexis Computer Database	LexisNexis
LRRM	Labor Relations Reference Manual	BNA
N.E.2d	Northeast Reporter, 2nd Series	West Group
NPER	National Public Employment Reporter	LRP Publications.
N.W.2d	Northwest Reporter, 2nd Series	West Group
N.Y.S.2d	New York Supplement Reporter, 2nd Series	West Group
P.2d	Pacific Reporter, 2nd Series	West Group
So.2d	Southern Reporter, 2nd Series	West Group
S.Ct.	Supreme Court Reporter	West Group
S.E.2d	Southeast Reporter, 2nd Series	West Group
U.S.	United States Reporter	West Group

U.S.C.	United States Code	Office of the Law Revision Counsel, U.S. House of Representatives
U.S.C.A.	United States Code Annotated	West Group
WH Cas.	Wage and Hour Cases	BNA
WL	Westlaw Computer Database	West Group

Legal citations not only follow a standard format, they often are preceded by modifying words that have specific meanings. The following table is taken from the bible of legal citation format, *The Bluebook: A Uniform System of Citation*, published by the Harvard Law Review and known colloquially as the "Bluebook" because of its occasionally blue cover:

See	Cited authority *directly states* or *clearly supports* the proposition set forth in the text.
See also	Cited authority *constitutes additional source material that supports* the proposition. "*See also*" is commonly used to cite an authority supporting a proposition when authorities that state or directly support the proposition already have been cited or discussed.
Cf.	Cited authority *supports a proposition different from the main proposition but sufficiently analogous to lend support.* Literally, "*cf.*" means "compare."
See generally	*Cited authority presents helpful background material related to the proposition.*

Today, locating court decisions is easier and less expensive than at any time in the past. Most court decisions of the last five years are available through the Internet without cost. The following table lists on-line resources for the most common sources of FMLA opinions:

On-Line FMLA Resources.

There is a tremendous wealth of information on the Internet concerning the FMLA. The following table summarizes some of the best on-line resources available:

Benefitsnext	A series of articles on compliance with the FMLA.	http://www.benefitsnext.com/Article_List.cfm/Nav/1.39.293.2
Commerce Clearing House	The "Business Owner's Toolkit" on the FMLA.	http://www.toolkit.cch.com/text/P05_4370.asp
Employer-Employee.com	A collection of articles on the FMLA, and information on how to order books on the FMLA.	http://www.employer-employee.com/fmla.html
Employment Law Information Network	A good short summary of the requirements of the FMLA.	http://www.elinfonet.com/FMLAsum.php
FMLA Survey and Information Site	A good collection of links and information on articles and other FMLA publications.	http://www.familyleavesurvey.homestead.com/FMLAHome.html
FMLA Technical Corrections Coalition	An advocacy page describing reasons why the publisher believes the FMLA should be amended.	http://www.workingforthefuture.org/
Hrnext	Several articles on FMLA compliance, as well as periodic discussion of FMLA cases.	http://www.hrnext.com/content/ subs.cfm?subs_id=144
HRTools.com	Several articles and forms related to the FMLA.	http://www.hrtools.com
International Foundation of Employee Benefit Plans	General and technical articles on the FMLA.	http://www.ifebp.org/
My Employment Lawyer	A series of questions and answers on the FMLA.	http://www.myemploymentlawyer.com/family-medical-leave-FAQs.htm
National Association of Letter Carriers	A series of forms for use with FMLA leave.	http://www.nalc.org/depart/cau/fmla.html

Parents Place	Questions and answers about the FMLA.	http://www.parentsplace.com
Strata Systems	"FMLA Pro" software to track FMLA issues.	http://www.fmla.com/
The Bonnett Group	"TBG FMLA" software.	http://www.tbginc.com/TBG_FMLA.htm
United States Department of Labor	The DOL's "FMLA Fact Sheet."	http://www.dol.gov/esa/regs/compliance/whd/whdfs28.htm
United States Department of Labor	The DOL's "Compliance Guide."	http://www.dol.gov/esa/regs/compliance/whd/1421.htm
United States Department of Labor	The DOL's FMLA Poster.	http://www.dol.gov/esa/regs/compliance/posters/fmla.htm
United States Department of Labor	The DOL's "Employer-Employee" Advisor on the FMLA.	http://www.dol.gov/elaws/fmla.htm

APPENDIX B

THE TEXT OF THE FMLA

The Text Of The FMLA.

What follows is the actual text of the FMLA as found in Title 29 of the United States Code. The United States Code can be accessed in virtually all law libraries and most public libraries. Good on-line resources to find the United States Code include the Legal Information Institute at Cornell Law School, located at http://www4.law.cornell.edu/uscode, and a web page maintained by the Government Printing Office, located at http://www.access.gpo.gov/congress/cong013.html.

THE FAMILY AND MEDICAL LEAVE ACT

Sec. 2601. Findings and purposes.

(a) Findings

Congress finds that -

(1) the number of single-parent households and two-parent households in which the single parent or both parents work is increasing significantly;

(2) it is important for the development of children and the family unit that fathers and mothers be able to participate in early childrearing and the care of family members who have serious health conditions;

(3) the lack of employment policies to accommodate working parents can force individuals to choose between job security and parenting;

(4) there is inadequate job security for employees who have serious health conditions that prevent them from working for temporary periods;

(5) due to the nature of the roles of men and women in our society, the primary responsibility for family caretaking often falls on women, and such responsibility affects the working lives of women more than it affects the working lives of men; and

(6) employment standards that apply to one gender only have serious potential for encouraging employers to discriminate against employees and applicants for employment who are of that gender.

(b) Purposes

It is the purpose of this Act -

(1) to balance the demands of the workplace with the needs of families, to promote the stability and economic security of families, and to promote national interests in preserving family integrity;

(2) to entitle employees to take reasonable leave for medical reasons, for the birth or adoption of a child, and for the care of a child, spouse, or parent who has a serious health condition;

(3) to accomplish the purposes described in paragraphs (1) and (2) in a manner that accommodates the legitimate interests of employers;

(4) to accomplish the purposes described in paragraphs (1) and (2) in a manner that, consistent with the Equal Protection Clause of the Fourteenth Amendment, minimizes the potential for employment discrimination on the basis of sex by ensuring generally that leave is available for eligible medical reasons (including maternity-related disability) and for compelling family reasons, on a gender-neutral basis; and

(5) to promote the goal of equal employment opportunity for women and men, pursuant to such clause.

Sec. 2611. Definitions

As used in this subchapter:

(1) Commerce

The terms "commerce" and "industry or activity affecting commerce" mean any activity, business, or industry in commerce or in which a labor dispute would hinder or obstruct commerce or the free flow of commerce, and include "commerce" and any "industry affecting commerce", as defined in paragraphs (1) and (3) of section 142 of this title.

(2) Eligible employee

(A) In general the term "eligible employee" means an employee who has been employed -

(i) for at least 12 months by the employer with respect to whom leave is requested under section 2612 of this title; and

(ii) for at least 1,250 hours of service with such employer during the previous 12-month period.

(B) Exclusions

The term "eligible employee" does not include -

(i) any Federal officer or employee covered under subchapter V of chapter 63 of title 5; or

(ii) any employee of an employer who is employed at a worksite at which such employer employs less than 50 employees if the total number of employees employed by that employer within 75 miles of that worksite is less than 50.

(C) Determination

For purposes of determining whether an employee meets the hours of service requirement specified in subparagraph (A)(ii), the legal standards established under section 207 of this title shall apply.

(3) Employ; employee; State

The terms "employ", "employee", and "State" have the same meanings given such terms in subsections (c), (e), and (g) of section 203 of this title.

(4) Employer

(A) In general

The term "employer" -

> (i) means any person engaged in commerce or in any industry or activity affecting commerce who employs 50 or more employees for each working day during each of 20 or more calendar work-weeks in the current or preceding calendar year;

> (ii) includes -

>> (I) any person who acts, directly or indirectly, in the interest of an employer to any of the employees of such employer; and (II) any successor in interest of an employer;

> (iii) includes any "public agency", as defined in section 203(x) of this title; and (iv) includes the General Accounting Office and the Library of Congress.

(B) Public agency

For purposes of subparagraph (A)(iii), a public agency shall be considered to be a person engaged in commerce or in an industry or activity affecting commerce.

(5) Employment benefits

The term "employment benefits" means all benefits provided or made available to employees by an employer, including group life insurance, health insurance, disability insurance, sick leave, annual leave, educational benefits, and pensions, regardless of whether such benefits are provided by a practice or written policy of an employer or through an "employee benefit plan", as defined in section 1002(3) of this title.

(6) Health care provider

The term "health care provider" means -

(A) a doctor of medicine or osteopathy who is authorized to practice medicine or surgery (as appropriate) by the State in which the doctor practices; or

(B) any other person determined by the Secretary to be capable of providing health care services.

(7) Parent

The term "parent" means the biological parent of an employee or an individual who stood in loco parentis to an employee when the employee was a son or daughter.

(8) Person

The term "person" has the same meaning given such term in section 203(a) of this title.

(9) Reduced leave schedule

The term "reduced leave schedule" means a leave schedule that reduces the usual number of hours per workweek, or hours per workday, of an employee.

(10) Secretary

The term "Secretary" means the Secretary of Labor.

(11) Serious health condition

The term "serious health condition" means an illness, injury, impairment, or physical or mental condition that involves -

  (A) inpatient care in a hospital, hospice, or residential medical care facility; or

  (B) continuing treatment by a health care provider.

(12) Son or daughter

The term "son or daughter" means a biological, adopted, or foster child, a stepchild, a legal ward, or a child of a person standing in loco parentis, who is -

  (A) under 18 years of age; or

  (B) 18 years of age or older and incapable of self-care because of a mental or physical disability.

(13) Spouse

The term "spouse" means a husband or wife, as the case may be.

Sec. 2612. Leave requirement

(a) In general

(1) Entitlement to leave

Subject to section 2613 of this title, an eligible employee shall be entitled to a total of 12 workweeks of leave during any 12-month period for one or more of the following:

  (A) Because of the birth of a son or daughter of the employee and in order to care for such son or daughter.

  (B) Because of the placement of a son or daughter with the employee for adoption or foster care.

  (C) In order to care for the spouse, or a son, daughter, or parent, of the employee, if such spouse, son, daughter, or parent has a serious health condition.

  (D) Because of a serious health condition that makes the employee unable to perform the functions of the position of such employee.

(2) Expiration of entitlement

The entitlement to leave under subparagraphs (A) and (B) of paragraph (1) for a birth or placement of a son or daughter shall expire at the end of the 12-month period beginning on the date of such birth or placement.

(b) Leave taken intermittently or on reduced leave schedule

(1) In general

Leave under subparagraph (A) or (B) of subsection (a)(1) of this section shall not be taken by an employee intermittently or on a reduced leave schedule unless the employee and the employer of the employee agree otherwise. Subject to paragraph (2), subsection (e)(2) of this section, and section 2613(b)(5) of this title, leave under subparagraph (C) or (D) of subsection (a)(1) of this section may be taken intermittently or on a reduced leave schedule when medically necessary. The taking of leave intermittently or on a reduced leave schedule pursuant to this paragraph shall not result in a reduction in the total amount of leave to which the employee is entitled under subsection (a) of this section beyond the amount of leave actually taken.

(2) Alternative position

If an employee requests intermittent leave, or leave on a reduced leave schedule, under subparagraph (C) or (D) of subsection (a)(1) of this section, that is foreseeable based on planned medical treatment, the employer may require such employee to transfer temporarily to an available alternative position offered by the employer for which the employee is qualified and that -

> (A) has equivalent pay and benefits; and (B) better accommodates recurring periods of leave than the regular employment position of the employee.

(c) Unpaid leave permitted

Except as provided in subsection (d) of this section, leave granted under subsection (a) may consist of unpaid leave. Where an employee is otherwise exempt under regulations issued by the Secretary pursuant to section 213(a)(1) of this title, the compliance of an employer with this subchapter by providing unpaid leave shall not affect the exempt status of the employee under such section.

(d) Relationship to paid leave

(1) Unpaid leave

If an employer provides paid leave for fewer than 12 workweeks, the additional weeks of leave necessary to attain the 12 workweeks of leave required under this subchapter may be provided without compensation.

(2) Substitution of paid leave

> (A) In general

> An eligible employee may elect, or an employer may require the employee, to substitute any of the accrued paid vacation leave, personal leave, or family leave of the employee for leave provided under subparagraph (A), (B), or (C) of subsection (a)(1) of this section for any part of the 12-week period of such leave under such subsection.

> (B) Serious health condition

> An eligible employee may elect, or an employer may require the employee, to substitute any of the accrued paid vacation leave, personal leave, or medical or sick leave of the employee for leave provided

under subparagraph (C) or (D) of subsection (a)(1) of this section for any part of the 12-week period of such leave under such subsection, except that nothing in this subchapter shall require an employer to provide paid sick leave or paid medical leave in any situation in which such employer would not normally provide any such paid leave.

(e) Foreseeable leave

(1) Requirement of notice

In any case in which the necessity for leave under subparagraph (A) or (B) of subsection (a)(1) of this section is foreseeable based on an expected birth or placement, the employee shall provide the employer with not less than 30 days' notice, before the date the leave is to begin, of the employee's intention to take leave under such subparagraph, except that if the date of the birth or placement requires leave to begin in less than 30 days, the employee shall provide such notice as is practicable.

(2) Duties of employee

In any case in which the necessity for leave under subparagraph (C) or (D) of subsection (a)(1) of this section is foreseeable based on planned medical treatment, the employee -

> (A) shall make a reasonable effort to schedule the treatment so as not to disrupt unduly the operations of the employer, subject to the approval of the health care provider of the employee or the health care provider of the son, daughter, spouse, or parent of the employee, as appropriate; and (B) shall provide the employer with not less than 30 days' notice, before the date the leave is to begin, of the employee's intention to take leave under such subparagraph, except that if the date of the treatment requires leave to begin in less than 30 days, the employee shall provide such notice as is practicable.

(f) Spouses employed by same employer

In any case in which a husband and wife entitled to leave under subsection (a) of this section are employed by the same employer, the aggregate number of workweeks of leave to which both may be entitled may be limited to 12 workweeks during any 12-month period, if such leave is taken -

(1) under subparagraph (A) or (B) of subsection (a)(1) of this section; or

(2) to care for a sick parent under subparagraph (C) of such subsection.

Sec. 2613. Certification

(a) In general

An employer may require that a request for leave under subparagraph (C) or (D) of section 2612(a)(1) of this title be supported by a certification issued by the health care provider of the eligible employee or of the son, daughter, spouse, or parent of the employee, as appropriate. The employee shall provide, in a timely manner, a copy of such certification to the employer.

(b) Sufficient certification

Certification provided under subsection (a) of this section shall be sufficient if it states -

(1) the date on which the serious health condition commenced;

(2) the probable duration of the condition;

(3) the appropriate medical facts within the knowledge of the health care provider regarding the condition;

(4)

(A) for purposes of leave under section 2612(a)(1)(C) of this title, a statement that the eligible employee is needed to care for the son, daughter, spouse, or parent and an estimate of the amount of time that such employee is needed to care for the son, daughter, spouse, or parent; and (B) for purposes of leave under section 2612(a)(1)(D) of this title, a statement that the employee is unable to perform the functions of the position of the employee;

(5) in the case of certification for intermittent leave, or leave on a reduced leave schedule, for planned medical treatment, the dates on which such treatment is expected to be given and the duration of such treatment;

(6) in the case of certification for intermittent leave, or leave on a reduced leave schedule, under section 2612(a)(1)(D) of this title, a statement of the medical necessity for the intermittent leave or leave on a reduced leave schedule, and the expected duration of the intermittent leave or reduced leave schedule; and

(7) in the case of certification for intermittent leave, or leave on a reduced leave schedule, under section 2612(a)(1)(C) of this title, a statement that the employee's intermittent leave or leave on a reduced leave schedule is necessary for the care of the son, daughter, parent, or spouse who has a serious health condition, or will assist in their recovery, and the expected duration and schedule of the intermittent leave or reduced leave schedule.

(c) Second opinion

(1) In general

In any case in which the employer has reason to doubt the validity of the certification provided under subsection (a) of this section for leave under subparagraph (C) or (D) of section 2612(a)(1) of this title, the employer may require, at the expense of the employer, that the eligible employee obtain the opinion of a second health care provider designated or approved by the employer concerning any information certified under subsection (b) of this section for such leave.

(2) Limitation

A health care provider designated or approved under paragraph (1) shall not be employed on a regular basis by the employer.

(d) Resolution of conflicting opinions

(1) In general

In any case in which the second opinion described in subsection (c) of this section differs from the opinion in the original certification provided under subsection (a) of this section, the employer may require, at the expense of the employer, that the employee obtain the opinion of a third health care provider designated or approved jointly by the employer and the employee concerning the information certified under subsection (b) of this section.

(2) Finality

The opinion of the third health care provider concerning the information certified under subsection (b) of this section shall be considered to be final and shall be binding on the employer and the employee.

(e) Subsequent recertification

The employer may require that the eligible employee obtain subsequent recertifications on a reasonable basis.

Sec. 2614. Employment and benefits protection

(a) Restoration to position

(1) In general

Except as provided in subsection (b) of this section, any eligible employee who takes leave under section 2612 of this title for the intended purpose of the leave shall be entitled, on return from such leave -

(A) to be restored by the employer to the position of employment held by the employee when the leave commenced; or

(B) to be restored to an equivalent position with equivalent employment benefits, pay, and other terms and conditions of employment.

(2) Loss of benefits

The taking of leave under section 2612 of this title shall not result in the loss of any employment benefit accrued prior to the date on which the leave commenced.

(3) Limitations Nothing in this section shall be construed to entitle any restored employee to -

(A) the accrual of any seniority or employment benefits during any period of leave; or

(B) any right, benefit, or position of employment other than any right, benefit, or position to which the employee would have been entitled had the employee not taken the leave.

(4) Certification

As a condition of restoration under paragraph (1) for an employee who has taken leave under section 2612(a)(1)(D) of this title, the employer may have a uniformly applied practice or policy that requires each such employee to receive certification from the health care provider of the employee that the employee is able to resume work, except that nothing in this paragraph shall supersede a valid State or local law or a collective bargaining agreement that governs the return to work of such employees.

(5) Construction

Nothing in this subsection shall be construed to prohibit an employer from requiring an employee on leave under section 2612 of this title to report periodically to the employer on the status and intention of the employee to return to work.

(b) Exemption concerning certain highly compensated employees

(1) Denial of restoration

An employer may deny restoration under subsection (a) of this section to any eligible employee described in paragraph (2) if -

   (A) such denial is necessary to prevent substantial and grievous economic injury to the operations of the employer;

   (B) the employer notifies the employee of the intent of the employer to deny restoration on such basis at the time the employer determines that such injury would occur; and

   (C) in any case in which the leave has commenced, the employee elects not to return to employment after receiving such notice.

(2) Affected employees

An eligible employee described in paragraph (1) is a salaried eligible employee who is among the highest paid 10 percent of the employees employed by the employer within 75 miles of the facility at which the employee is employed.

(c) Maintenance of health benefits

(1) Coverage

Except as provided in paragraph (2), during any period that an eligible employee takes leave under section 2612 of this title, the employer shall maintain coverage under any "group health plan" (as defined in section 5000(b)(1) of title 26) for the duration of such leave at the level and under the conditions coverage would have been provided if the employee had continued in employment continuously for the duration of such leave.

(2) Failure to return from leave

The employer may recover the premium that the employer paid for maintaining coverage for the employee under such group health plan during any period of unpaid leave under section 2612 of this title if -

   (A) the employee fails to return from leave under section 2612 of this title after the period of leave to which the employee is entitled has expired; and

   (B) the employee fails to return to work for a reason other than -

      (i) the continuation, recurrence, or onset of a serious health condition that entitles the employee to leave under subparagraph (C) or (D) of section 2612(a)(1) of this title; or

      (ii) other circumstances beyond the control of the employee.

(3) Certification

(A) Issuance

An employer may require that a claim that an employee is unable to return to work because of the continuation, recurrence, or onset of the serious health condition described in paragraph (2)(B)(i) be supported by -

> (i) a certification issued by the health care provider of the son, daughter, spouse, or parent of the employee, as appropriate, in the case of an employee unable to return to work because of a condition specified in section 2612(a)(1)(C) of this title; or

> (ii) a certification issued by the health care provider of the eligible employee, in the case of an employee unable to return to work because of a condition specified in section 2612(a)(1)(D) of this title.

(B) Copy

The employee shall provide, in a timely manner, a copy of such certification to the employer.

(C) Sufficiency of certification

> (i) Leave due to serious health condition of employee The certification described in subparagraph (A)(ii) shall be sufficient if the certification states that a serious health condition prevented the employee from being able to perform the functions of the position of the employee on the date that the leave of the employee expired.

> (ii) Leave due to serious health condition of family member The certification described in subparagraph (A)(i) shall be sufficient if the certification states that the employee is needed to care for the son, daughter, spouse, or parent who has a serious health condition on the date that the leave of the employee expired.

Sec. 2615. Prohibited acts

(a) Interference with rights

(1) Exercise of rights

It shall be unlawful for any employer to interfere with, restrain, or deny the exercise of or the attempt to exercise, any right provided under this subchapter.

(2) Discrimination

It shall be unlawful for any employer to discharge or in any other manner discriminate against any individual for opposing any practice made unlawful by this subchapter.

(b) Interference with proceedings or inquiries

It shall be unlawful for any person to discharge or in any other manner discriminate against any individual because such individual -

(1) has filed any charge, or has instituted or caused to be instituted any proceeding, under or related to this subchapter;

(2) has given, or is about to give, any information in connection with any inquiry or proceeding relating to any right provided under this subchapter; or

(3) has testified, or is about to testify, in any inquiry or proceeding relating to any right provided under this subchapter.

Sec. 2616. Investigative authority

(a) In general

To ensure compliance with the provisions of this subchapter, or any regulation or order issued under this subchapter, the Secretary shall have, subject to subsection (c) of this section, the investigative authority provided under section 211(a) of this title.

(b) Obligation to keep and preserve records

Any employer shall make, keep, and preserve records pertaining to compliance with this subchapter in accordance with section 211(c) of this title and in accordance with regulations issued by the Secretary.

(c) Required submissions generally limited to annual basis

The Secretary shall not under the authority of this section require any employer or any plan, fund, or program to submit to the Secretary any books or records more than once during any 12-month period, unless the Secretary has reasonable cause to believe there may exist a violation of this subchapter or any regulation or order issued pursuant to this subchapter, or is investigating a charge pursuant to section 2617(b) of this title.

(d) Subpoena powers

For the purposes of any investigation provided for in this section, the Secretary shall have the subpoena authority provided for under section 209 of this title.

Sec. 2617. Enforcement

(a) Civil action by employees

(1) Liability

Any employer who violates section 2615 of this title shall be liable to any eligible employee affected -

(A) for damages equal to -

(i) the amount of -

(I) any wages, salary, employment benefits, or other compensation denied or lost to such employee by reason of the violation; or

(II) in a case in which wages, salary, employment benefits, or other compensation have not been denied or lost to the employee, any actual monetary losses sustained by the employee as a direct result of the violation, such as the cost of providing care, up to a sum equal to 12 weeks of wages or salary for the employee;

(ii) the interest on the amount described in clause (i) calculated at the prevailing rate; and

(iii) an additional amount as liquidated damages equal to the sum of the amount described in clause (i) and the interest described in clause (ii), except that if an employer who has violated section 2615 of this title proves to the satisfaction of the court that the act or omission which violated section 2615 of this title was in good faith and that the employer had reasonable grounds for believing that the act or omission was not a violation of section 2615 of this title, such court may, in the discretion of the court, reduce the amount of the liability to the amount and interest determined under clauses (i) and (ii), respectively; and

(B) for such equitable relief as may be appropriate, including employment, reinstatement, and promotion.

(2) Right of action

An action to recover the damages or equitable relief prescribed in paragraph (1) may be maintained against any employer (including a public agency) in any Federal or State court of competent jurisdiction by any one or more employees for and in behalf of -

(A) the employees; or

(B) the employees and other employees similarly situated.

(3) Fees and costs

The court in such an action shall, in addition to any judgment awarded to the plaintiff, allow a reasonable attorney's fee, reasonable expert witness fees, and other costs of the action to be paid by the defendant.

(4) Limitations

The right provided by paragraph (2) to bring an action by or on behalf of any employee shall terminate -

(A) on the filing of a complaint by the Secretary in an action under subsection (d) of this section in which restraint is sought of any further delay in the payment of the amount described in paragraph (1)(A) to such employee by an employer responsible under paragraph (1) for the payment; or

(B) on the filing of a complaint by the Secretary in an action under subsection (b) of this section in which a recovery is sought of the damages described in paragraph (1)(A) owing to an eligible employee by an employer liable under paragraph (1), unless the action described in subparagraph (A) or (B) is dismissed without prejudice on motion of the Secretary.

(b) Action by Secretary

(1) Administrative action

The Secretary shall receive, investigate, and attempt to resolve complaints of violations of section 2615 of this title in the same manner that the

Secretary receives, investigates, and attempts to resolve complaints of violations of sections 206 and 207 of this title.

(2) Civil action

The Secretary may bring an action in any court of competent jurisdiction to recover the damages described in subsection (a)(1)(A) of this section.

(3) Sums recovered

Any sums recovered by the Secretary pursuant to paragraph (2) shall be held in a special deposit account and shall be paid, on order of the Secretary, directly to each employee affected. Any such sums not paid to an employee because of inability to do so within a period of 3 years shall be deposited into the Treasury of the United States as miscellaneous receipts.

(c) Limitation

(1) In general

Except as provided in paragraph (2), an action may be brought under this section not later than 2 years after the date of the last event constituting the alleged violation for which the action is brought.

(2) Willful violation

In the case of such action brought for a willful violation of section 2615 of this title, such action may be brought within 3 years of the date of the last event constituting the alleged violation for which such action is brought.

(3) Commencement

In determining when an action is commenced by the Secretary under this section for the purposes of this subsection, it shall be considered to be commenced on the date when the complaint is filed.

(d) Action for injunction by Secretary

The district courts of the United States shall have jurisdiction, for cause shown, in an action brought by the Secretary -

(1) to restrain violations of section 2615 of this title, including the restraint of any withholding of payment of wages, salary, employment benefits, or other compensation, plus interest, found by the court to be due to eligible employees; or

(2) to award such other equitable relief as may be appropriate, including employment, reinstatement, and promotion.

(e) Solicitor of Labor

The Solicitor of Labor may appear for and represent the Secretary on any litigation brought under this section.

(f) General Accounting Office and Library of Congress

In the case of the General Accounting Office and the Library of Congress, the authority of the Secretary of Labor under this subchapter shall be exercised respectively by the Comptroller General of the United States and the Librarian of Congress.

Sec. 2618. Special rules concerning employees of local educational agencies

(a) Application

(1) In general

Except as otherwise provided in this section, the rights (including the rights under section 2614 of this title, which shall extend throughout the period of leave of any employee under this section), remedies, and procedures under this subchapter shall apply to -

> (A) any "local educational agency" (as defined in section 8801 of title 20) and an eligible employee of the agency; and (B) any private elementary or secondary school and an eligible employee of the school.

(2) Definitions

For purposes of the application described in paragraph (1):

> (A) Eligible employee
>
> The term "eligible employee" means an eligible employee of an agency or school described in paragraph (1).
>
> (B) Employer
>
> The term "employer" means an agency or school described in paragraph (1).

(b) Leave does not violate certain other Federal laws

A local educational agency and a private elementary or secondary school shall not be in violation of the Individuals with Disabilities Education Act (20 U.S.C. 1400 et seq.), section 794 of this title), or title VI of the Civil Rights Act of 1964 (42 U.S.C. 2000d et seq.), solely as a result of an eligible employee of such agency or school exercising the rights of such employee under this subchapter.

(c) Intermittent leave or leave on reduced schedule for instructional employees

(1) In general

Subject to paragraph (2), in any case in which an eligible employee employed principally in an instructional capacity by any such educational agency or school requests leave under subparagraph (C) or (D) of section 2612(a)(1) of this title that is foreseeable based on planned medical treatment and the employee would be on leave for greater than 20 percent of the total number of working days in the period during which the leave would extend, the agency or school may require that such employee elect either -

> (A) to take leave for periods of a particular duration, not to exceed the duration of the planned medical treatment; or
>
> (B) to transfer temporarily to an available alternative position offered by the employer for which the employee is qualified, and that -

(i) has equivalent pay and benefits; and (ii) better accommodates recurring periods of leave than the regular employment position of the employee.

(2) Application

The elections described in subparagraphs (A) and (B) of paragraph (1) shall apply only with respect to an eligible employee who complies with section 2612(e)(2) of this title.

(d) Rules applicable to periods near conclusion of academic term

The following rules shall apply with respect to periods of leave near the conclusion of an academic term in the case of any eligible employee employed principally in an instructional capacity by any such educational agency or school:

(1) Leave more than 5 weeks prior to end of term

If the eligible employee begins leave under section 2612 of this title more than 5 weeks prior to the end of the academic term, the agency or school may require the employee to continue taking leave until the end of such term, if -

(A) the leave is of at least 3 weeks duration; and (B) the return to employment would occur during the 3-week period before the end of such term.

(2) Leave less than 5 weeks prior to end of term

If the eligible employee begins leave under subparagraph (A), that commences 5 weeks prior to the end of the academic term, the agency or school may require the employee to continue taking leave until the end of such term, if -

(A) the leave is of greater than 2 weeks duration; and (B) the return to employment would occur during the 2-week period before the end of such term.

(3) Leave less than 3 weeks prior to end of term

If the eligible employee begins leave under subparagraph (A), that commences 3 weeks prior to the end of the academic term and the duration of the leave is greater than 5 working days, the agency or school may require the employee to continue to take leave until the end of such term.

(e) Restoration to equivalent employment position

For purposes of determinations under section 2614(a)(1)(B) of this title (relating to the restoration of an eligible employee to an equivalent position), in the case of a local educational agency or a private elementary or secondary school, such determination shall be made on the basis of established school board policies and practices, private school policies and practices, and collective bargaining agreements.

(f) Reduction of amount of liability

If a local educational agency or a private elementary or secondary school that has violated this subchapter proves to the satisfaction of the court that the agency, school, or department had reasonable grounds for believing that the underlying act or omission was not a violation of this subchapter, such court may, in the discretion of the court, reduce the amount of the liability provided for under section 2617(a)(1)(A) of this title to the amount and interest determined under clauses (i) and (ii), respectively, of such section.

Sec. 2619. Notice

(a) In general

Each employer shall post and keep posted, in conspicuous places on the premises of the employer where notices to employees and applicants for employment are customarily posted, a notice, to be prepared or approved by the Secretary, setting forth excerpts from, or summaries of, the pertinent provisions of this subchapter and information pertaining to the filing of a charge.

(b) Penalty

Any employer that willfully violates this section may be assessed a civil money penalty not to exceed $100 for each separate offense.

Sec. 2651. Effect on other laws

(a) Federal and State antidiscrimination laws

Nothing in this Act or any amendment made by this Act shall be construed to modify or affect any Federal or State law prohibiting discrimination on the basis of race, religion, color, national origin, sex, age, or disability.

(b) State and local laws

Nothing in this Act or any amendment made by this Act shall be construed to supersede any provision of any State or local law that provides greater family or medical leave rights than the rights established under this Act or any amendment made by this Act.

Sec. 2652. Effect on existing employment benefits

(a) More protective

Nothing in this Act or any amendment made by this Act shall be construed to diminish the obligation of an employer to comply with any collective bargaining agreement or any employment benefit program or plan that provides greater family or medical leave rights to employees than the rights established under this Act or any amendment made by this Act.

(b) Less protective

The rights established for employees under this Act or any amendment made by this Act shall not be diminished by any collective bargaining agreement or any employment benefit program or plan.

Sec. 2653. Encouragement of more generous leave policies

Nothing in this Act or any amendment made by this Act shall be construed to discourage employers from adopting or retaining leave policies more generous than any policies that comply with the requirements under this Act or any amendment made by this Act.

Sec. 2654. Regulations

The Secretary of Labor shall prescribe such regulations as are necessary to carry out subchapter I of this chapter and this subchapter not later than 120 days after February 5, 1993.

APPENDIX C

FMLA REGULATIONS

The DOL's regulations interpreting and applying the FMLA are, for federal regulations, unusually clear, straightforward, and lucid. Just kidding. What follows is the complete text of those regulations.

Section Number: 825.100

Section Name: What is the Family and Medical Leave Act?

(a) The Family and Medical Leave Act of 1993 (FMLA or Act) allows "eligible" employees of a covered employer to take job-protected, unpaid leave, or to substitute appropriate paid leave if the employee has earned or accrued it, for up to a total of 12 workweeks in any 12 months because of the birth of a child and to care for the newborn child, because of the placement of a child with the employee for adoption or foster care, because the employee is needed to care for a family member (child, spouse, or parent) with a serious health condition, or because the employee's own serious health condition makes the employee unable to perform the functions of his or her job (see Sec. 825.306(b)(4)). In certain cases, this leave may be taken on an intermittent basis rather than all at once, or the employee may work a part-time schedule.

(b) An employee on FMLA leave is also entitled to have health benefits maintained while on leave as if the employee had continued to work instead of taking the leave. If an employee was paying all or part of the premium payments prior to leave, the employee would continue to pay his or her share during the leave period. The employer may recover its share only if the employee does not return to work for a reason other than the serious health condition of the employee or the employee's immediate family member, or another reason beyond the employee's control.

(c) An employee generally has a right to return to the same position or an equivalent position with equivalent pay, benefits and working conditions at the conclusion of the leave. The taking of FMLA leave cannot result in the loss of any benefit that accrued prior to the start of the leave.

(d) The employer has a right to 30 days advance notice from the employee where practicable. In addition, the employer may require an employee to submit certification from a health care provider to substantiate that the leave is due to the serious health condition of the employee or the employee's immediate family member. Failure to comply with these requirements may result in a delay in the start of FMLA leave. Pursuant to a uniformly applied policy, the employer may also require that an employee present a certification of fitness to return to work when the absence was caused by the employee's serious health condition (see Sec. 825.311(c)). The employer may delay restoring the employee to employment without such certificate relating to the health condition which caused the employee's absence. [60 FR 2237, Jan. 6, 1995; 60 FR 16383, Mar. 30, 1995]

Section Number: 825.101

Section Name: What is the purpose of the Act?

(a) FMLA is intended to allow employees to balance their work and family life by taking reasonable unpaid leave for medical reasons, for the birth or adoption of a child, and for the care of a child, spouse, or parent who has a serious health condition. The Act is intended to balance the demands of the workplace with the needs of families, to promote the stability and economic security of families, and to promote national interests in preserving family integrity. It was intended that the Act accomplish these purposes in a manner that accommodates the legitimate interests of employers, and in a manner consistent with the Equal Protection Clause of the Fourteenth Amendment in minimizing the potential for employment discrimination on the basis of sex, while promoting equal employment opportunity for men and women.

(b) The enactment of FMLA was predicated on two fundamental concerns – the needs of the American workforce, and the development of high-performance organizations. Increasingly, America's children and elderly are dependent upon family members who must spend long hours at work. When a family emergency arises, requiring workers to attend to seriously-ill children or parents, or to newly-born or adopted infants, or even to their own serious illness, workers need reassurance that they will not be asked to choose between continuing their employment, and meeting their personal and family obligations or tending to vital needs at home.

(c) The FMLA is both intended and expected to benefit employers as well as their employees. A direct correlation exists between stability in the family and productivity in the workplace. FMLA will encourage the development of high-performance organizations. When workers can count on durable links to their workplace they are able to make their own full commitments to their jobs. The record of hearings on family and medical leave indicate the powerful productive advantages of stable workplace relationships, and the comparatively small costs of guaranteeing that those relationships will not be dissolved while workers attend to pressing family health obligations or their own serious illness.

Section Number: 825.102

Section Name: When was the Act effective?

(a) The Act became effective on August 5, 1993, for most employers. If a collective bargaining agreement was in effect on that date, the Act's effective date was delayed until February 5, 1994, or the date the agreement expired, whichever date occurred sooner. This delayed effective date was applicable only to employees covered by a collective bargaining agreement that was in effect on August 5, 1993, and not, for example, to employees outside the bargaining unit. Application of FMLA to collective bargaining agreements is discussed further in Sec. 825.700(c).

(b) The period prior to the Act's effective date must be considered in determining employer coverage and employee eligibility. For example, as discussed further below, an employer with no collective bargaining agreements in effect as of August 5, 1993, must count employees/ workweeks for calendar year 1992 and calendar year 1993. If 50 or more employees were employed during 20 or more workweeks in either 1992 or 1993 (through August 5, 1993), the employer was covered under FMLA on August 5, 1993. If not, the employer was not covered on August 5, 1993, but must continue to monitor employment levels each workweek remaining in 1993 and thereafter to determine if and when it might become covered.

Section Number: 825.103

Section Name: How did the Act affect leave in progress on, or taken before, the effective date of the Act?

(a) An eligible employee's right to take FMLA leave began on the date that the Act went into effect for the employer (see the discussion of differing effective dates for collective bargaining agreements in Secs. 825.102(a) and 825.700(c)). Any leave taken prior to the Act's effective date may not be counted for purposes of FMLA. If leave qualifying as FMLA leave was underway prior to the effective date of the Act and continued after the Act's effective date, only that portion of leave taken on or after the Act's effective date may be counted against the employee's leave entitlement under the FMLA.

(b) If an employer-approved leave was underway when the Act took effect, no further notice would be required of the employee unless the employee requested an extension of the leave. For leave which commenced on the effective date or shortly thereafter, such notice must have been given which was practicable, considering the foreseeability of the need for leave and the effective date of the statute.

(c) Starting on the Act's effective date, an employee is entitled to FMLA leave if the reason for the leave is qualifying under the Act, even if the event occasioning the need for leave (e.g., the birth of a child) occurred before the effective date (so long as any other requirements are satisfied).

Section Number: 825.104

Section Name: What employers are covered by the Act?

(a) An employer covered by FMLA is any person engaged in commerce or in any industry or activity affecting commerce, who employs 50 or more employees for each working day during each of 20 or more calendar workweeks in the current or preceding calendar year. Employers covered by FMLA also include any person acting, directly or indirectly, in the interest of a covered employer to any of the employees of the employer, any successor in interest of a covered employer, and any public agency. Public agencies are covered employers without regard to the number of employees employed. Public as well as private elementary and secondary schools are also covered employers without regard to the number of employees employed. (See Sec. 825.600.)

(b) The terms "commerce" and "industry affecting commerce" are defined in accordance with section 501(1) and (3) of the Labor Management Relations Act of 1947 (LMRA) (29 U.S.C. 142 (1) and (3)), as set forth in the definitions at section 825.800 of this part. For purposes of the FMLA, employers who meet the 50-employee coverage test are deemed to be engaged in commerce or in an industry or activity affecting commerce.

(c) Normally the legal entity which employs the employee is the employer under FMLA. Applying this principle, a corporation is a single employer rather than its separate establishments or divisions.

(1) Where one corporation has an ownership interest in another corporation, it is a separate employer unless it meets the "joint employment" test discussed in Sec. 825.106, or the "integrated employer" test contained in paragraph (c)(2) of this section.

(2) Separate entities will be deemed to be parts of a single employer for purposes of FMLA if they meet the "integrated employer" test. Where this test is met, the employees of all entities making up the integrated employer will be counted in determining employer coverage and employee eligibility. A determination of whether or not separate entities are an integrated employer is not determined by the application of any single criterion, but rather the entire relationship is to be reviewed in its totality. Factors considered in determining whether two or more entities are an integrated employer include:

(i) Common management;

(ii) Interrelation between operations;

(iii) Centralized control of labor relations; and

(iv) Degree of common ownership/financial control.

(d) An "employer" includes any person who acts directly or indirectly in the interest of an employer to any of the employer's employees. The definition of "employer" in section 3(d) of the Fair Labor Standards Act (FLSA), 29 U.S.C. 203(d), similarly includes any person acting directly or indirectly in the interest of an employer in relation to an employee. As under the FLSA, individuals such as corporate officers "acting in the interest of an employer" are individually liable for any violations of the requirements of FMLA.

Section Number: 825.105

Section Name: In determining whether an employer is covered by FMLA, what

does it mean to employ 50 or more employees for each working day during each of 20 or more calendar workweeks in the current or preceding calendar year?

(a) The definition of "employ" for purposes of FMLA is taken from the Fair Labor Standards Act, Sec. 3(g). The courts have made it clear that the employment relationship under the FLSA is broader than the traditional common law concept of master and servant. The difference between the employment relationship under the FLSA and that under the common law arises from the fact that the term "employ" as defined in the Act includes "to suffer or permit to work". The courts have indicated that, while "to permit" requires a more positive action than "to suffer", both terms imply much less positive action than required by the common law. Mere knowledge by an employer of work done for the employer by another is sufficient to create the employment relationship under the Act. The courts have said that there is no definition that solves all problems as to the limitations of the employer-employee relationship under the Act; and that determination of the relation cannot be based on "isolated factors" or upon a single characteristic or "technical concepts", but depends "upon the circumstances of the whole activity" including the underlying "economic reality." In general an employee, as distinguished from an independent contractor who is engaged in a business of his/her own, is one who "follows the usual path of an employee" and is dependent on the business which he/she serves.

(b) Any employee whose name appears on the employer's payroll will be considered employed each working day of the calendar week, and must be counted whether or not any compensation is received for the week. However, the FMLA applies only to employees who are employed within any State of the United States, the District of Columbia or any Territory or possession of the United States. Employees who are employed outside these areas are not counted for purposes of determining employer coverage or employee eligibility.

(c) Employees on paid or unpaid leave, including FMLA leave, leaves of absence, disciplinary suspension, etc., are counted as long as the employer has a reasonable expectation that the employee will later return to active employment. If there is no employer/employee relationship (as when an employee is laid off, whether temporarily or permanently) such individual is not counted. Part-time employees, like full-time employees, are considered to be employed each working day of the calendar week, as long as they are maintained on the payroll.

(d) An employee who does not begin to work for an employer until after the first working day of a calendar week, or who terminates employment before the last working day of a calendar week, is not considered employed on each working day of that calendar week.

(e) A private employer is covered if it maintained 50 or more employees on the payroll during 20 or more calendar workweeks (not necessarily consecutive workweeks) in either the current or the preceding calendar year.

(f) Once a private employer meets the 50 employees/20 workweeks threshold, the employer remains covered until it reaches a future point where it no longer has employed 50 employees for 20 (nonconsecutive) workweeks in the current and preceding calendar year. For example, if an employer who met the 50 employees/20 workweeks test in the calendar year as of August 5, 1993, subsequently dropped below 50 employees before the end of 1993 and continued to employ fewer than 50 employees in all workweeks throughout calendar year 1994, the employer would continue to be covered throughout calendar year 1994 because it met the coverage criteria for 20 workweeks of the preceding (i.e., 1993) calendar year.

Section Number: 825.106

Section Name: How is "joint employment" treated under FMLA?

(a) Where two or more businesses exercise some control over the work or working conditions of the employee, the businesses may be joint employers under FMLA. Joint employers may be separate and distinct entities with separate owners, managers and facilities. Where the employee performs work which simultaneously benefits two or more employers, or works for two or more employers at different times during the workweek, a joint employment relationship generally will be considered to exist in situations such as:

(1) Where there is an arrangement between employers to share an employee's services or to interchange employees;

(2) Where one employer acts directly or indirectly in the interest of the other employer in relation to the employee; or,

(3) Where the employers are not completely disassociated with respect to the employee's employment and may be deemed to share control of the employee, directly or indirectly, because one employer controls, is controlled by, or is under common control with the other employer.

(b) A determination of whether or not a joint employment relationship exists is not determined by the application of any single criterion, but rather the entire relationship is to be viewed in its totality. For example, joint employment will ordinarily be found to exist when a temporary or leasing agency supplies employees to a second employer.

(c) In joint employment relationships, only the primary employer is responsible for giving required notices to its employees, providing FMLA leave, and maintenance of health benefits. Factors considered in determining which is the "primary" employer include authority/responsibility to hire and fire, assign/place the employee, make payroll, and provide employment benefits. For employees of temporary help or leasing agencies, for example, the placement agency most commonly would be the primary employer.

(d) Employees jointly employed by two employers must be counted by both employers, whether or not maintained on one of the employer's payroll, in determining employer coverage and employee eligibility. For example, an employer who jointly employs 15 workers from a leasing or temporary help agency and 40 permanent workers is covered by FMLA. An employee on leave who is working for a secondary employer is considered employed by the secondary employer, and must be counted for coverage and eligibility purposes, as long as the employer has a reasonable expectation that that employee will return to employment with that employer.

(e) Job restoration is the primary responsibility of the primary employer. The secondary employer is responsible for accepting the employee returning from FMLA leave in place of the replacement employee if the secondary employer continues to utilize an employee from the temporary or leasing agency, and the agency chooses to place the employee with the secondary employer. A secondary employer is also responsible for compliance with the prohibited acts provisions with respect to its temporary/leased employees, whether or not the secondary employer is covered by FMLA (see Sec. 825.220(a)). The prohibited acts include prohibitions against interfering with an employee's attempt to exercise rights under the Act, or discharging or discriminating against an employee for opposing a practice which is unlawful under FMLA. A covered secondary employer will be responsible for compliance with all the provisions of the FMLA with respect to its regular, permanent workforce.

Section Number: 825.107

Section Name: What is meant by "successor in interest"?

(a) For purposes of FMLA, in determining whether an employer is covered because it is a "successor in interest" to a covered employer, the factors used under Title VII of the Civil Rights Act and the Vietnam Era Veterans' Adjustment Act will be considered. However, unlike Title VII, whether the successor has notice of the employee's claim is not a consideration. Notice may be relevant, however, in determining successor liability for violations of the predecessor. The factors to be considered include:

(1) Substantial continuity of the same business operations;

(2) Use of the same plant;

(3) Continuity of the work force;

(4) Similarity of jobs and working conditions;

(5) Similarity of supervisory personnel;

(6) Similarity in machinery, equipment, and production methods;

(7) Similarity of products or services; and

(8) The ability of the predecessor to provide relief.

(b) A determination of whether or not a "successor in interest" exists is not determined by the application of any single criterion, but rather the entire circumstances are to be viewed in their totality.

(c) When an employer is a "successor in interest," employees' entitlements are the same as if the employment by the predecessor and successor were continuous employment by a single employer. For example, the successor, whether or not it meets FMLA coverage criteria, must grant leave for eligible employees who had provided appropriate notice to the predecessor, or continue leave begun while employed by the predecessor, including maintenance of group health benefits during the leave and job restoration at the conclusion of the leave. A successor which meets FMLA's coverage criteria must count periods of employment and hours worked for the predecessor for purposes of determining employee eligibility for FMLA leave.

Section Number: 825.108

Section Name: What is a "public agency"?

(a) An "employer" under FMLA includes any "public agency," as defined in section 3(x) of the Fair Labor Standards Act, 29 U.S.C. 203(x). Section 3(x) of the FLSA defines "public agency" as the government of the United States; the government of a State or political subdivision of a State; or an agency of the United States, a State, or a political subdivision of a State, or any interstate governmental agency. "State" is further defined in Section 3(c) of the FLSA to include any State of the United States, the District of Columbia, or any Territory or possession of the United States.

(b) The determination of whether an entity is a "public" agency, as distinguished from a private employer, is determined by whether the agency has taxing authority, or whether the chief administrative officer or board, etc., is elected by the voters-at-large or their appointment is subject to approval by an elected official.

(c)(1) A State or a political subdivision of a State constitutes a single public agency and, therefore, a single employer for purposes of determining employee eligibility. For example, a State is a single employer; a county is a single employer; a city or town is a single employer. Where there is any question about whether a public entity is a public agency, as distinguished from a part of another public agency, the U.S. Bureau of the Census' "Census of Governments" will be determinative, except for new entities formed since the most recent publication of the "Census." For new entities, the criteria used by the Bureau of Census will be used to determine whether an entity is a public agency or a part of another agency, including existence as an organized entity, governmental character, and substantial autonomy of the entity.

(2) The Census Bureau takes a census of governments at 5-year intervals. Volume I, Government Organization, contains the official counts of the number of State and local governments. It includes tabulations of governments by State, type of government, size, and county location. Also produced is a universe list of governmental units, classified according to type of government. Copies of Volume I, Government Organization, and subsequent volumes are available from

the Superintendent of Documents, U.S. Government Printing Office, Washington, D.C., 20402, U.S. Department of Commerce District Offices, or can be found in Regional and selective depository libraries. For a list of all depository libraries, write to the Government Printing Office, 710 N. Capitol St., NW, Washington, D.C. 20402.

(d) All public agencies are covered by FMLA regardless of the number of employees; they are not subject to the coverage threshold of 50 employees carried on the payroll each day for 20 or more weeks in a year. However, employees of public agencies must meet all of the requirements of eligibility, including the requirement that the employer (e.g., State) employ 50 employees at the work site or within 75 miles.

Section Number: 825.109

Section Name: Are Federal agencies covered by these regulations?

(a) Most employees of the government of the United States, if they are covered by the FMLA, are covered under Title II of the FMLA (incorporated in Title V, Chapter 63, Subchapter 5 of the United States Code) which is administered by the U.S. Office of Personnel Management (OPM). OPM has separate regulations at 5 CFR Part 630, Subpart L. In addition, employees of the Senate and House of Representatives are covered by Title V of the FMLA.

(b) The Federal Executive Branch employees within the jurisdiction of these regulations include:

(1) Employees of the Postal Service;

(2) Employees of the Postal Rate Commission;

(3) A part-time employee who does not have an established regular tour of duty during the administrative workweek; and,

(4) An employee serving under an intermittent appointment or temporary appointment with a time limitation of one year or less.

(c) Employees of other Federal executive agencies are also covered by these regulations if they are not covered by Title II of FMLA.

(d) Employees of the legislative or judicial branch of the United States are covered by these regulations only if they are employed in a unit which has employees in the competitive service. Examples include employees of the Government Printing Office and the U.S. Tax Court.

(e) For employees covered by these regulations, the U.S. Government constitutes a single employer for purposes of determining employee eligibility. These employees must meet all of the requirements for eligibility, including the requirement that the Federal Government employ 50 employees at the work site or within 75 miles.

Section Number: 825.110

Section Name: Which employees are "eligible" to take leave under FMLA?

(a) An "eligible employee" is an employee of a covered employer who:

(1) Has been employed by the employer for at least 12 months, and

(2) Has been employed for at least 1,250 hours of service during the 12-month period immediately preceding the commencement of the leave, and

(3) Is employed at a work site where 50 or more employees are employed by the employer within 75 miles of that work site. (See Sec. 825.105(a) regarding employees who work outside the U.S.)

(b) The 12 months an employee must have been employed by the employer need not be consecutive months. If an employee is maintained on the payroll for any part of a week, including any periods of paid or unpaid leave (sick, vacation) during which other benefits or compensation are provided by the employer (e.g., workers' compensation, group health plan benefits, etc.), the week counts as a week of employment. For purposes of determining whether intermittent/occasional/ casual employment qualifies as "at least 12 months," 52 weeks is deemed to be equal to 12 months.

(c) Whether an employee has worked the minimum 1,250 hours of service is determined according to the principles established under the Fair Labor Standards Act (FLSA) for determining compensable hours of work (see 29 CFR Part 785). The determining factor is the number of hours an employee has worked for the employer within the meaning of the FLSA. The determination is not limited by methods of recordkeeping, or by compensation agreements that do not accurately reflect all of the hours an employee has worked for or been in service to the employer. Any accurate accounting of actual hours worked under FLSA's principles may be used. In the event an employer does not maintain an accurate record of hours worked by an employee, including for employees who are exempt from FLSA's requirement that a record be kept of their hours worked (e.g., bona fide executive, administrative, and professional employees as defined in FLSA Regulations, 29 CFR Part 541), the employer has the burden of showing that the employee has not worked the requisite hours. In the event the employer is unable to meet this burden the employee is deemed to have met this test. See also Sec. 825.500(f). For this purpose, full-time teachers (see Sec. 825.800 for definition) of an elementary or secondary school system, or institution of higher education, or other educational establishment or institution are deemed to meet the 1,250 hour test. An employer must be able to clearly demonstrate that such an employee did not work 1,250 hours during the previous 12 months in order to claim that the employee is not "eligible" for FMLA leave.

(d) The determinations of whether an employee has worked for the employer for at least 1,250 hours in the past 12 months and has been employed by the employer for a total of at least 12 months must be made as of the date leave commences. If an employee notifies the employer of need for FMLA leave before the employee meets these eligibility criteria, the employer must either confirm the employee's eligibility based upon a projection that the employee will be eligible on the date leave would commence or must advise the employee when the eligibility requirement is met. If the employer confirms eligibility at the time the notice for leave is received, the employer may not subsequently challenge the employee's eligibility. In the latter case, if the employer does not advise the employee whether the employee is eligible as soon as practicable (i.e., two business days absent extenuating circumstances) after the date employee eligibility is determined, the employee will have satisfied the notice requirements and the notice of leave is considered current and outstanding until the employer does advise. If the employer fails to advise the employee whether the employee is eligible prior to the date the requested leave is to commence, the employee will be deemed eligible. The employer may not, then, deny the leave. Where the employee does not give notice of the need for leave more than two business days prior to commencing leave, the employee will be deemed to be eligible if the employer fails to advise the employee that the employee is not eligible within two business days of receiving the employee's notice.

(e) The period prior to the FMLA's effective date must be considered in determining employee's eligibility.

(f) Whether 50 employees are employed within 75 miles to ascertain an employee's eligibility for FMLA benefits is determined when the employee gives notice of the need for leave. Whether the leave is to be taken at one time or on an intermittent or reduced leave schedule basis, once an employee is determined eligible in response to that notice of the need for leave, the employee's eligibility is not affected by any subsequent change in the number of employees employed at or within 75 miles of the employee's work site, for that specific notice of the need for leave. Similarly, an employer may not terminate employee leave that has already started if the employee-count drops below 50. For example, if an employer employs 60 employees in August, but expects that the number of employees will drop to 40 in December, the employer must grant FMLA benefits to an otherwise eligible employee who gives notice of the need for leave in August for a period of leave to begin in December. [60 FR 2237, Jan. 6, 1995; 60 FR 16383, Mar. 30, 1995]

Section Number: 825.111

Section Name: In determining if an employee is "eligible" under FMLA, how is the determination made whether the employer employs 50 employees within 75 miles of the work site where the employee needing leave is employed?

(a) Generally, a work site can refer to either a single location or a group of contiguous locations. Structures which form a campus or industrial park, or separate facilities in proximity with one another, may be considered a single site of employment. On the other hand, there may be several single sites of employment within a single building, such as an office building, if separate employers conduct activities within the building. For example, an office building with 50 different businesses as tenants will contain 50 sites of employment. The offices of each employer will be considered separate sites of employment for purposes of FMLA. An employee's work site under FMLA will ordinarily be the site the employee reports to or, if none, from which the employee's work is assigned.

(1) Separate buildings or areas which are not directly connected or in immediate proximity are a single work site if they are in reasonable geographic proximity, are used for the same purpose, and share the same staff and equipment. For example, if an employer manages a number of warehouses in a metropolitan area but regularly shifts or rotates the same employees from one building to another, the multiple warehouses would be a single work site.

(2) For employees with no fixed work site, e.g., construction workers, transportation workers (e.g., truck drivers, seamen, pilots), salespersons, etc., the "work site" is the site to which they are assigned as their home base, from which their work is assigned, or to which they report. For example, if a construction company headquartered in New Jersey opened a construction site in Ohio, and set up a mobile trailer on the construction site as the company's on-site office, the construction site in Ohio would be the work site for any employees hired locally who report to the mobile trailer/company office daily for work assignments, etc. If that construction company also sent personnel such as job superintendents, foremen, engineers, an office manager, etc., from New Jersey to the job site in Ohio, those workers sent from New Jersey continue to have the headquarters in New Jersey as their "work site." The workers who have New Jersey as their work site would not be counted in determining eligibility of employees whose home base is the Ohio work site, but would be counted in determining eligibility of employees whose home base is New Jersey. For transportation employees, their work site is the terminal to which they are assigned, report for work, depart, and return after completion of a work assignment. For example, an airline pilot may work for an airline with headquarters in New York, but the pilot regularly reports for duty and originates or begins flights from the company's facilities located in an airport in Chicago and returns to Chicago at the completion of one or more flights to go off duty. The pilot's work site is the facility in Chicago. An employee's personal residence is not a work site in the case of employees such as salespersons who travel a sales territory and who generally leave to work and return from work to their personal residence, or employees who work at home, as under the new concept of flexiplace. Rather, their work site is the office to which the report and from which assignments are made.

(3) For purposes of determining that employee's eligibility, when an employee is jointly employed by two or more employers (see Sec. 825.106), the employee's work site is the primary employer's office from which the employee is assigned or reports. The employee is also counted by the secondary employer to determine eligibility for the secondary employer's full-time or permanent employees.

(b) The 75-mile distance is measured by surface miles, using surface transportation over public streets, roads, highways and waterways, by the shortest route from the facility where the eligible employee needing leave is employed. Absent available surface transportation between work sites, the distance is measured by using the most frequently utilized mode of transportation (e.g., airline miles).

(c) The determination of how many employees are employed within 75 miles of the work site of an employee is based on the number of employees maintained on the payroll. Employees of educational institutions who are employed permanently or who are under contract are "maintained on the payroll" during any portion of the year when school is not in session. See Sec. 825.105(c). [60 FR 2237, Jan. 6, 1995; 60 FR 16383, Mar. 30, 1995]

Section Number: 825.112

Section Name: Under what kinds of circumstances are employers required to grant family or medical leave?

(a) Employers covered by FMLA are required to grant leave to eligible employees:

(1) For birth of a son or daughter, and to care for the newborn child;

(2) For placement with the employee of a son or daughter for adoption or foster care;

(3) To care for the employee's spouse, son, daughter, or parent with a serious health condition; and

(4) Because of a serious health condition that makes the employee unable to perform the functions of the employee's job.

(b) The right to take leave under FMLA applies equally to male and female employees. A father, as well as a mother, can take family leave for the birth, placement for adoption or foster care of a child.

(c) Circumstances may require that FMLA leave begin before the actual date of birth of a child. An expectant mother may take FMLA leave pursuant to paragraph (a)(4) of this section before the birth of the child for prenatal care or if her condition makes her unable to work.

(d) Employers covered by FMLA are required to grant FMLA leave pursuant to paragraph (a)(2) of this section before the actual placement or adoption of a child if an absence from work is required for the placement for adoption or foster care to proceed. For example, the employee may be required to attend counseling sessions, appear in court, consult with his or her attorney or the doctor(s) representing the birth parent, or submit to a physical examination. The source of an adopted child (e.g., whether from a licensed placement agency or otherwise) is not a factor in determining eligibility for leave for this purpose.

(e) Foster care is 24-hour care for children in substitution for, and away from, their parents or guardian. Such placement is made by or with the agreement of the State as a result of a voluntary agreement between the parent or guardian that the child be removed from the home, or pursuant to a judicial determination of the necessity for foster care, and involves agreement between the State and foster family that the foster family will take care of the child. Although foster care may be with relatives of the child, State action is involved in the removal of the child from parental custody.

(f) In situations where the employer/employee relationship has been interrupted, such as an employee who has been on layoff, the employee must be recalled or otherwise be re-employed before being eligible for FMLA leave. Under such circumstances, an eligible employee is immediately entitled to further FMLA leave for a qualifying reason.

(g) FMLA leave is available for treatment for substance abuse provided the conditions of Sec. 825.114 are met. However, treatment for substance abuse does not prevent an employer from taking employment action against an employee. The employer may not take action against the employee because the employee has exercised his or her right to take FMLA leave for treatment. However, if the employer has an established policy, applied in a non-discriminatory manner that has been communicated to all employees, that provides under certain circumstances an employee may be terminated for substance abuse, pursuant to that policy the employee may be terminated whether or not the employee is presently taking FMLA leave. An employee may also take FMLA leave to care for an immediate family member who is receiving treatment for substance abuse. The employer may not take action against an employee who is providing care for an immediate family member receiving treatment for substance abuse.

Section Number: 825.113

Section Name: What do "spouse," "parent," and "son or daughter" mean for purposes of an employee qualifying to take FMLA leave?

(a) Spouse means a husband or wife as defined or recognized under State law for purposes of marriage in the State where the employee resides, including common law marriage in States where it is recognized.

(b) Parent means a biological parent or an individual who stands or stood in loco parentis to an employee when the employee was a son or daughter as defined in (c) below. This term does not include parents "in law".

(c) Son or daughter means a biological, adopted, or foster child, a stepchild, a legal ward, or a child of a person standing in loco parentis, who is either under age 18, or age 18 or older and "incapable of self-care because of a mental or physical disability."

(1) "Incapable of self-care" means that the individual requires active assistance or supervision to provide daily self-care in three or more of the "activities of daily living" (ADLs) or "instrumental activities of daily living" (IADLs). Activities of daily living include adaptive activities such as caring appropriately for one's grooming and hygiene, bathing, dressing and eating. Instrumental activities of daily living include cooking, cleaning, shopping, taking public transportation, paying bills, maintaining a residence, using telephones and directories, using a post office, etc.

(2) "Physical or mental disability" means a physical or mental impairment that substantially limits one or more of the major life activities of an individual. Regulations at 29 CFR Sec. 1630.2(h), (i), and (j), issued by the Equal Employment Opportunity Commission under the Americans with Disabilities Act (ADA), 42 U.S.C. 12101 et seq., define these terms.

(3) Persons who are "in loco parentis" include those with day-to- day responsibilities to care for and financially support a child or, in the case of an employee, who had such responsibility for the employee when the employee was a child. A biological or legal relationship is not necessary.

(d) For purposes of confirmation of family relationship, the employer may require the employee giving notice of the need for leave to provide reasonable documentation or statement of family relationship. This documentation may take the form of a simple statement from the employee, or a child's birth certificate, a court document, etc. The employer is entitled to examine documentation such as a birth certificate, etc., but the employee is entitled to the return of the official document submitted for this purpose.

Section Number: 825.114

Section Name: What is a "serious health condition" entitling an employee to

FMLA leave?

(a) For purposes of FMLA, "serious health condition" entitling an employee to FMLA leave means an illness, injury, impairment, or physical or mental condition that involves:

(1) Inpatient care (i.e., an overnight stay) in a hospital, hospice, or residential medical care facility, including any period of incapacity (for purposes of this section, defined to mean inability to work, attend school or perform other regular daily activities due to the serious health condition, treatment therefor, or recovery therefrom), or any subsequent treatment in connection with such inpatient care; or

(2) Continuing treatment by a health care provider. A serious health condition involving continuing treatment by a health care provider includes any one or more of the following:

(i) A period of incapacity (i.e., inability to work, attend school or perform other regular daily activities due to the serious health condition, treatment therefor, or recovery therefrom) of more than three consecutive calendar days, and any subsequent treatment or period of incapacity relating to the same condition, that also involves:

(A) Treatment two or more times by a health care provider, by a nurse or physician's assistant under direct supervision of a health care provider, or by a provider of health care services (e.g., physical therapist) under orders of, or on referral by, a health care provider; or

(B) Treatment by a health care provider on at least one occasion which results in a regimen of continuing treatment under the supervision of the health care provider.

(ii) Any period of incapacity due to pregnancy, or for prenatal care.

(iii) Any period of incapacity or treatment for such incapacity due to a chronic serious health condition. A chronic serious health condition is one which:

(A) Requires periodic visits for treatment by a health care provider, or by a nurse or physician's assistant under direct supervision of a health care provider;

(B) Continues over an extended period of time (including recurring episodes of a single underlying condition); and

(C) May cause episodic rather than a continuing period of incapacity (e.g., asthma, diabetes, epilepsy, etc.).

(iv) A period of incapacity which is permanent or long-term due to a condition for which treatment may not be effective. The employee or family member must be under the continuing supervision of, but need not be receiving active treatment by, a health care provider. Examples include Alzheimer's, a severe stroke, or the terminal stages of a disease.

(v) Any period of absence to receive multiple treatments (including any period of recovery therefrom) by a health care provider or by a provider of health care services under orders of, or on referral by, a health care provider, either for restorative surgery after an accident or other injury, or for a condition that would likely result in a period of incapacity of more than three consecutive calendar days in the absence of medical intervention or treatment, such as cancer (chemotherapy, radiation, etc.), severe arthritis (physical therapy), kidney disease (dialysis).

(b) Treatment for purposes of paragraph (a) of this section includes (but is not limited to) examinations to determine if a serious health condition exists and evaluations of the condition. Treatment does not include routine physical examinations, eye examinations, or dental examinations. Under paragraph (a)(2)(i)(B), a regimen of continuing treatment includes, for example, a course of prescription medication (e.g., an antibiotic) or therapy requiring special equipment to resolve or alleviate the health condition (e.g., oxygen). A regimen of continuing treatment that includes the taking of over-the-counter medications such as aspirin, antihistamines, or salves; or bed-rest, drinking fluids, exercise, and other similar activities that can be initiated without a visit to a health care provider, is not, by itself, sufficient to constitute a regimen of continuing treatment for purposes of FMLA leave.

(c) Conditions for which cosmetic treatments are administered (such as most treatments for acne or plastic surgery) are not "serious health conditions" unless inpatient hospital care is required or unless complications develop. Ordinarily, unless complications arise, the common cold, the flu, ear aches, upset stomach, minor ulcers, headaches other than migraine, routine dental or orthodontia problems, periodontal disease, etc., are examples of conditions that do not meet the definition of a serious health condition and do not qualify for FMLA leave. Restorative dental or plastic surgery after an injury or removal of cancerous growths are serious health conditions provided all the other conditions of this regulation are met. Mental illness resulting from stress or allergies may be serious health conditions, but only if all the conditions of this section are met.

(d) Substance abuse may be a serious health condition if the conditions of this section are met. However, FMLA leave may only be taken for treatment for substance abuse by a health care provider or by a provider of health care services on referral by a health care provider. On the other hand, absence because of the employee's use of the substance, rather than for treatment, does not qualify for FMLA leave.

(e) Absences attributable to incapacity under paragraphs (a)(2) (ii) or (iii) qualify for FMLA leave even though the employee or the immediate family member does not receive treatment from a health care provider during the absence, and even if the absence does not last more than three days. For example, an employee with asthma may be unable to report for work due to the onset of an asthma attack or because the employee's health care provider has advised the employee to stay home when the pollen count exceeds a certain level. An employee who is pregnant may be unable to report to work because of severe morning sickness.

Section Number: 825.115

Section Name: What does it mean that "the employee is unable to perform the functions of the position of the employee"?

An employee is "unable to perform the functions of the position" where the health care provider finds that the employee is unable to work at all or is unable to perform any one of the essential functions of the employee's position within the meaning of the Americans with Disabilities Act (ADA), 42 U.S.C. 12101 et seq., and the regulations at 29 CFR Sec. 1630.2(n). An employee who must be absent from work to receive medical treatment for a serious health condition is considered to be unable to perform the essential functions of the position during the absence for treatment. An employer has the option, in requiring certification from a health care provider, to provide a statement of the essential functions of the employee's position for the health care provider to review. For purposes of FMLA, the essential functions of the employee's position are to be determined with reference to the position the employee held at the time notice is given or leave commenced, whichever is earlier.

Section Number: 825.116

Section Name: What does it mean that an employee is "needed to care for" a

family member?

(a) The medical certification provision that an employee is "needed to care for" a family member encompasses both physical and psychological care. It includes situations where, for example, because of a serious health condition, the family member is unable to care for his or her own basic medical, hygienic, or nutritional needs or safety, or is unable to transport himself or herself to the doctor, etc. The term also includes providing psychological comfort and reassurance which would be beneficial to a child, spouse or parent with a serious health condition who is receiving inpatient or home care.

(b) The term also includes situations where the employee may be needed to fill in for others who are caring for the family member, or to make arrangements for changes in care, such as transfer to a nursing home.

(c) An employee's intermittent leave or a reduced leave schedule necessary to care for a family member includes not only a situation where the family member's condition itself is intermittent, but also where the employee is only needed intermittently - such as where other care is normally available, or care responsibilities are shared with another member of the family or a third party.

Section Number: 825.117

Section Name: For an employee seeking intermittent FMLA leave or leave on a reduced leave schedule, what is meant by "the medical necessity for" such leave?

For intermittent leave or leave on a reduced leave schedule, there must be a medical need for leave (as distinguished from voluntary treatments and procedures) and it must be that such medical need can be best accommodated through an intermittent or reduced leave schedule. The treatment regimen and other information described in the certification of a serious health condition (see Sec. 825.306) meets the requirement for certification of the medical necessity of intermittent FMLA leave or leave on a reduced leave schedule. Employees needing intermittent FMLA leave or leave on a reduced leave schedule must attempt to schedule their leave so as not to disrupt the employer's operations. In addition, an employer may assign an employee to an alternative position with equivalent pay and benefits that better accommodates the employee's intermittent or reduced leave schedule.

Section Number: 825.118

Section Name: What is a "health care provider"?

(a) The Act defines "health care provider" as:

(1) A doctor of medicine or osteopathy who is authorized to practice medicine or surgery (as appropriate) by the State in which the doctor practices; or

(2) Any other person determined by the Secretary to be capable of providing health care services.

(b) Others "capable of providing health care services" include only:

(1) Podiatrists, dentists, clinical psychologists, optometrists, and chiropractors (limited to treatment consisting of manual manipulation of the spine to correct a subluxation as demonstrated by X-ray to exist) authorized to practice in the State and performing within the scope of their practice as defined under State law;

(2) Nurse practitioners, nurse-midwives and clinical social workers who are authorized to practice under State law and who are performing within the scope of their practice as defined under State law;

(3) Christian Science practitioners listed with the First Church of Christ, Scientist in Boston, Massachusetts. Where an employee or family member is receiving treatment from a Christian Science practitioner, an employee may not object to any requirement from an employer that the employee or family member submit to examination (though not treatment) to obtain a second or third certification from a health care provider other than a Christian Science practitioner except as otherwise provided under applicable State or local law or collective bargaining agreement.

(4) Any health care provider from whom an employer or the employer's group health plan's benefits manager will accept certification of the existence of a serious health condition to substantiate a claim for benefits; and

(5) A health care provider listed above who practices in a country other than the United States, who is authorized to practice in accordance with the law of that country, and who is performing within the scope of his or her practice as defined under such law.

(c) The phrase "authorized to practice in the State" as used in this section means that the provider must be authorized to diagnose and treat physical or mental health conditions without supervision by a doctor or other health care provider.

Section Number: 825.200

Section Name: How much leave may an employee take?

(a) An eligible employee's FMLA leave entitlement is limited to a total of 12 workweeks of leave during any 12-month period for any one, or more, of the following reasons:

(1) The birth of the employee's son or daughter, and to care for the newborn child;

(2) The placement with the employee of a son or daughter for adoption or foster care, and to care for the newly placed child;

(3) To care for the employee's spouse, son, daughter, or parent with a serious health condition; and,

(4) Because of a serious health condition that makes the employee unable to perform one or more of the essential functions of his or her job.

(b) An employer is permitted to choose any one of the following methods for determining the "12-month period" in which the 12 weeks of leave entitlement occurs:

(1) The calendar year;

(2) Any fixed 12-month "leave year," such as a fiscal year, a year required by State law, or a year starting on an employee's "anniversary" date;

(3) The 12-month period measured forward from the date any employee's first FMLA leave begins; or,

(4) A "rolling" 12-month period measured backward from the date an employee uses any FMLA leave (except that such measure may not extend back before August 5, 1993).

(c) Under methods in paragraphs (b)(1) and (b)(2) of this section an employee would be entitled to up to 12 weeks of FMLA leave at any time in the fixed 12-month period selected. An employee could, therefore, take 12 weeks of leave at the end of the year and 12 weeks at the beginning of the following year. Under the method in paragraph (b)(3) of this section, an employee would be entitled to 12 weeks of leave during the year beginning on the first date FMLA leave is taken; the next 12- month period would begin the first time FMLA leave is taken after completion of any previous 12-month period. Under the method in paragraph (b)(4) of this section, the "rolling" 12-month period, each time an employee takes FMLA leave the remaining leave entitlement would be any balance of the 12 weeks which has not been used during the immediately preceding 12 months. For example, if an employee has taken eight weeks of leave during the past 12 months, an additional four weeks of leave could be taken. If an employee used four weeks beginning February 1, 1994, four weeks beginning June 1, 1994, and four weeks beginning December 1, 1994, the employee would not be entitled to any additional leave until February 1, 1995. However, beginning on February 1, 1995, the employee would be entitled to four weeks of leave, on June 1 the employee would be entitled to an additional four weeks, etc.

(d)(1) Employers will be allowed to choose any one of the alternatives in paragraph (b) of this section provided the alternative chosen is applied consistently and uniformly to all employees. An employer wishing to change to another alternative is required to give at least 60 days notice to all employees, and the transition must take place in such a way that the employees retain the full benefit of 12 weeks of leave under whichever method affords the greatest benefit to the employee. Under no circumstances may a new method be implemented in order to avoid the Act's leave requirements.

(2) An exception to this required uniformity would apply in the case of a multi-State employer who has eligible employees in a State which has a family and medical leave statute. The State may require a single method of determining the period during which use of the leave entitlement is measured. This method may conflict with the method chosen by the employer to determine "any 12 months" for purposes of the Federal statute. The employer may comply with the State provision for all employees employed within that State, and uniformly use another method provided by this regulation for all other employees.

(e) If an employer fails to select one of the options in paragraph (b) of this section for measuring the 12-month period, the option that provides the most beneficial outcome for the employee will be used. The employer may subsequently select an option only by providing the 60-day notice to all employees of the option the employer intends to implement. During the running of the 60-day period any other employee who needs FMLA leave may use the option providing the most beneficial outcome to that employee. At the conclusion of the 60-day period the employer may implement the selected option.

(f) For purposes of determining the amount of leave used by an employee, the fact that a holiday may occur within the week taken as FMLA leave has no effect; the week is counted as a week of FMLA leave. However, if for some reason the employer's business activity has temporarily ceased and employees generally are not expected to report for work for one or more weeks (e.g., a school closing two weeks for the Christmas/New Year holiday or the summer vacation or an employer closing the plant for retooling or repairs), the days the employer's activities have ceased do not count against the employee's FMLA leave entitlement. Methods for determining an employee's 12-week leave entitlement are also described in Sec. 825.205.

Section Number: 825.201

Section Name: If leave is taken for the birth of a child, or for placement of a child for adoption or foster care, when must the leave be concluded?

An employee's entitlement to leave for a birth or placement for adoption or foster care expires at the end of the 12-month period beginning on the date of the birth or placement, unless state law allows, or the employer permits, leave to be taken for a longer period. Any such FMLA leave must be concluded within this one-year period. However, see Sec. 825.701 regarding non-FMLA leave which may be available under applicable State laws.

Section Number: 825.202

Section Name: How much leave may a husband and wife take if they are employed by the same employer?

(a) A husband and wife who are eligible for FMLA leave and are employed by the same covered employer may be limited to a combined total of 12 weeks of leave during any 12-month period if the leave is taken:

(1) for birth of the employee's son or daughter or to care for the child after birth;

(2) for placement of a son or daughter with the employee for adoption or foster care, or to care for the child after placement; or

(3) to care for the employee's parent with a serious health condition.

(b) This limitation on the total weeks of leave applies to leave taken for the reasons specified in paragraph (a) of this section as long as a husband and wife are employed by the "same employer." It would apply, for example, even though the spouses are employed at two different work sites of an employer located more than 75 miles from each other, or by two different operating divisions of the same company. On the other hand, if one spouse is ineligible for FMLA leave, the other spouse would be entitled to a full 12 weeks of FMLA leave.

(c) Where the husband and wife both use a portion of the total 12- week FMLA leave entitlement for one of the purposes in paragraph (a) of this section, the husband and wife would each be entitled to the difference between the amount he or she has taken individually and 12 weeks for FMLA leave for a purpose other than those contained in paragraph (a) of this section. For example, if each spouse took 6 weeks of leave to care for a healthy, newborn child, each could use an additional 6 weeks due to his or her own serious health condition or to care for a child with a serious health condition. Note, too, that many State pregnancy disability laws specify a period of disability either before or after the birth of a child; such periods would also be considered FMLA leave for a serious health condition of the mother, and would not be subject to the combined limit. [60 FR 2237, Jan. 6, 1995; 60 FR 16383, Mar. 30, 1995]

Section Number: 825.203

Section Name: Does FMLA leave have to be taken all at once, or can it be taken in parts?

(a) FMLA leave may be taken "intermittently or on a reduced leave schedule" under certain circumstances. Intermittent leave is FMLA leave taken in separate blocks of time due to a single qualifying reason. A reduced leave schedule is a leave schedule that reduces an employee's usual number of working hours per workweek, or hours per workday. A reduced leave schedule is a change in the employee's schedule for a period of time, normally from full-time to part-time.

(b) When leave is taken after the birth or placement of a child for adoption or foster care, an employee may take leave intermittently or on a reduced leave schedule only if the employer agrees. Such a schedule reduction might occur, for example, where an employee, with the employer's agreement, works part-time after the birth of a child, or takes leave in several segments. The employer's agreement is not required, however, for leave during which the mother has a serious health condition in connection with the birth of her child or if the newborn child has a serious health condition.

(c) Leave may be taken intermittently or on a reduced leave schedule when medically necessary for planned and/or unanticipated medical treatment of a related serious health condition by or under the supervision of a health care provider, or for recovery from treatment or recovery from a serious health condition. It may also be taken to provide care or psychological comfort to an immediate family member with a serious health condition.

(1) Intermittent leave may be taken for a serious health condition which requires treatment by a health care provider periodically, rather than for one continuous period of time, and may include leave of periods from an hour or more to several weeks. Examples of intermittent leave would include leave taken on an occasional basis for medical appointments, or leave taken several days at a time spread over a period of six months, such as for chemotherapy. A pregnant employee may take leave intermittently for prenatal examinations or for her own condition, such as for periods of severe morning sickness. An example of an employee taking leave on a reduced leave schedule is an employee who is recovering from a serious health condition and is not strong enough to work a full-time schedule.

(2) Intermittent or reduced schedule leave may be taken for absences where the employee or family member is incapacitated or unable to perform the essential functions of the position because of a chronic serious health condition even if he or she does not receive treatment by a health care provider.

(d) There is no limit on the size of an increment of leave when an employee takes intermittent leave or leave on a reduced leave schedule. However, an employer may limit leave increments to the shortest period of time that the employer's payroll system uses to account for absences or use of leave, provided it is one hour or less. For example, an employee might take two hours off for a medical appointment, or might work a reduced day of four hours over a period of several weeks while recuperating from an illness. An employee may not be required to take more FMLA leave than necessary to address the circumstance that precipitated the need for the leave, except as provided in Secs. 825.601 and 825.602.

Section Number: 825.204

Section Name: May an employer transfer an employee to an "alternative position" in order to accommodate intermittent leave or a reduced leave schedule?

(a) If an employee needs intermittent leave or leave on a reduced leave schedule that is foreseeable based on planned medical treatment for the employee or a family member, including during a period of recovery from a serious health condition, or if the employer agrees to permit intermittent or reduced schedule leave for the birth of a child or for placement of a child for adoption or foster care, the employer may require the employee to transfer temporarily, during the period the intermittent or reduced leave schedule is required, to an available alternative position for which the employee is qualified and which better accommodates recurring periods of leave than does the employee's regular position. See Sec. 825.601 for special rules applicable to instructional employees of schools.

(b) Transfer to an alternative position may require compliance with any applicable collective bargaining agreement, federal law (such as the Americans with Disabilities Act), and State law. Transfer to an alternative position may include altering an existing job to better accommodate the employee's need for intermittent or reduced leave.

(c) The alternative position must have equivalent pay and benefits. An alternative position for these purposes does not have to have equivalent duties. The employer may increase the pay and benefits of an existing alternative position, so as to make them equivalent to the pay and benefits of the employee's regular job. The employer may also transfer the employee to a part-time job with the same hourly rate of pay and benefits, provided the employee is not required to take more leave than is medically necessary. For example, an employee desiring to take leave in increments of four hours per day could be transferred to a half-time job, or could remain in the employee's same job on a part-time schedule, paying the same hourly rate as the employee's previous job and enjoying the same benefits. The employer may not eliminate benefits which otherwise would not be provided to part-time employees; however, an employer may proportionately reduce benefits such as vacation leave where an employer's normal practice is to base such benefits on the number of hours worked.

(d) An employer may not transfer the employee to an alternative position in order to discourage the employee from taking leave or otherwise work a hardship on the employee. For example, a white collar employee may not be assigned to perform laborer's work; an employee working the day shift may not be reassigned to the graveyard shift; an employee working in the headquarters facility may not be reassigned to a branch a significant distance away from the employee's normal job location. Any such attempt on the part of the employer to make such a transfer will be held to be contrary to the prohibited acts of the FMLA.

(e) When an employee who is taking leave intermittently or on a reduced leave schedule and has been transferred to an alternative position, no longer needs to continue on leave and is able to return to full-time work, the employee must be placed in the same or equivalent job as the job he/she left when the leave commenced. An employee may not be required to take more leave than necessary to address the circumstance that precipitated the need for leave.

Section Number: 825.205

Section Name: How does one determine the amount of leave used where an employee takes leave intermittently or on a reduced leave schedule?

(a) If an employee takes leave on an intermittent or reduced leave schedule, only the amount of leave actually taken may be counted toward the 12 weeks of leave to which an employee is entitled. For example, if an employee who normally works five days a week takes off one day, the employee would use 1/5 of a week of FMLA leave. Similarly, if a full-time employee who normally works 8-hour days works 4-hour days under a reduced leave schedule, the employee would use 1/2 week of FMLA leave each week.

(b) Where an employee normally works a part-time schedule or variable hours, the amount of leave to which an employee is entitled is determined on a pro rata or proportional basis by comparing the new schedule with the employee's normal schedule. For example, if an employee who normally works 30 hours per week works only 20 hours a week under a reduced leave schedule, the employee's ten hours of leave would constitute one-third of a week of FMLA leave for each week the employee works the reduced leave schedule.

(c) If an employer has made a permanent or long-term change in the employee's schedule (for reasons other than FMLA, and prior to the notice of need for FMLA leave), the hours worked under the new schedule are to be used for making this calculation.

(d) If an employee's schedule varies from week to week, a weekly average of the hours worked over the 12 weeks prior to the beginning of the leave period would be used for calculating the employee's normal workweek.

Section Number: 825.206

Section Name: May an employer deduct hourly amounts from an employee's salary, when providing unpaid leave under FMLA, without affecting the employee's qualification for exemption as an executive, administrative, or professional employee, or when utilizing the fluctuating workweek method for payment of overtime, under the Fair Labor Standards Act?

(a) Leave taken under FMLA may be unpaid. If an employee is otherwise exempt from minimum wage and overtime requirements of the Fair Labor Standards Act (FLSA) as a salaried executive, administrative, or professional employee (under regulations issued by the Secretary), 29 CFR Part 541, providing unpaid FMLA-qualifying leave to such an employee will not cause the employee to lose the FLSA exemption. This means that under regulations currently in effect, where an employee meets the specified duties test, is paid on a salary basis, and is paid a salary of at least the amount specified in the regulations, the employer may make deductions from the employee's salary for any hours taken as intermittent or reduced FMLA leave within a workweek, without affecting the exempt status of the employee.

The fact that an employer provides FMLA leave, whether paid or unpaid, and maintains records required by this part regarding FMLA leave, will not be relevant to the determination whether an employee is exempt within the meaning of 29 CFR Part 541.

(b) For an employee paid in accordance with the fluctuating workweek method of payment for overtime (see 29 CFR 778.114), the employer, during the period in which intermittent or reduced schedule FMLA leave is scheduled to be taken, may compensate an employee on an hourly basis and pay only for the hours the employee works, including time and one- half the employee's regular rate for overtime hours. The change to payment on an hourly basis would include the entire period during which the employee is taking intermittent leave, including weeks in which no leave is taken. The hourly rate shall be determined by dividing the employee's weekly salary by the employee's normal or average schedule of hours worked during weeks in which FMLA leave is not being taken. If an employer chooses to follow this exception from the fluctuating workweek method of payment, the employer must do so uniformly, with respect to all employees paid on a fluctuating workweek basis for whom FMLA leave is taken on an intermittent or reduced leave schedule basis. If an employer does not elect to convert the employee's compensation to hourly pay, no deduction may be taken for FMLA leave absences. Once the need for intermittent or reduced scheduled leave is over, the employee may be restored to payment on a fluctuating work week basis.

(c) This special exception to the "salary basis" requirements of the FLSA exemption or fluctuating workweek payment requirements applies only to employees of covered employers who are eligible for FMLA leave, and to leave which qualifies as (one of the four types of) FMLA leave. Hourly or other deductions which are not in accordance with 29 CFR Part 541 or 29 CFR Sec. 778.114 may not be taken, for example, from the salary of an employee who works for an employer with fewer than 50 employees, or where the employee has not worked long enough to be eligible for FMLA leave without potentially affecting the employee's eligibility for exemption. Nor may deductions which are not permitted by 29 CFR Part 541 or 29 CFR Sec. 778.114 be taken from such an employee's salary for any leave which does not qualify as FMLA leave, for example, deductions from an employee's pay for leave required under State law or under an employer's policy or practice for a reason which does not qualify as FMLA leave, e.g., leave to care for a grandparent or for a medical condition which does not qualify as a serious health condition; or for leave which is more generous than provided by FMLA, such as leave in excess of 12 weeks in a year. Employers may comply with State law or the employer's own policy/practice under these circumstances and maintain the employee's eligibility for exemption or for the fluctuating workweek method of pay by not taking hourly deductions from the employee's pay, in accordance with FLSA requirements, or may take such deductions, treating the employee as an "hourly" employee and pay overtime premium pay for hours worked over 40 in a workweek.

Section Number: 825.207

Section Name: Is FMLA leave paid or unpaid?

(a) Generally, FMLA leave is unpaid. However, under the circumstances described in this section, FMLA permits an eligible employee to choose to substitute paid leave for FMLA leave. If an employee does not choose to substitute accrued paid leave, the employer may require the employee to substitute accrued paid leave for FMLA leave.

(b) Where an employee has earned or accrued paid vacation, personal or family leave, that paid leave may be substituted for all or part of any (otherwise) unpaid FMLA leave relating to birth, placement of a child for adoption or foster care, or care for a spouse, child or parent who has a serious health condition. The term "family leave" as used in FMLA refers to paid leave provided by the employer covering the particular circumstances for which the employee seeks leave for either the birth of a child and to care for such child, placement of a child for adoption or foster care, or care for a spouse, child or parent with a serious health condition. For example, if the employer's leave plan allows use of family leave to care for a child but not for a parent, the employer is not required to allow accrued family leave to be substituted for FMLA leave used to care for a parent.

(c) Substitution of paid accrued vacation, personal, or medical/sick leave may be made for any (otherwise) unpaid FMLA leave needed to care for a family member or the employee's own serious health condition. Substitution of paid sick/medical leave may be elected to the extent the circumstances meet the employer's usual requirements for the use of sick/medical leave. An employer is not required to allow substitution of paid sick or medical leave for unpaid FMLA leave "in any situation" where the employer's uniform policy would not normally allow such paid leave. An employee, therefore, has a right to substitute paid medical/sick leave to care for a seriously ill family member only if the employer's leave plan allows paid leave to be used for that purpose. Similarly, an employee does not have a right to substitute paid medical/ sick leave for a serious health condition which is not covered by the employer's leave plan.

(d)(1) Disability leave for the birth of a child would be considered FMLA leave for a serious health condition and counted in the 12 weeks of leave permitted under FMLA. Because the leave pursuant to a temporary disability benefit plan is not unpaid, the provision for substitution of paid leave is inapplicable. However, the employer may designate the leave as FMLA leave and count the leave as running concurrently for purposes of both the benefit plan and the FMLA leave entitlement. If the requirements to qualify for payments pursuant to the employer's temporary disability plan are more stringent than those of FMLA, the employee must meet the more stringent requirements of the plan, or may choose not to meet the requirements of the plan and instead receive no payments from the plan and use unpaid FMLA leave or substitute available accrued paid leave.

(2) The Act provides that a serious health condition may result from injury to the employee "on or off" the job. If the employer designates the leave as FMLA leave in accordance with Sec. 825.208, the employee's FMLA 12-week leave entitlement may run concurrently with a workers' compensation absence when the injury is one that meets the criteria for a serious health condition. As the workers' compensation absence is not unpaid leave, the provision for substitution of the employee's accrued paid leave is not applicable. However, if the health care provider treating the employee for the workers' compensation injury certifies the employee is able to return to a "light duty job" but is unable to return to the same or equivalent job, the employee may decline the employer's offer of a "light duty job". As a result the employee may lose workers' compensation payments, but is entitled to remain on unpaid FMLA leave until the 12-week entitlement is exhausted. As of the date workers' compensation benefits cease, the substitution provision becomes applicable and either the employee may elect or the employer may require the use of accrued paid leave. See also Secs. 825.210(f), 825.216(d), 825.220(d), 825.307(a)(1) and 825.702(d) (1) and (2) regarding the relationship between workers' compensation absences and FMLA leave.

(e) Paid vacation or personal leave, including leave earned or accrued under plans allowing "paid time off," may be substituted, at either the employee's or the employer's option, for any qualified FMLA leave. No limitations may be placed by the employer on substitution of paid vacation or personal leave for these purposes.

(f) If neither the employee nor the employer elects to substitute paid leave for unpaid FMLA leave under the above conditions and circumstances, the employee will remain entitled to all the paid leave which is earned or accrued under the terms of the employer's plan.

(g) If an employee uses paid leave under circumstances which do not qualify as FMLA leave, the leave will not count against the 12 weeks of FMLA leave to which the employee is entitled. For example, paid sick leave used for a medical condition which is not a serious health condition does not count against the 12 weeks of FMLA leave entitlement.

(h) When an employee or employer elects to substitute paid leave (of any type) for unpaid FMLA leave under circumstances permitted by these regulations, and the employer's procedural requirements for taking that kind of leave are less stringent than the requirements of FMLA (e.g., notice or certification requirements), only the less stringent requirements may be imposed. An employee who complies with an employer's less stringent leave plan requirements in such cases may not have leave for an FMLA purpose delayed or denied on the grounds that the employee has not complied with stricter requirements of FMLA. However, where accrued paid vacation or personal leave is substituted for unpaid FMLA leave for a serious health condition, an employee may be required to comply with any less stringent medical certification requirements of the employer's sick leave program. See Secs. 825.302(g), 825.305(e) and 825.306(c).

(i) Section 7(o) of the Fair Labor Standards Act (FLSA) permits public employers under prescribed circumstances to substitute compensatory time off accrued at one and one-half hours for each overtime hour worked in lieu of paying cash to an employee when the employee works overtime hours as prescribed by the Act. There are limits to the amounts of hours of compensatory time an employee may accumulate depending upon whether the employee works in fire protection or law enforcement (480 hours) or elsewhere for a public agency (240 hours). Compensatory time off is not a form of accrued paid leave that an employer may require the employee to substitute for unpaid FMLA leave. The employee may request to use his/her balance of compensatory time for an FMLA reason. If the employer permits the accrual to be used in compliance with regulations, 29 CFR 553.25, the absence which is paid from the employee's accrued compensatory time "account" may not be counted against the employee's FMLA leave entitlement. [60 FR 2237, Jan. 6, 1995; 60 FR 16383, Mar. 30, 1995]

Section Number: 825.208

Section Name: Under what circumstances may an employer designate leave, paid or unpaid, as FMLA leave and, as a result, count it against the employee's total FMLA leave entitlement?

(a) In all circumstances, it is the employer's responsibility to designate leave, paid or unpaid, as FMLA-qualifying, and to give notice of the designation to the employee as provided in this section. In the case of intermittent leave or leave on a reduced schedule, only one such notice is required unless the circumstances regarding the leave have changed. The employer's designation decision must be based only on information received from the employee or the employee's spokesperson (e.g., if the employee is incapacitated, the employee's spouse, adult child, parent, doctor, etc., may provide notice to the employer of the need to take FMLA leave). In any circumstance where the employer does not have sufficient information about the reason for an employee's use of paid leave, the employer should inquire further of the employee or the spokesperson to ascertain whether the paid leave is potentially FMLA-qualifying.

(1) An employee giving notice of the need for unpaid FMLA leave must explain the reasons for the needed leave so as to allow the employer to determine that the leave qualifies under the Act. If the employee fails to explain the reasons, leave may be denied. In many cases, in explaining the reasons for a request to use paid leave, especially when the need for the leave was unexpected or unforeseen, an employee will provide sufficient information for the employer to designate the paid leave as FMLA leave. An employee using accrued paid leave, especially vacation or personal leave, may in some cases not spontaneously explain the reasons or their plans for using their accrued leave.

(2) As noted in Sec. 825.302(c), an employee giving notice of the need for unpaid FMLA leave does not need to expressly assert rights under the Act or even mention the FMLA to meet his or her obligation to provide notice, though the employee would need to state a qualifying reason for the needed leave. An employee requesting or notifying the employer of an intent to use accrued paid leave, even if for a purpose covered by FMLA, would not need to assert such right either. However, if an employee requesting to use paid leave for an FMLA-qualifying purpose does not explain the reason for the leave - consistent with the employer's established policy or practice - and the employer denies the employee's request, the employee will need to provide sufficient information to establish an FMLA-qualifying

reason for the needed leave so that the employer is aware of the employee's entitlement (i.e., that the leave may not be denied) and, then, may designate that the paid leave be appropriately counted against (substituted for) the employee's 12-week entitlement. Similarly, an employee using accrued paid vacation leave who seeks an extension of unpaid leave for an FMLA-qualifying purpose will need to state the reason. If this is due to an event which occurred during the period of paid leave, the employer may count the leave used after the FMLA-qualifying event against the employee's 12-week entitlement.

(b)(1) Once the employer has acquired knowledge that the leave is being taken for an FMLA required reason, the employer must promptly (within two business days absent extenuating circumstances) notify the employee that the paid leave is designated and will be counted as FMLA leave. If there is a dispute between an employer and an employee as to whether paid leave qualifies as FMLA leave, it should be resolved through discussions between the employee and the employer. Such discussions and the decision must be documented.

(2) The employer's notice to the employee that the leave has been designated as FMLA leave may be orally or in writing. If the notice is oral, it shall be confirmed in writing, no later than the following payday (unless the payday is less than one week after the oral notice, in which case the notice must be no later than the subsequent payday). The written notice may be in any form, including a notation on the employee's pay stub.

(c) If the employer requires paid leave to be substituted for unpaid leave, or that paid leave taken under an existing leave plan be counted as FMLA leave, this decision must be made by the employer within two business days of the time the employee gives notice of the need for leave, or, where the employer does not initially have sufficient information to make a determination, when the employer determines that the leave qualifies as FMLA leave if this happens later. The employer's designation must be made before the leave starts, unless the employer does not have sufficient information as to the employee's reason for taking the leave until after the leave commenced. If the employer has the requisite knowledge to make a determination that the paid leave is for an FMLA reason at the time the employee either gives notice of the need for leave or commences leave and fails to designate the leave as FMLA leave (and so notify the employee in accordance with paragraph (b)), the employer may not designate leave as FMLA leave retroactively, and may designate only prospectively as of the date of notification to the employee of the designation. In such circumstances, the employee is subject to the full protections of the Act, but none of the absence preceding the notice to the employee of the designation may be counted against the employee's 12-week FMLA leave entitlement.

(d) If the employer learns that leave is for an FMLA purpose after leave has begun, such as when an employee gives notice of the need for an extension of the paid leave with unpaid FMLA leave, the entire or some portion of the paid leave period may be retroactively counted as FMLA leave, to the extent that the leave period qualified as FMLA leave. For example, an employee is granted two weeks paid vacation leave for a skiing trip. In mid-week of the second week, the employee contacts the employer for an extension of leave as unpaid leave and advises that at the beginning of the second week of paid vacation leave the employee suffered a severe accident requiring hospitalization. The employer may notify the employee that both the extension and the second week of paid vacation leave (from the date of the injury) is designated as FMLA leave. On the other hand, when the employee takes sick leave that turns into a serious health condition (e.g., bronchitis that turns into bronchial pneumonia) and the employee gives notice of the need for an extension of leave, the entire period of the serious health condition may be counted as FMLA leave.

(e) Employers may not designate leave as FMLA leave after the employee has returned to work with two exceptions:

(1) If the employee was absent for an FMLA reason and the employer did not learn the reason for the absence until the employee's return (e.g., where

the employee was absent for only a brief period), the employer may, upon the employee's return to work, promptly (within two business days of the employee's return to work) designate the leave retroactively with appropriate notice to the employee. If leave is taken for an FMLA reason but the employer was not aware of the reason, and the employee desires that the leave be counted as FMLA leave, the employee must notify the employer within two business days of returning to work of the reason for the leave. In the absence of such timely notification by the employee, the employee may not subsequently assert FMLA protections for the absence.

(2) If the employer knows the reason for the leave but has not been able to confirm that the leave qualifies under FMLA, or where the employer has requested medical certification which has not yet been received or the parties are in the process of obtaining a second or third medical opinion, the employer should make a preliminary designation, and so notify the employee, at the time leave begins, or as soon as the reason for the leave becomes known. Upon receipt of the requisite information from the employee or of the medical certification which confirms the leave is for an FMLA reason, the preliminary designation becomes final. If the medical certifications fail to confirm that the reason for the absence was an FMLA reason, the employer must withdraw the designation (with written notice to the employee). [60 FR 2237, Jan. 6, 1995; 60 FR 16383, Mar. 30, 1995]

Section Number: 825.209

Section Name: Is an employee entitled to benefits while using FMLA leave?

(a) During any FMLA leave, an employer must maintain the employee's coverage under any group health plan (as defined in the Internal Revenue Code of 1986 at 26 U.S.C. 5000(b)(1)) on the same conditions as coverage would have been provided if the employee had been continuously employed during the entire leave period. All employers covered by FMLA, including public agencies, are subject to the Act's requirements to maintain health coverage. The definition of "group health plan" is set forth in Sec. 825.800. For purposes of FMLA, the term "group health plan" shall not include an insurance program providing health coverage under which employees purchase individual policies from insurers provided that:

(1) no contributions are made by the employer;

(2) participation in the program is completely voluntary for employees;

(3) the sole functions of the employer with respect to the program are, without endorsing the program, to permit the insurer to publicize the program to employees, to collect premiums through payroll deductions and to remit them to the insurer;

(4) the employer receives no consideration in the form of cash or otherwise in connection with the program, other than reasonable compensation, excluding any profit, for administrative services actually rendered in connection with payroll deduction; and,

(5) the premium charged with respect to such coverage does not increase in the event the employment relationship terminates.

(b) The same group health plan benefits provided to an employee prior to taking FMLA leave must be maintained during the FMLA leave. For example, if family member coverage is provided to an employee, family member coverage must be maintained during the FMLA leave. Similarly, benefit coverage during FMLA leave for medical care, surgical care, hospital care, dental care, eye care, mental health counseling, substance abuse treatment, etc., must be maintained during leave if provided in an employer's group health plan, including a supplement to a group health plan, whether or not provided through a flexible spending account or other component of a cafeteria plan.

(c) If an employer provides a new health plan or benefits or changes health benefits or plans while an employee is on FMLA leave, the employee is entitled to the new or changed plan/benefits to the same extent as if the employee were not on leave. For example, if an employer changes a group health plan so that dental care becomes covered under the plan, an employee on FMLA leave must be given the same opportunity as other employees to receive (or obtain) the dental care coverage. Any other plan changes (e.g., in coverage, premiums, deductibles, etc.) which apply to all employees of the workforce would also apply to an employee on FMLA leave.

(d) Notice of any opportunity to change plans or benefits must also be given to an employee on FMLA leave. If the group health plan permits an employee to change from single to family coverage upon the birth of a child or otherwise add new family members, such a change in benefits must be made available while an employee is on FMLA leave. If the employee requests the changed coverage it must be provided by the employer.

(e) An employee may choose not to retain group health plan coverage during FMLA leave. However, when an employee returns from leave, the employee is entitled to be reinstated on the same terms as prior to taking the leave, including family or dependent coverages, without any qualifying period, physical examination, exclusion of pre- existing conditions, etc. See Sec. 825.212(c).

(f) Except as required by the Consolidated Omnibus Budget Reconciliation Act of 1986 (COBRA) and for "key" employees (as discussed below), an employer's obligation to maintain health benefits during leave (and to restore the employee to the same or equivalent employment) under FMLA ceases if and when the employment relationship would have terminated if the employee had not taken FMLA leave (e.g., if the employee's position is eliminated as part of a nondiscriminatory reduction in force and the employee would not have been transferred to another position); an employee informs the employer of his or her intent not to return from leave (including before starting the leave if the employer is so informed before the leave starts); or the employee fails to return from leave or continues on leave after exhausting his or her FMLA leave entitlement in the 12-month period.

(g) If a "key employee" (see Sec. 825.218) does not return from leave when notified by the employer that substantial or grievous economic injury will result from his or her reinstatement, the employee's entitlement to group health plan benefits continues unless and until the employee advises the employer that the employee does not desire restoration to employment at the end of the leave period, or FMLA leave entitlement is exhausted, or reinstatement is actually denied.

(h) An employee's entitlement to benefits other than group health benefits during a period of FMLA leave (e.g., holiday pay) is to be determined by the employer's established policy for providing such benefits when the employee is on other forms of leave (paid or unpaid, as appropriate). [60 FR 2237, Jan. 6, 1995; 60 FR 16383, Mar. 30, 1995]

Section Number: 825.210

Section Name: How may employees on FMLA leave pay their share of group health benefit premiums?

(a) Group health plan benefits must be maintained on the same basis as coverage would have been provided if the employee had been continuously employed during the FMLA leave period. Therefore, any share of group health plan premiums which had been paid by the employee prior to FMLA leave must continue to be paid by the employee during the FMLA leave period. If premiums are raised or lowered, the employee would be required to pay the new premium rates. Maintenance of health insurance policies which are not a part of the employer's group health plan, as described in Sec. 825.209(a)(1), are the sole responsibility of the employee. The employee and the insurer should make necessary arrangements for payment of premiums during periods of unpaid FMLA leave.

(b) If the FMLA leave is substituted paid leave, the employee's share of premiums must be paid by the method normally used during any paid leave, presumably as a payroll deduction.

(c) If FMLA leave is unpaid, the employer has a number of options for obtaining payment from the employee. The employer may require that payment be made to the employer or to the insurance carrier, but no additional charge may be added to the employee's premium payment for administrative expenses. The employer may require employees to pay their share of premium payments in any of the following ways:

(1) Payment would be due at the same time as it would be made if by payroll deduction;

(2) Payment would be due on the same schedule as payments are made under COBRA;

(3) Payment would be prepaid pursuant to a cafeteria plan at the employee's option;

(4) The employer's existing rules for payment by employees on "leave without pay" would be followed, provided that such rules do not require prepayment (i.e., prior to the commencement of the leave) of the premiums that will become due during a period of unpaid FMLA leave or payment of higher premiums than if the employee had continued to work instead of taking leave; or,

(5) Another system voluntarily agreed to between the employer and the employee, which may include prepayment of premiums (e.g., through increased payroll deductions when the need for the FMLA leave is foreseeable).

(d) The employer must provide the employee with advance written notice of the terms and conditions under which these payments must be made. (See Sec. 825.301.)

(e) An employer may not require more of an employee using FMLA leave than the employer requires of other employees on "leave without pay."

(f) An employee who is receiving payments as a result of a workers' compensation injury must make arrangements with the employer for payment of group health plan benefits when simultaneously taking unpaid FMLA leave. See paragraph (c) of this section and Sec. 825.207(d)(2). [60 FR 2237, Jan. 6, 1995; 60 FR 16383, Mar. 30, 1995]

Section Number: 825.211

Section Name: What special health benefits maintenance rules apply to multi-employer health plans?

(a) A multi-employer health plan is a plan to which more than one employer is required to contribute, and which is maintained pursuant to one or more collective bargaining agreements between employee organization(s) and the employers.

(b) An employer under a multi-employer plan must continue to make contributions on behalf of an employee using FMLA leave as though the employee had been continuously employed, unless the plan contains an explicit FMLA provision for maintaining coverage such as through pooled contributions by all employers party to the plan.

(c) During the duration of an employee's FMLA leave, coverage by the group health plan, and benefits provided pursuant to the plan, must be maintained at the level of coverage and benefits which were applicable to the employee at the time FMLA leave commenced.

(d) An employee using FMLA leave cannot be required to use "banked" hours or pay a greater premium than the employee would have been required to pay if the employee had been continuously employed.

(e) As provided in Sec. 825.209(f) of this part, group health plan coverage must be maintained for an employee on FMLA leave until:

> (1) the employee's FMLA leave entitlement is exhausted;

> (2) the employer can show that the employee would have been laid off and the employment relationship terminated; or,

> (3) the employee provides unequivocal notice of intent not to return to work.

Section Number: 825.212

Section Name: What are the consequences of an employee's failure to make timely health plan premium payments?

(a)(1) In the absence of an established employer policy providing a longer grace period, an employer's obligations to maintain health insurance coverage cease under FMLA if an employee's premium payment is more than 30 days late. In order to drop the coverage for an employee whose premium payment is late, the employer must provide written notice to the employee that the payment has not been received. Such notice must be mailed to the employee at least 15 days before coverage is to cease, advising that coverage will be dropped on a specified date at least 15 days after the date of the letter unless the payment has been received by that date. If the employer has established policies regarding other forms of unpaid leave that provide for the employer to cease coverage retroactively to the date the unpaid premium payment was due, the employer may drop the employee from coverage retroactively in accordance with that policy, provided the 15-day notice was given. In the absence of such a policy, coverage for the employee may be terminated at the end of the 30-day grace period, where the required 15-day notice has been provided.

> (2) An employer has no obligation regarding the maintenance of a health insurance policy which is not a "group health plan." See Sec. 825.209(a).

> (3) All other obligations of an employer under FMLA would continue; for example, the employer continues to have an obligation to reinstate an employee upon return from leave.

(b) The employer may recover the employee's share of any premium payments missed by the employee for any FMLA leave period during which the employer maintains health coverage by paying the employee's share after the premium payment is missed.

(c) If coverage lapses because an employee has not made required premium payments, upon the employee's return from FMLA leave the employer must still restore the employee to coverage/benefits equivalent to those the employee would have had if leave had not been taken and the premium payment(s) had not been missed, including family or dependent coverage. See Sec. 825.215(d)(1)-(5). In such case, an employee may not be required to meet any qualification requirements imposed by the plan, including any new preexisting condition waiting period, to wait for an open season, or to pass a medical examination to obtain reinstatement of coverage.

Section Number: 825.213

Section Name: May an employer recover costs it incurred for maintaining "group health plan" or other non-health benefits coverage during FMLA leave?

(a) In addition to the circumstances discussed in Sec. 825.212(b), an employer may recover its share of health plan premiums during a period of unpaid FMLA leave from an employee if the employee fails to return to work after the employee's FMLA leave entitlement has been exhausted or expires, unless the reason the employee does not return is due to:

(1) The continuation, recurrence, or onset of a serious health condition of the employee or the employee's family member which would otherwise entitle the employee to leave under FMLA; or

(2) Other circumstances beyond the employee's control. Examples of "other circumstances beyond the employee's control" are necessarily broad. They include such situations as where a parent chooses to stay home with a newborn child who has a serious health condition; an employee's spouse is unexpectedly transferred to a job location more than 75 miles from the employee's work site; a relative or individual other than an immediate family member has a serious health condition and the employee is needed to provide care; the employee is laid off while on leave; or, the employee is a "key employee" who decides not to return to work upon being notified of the employer's intention to deny restoration because of substantial and grievous economic injury to the employer's operations and is not reinstated by the employer. Other circumstances beyond the employee's control would not include a situation where an employee desires to remain with a parent in a distant city even though the parent no longer requires the employee's care, or a parent chooses not to return to work to stay home with a well, newborn child.

(3) When an employee fails to return to work because of the continuation, recurrence, or onset of a serious health condition, thereby precluding the employer from recovering its (share of) health benefit premium payments made on the employee's behalf during a period of unpaid FMLA leave, the employer may require medical certification of the employee's or the family member's serious health condition. Such certification is not required unless requested by the employer. The employee is required to provide medical certification in a timely manner which, for purposes of this section, is within 30 days from the date of the employer's request. For purposes of medical certification, the employee may use the optional DOL form developed for this purpose (see Sec. 825.306(a) and Appendix B of this part). If the employer requests medical certification and the employee does not provide such certification in a timely manner (within 30 days), or the reason for not returning to work does not meet the test of other circumstances beyond the employee's control, the employer may recover 100% of the health benefit premiums it paid during the period of unpaid FMLA leave.

(b) Under some circumstances an employer may elect to maintain other benefits, e.g., life insurance, disability insurance, etc., by paying the employee's (share of) premiums during periods of unpaid FMLA leave. For example, to ensure the employer can meet its responsibilities to provide equivalent benefits to the employee upon return from unpaid FMLA leave, it may be necessary that premiums be paid continuously to avoid a lapse of coverage. If the employer elects to maintain such benefits during the leave, at the conclusion of leave, the employer is entitled to recover only the costs incurred for paying the employee's share of any premiums whether or not the employee returns to work.

(c) An employee who returns to work for at least 30 calendar days is considered to have "returned" to work. An employee who transfers directly from taking FMLA leave to retirement, or who retires during the first 30 days after the employee returns to work, is deemed to have returned to work.

(d) When an employee elects or an employer requires paid leave to be substituted for FMLA leave, the employer may not recover its (share of) health insurance or other non-health benefit premiums for any period of FMLA leave covered by paid leave. Because paid leave provided under a plan covering temporary disabilities (including workers' compensation) is not unpaid, recovery of health insurance premiums does not apply to such paid leave.

(e) The amount that self-insured employers may recover is limited to only the employer's share of allowable "premiums" as would be calculated under COBRA, excluding the 2 percent fee for administrative costs.

(f) When an employee fails to return to work, any health and non- health benefit premiums which this section of the regulations permits an employer to recover are a debt owed by the non-returning employee to the employer. The existence of this debt caused by the employee's failure to return to work does not alter the employer's responsibilities for health benefit coverage and, under a self-insurance plan, payment of claims incurred during the period of FMLA leave. To the extent recovery is allowed, the employer may recover the costs through deduction from any sums due to the employee (e.g., unpaid wages, vacation pay, profit sharing, etc.), provided such deductions do not otherwise violate applicable Federal or State wage payment or other laws. Alternatively, the employer may initiate legal action against the employee to recover such costs.

Section Number: 825.214

Section Name: What are an employee's rights on returning to work from FMLA leave?

(a) On return from FMLA leave, an employee is entitled to be returned to the same position the employee held when leave commenced, or to an equivalent position with equivalent benefits, pay, and other terms and conditions of employment. An employee is entitled to such reinstatement even if the employee has been replaced or his or her position has been restructured to accommodate the employee's absence. See also Sec. 825.106(e) for the obligations of joint employers.

(b) If the employee is unable to perform an essential function of the position because of a physical or mental condition, including the continuation of a serious health condition, the employee has no right to restoration to another position under the FMLA. However, the employer's obligations may be governed by the Americans with Disabilities Act (ADA). See Sec. 825.702. [60 FR 2237, Jan. 6, 1995; 60 FR 16383, Mar. 30, 1995]

Section Number: 825.215

Section Name: What is an equivalent position?

(a) An equivalent position is one that is virtually identical to the employee's former position in terms of pay, benefits and working conditions, including privileges, perquisites and status. It must involve the same or substantially similar duties and responsibilities, which must entail substantially equivalent skill, effort, responsibility, and authority.

(b) If an employee is no longer qualified for the position because of the employee's inability to attend a necessary course, renew a license, fly a minimum number of hours, etc., as a result of the leave, the employee shall be given a reasonable opportunity to fulfill those conditions upon return to work.

(c) Equivalent Pay. (1) An employee is entitled to any unconditional pay increases which may have occurred during the FMLA leave period, such as cost of living increases. Pay increases conditioned upon seniority, length of service, or work performed would not have to be granted unless it is the employer's policy or practice to do so with respect to other employees on "leave without pay." In such case, any pay increase would be granted based on the employee's seniority, length of service, work performed, etc., excluding the period of unpaid FMLA leave. An employee is entitled to be restored to a position with the same or equivalent pay premiums, such as a shift differential. If an employee departed from a position averaging ten hours of overtime (and corresponding overtime pay) each week, an employee is ordinarily entitled to such a position on return from FMLA leave.

(2) Many employers pay bonuses in different forms to employees for job-related performance such as for perfect attendance, safety (absence of injuries or accidents on the job) and exceeding production goals. Bonuses for perfect attendance and safety do not require performance by the employee but rather contemplate the absence of occurrences. To the extent an employee who takes

FMLA leave had met all the requirements for either or both of these bonuses before FMLA leave began, the employee is entitled to continue this entitlement upon return from FMLA leave, that is, the employee may not be disqualified for the bonus(es) for the taking of FMLA leave. See Sec. 825.220 (b) and (c). A monthly production bonus, on the other hand does require performance by the employee. If the employee is on FMLA leave during any part of the period for which the bonus is computed, the employee is entitled to the same consideration for the bonus as other employees on paid or unpaid leave (as appropriate). See paragraph (d)(2) of this section.

(d) Equivalent Benefits. "Benefits" include all benefits provided or made available to employees by an employer, including group life insurance, health insurance, disability insurance, sick leave, annual leave, educational benefits, and pensions, regardless of whether such benefits are provided by a practice or written policy of an employer through an employee benefit plan as defined in Section 3(3) of the Employee Retirement Income Security Act of 1974, 29 U.S.C. 1002(3).

(1) At the end of an employee's FMLA leave, benefits must be resumed in the same manner and at the same levels as provided when the leave began, and subject to any changes in benefit levels that may have taken place during the period of FMLA leave affecting the entire workforce, unless otherwise elected by the employee. Upon return from FMLA leave, an employee cannot be required to requalify for any benefits the employee enjoyed before FMLA leave began (including family or dependent coverages). For example, if an employee was covered by a life insurance policy before taking leave but is not covered or coverage lapses during the period of unpaid FMLA leave, the employee cannot be required to meet any qualifications, such as taking a physical examination, in order to requalify for life insurance upon return from leave. Accordingly, some employers may find it necessary to modify life insurance and other benefits programs in order to restore employees to equivalent benefits upon return from FMLA leave, make arrangements for continued payment of costs to maintain such benefits during unpaid FMLA leave, or pay these costs subject to recovery from the employee on return from leave. See Sec. 825.213(b).

(2) An employee may, but is not entitled to, accrue any additional benefits or seniority during unpaid FMLA leave. Benefits accrued at the time leave began, however, (e.g., paid vacation, sick or personal leave to the extent not substituted for FMLA leave) must be available to an employee upon return from leave.

(3) If, while on unpaid FMLA leave, an employee desires to continue life insurance, disability insurance, or other types of benefits for which he or she typically pays, the employer is required to follow established policies or practices for continuing such benefits for other instances of leave without pay. If the employer has no established policy, the employee and the employer are encouraged to agree upon arrangements before FMLA leave begins.

(4) With respect to pension and other retirement plans, any period of unpaid FMLA leave shall not be treated as or counted toward a break in service for purposes of vesting and eligibility to participate. Also, if the plan requires an employee to be employed on a specific date in order to be credited with a year of service for vesting, contributions or participation purposes, an employee on unpaid FMLA leave on that date shall be deemed to have been employed on that date. However, unpaid FMLA leave periods need not be treated as credited service for purposes of benefit accrual, vesting and eligibility to participate.

(5) Employees on unpaid FMLA leave are to be treated as if they continued to work for purposes of changes to benefit plans. They are entitled to changes in benefits plans, except those which may be dependent upon seniority or accrual during the leave period, immediately upon return from leave or to the same extent they would have qualified if no leave had been taken. For example if the

benefit plan is predicated on a pre-established number of hours worked each year and the employee does not have sufficient hours as a result of taking unpaid FMLA leave, the benefit is lost. (In this regard, Sec. 825.209 addresses health benefits.)

(e) Equivalent Terms and Conditions of Employment. An equivalent position must have substantially similar duties, conditions, responsibilities, privileges and status as the employee's original position.

(1) The employee must be reinstated to the same or a geographically proximate work site (i.e., one that does not involve a significant increase in commuting time or distance) from where the employee had previously been employed. If the employee's original work site has been closed, the employee is entitled to the same rights as if the employee had not been on leave when the work site closed. For example, if an employer transfers all employees from a closed work site to a new work site in a different city, the employee on leave is also entitled to transfer under the same conditions as if he or she had continued to be employed.

(2) The employee is ordinarily entitled to return to the same shift or the same or an equivalent work schedule.

(3) The employee must have the same or an equivalent opportunity for bonuses, profit-sharing, and other similar discretionary and non- discretionary payments.

(4) FMLA does not prohibit an employer from accommodating an employee's request to be restored to a different shift, schedule, or position which better suits the employee's personal needs on return from leave, or to offer a promotion to a better position. However, an employee cannot be induced by the employer to accept a different position against the employee's wishes.

(f) The requirement that an employee be restored to the same or equivalent job with the same or equivalent pay, benefits, and terms and conditions of employment does not extend to de minimis or intangible, unmeasurable aspects of the job. However, restoration to a job slated for lay-off when the employee's original position is not would not meet the requirements of an equivalent position.

Section Number: 825.216

Section Name: Are there any limitations on an employer's obligation to reinstate an employee?

(a) An employee has no greater right to reinstatement or to other benefits and conditions of employment than if the employee had been continuously employed during the FMLA leave period. An employer must be able to show that an employee would not otherwise have been employed at the time reinstatement is requested in order to deny restoration to employment. For example:

(1) If an employee is laid off during the course of taking FMLA leave and employment is terminated, the employer's responsibility to continue FMLA leave, maintain group health plan benefits and restore the employee cease at the time the employee is laid off, provided the employer has no continuing obligations under a collective bargaining agreement or otherwise. An employer would have the burden of proving that an employee would have been laid off during the FMLA leave period and, therefore, would not be entitled to restoration.

(2) If a shift has been eliminated, or overtime has been decreased, an employee would not be entitled to return to work that shift or the original overtime hours upon restoration. However, if a position on, for example, a night shift has been filled by another employee, the employee is entitled to return to the same shift on which employed before taking FMLA leave.

(b) If an employee was hired for a specific term or only to perform work on a discrete project, the employer has no obligation to restore the employee if the employment term or project is over and the employer would not otherwise have continued to employ the employee. On the other hand, if an employee was hired to perform work on a contract, and after that contract period the contract was awarded to another contractor, the successor contractor may be required to restore the employee if it is a successor employer. See Sec. 825.107.

(c) In addition to the circumstances explained above, an employer may deny job restoration to salaried eligible employees ("key employees," as defined in paragraph (c) of Sec. 825.217) if such denial is necessary to prevent substantial and grievous economic injury to the operations of the employer; or may delay restoration to an employee who fails to provide a fitness for duty certificate to return to work under the conditions described in Sec. 825.310.

(d) If the employee has been on a workers' compensation absence during which FMLA leave has been taken concurrently, and after 12 weeks of FMLA leave the employee is unable to return to work, the employee no longer has the protections of FMLA and must look to the workers' compensation statute or ADA for any relief or protections.

Section Number: 825.217

Section Name: What is a "key employee"?

(a) A "key employee" is a salaried FMLA-eligible employee who is among the highest paid 10 percent of all the employees employed by the employer within 75 miles of the employee's work site.

(b) The term "salaried" means "paid on a salary basis," as defined in 29 CFR 541.118. This is the Department of Labor regulation defining employees who may qualify as exempt from the minimum wage and overtime requirements of the FLSA as executive, administrative, and professional employees.

(c) A "key employee" must be "among the highest paid 10 percent" of all the employees--both salaried and non-salaried, eligible and ineligible--who are employed by the employer within 75 miles of the work site.

(1) In determining which employees are among the highest paid 10 percent, year-to-date earnings are divided by weeks worked by the employee (including weeks in which paid leave was taken). Earnings include wages, premium pay, incentive pay, and non-discretionary and discretionary bonuses. Earnings do not include incentives whose value is determined at some future date, e.g., stock options, or benefits or perquisites.

(2) The determination of whether a salaried employee is among the highest paid 10 percent shall be made at the time the employee gives notice of the need for leave. No more than 10 percent of the employer's employees within 75 miles of the work site may be "key employees."

Section Number: 825.218

Section Name: What does "substantial and grievous economic injury" mean?

(a) In order to deny restoration to a key employee, an employer must determine that the restoration of the employee to employment will cause "substantial and grievous economic injury" to the operations of the employer, not whether the absence of the employee will cause such substantial and grievous injury.

(b) An employer may take into account its ability to replace on a temporary basis (or temporarily do without) the employee on FMLA leave. If permanent replacement is unavoidable, the cost of then reinstating the employee can be considered in evaluating whether substantial and grievous economic injury will occur from restoration; in other words, the effect on the operations of the company of reinstating the employee in an equivalent position.

(c) A precise test cannot be set for the level of hardship or injury to the employer which must be sustained. If the reinstatement of a "key employee" threatens the economic viability of the firm, that would constitute "substantial and grievous economic injury." A lesser injury which causes substantial, long-term economic injury would also be sufficient. Minor inconveniences and costs that the employer would experience in the normal course of doing business would certainly not constitute "substantial and grievous economic injury."

(d) FMLA's "substantial and grievous economic injury" standard is different from and more stringent than the "undue hardship" test under the ADA (see, also Sec. 825.702).

Section Number: 825.219

Section Name: What are the rights of a key employee?

(a) An employer who believes that reinstatement may be denied to a key employee, must give written notice to the employee at the time the employee gives notice of the need for FMLA leave (or when FMLA leave commences, if earlier) that he or she qualifies as a key employee. At the same time, the employer must also fully inform the employee of the potential consequences with respect to reinstatement and maintenance of health benefits if the employer should determine that substantial and grievous economic injury to the employer's operations will result if the employee is reinstated from FMLA leave. If such notice cannot be given immediately because of the need to determine whether the employee is a key employee, it shall be given as soon as practicable after being notified of a need for leave (or the commencement of leave, if earlier). It is expected that in most circumstances there will be no desire that an employee be denied restoration after FMLA leave and, therefore, there would be no need to provide such notice. However, an employer who fails to provide such timely notice will lose its right to deny restoration even if substantial and grievous economic injury will result from reinstatement.

(b) As soon as an employer makes a good faith determination, based on the facts available, that substantial and grievous economic injury to its operations will result if a key employee who has given notice of the need for FMLA leave or is using FMLA leave is reinstated, the employer shall notify the employee in writing of its determination, that it cannot deny FMLA leave, and that it intends to deny restoration to employment on completion of the FMLA leave. It is anticipated that an employer will ordinarily be able to give such notice prior to the employee starting leave. The employer must serve this notice either in person or by certified mail. This notice must explain the basis for the employer's finding that substantial and grievous economic injury will result, and, if leave has commenced, must provide the employee a reasonable time in which to return to work, taking into account the circumstances, such as the length of the leave and the urgency of the need for the employee to return.

(c) If an employee on leave does not return to work in response to the employer's notification of intent to deny restoration, the employee continues to be entitled to maintenance of health benefits and the employer may not recover its cost of health benefit premiums. A key employee's rights under FMLA continue unless and until the employee either gives notice that he or she no longer wishes to return to work, or the employer actually denies reinstatement at the conclusion of the leave period.

(d) After notice to an employee has been given that substantial and grievous economic injury will result if the employee is reinstated to employment, an employee is still entitled to request reinstatement at the end of the leave period even if the employee did not return to work in response to the employer's notice. The employer must then again determine whether there will be substantial and grievous economic injury from reinstatement, based on the facts at that time. If it is determined that substantial and grievous economic injury will result, the employer shall notify the employee in writing (in person or by certified mail) of the denial of restoration.

Section Number: 825.220

Section Name: How are employees protected who request leave or otherwise assert FMLA rights?

(a) The FMLA prohibits interference with an employee's rights under the law, and with legal proceedings or inquiries relating to an employee's rights. More specifically, the law contains the following employee protections:

(1) An employer is prohibited from interfering with, restraining, or denying the exercise of (or attempts to exercise) any rights provided by the Act.

(2) An employer is prohibited from discharging or in any other way discriminating against any person (whether or not an employee) for opposing or complaining about any unlawful practice under the Act.

(3) All persons (whether or not employers) are prohibited from discharging or in any other way discriminating against any person (whether or not an employee) because that person has--

(i) Filed any charge, or has instituted (or caused to be instituted) any proceeding under or related to this Act;

(ii) Given, or is about to give, any information in connection with an inquiry or proceeding relating to a right under this Act;

(iii) Testified, or is about to testify, in any inquiry or proceeding relating to a right under this Act.

(b) Any violations of the Act or of these regulations constitute interfering with, restraining, or denying the exercise of rights provided by the Act. "Interfering with" the exercise of an employee's rights would include, for example, not only refusing to authorize FMLA leave, but discouraging an employee from using such leave. It would also include manipulation by a covered employer to avoid responsibilities under FMLA, for example:

(1) transferring employees from one work site to another for the purpose of reducing work sites, or to keep work sites, below the 50- employee threshold for employee eligibility under the Act;

(2) changing the essential functions of the job in order to preclude the taking of leave;

(3) reducing hours available to work in order to avoid employee eligibility.

(c) An employer is prohibited from discriminating against employees or prospective employees who have used FMLA leave. For example, if an employee on leave without pay would otherwise be entitled to full benefits (other than health benefits), the same benefits would be required to be provided to an employee on unpaid FMLA leave. By the same token, employers cannot use the taking of FMLA leave as a negative factor in employment actions, such as hiring, promotions or disciplinary actions; nor can FMLA leave be counted under "no fault" attendance policies.

(d) Employees cannot waive, nor may employers induce employees to waive, their rights under FMLA. For example, employees (or their collective bargaining representatives) cannot "trade off" the right to take FMLA leave against some other benefit offered by the employer. This does not prevent an employee's voluntary and uncoerced acceptance (not as a condition of employment) of a "light duty" assignment while recovering from a serious health condition (see Sec. 825.702(d)). In such a circumstance the employee's right to restoration to the same or an equivalent position is available until 12 weeks have passed within the 12-month period, including all FMLA leave taken and the period of "light duty."

(e) Individuals, and not merely employees, are protected from retaliation for opposing (e.g., file a complaint about) any practice which is unlawful under the Act. They are similarly protected if they oppose any practice which they reasonably believe to be a violation of the Act or regulations.

Section Number: 825.300

Section Name: What posting requirements does the Act place on employers?

(a) Every employer covered by the FMLA is required to post and keep posted on its premises, in conspicuous places where employees are employed, whether or not it has any "eligible" employees, a notice explaining the Act's provisions and providing information concerning the procedures for filing complaints of violations of the Act with the Wage and Hour Division. The notice must be posted prominently where it can be readily seen by employees and applicants for employment. Employers may duplicate the text of the notice contained in Appendix C of this part, or copies of the required notice may be obtained from local offices of the Wage and Hour Division. The poster and the text must be large enough to be easily read and contain fully legible text.

(b) An employer that willfully violates the posting requirement may be assessed a civil money penalty by the Wage and Hour Division not to exceed $100 for each separate offense. Furthermore, an employer that fails to post the required notice cannot take any adverse action against an employee, including denying FMLA leave, for failing to furnish the

employer with advance notice of a need to take FMLA leave.

Section Number: 825.301

Section Name: What other notices to employees are required of employers under the FMLA?

(a)(1) If an FMLA-covered employer has any eligible employees and has any written guidance to employees concerning employee benefits or leave rights, such as in an employee handbook, information concerning FMLA entitlements and employee obligations under the FMLA must be included in the handbook or other document. For example, if an employer provides an employee handbook to all employees that describes the employer's policies regarding leave, wages, attendance, and similar matters, the handbook must incorporate information on FMLA rights and responsibilities and the employer's policies regarding the FMLA. Informational publications describing the Act's provisions are available from local offices of the Wage and Hour Division and may be incorporated in such employer handbooks or written policies.

(2) If such an employer does not have written policies, manuals, or handbooks describing employee benefits and leave provisions, the employer shall provide written guidance to an employee concerning all the employee's rights and obligations under the FMLA. This notice shall be provided to employees each time notice is given pursuant to paragraph (b), and in accordance with the provisions of that paragraph. Employers may duplicate and provide the employee a copy of the FMLA Fact Sheet available from the nearest office of the Wage and Hour Division to provide such guidance.

(b)(1) The employer shall also provide the employee with written notice detailing the specific expectations and obligations of the employee and explaining any consequences of a failure to meet these obligations. The written notice must be provided to the employee in a language in which the employee is literate (see Sec. 825.300(c)). Such specific notice must include, as appropriate:

(i) that the leave will be counted against the employee's annual FMLA leave entitlement (see Sec. 825.208);

(ii) any requirements for the employee to furnish medical certification of a serious health condition and the consequences of failing to do so (see Sec. 825.305);

(iii) the employee's right to substitute paid leave and whether the employer will require the substitution of paid leave, and the conditions related to any substitution;

(iv) any requirement for the employee to make any premium payments to maintain health benefits and the arrangements for making such payments (see Sec. 825.210), and the possible consequences of failure to make such payments on a timely basis (i.e., the circumstances under which coverage may lapse);

(v) any requirement for the employee to present a fitness-for-duty certificate to be restored to employment (see Sec. 825.310);

(vi) the employee's status as a "key employee" and the potential consequence that restoration may be denied following FMLA leave, explaining the conditions required for such denial (see Sec. 825.218);

(vii) the employee's right to restoration to the same or an equivalent job upon return from leave (see Secs. 825.214 and 825.604); and,

(viii) the employee's potential liability for payment of health insurance premiums paid by the employer during the employee's unpaid FMLA leave if the employee fails to return to work after taking FMLA leave (see Sec. 825.213).

(2) The specific notice may include other information--e.g., whether the employer will require periodic reports of the employee's status and intent to return to work, but is not required to do so. A prototype notice is contained in Appendix D of this part, or may be obtained from local offices of the Department of Labor's Wage and Hour Division, which employers may adapt for their use to meet these specific notice requirements.

(c) Except as provided in this subparagraph, the written notice required by paragraph (b) (and by subparagraph (a)(2) where applicable) must be provided to the employee no less often than the first time in each six-month period that an employee gives notice of the need for FMLA leave (if FMLA leave is taken during the six-month period). The notice shall be given within a reasonable time after notice of the need for leave is given by the employee--within one or two business days if feasible. If leave has already begun, the notice should be mailed to the employee's address of record.

(1) If the specific information provided by the notice changes with respect to a subsequent period of FMLA leave during the six-month period, the employer shall, within one or two business days of receipt of the employee's notice of need for leave, provide written notice referencing the prior notice and setting forth any of the information in subparagraph (b) which has changed. For example, if the initial leave period were paid leave and the subsequent leave period would be unpaid leave, the employer may need to give notice of the arrangements for making premium payments.

(2)(i) Except as provided in subparagraph (ii), if the employer is requiring medical certification or a "fitness-for-duty" report, written notice of the requirement shall be given with respect to each employee notice of a need for leave.

(ii) Subsequent written notification shall not be required if the initial notice in the six-months period and the employer handbook or other written documents (if any) describing the employer's leave policies, clearly provided that certification or a "fitness-for-duty" report would be required (e.g., by stating that certification would be required in all cases, by stating that certification would be required in all cases in which leave of more than a specified number of days is taken, or by stating that a "fitness-for-duty" report would be required in all cases for back injuries for employees in a certain occupation). Where subsequent written notice is not required, at least oral notice shall be provided. (See Sec. 825.305(a).)

(d) Employers are also expected to responsively answer questions from employees concerning their rights and responsibilities under the FMLA.

(e) Employers furnishing FMLA-required notices to sensory impaired individuals must also comply with all applicable requirements under Federal or State law.

(f) If an employer fails to provide notice in accordance with the provisions of this section, the employer may not take action against an employee for failure to comply with any provision required to be set forth in the notice. [60 FR 2237, Jan. 6, 1995; 60 FR 16383, Mar. 30, 1995]

(c) Where an employer's workforce is comprised of a significant portion of workers who are not literate in English, the employer shall be responsible for providing the notice in a language in which the employees are literate.

Section Number: 825.302

Section Name: What notice does an employee have to give an employer when the need for FMLA leave is foreseeable?

(a) An employee must provide the employer at least 30 days advance notice before FMLA leave is to begin if the need for the leave is foreseeable based on an expected birth, placement for adoption or foster care, or planned medical treatment for a serious health condition of the employee or of a family member. If 30 days notice is not practicable, such as because of a lack of knowledge of approximately when leave will be required to begin, a change in circumstances, or a medical emergency, notice must be given as soon as practicable. For example, an employee's health condition may require leave to commence earlier than anticipated before the birth of a child. Similarly, little opportunity for notice may be given before placement for adoption. Whether the leave is to be continuous or is to be taken intermittently or on a reduced schedule basis, notice need only be given one time, but the employee shall advise the employer as soon as practicable if dates of scheduled leave change or are extended, or were initially unknown.

(b) "As soon as practicable" means as soon as both possible and practical, taking into account all of the facts and circumstances in the individual case. For foreseeable leave where it is not possible to give as much as 30 days notice, "as soon as practicable" ordinarily would mean at least verbal notification to the employer within one or two business days of when the need for leave becomes known to the employee.

(c) An employee shall provide at least verbal notice sufficient to make the employer aware that the employee needs FMLA-qualifying leave, and the anticipated timing and duration of the leave. The employee need not expressly assert rights under the FMLA or even mention the FMLA, but may only state that leave is needed for an expected birth or adoption, for example. The employer should inquire further of the employee if it is necessary to have more information about whether FMLA leave is being sought by the employee, and obtain the necessary details of the leave to be taken. In the case of medical conditions, the employer may find it necessary to inquire further to determine if the leave is because of a serious health condition and may request medical certification to support the need for such leave (see Sec. 825.305).

(d) An employer may also require an employee to comply with the employer's usual and customary notice and procedural requirements for requesting leave. For example, an employer may require that written notice set forth the reasons for the requested leave, the anticipated duration of the leave, and the anticipated start of the leave. However, failure to follow such internal employer procedures will not permit an employer to disallow or delay an employee's taking FMLA leave if the employee gives timely verbal or other notice.

(e) When planning medical treatment, the employee must consult with the employer and make a reasonable effort to schedule the leave so as not to disrupt unduly the employer's operations, subject to the approval of the health care provider. Employees are ordinarily expected to consult with their employers prior to the scheduling of treatment in order to work out a treatment schedule which best suits the needs of both the employer and the employee. If an employee who provides notice of the need to take FMLA leave on an intermittent basis for planned medical treatment neglects to consult with the employer to make a reasonable attempt to arrange the schedule of treatments so as not to unduly disrupt the employer's operations, the employer may initiate discussions with the employee and require the employee to attempt to make such arrangements, subject to the approval of the health care provider.

(f) In the case of intermittent leave or leave on a reduced leave schedule which is medically necessary, an employee shall advise the employer, upon request, of the reasons why the intermittent/reduced leave schedule is necessary and of the schedule for treatment, if applicable. The employee and employer shall attempt to work out a schedule which meets the employee's needs without unduly disrupting the employer's operations, subject to the approval of the health care provider.

(g) An employer may waive employees' FMLA notice requirements. In addition, an employer may not require compliance with stricter FMLA notice requirements where the provisions of a collective bargaining agreement, State law, or applicable leave plan allow less advance notice to the employer. For example, if an employee (or employer) elects to substitute paid vacation leave for unpaid FMLA leave (see Sec. 825.207), and the employer's paid vacation leave plan imposes no prior notification requirements for taking such vacation leave, no advance notice may be required for the FMLA leave taken in these circumstances. On the other hand, FMLA notice requirements would apply to a period of unpaid FMLA leave, unless the employer imposes lesser notice requirements on employees taking leave without pay.

Section Number: 825.303

Section Name: What are the requirements for an employee to furnish notice to an employer where the need for FMLA leave is not foreseeable?

(a) When the approximate timing of the need for leave is not foreseeable, an employee should give notice to the employer of the need for FMLA leave as soon as practicable under the facts and circumstances of the particular case. It is expected that an employee will give notice to the employer within no more than one or two working days of learning of the need for leave, except in extraordinary circumstances where such notice is not feasible. In the case of a medical emergency requiring leave because of an employee's own serious health condition or to care for a family member with a serious health condition, written advance notice pursuant to an employer's internal rules and procedures may not be required when FMLA leave is involved.

(b) The employee should provide notice to the employer either in person or by telephone, telegraph, facsimile ("fax") machine or other electronic means. Notice may be given by the employee's spokesperson (e.g., spouse, adult family member or other responsible party) if the employee is unable to do so personally. The employee need not expressly assert rights under the FMLA or even mention the FMLA, but may only state that leave is needed. The employer will be expected to obtain any additional required information through informal means. The employee or spokesperson will be expected to provide more information when it can readily be accomplished as a practical matter, taking into consideration the exigencies of the situation.

Section Number: 825.304

Section Name: What recourse do employers have if employees fail to provide the required notice?

(a) An employer may waive employees' FMLA notice obligations or the employer's own internal rules on leave notice requirements.

(b) If an employee fails to give 30 days notice for foreseeable leave with no reasonable excuse for the delay, the employer may delay the taking of FMLA leave until at least 30 days after the date the employee provides notice to the employer of the need for FMLA leave.

(c) In all cases, in order for the onset of an employee's FMLA leave to be delayed due to lack of required notice, it must be clear that the employee had actual notice of the FMLA notice requirements. This condition would be satisfied by the employer's proper posting of the required notice at the work site where the employee is employed. Furthermore, the need for leave and the approximate date leave would be taken must have been clearly foreseeable to the employee 30 days in advance of the leave. For example, knowledge that an employee would receive a telephone call about the availability of a child for adoption at some unknown point in the future would not be sufficient.

Section Number: 825.305

Section Name: When must an employee provide medical certification to support FMLA leave?

(a) An employer may require that an employee's leave to care for the employee's seriously-ill spouse, son, daughter, or parent, or due to the employee's own serious health condition that makes the employee unable to perform one or more of the essential functions of the employee's position, be supported by a certification issued by the health care provider of the employee or the employee's ill family member. An employer must give notice of a requirement for medical certification each time a certification is required; such notice must be written notice whenever required by Sec. 825.301. An employer's oral request to an employee to furnish any subsequent medical certification is sufficient.

(b) When the leave is foreseeable and at least 30 days notice has been provided, the employee should provide the medical certification before the leave begins. When this is not possible, the employee must provide the requested certification to the employer within the time frame requested by the employer (which must allow at least 15 calendar days after the employer's request), unless it is not practicable under the particular circumstances to do so despite the employee's diligent, good faith efforts.

(c) In most cases, the employer should request that an employee furnish certification from a health care provider at the time the employee gives notice of the need for leave or within two business days thereafter, or, in the case of unforeseen leave, within two business days after the leave commences. The employer may request certification at some later date if the employer later has reason to question the appropriateness of the leave or its duration.

(d) At the time the employer requests certification, the employer must also advise an employee of the anticipated consequences of an employee's failure to provide adequate certification. The employer shall advise an employee whenever the employer finds a certification incomplete, and provide the employee a reasonable opportunity to cure any such deficiency.

(e) If the employer's sick or medical leave plan imposes medical certification requirements that are less stringent than the certification requirements of these regulations, and the employee or employer elects to substitute paid sick, vacation, personal or family leave for unpaid FMLA leave where authorized (see Sec. 825.207), only the employer's less stringent sick leave certification requirements may be imposed.

Section Number: 825.306

Section Name: How much information may be required in medical certifications of a serious health condition?

(a) DOL has developed an optional form (Form WH-380, as revised) for employees' (or their family members') use in obtaining medical certification, including second and third opinions, from health care providers that meets FMLA's certification requirements. (See Appendix B to these regulations.) This optional form reflects certification requirements so as to permit the health care provider to furnish appropriate medical information within his or her knowledge.

(b) Form WH-380, as revised, or another form containing the same basic information, may be used by the employer; however, no additional information may be required. In all instances the information on the form must relate only to the serious health condition for which the current need for leave exists. The form identifies the health care provider and type of medical practice (including pertinent specialization, if any), makes maximum use of checklist entries for ease in completing the form, and contains required entries for:

(1) A certification as to which part of the definition of "serious health condition" (see Sec. 825.114), if any, applies to the patient's condition, and the medical facts which support the certification, including a brief statement as to how the medical facts meet the criteria of the definition.

(2)(i) The approximate date the serious health condition commenced, and its probable duration, including the probable duration of the patient's present incapacity (defined to mean inability to work, attend school or perform other regular daily activities due to the serious health condition, treatment therefor, or recovery therefrom) if different.

(ii) Whether it will be necessary for the employee to take leave intermittently or to work on a reduced leave schedule basis (i.e., part-time) as a result of the serious health condition (see Sec. 825.117 and Sec. 825.203), and if so, the probable duration of such schedule.

(iii) If the condition is pregnancy or a chronic condition within the meaning of Sec. 825.114(a)(2)(iii), whether the patient is presently incapacitated and the likely duration and frequency of episodes of incapacity.

(3)(i)(A) If additional treatments will be required for the condition, an estimate of the probable number of such treatments.

(B) If the patient's incapacity will be intermittent, or will require a reduced leave schedule, an estimate of the probable number and interval between such treatments, actual or estimated dates of treatment if known, and period required for recovery if any.

(ii) If any of the treatments referred to in subparagraph (i) will be provided by another provider of health services (e.g., physical therapist), the nature of the treatments.

(iii) If a regimen of continuing treatment by the patient is required under the supervision of the health care provider, a general description of the regimen (see Sec. 825.114(b)).

(4) If medical leave is required for the employee's absence from work because of the employee's own condition (including absences due to pregnancy or a chronic condition), whether the employee:

(i) Is unable to perform work of any kind;

(ii) Is unable to perform any one or more of the essential functions of the employee's position, including a statement of the essential functions the employee is unable to perform (see Sec. 825.115), based on either information provided on a statement from the employer of the essential functions of the position or, if not provided, discussion with the employee about the employee's job functions; or

(iii) Must be absent from work for treatment.

(5)(i) If leave is required to care for a family member of the employee with a serious health condition, whether the patient requires assistance for basic medical or personal needs or safety, or for transportation; or if not, whether the employee's presence to provide psychological comfort would be beneficial to the patient or assist in the patient's recovery. The employee is required to indicate on the form the care he or she will provide and an estimate of the time period.

(ii) If the employee's family member will need care only intermittently or on a reduced leave schedule basis (i.e., part-time), the probable duration of the need.

(c) If the employer's sick or medical leave plan requires less information to be furnished in medical certifications than the certification requirements of these regulations, and the employee or employer elects to substitute paid sick, vacation, personal or family leave for unpaid FMLA leave where authorized (see Sec. 825.207), only the employer's lesser sick leave certification requirements may be imposed.

Section Number: 825.307

Section Name: What may an employer do if it questions the adequacy of a medical certification?

(a) If an employee submits a complete certification signed by the health care provider, the employer may not request additional information from the employee's health care provider. However, a health care provider representing the employer may contact the employee's health care provider, with the employee's permission, for purposes of clarification and authenticity of the medical certification.

(1) If an employee is on FMLA leave running concurrently with a workers' compensation absence, and the provisions of the workers' compensation statute permit the employer or the employer's representative to have direct contact with the employee's workers' compensation health care provider, the employer may follow the workers' compensation provisions.

(2) An employer who has reason to doubt the validity of a medical certification may require the employee to obtain a second opinion at the employer's expense. Pending receipt of the second (or third) medical opinion, the employee is provisionally entitled to the benefits of the Act, including maintenance of group health benefits. If the certifications do not ultimately establish the employee's entitlement to FMLA leave, the leave shall not be designated as FMLA leave and may be treated as paid or unpaid leave under the employer's established leave policies. The employer is permitted to designate the health care provider to furnish the second opinion, but the selected health care provider may not be employed on a regular basis by the employer. See also paragraphs (e) and (f) of this section.

(b) The employer may not regularly contract with or otherwise regularly utilize the services of the health care provider furnishing the second opinion unless the employer is located in an area where access to health care is extremely limited (e.g., a rural area where no more than one or two doctors practice in the relevant specialty in the vicinity).

(c) If the opinions of the employee's and the employer's designated health care providers differ, the employer may require the employee to obtain certification from a third health care provider, again at the employer's expense. This third opinion shall be final and binding. The third health care provider must be designated or approved jointly by the employer and the employee. The employer and the employee must each act in good faith to attempt to reach agreement on whom to select for the third opinion provider. If the employer does not attempt in good faith to reach agreement, the employer will be bound by the first certification. If the employee does not attempt in good faith to reach agreement, the employee will be bound by the second certification. For example, an employee who refuses to agree to see a doctor in the specialty in question may be failing to act in good faith. On the other hand, an employer that refuses to agree to any doctor on a list of specialists in the appropriate field provided by the employee and whom the employee has not previously consulted may be failing to act in good faith.

(d) The employer is required to provide the employee with a copy of the second and third medical opinions, where applicable, upon request by the employee. Requested copies are to be provided within two business days unless extenuating circumstances prevent such action.

(e) If the employer requires the employee to obtain either a second or third opinion the employer must reimburse an employee or family member for any reasonable "out of pocket" travel expenses incurred to obtain the second and third medical opinions. The employer may not require the employee or family member to travel outside normal commuting distance for purposes of obtaining the second or third medical opinions except in very unusual circumstances.

(f) In circumstances when the employee or a family member is visiting in another country, or a family member resides in another country, and a serious health condition develops, the employer shall accept a medical certification as well as second and third opinions from a health care provider who practices in that country. [60 FR 2237, Jan. 6, 1995; 60 FR 16383, Mar. 30, 1995]

Section Number: 825.308

Section Name: Under what circumstances may an employer request subsequent recertifications of medical conditions?

(a) For pregnancy, chronic, or permanent/long-term conditions under continuing supervision of a health care provider (as defined in Sec. 825.114(a)(2)(ii), (iii) or (iv)), an employer may request recertification no more often than every 30 days and only in connection with an absence by the employee, unless:

(1) Circumstances described by the previous certification have changed significantly (e.g., the duration or frequency of absences, the severity of the condition, complications); or

(2) The employer receives information that casts doubt upon the employee's stated reason for the absence.

(b)(1) If the minimum duration of the period of incapacity specified on a certification furnished by the health care provider is more than 30 days, the employer may not request recertification until that minimum duration has passed unless one of the conditions set forth in paragraph (c)(1), (2) or (3) of this section is met.

(2) For FMLA leave taken intermittently or on a reduced leave schedule basis, the employer may not request recertification in less than the minimum period specified on the certification as necessary for such leave (including treatment) unless one of the conditions set forth in paragraph (c)(1), (2) or (3) of this section is met.

(c) For circumstances not covered by paragraphs (a) or (b) of this section, an employer may request recertification at any reasonable interval, but not more often than every 30 days, unless:

(1) The employee requests an extension of leave;

(2) Circumstances described by the previous certification have changed significantly (e.g., the duration of the illness, the nature of the illness, complications); or

(3) The employer receives information that casts doubt upon the continuing validity of the certification.

(d) The employee must provide the requested recertification to the employer within the time frame requested by the employer (which must allow at least 15 calendar days after the employer's request), unless it is not practicable under the particular circumstances to do so despite the employee's diligent, good faith efforts.

(e) Any recertification requested by the employer shall be at the employee's expense unless the employer provides otherwise. No second or third opinion on recertification may be required.

Section Number: 825.309

Section Name: What notice may an employer require regarding an employee's intent to return to work?

(a) An employer may require an employee on FMLA leave to report periodically on the employee's status and intent to return to work. The employer's policy regarding such reports may not be discriminatory and must take into account all of the relevant facts and circumstances related to the individual employee's leave situation.

(b) If an employee gives unequivocal notice of intent not to return to work, the employer's obligations under FMLA to maintain health benefits (subject to COBRA requirements) and to restore the employee cease. However, these obligations continue if an employee indicates he or she may be unable to return to work but expresses a continuing desire to do so.

(c) It may be necessary for an employee to take more leave than originally anticipated. Conversely, an employee may discover after beginning leave that the circumstances have changed and the amount of leave originally anticipated is no longer necessary. An employee may not be required to take more FMLA leave than necessary to resolve the circumstance that precipitated the need for leave. In both of these situations, the employer may require that the employee provide the employer reasonable notice (i.e., within two business days) of the changed circumstances where foreseeable. The employer may also obtain information on such changed circumstances through requested status reports.

Section Number: 825.310

Section Name: Under what circumstances may an employer require that an employee submit a medical certification that the employee is able (or unable) to return to work (i.e., a "fitness-for-duty" report)?

(a) As a condition of restoring an employee whose FMLA leave was occasioned by the employee's own serious health condition that made the employee unable to perform the employee's job, an employer may have a uniformly-applied policy or practice that requires all similarly- situated employees (i.e., same occupation, same serious health condition) who take leave for such conditions to obtain and present certification from the employee's health care provider that the employee is able to resume work.

(b) If State or local law or the terms of a collective bargaining agreement govern an employee's return to work, those provisions shall be applied. Similarly, requirements under the Americans with Disabilities Act (ADA) that any return-to-work physical be job-related and consistent with business necessity apply. For example, an attorney could not be required to submit to a medical examination or inquiry just because her leg had been amputated. The essential functions of an attorney's job do not require use of both legs; therefore such an inquiry would not be job related. An employer may require a warehouse laborer, whose back impairment affects the ability to lift, to be examined by an orthopedist, but may not require this employee to submit to an HIV test where the test is not related to either the essential functions of his/her job or to his/her impairment.

(c) An employer may seek fitness-for-duty certification only with regard to the particular health condition that caused the employee's need for FMLA leave. The certification itself need only be a simple statement of an employee's ability to return to work. A health care provider employed by the employer may contact the employee's health care provider with the employee's permission, for purposes of clarification of the employee's fitness to return to work. No additional information may be acquired, and clarification may be requested only for the serious health condition for which FMLA leave was taken. The employer may not delay the employee's return to work while contact with the health care provider is being made.

(d) The cost of the certification shall be borne by the employee and the employee is not entitled to be paid for the time or travel costs spent in acquiring the certification.

(e) The notice that employers are required to give to each employee giving notice of the need for FMLA leave regarding their FMLA rights and obligations (see Sec. 825.301) shall advise the employee if the employer will require fitness-for-duty certification to return to work. If the employer has a handbook explaining employment policies and benefits, the handbook should explain the employer's general policy regarding any requirement for fitness-for-duty certification to return to work. Specific notice shall also be given to any employee from whom fitness- for-duty certification will be required either at the time notice of the need for leave is given or immediately after leave commences and the employer is advised of the medical circumstances requiring the leave, unless the employee's condition changes from one that did not previously require certification pursuant to the employer's practice or policy. No second or third fitness-for-duty certification may be required.

(f) An employer may delay restoration to employment until an employee submits a required fitness-for-duty certification unless the employer has failed to provide the notices required in paragraph (e) of this section.

(g) An employer is not entitled to certification of fitness to return to duty when the employee takes intermittent leave as described in Sec. 825.203.

(h) When an employee is unable to return to work after FMLA leave because of the continuation, recurrence, or onset of the employee's or family member's serious health condition, thereby preventing the employer from recovering its share of health benefit premium payments made on the employee's behalf during a period of unpaid FMLA leave, the employer may require medical certification of the employee's or the family member's serious health condition. (See Sec. 825.213(a)(3).) The cost of the certification shall be borne by the employee and the employee is not entitled to be paid for the time or travel costs spent in acquiring the certification. [60 FR 2237, Jan. 6, 1995; 60 FR 16383, Mar. 30, 1995]

Section Number: 825.311

Section Name: What happens if an employee fails to satisfy the medical certification and/or recertification requirements?

(a) In the case of foreseeable leave, an employer may delay the taking of FMLA leave to an employee who fails to provide timely certification after being requested by the employer to furnish such certification (i.e., within 15 calendar days, if practicable), until the required certification is provided.

(b) When the need for leave is not foreseeable, or in the case of recertification, an employee must provide certification (or recertification) within the time frame requested by the employer (which must allow at least 15 days after the employer's request) or as soon as reasonably possible under the particular facts and circumstances. In the case of a medical emergency, it may not be practicable for an employee to provide the required certification within 15 calendar days. If an employee fails to provide a medical certification within a reasonable time under the pertinent circumstances, the employer may delay the employee's continuation of FMLA leave. If the employee never produces the certification, the leave is not FMLA leave.

(c) When requested by the employer pursuant to a uniformly applied policy for similarly-situated employees, the employee must provide medical certification at the time the employee seeks reinstatement at the end of FMLA leave taken for the employee's serious health condition, that the employee is fit for duty and able to return to work (see Sec. 825.310(a)) if the employer has provided the required notice (see Sec. 825.301(c); the employer may delay restoration until the certification is provided. In this situation, unless the employee provides either a fitness-for-duty certification or a new medical certification for a serious health condition at the time FMLA leave is concluded, the employee may be terminated. See also Sec. 825.213(a)(3).

Section Number: 825.312

Section Name: Under what circumstances may a covered employer refuse to provide FMLA leave or reinstatement to eligible employees?

(a) If an employee fails to give timely advance notice when the need for FMLA leave is foreseeable, the employer may delay the taking of FMLA leave until 30 days after the date the employee provides notice to the employer of the need for FMLA leave. (See Sec. 825.302.)

(b) If an employee fails to provide in a timely manner a requested medical certification to substantiate the need for FMLA leave due to a serious health condition, an employer may delay continuation of FMLA leave until an employee submits the certificate. (See Secs. 825.305 and 825.311.) If the employee never produces the certification, the leave is not FMLA leave.

(c) If an employee fails to provide a requested fitness-for-duty certification to return to work, an employer may delay restoration until the employee submits the certificate. (See Secs. 825.310 and 825.311.)

(d) An employee has no greater right to reinstatement or to other benefits and conditions of employment than if the employee had been continuously employed during the FMLA leave period. Thus, an employee's rights to continued leave, maintenance of health benefits, and restoration cease under FMLA if and when the employment relationship terminates (e.g., layoff), unless that relationship continues, for example, by the employee remaining on paid FMLA leave. If the employee is recalled or otherwise re-employed, an eligible employee is immediately entitled to further FMLA leave for an FMLA-qualifying reason. An employer must be able to show, when an employee requests restoration, that the employee would not otherwise have been employed if leave had not been taken in order to deny restoration to employment. (See Sec. 825.216.)

(e) An employer may require an employee on FMLA leave to report periodically on the employee's status and intention to return to work. (See Sec. 825.309.) If an employee unequivocally advises the employer either before or during the taking of leave that the employee does not intend to return to work, and the employment relationship is terminated, the employee's entitlement to continued leave, maintenance of health benefits, and restoration ceases unless the employment relationship continues, for example, by the employee remaining on paid leave. An employee may not be required to take more leave than necessary to address the circumstances for which leave was taken. If the employee is able to return to work earlier than anticipated, the employee shall provide the employer two business days notice where feasible; the employer is required to restore the employee once such notice is given, or where such prior notice was not feasible.

(f) An employer may deny restoration to employment, but not the taking of FMLA leave and the maintenance of health benefits, to an eligible employee only under the terms of the "key employee" exemption. Denial of reinstatement must be necessary to prevent "substantial and grievous economic injury" to the employer's operations. The employer must notify the employee of the employee's status as a "key employee" and of the employer's intent to deny reinstatement on that basis when the employer makes these determinations. If leave has started, the employee must be given a reasonable opportunity to return to work after being so notified. (See Sec. 825.219.)

(g) An employee who fraudulently obtains FMLA leave from an employer is not protected by FMLA's job restoration or maintenance of health benefits provisions.

(h) If the employer has a uniformly-applied policy governing outside or supplemental employment, such a policy may continue to apply to an employee while on FMLA leave. An employer which does not have such a policy may not deny benefits to which an employee is entitled under FMLA on this basis unless the FMLA leave was fraudulently obtained as in paragraph (g) of this section. [60 FR 2237, Jan. 6, 1995; 60 FR 16383, Mar. 30, 1995]

Section Number: 825.400

Section Name: What can employees do who believe that their rights under FMLA have been violated?

(a) The employee has the choice of:

(1) Filing, or having another person file on his or her behalf, a complaint with the Secretary of Labor, or

(2) Filing a private lawsuit pursuant to section 107 of FMLA.

(b) If the employee files a private lawsuit, it must be filed within two years after the last action which the employee contends was in violation of the Act, or three years if the violation was willful.

(c) If an employer has violated one or more provisions of FMLA, and if justified by the facts of a particular case, an employee may receive one or more of the following: wages, employment benefits, or other compensation denied or lost to such employee by reason of the violation; or, where no such tangible loss has occurred, such as when FMLA leave was unlawfully denied, any actual monetary loss sustained by the employee as a direct result of the violation, such as the cost of providing care, up to a sum equal to 12 weeks of wages for the employee. In addition, the employee may be entitled to interest on such sum, calculated at the prevailing rate. An amount equaling the preceding sums may also be awarded as liquidated damages unless such amount is reduced by the court because the violation was in good faith and the employer had reasonable grounds for believing the employer had not violated the Act. When appropriate, the employee may also obtain appropriate equitable relief, such as employment, reinstatement and promotion. When the employer is found in violation, the employee may recover a reasonable attorney's fee, reasonable expert witness fees, and other costs of the action from the employer in addition to any judgment awarded by the court.

Section Number: 825.401

Section Name: Where may an employee file a complaint of FMLA violations with the Federal government?

(a) A complaint may be filed in person, by mail or by telephone, with the Wage and Hour Division, Employment Standards Administration, U.S. Department of Labor. A complaint may be filed at any local office of the Wage and Hour Division; the address and telephone number of local offices may be found in telephone directories.

(b) A complaint filed with the Secretary of Labor should be filed within a reasonable time of when the employee discovers that his or her FMLA rights have been violated. In no event may a complaint be filed more than two years after the action which is alleged to be a violation of FMLA occurred, or three years in the case of a willful violation.

(c) No particular form of complaint is required, except that a complaint must be reduced to writing and should include a full statement of the acts and/or omissions, with pertinent dates, which are believed to constitute the violation.

Section Number: 825.402

Section Name: How is an employer notified of a violation of the posting requirement?

Section 825.300 describes the requirements for covered employers to post a notice for employees that explains the Act's provisions. If a representative of the Department of Labor determines that an employer has committed a willful violation of this posting requirement, and that the imposition of a civil money penalty for such violation is appropriate, the representative may issue and serve a notice of penalty on such employer in person or by certified mail. Where service by certified mail is not accepted, notice shall be deemed received on the date of attempted delivery. Where service is not accepted, the notice may be served by regular mail.

Section Number: 825.403

Section Name: How may an employer appeal the assessment of a penalty for willful violation of the posting requirement?

(a) An employer may obtain a review of the assessment of penalty from the Wage and Hour Regional Administrator for the region in which the alleged violation(s) occurred. If the employer does not seek such a review or fails to do so in a timely manner, the notice of the penalty constitutes the final ruling of the Secretary of Labor.

(b) To obtain review, an employer may file a petition with the Wage and Hour Regional Administrator for the region in which the alleged violations occurred. No particular form of petition for review is required, except that the petition must be in writing, should contain the legal and factual bases for the petition, and must be mailed to the Regional Administrator within 15 days of receipt of the notice of penalty. The employer may request an oral hearing which may be conducted by telephone.

(c) The decision of the Regional Administrator constitutes the final order of the Secretary.

Section Number: 825.404

Section Name: What are the consequences of an employer not paying the penalty assessment after a final order is issued?

The Regional Administrator may seek to recover the unpaid penalty pursuant to the Debt Collection Act (DCA), 31 U.S.C. 3711 et seq., and, in addition to seeking recovery of the unpaid final order, may seek interest and penalties as provided under the DCA. The final order may also be referred to the Solicitor of Labor for collection. The Secretary may file suit in any court of competent jurisdiction to recover the monies due as a result of the unpaid final order, interest, and penalties.

Section Number: 825.500

Section Name: What records must an employer keep to comply with the FMLA?

(a) FMLA provides that covered employers shall make, keep, and preserve records pertaining to their obligations under the Act in accordance with the recordkeeping requirements of section 11(c) of the Fair Labor Standards Act (FLSA) and in accordance with these regulations. FMLA also restricts the authority of the Department of Labor to require any employer or plan, fund or program to submit books or records more than once during any 12-month period unless the Department has reasonable cause to believe a violation of the FMLA exists or the DOL is investigating a complaint. These regulations establish no requirement for the submission of any records unless specifically requested by a Departmental official.

(b) Form of records. No particular order or form of records is required. These regulations establish no requirement that any employer revise its computerized payroll or personnel records systems to comply. However, employers must keep the records specified by these regulations for no less than three years and make them available for inspection, copying, and transcription by representatives of the Department of Labor upon request. The records may be maintained and preserved on microfilm or other basic source document of an automated data processing memory provided that adequate projection or viewing equipment is available, that the reproductions are clear and identifiable by date or pay period, and that extensions or transcriptions of the information required herein can be and are made available upon request. Records kept in computer form must be made available for transcription or copying.

(c) Items required. Covered employers who have eligible employees must maintain records that must disclose the following:

(1) Basic payroll and identifying employee data, including name, address, and occupation; rate or basis of pay and terms of compensation; daily and weekly hours worked per pay period; additions to or deductions from wages; and total compensation paid.

(2) Dates FMLA leave is taken by FMLA eligible employees (e.g., available from time records, requests for leave, etc., if so designated). Leave must be designated in records as FMLA leave; leave so designated may not include leave required under State law or an employer plan which is not also covered by FMLA.

(3) If FMLA leave is taken by eligible employees in increments of less than one full day, the hours of the leave.

(4) Copies of employee notices of leave furnished to the employer under FMLA, if in writing, and copies of all general and specific written notices given to employees as required under FMLA and these regulations (see Sec. 825.301(b)). Copies may be maintained in employee personnel files.

(5) Any documents (including written and electronic records) describing employee benefits or employer policies and practices regarding the taking of paid and unpaid leaves.

(6) Premium payments of employee benefits.

(7) Records of any dispute between the employer and an eligible employee regarding designation of leave as FMLA leave, including any written statement from the employer or employee of the reasons for the designation and for the disagreement.

(d) Covered employers with no eligible employees must maintain the records set forth in paragraph (c)(1) above.

(e) Covered employers in a joint employment situation (see Sec. 825.106) must keep all the records required by paragraph (c) of this section with respect to any primary employees, and must keep the records required by paragraph (c)(1) with respect to any secondary employees.

(f) If FMLA-eligible employees are not subject to FLSA's recordkeeping regulations for purposes of minimum wage or overtime compliance (i.e., not covered by or exempt from FLSA), an employer need not keep a record of actual hours worked (as otherwise required under FLSA, 29 CFR 516.2(a)(7)), provided that:

(1) eligibility for FMLA leave is presumed for any employee who has been employed for at least 12 months; and

(2) with respect to employees who take FMLA leave intermittently or on a reduced leave schedule, the employer and employee agree on the employee's normal schedule or average hours worked each week and reduce their agreement to a written record maintained in accordance with paragraph (b) of this section.

(g) Records and documents relating to medical certifications, recertifications or medical histories of employees or employees' family members, created for purposes of FMLA, shall be maintained as confidential medical records in separate files/records from the usual personnel files, and if ADA is also applicable, such records shall be maintained in conformance with ADA confidentiality requirements (see 29 CFR Sec. 1630.14(c)(1)), except that:

(1) Supervisors and managers may be informed regarding necessary restrictions on the work or duties of an employee and necessary accommodations;

(2) First aid and safety personnel may be informed (when appropriate) if the employee's physical or medical condition might require emergency treatment; and

(3) Government officials investigating compliance with FMLA (or other pertinent law) shall be provided relevant information upon request.

(Approved by the Office of Management and Budget under control number 1215-0181)

[60 FR 2237, Jan. 6, 1995; 60 FR 16383, Mar. 30, 1995]

Section Number: 825.600

Section Name: To whom do the special rules apply?

(a) Certain special rules apply to employees of "local educational agencies," including public school boards and elementary and secondary schools under their jurisdiction, and private elementary and secondary schools. The special rules do not apply to other kinds of educational institutions, such as colleges and universities, trade schools, and preschools.

(b) Educational institutions are covered by FMLA (and these special rules) and the Act's 50-employee coverage test does not apply. The usual requirements for employees to be "eligible" do apply, however, including employment at a work site where at least 50 employees are employed within 75 miles. For example, employees of a rural school would not be eligible for FMLA leave if the school has fewer than 50 employees and there are no other schools under the jurisdiction of the same employer (usually, a school board) within 75 miles.

(c) The special rules affect the taking of intermittent leave or leave on a reduced leave schedule, or leave near the end of an academic term (semester), by instructional employees. "Instructional employees" are those whose principal function is to teach and instruct students in a class, a small group, or an individual setting. This term includes not only teachers, but also athletic coaches, driving instructors, and special education assistants such as signers for the hearing impaired. It does not include, and the special rules do not apply to, teacher assistants or aides who do not have as their principal job actual teaching or instructing, nor does it include auxiliary personnel such as counselors, psychologists, or curriculum specialists. It also does not include cafeteria workers, maintenance workers, or bus drivers.

(d) Special rules which apply to restoration to an equivalent position apply to all employees of local educational agencies.

Section Number: 825.601

Section Name: What limitations apply to the taking of intermittent leave or leave on a reduced leave schedule?

(a) Leave taken for a period that ends with the school year and begins the next semester is leave taken consecutively rather than intermittently. The period during the summer vacation when the employee would not have been required to report for duty is not counted against the employee's FMLA leave entitlement. An instructional employee who is on FMLA leave at the end of the school year must be provided with any benefits over the summer vacation that employees would normally receive if they had been working at the end of the school year.

(1) If an eligible instructional employee needs intermittent leave or leave on a reduced leave schedule to care for a family member, or for the employee's own serious health condition, which is foreseeable based on planned medical treatment, and the employee would be on leave for more than 20 percent of the total number of working days over the period the leave would extend, the employer may require the employee to choose either to:

(i) Take leave for a period or periods of a particular duration, not greater than the duration of the planned treatment; or

(ii) Transfer temporarily to an available alternative position for which the employee is qualified, which has equivalent pay and benefits and which better accommodates recurring periods of leave than does the employee's regular position.

(2) These rules apply only to a leave involving more than 20 percent of the working days during the period over which the leave extends. For example, if an instructional employee who normally works five days each week needs to take two days of FMLA leave per week over a period of several weeks, the special rules would apply. Employees taking leave which constitutes 20 percent or less of the working days during the leave period would not be subject to transfer to an alternative position. "Periods of a particular duration" means a block, or blocks, of time beginning no earlier than the first day for which leave is needed and ending no later than the last day on which leave is needed, and may include one uninterrupted period of leave.

(b) If an instructional employee does not give required notice of foreseeable FMLA leave (see Sec. 825.302) to be taken intermittently or on a reduced leave schedule, the employer may require the employee to take leave of a particular duration, or to transfer temporarily to an alternative position. Alternatively, the employer may require the employee to delay the taking of leave until the notice provision is met. See Sec. 825.207(h).

Section Number: 825.602

Section Name: What limitations apply to the taking of leave near the end of an academic term?

(a) There are also different rules for instructional employees who begin leave more than five weeks before the end of a term, less than five weeks before the end of a term, and less than three weeks before the end of a term. Regular rules apply except in circumstances when:

(1) An instructional employee begins leave more than five weeks before the end of a term. The employer may require the employee to continue taking leave until the end of the term if--

(i) The leave will last at least three weeks, and

(ii) The employee would return to work during the three-week period before the end of the term.

(2) The employee begins leave for a purpose other than the employee's own serious health condition during the five-week period before the end of a term. The employer may require the employee to continue taking leave until the end of the term if--

(i) The leave will last more than two weeks, and

(ii) The employee would return to work during the two-week period before the end of the term.

(3) The employee begins leave for a purpose other than the employee's own serious health condition during the three-week period before the end of a term, and the leave will last more than five working days. The employer may require the employee to continue taking leave until the end of the term.

(b) For purposes of these provisions, "academic term" means the school semester, which typically ends near the end of the calendar year and the end of spring each school year. In no case may a school have more than two academic terms or semesters each year for purposes of FMLA. An example of leave falling within these provisions would be where an employee plans two weeks of leave to care for a family member which will begin three weeks before the end of the term. In that situation, the employer could require the employee to stay out on leave until the end of the term.

Section Number: 825.603

Section Name: Is all leave taken during "periods of a particular duration" counted against the FMLA leave entitlement?

(a) If an employee chooses to take leave for "periods of a particular duration" in the case of intermittent or reduced schedule leave, the entire period of leave taken will count as FMLA leave.

(b) In the case of an employee who is required to take leave until the end of an academic term, only the period of leave until the employee is ready and able to return to work shall be charged against the employee's FMLA leave entitlement. The employer has the option not to require the employee to stay on leave until the end of the school term. Therefore, any additional leave required by the employer to the end of the school term is not counted as FMLA leave; however, the employer shall be required to maintain the employee's group health insurance and restore the employee to the same or equivalent job including other benefits at the conclusion of the leave.

Section Number: 825.604

Section Name: What special rules apply to restoration to "an equivalent position?"

The determination of how an employee is to be restored to "an equivalent position" upon return from FMLA leave will be made on the basis of "established school board policies and practices, private school policies and practices, and collective bargaining agreements." The "established policies" and collective bargaining agreements used as a basis for restoration must be in writing, must be made known to the employee prior to the taking of FMLA leave, and must clearly explain the employee's restoration rights upon return from leave. Any established policy which is used as the basis for restoration of an employee to "an equivalent position" must provide substantially the same protections as provided in the Act for reinstated employees. See Sec. 825.215. In other words, the policy or collective bargaining agreement must provide for restoration to an "equivalent position" with equivalent employment benefits, pay, and other terms and conditions of employment. For example, an employee may not be restored to a position requiring additional licensure or certification.

Section Number: 825.700

Section Name: What if an employer provides more generous benefits than required by FMLA?

(a) An employer must observe any employment benefit program or plan that provides greater family or medical leave rights to employees than the rights established by the FMLA. Conversely, the rights established by the Act may not be diminished by any employment benefit program or plan. For example, a provision of a CBA which provides for reinstatement to a position that is not equivalent because of seniority (e.g., provides lesser pay) is superseded by FMLA. If an employer provides greater unpaid family leave rights than are afforded by FMLA, the employer is not required to extend additional rights afforded by FMLA, such as maintenance of health benefits (other than through COBRA), to the additional leave period not covered by FMLA. If an employee takes paid or unpaid leave and the employer does not designate the leave as FMLA leave, the leave taken does not count against an employee's FMLA entitlement.

(b) Nothing in this Act prevents an employer from amending existing leave and employee benefit programs, provided they comply with FMLA. However, nothing in the Act is intended to discourage employers from adopting or retaining more generous leave policies.

(c)(1) The Act does not apply to employees under a collective bargaining agreement (CBA) in effect on August 5, 1993, until February 5, 1994, or the date the agreement terminates (i.e., its expiration date), whichever is earlier. Thus, if the CBA contains family or medical leave benefits, whether greater or less than those under the Act, such benefits are not disturbed until the Act's provisions begin to apply to employees under that agreement. A CBA which provides no family or medical leave rights also continues in effect. For CBAs subject to the Railway Labor Act and other CBAs which do not have an expiration date for the general terms, but which may be reopened at specified times, e.g., to amend wages and benefits, the first time the agreement is amended after August 5, 1993, shall be considered the termination date of the CBA, and the effective date for FMLA.

(2) As discussed in Sec. 825.102(b), the period prior to the Act's delayed effective date must be considered in determining employer coverage and employee eligibility for FMLA leave.

Section Number: 825.701

Section Name: Do State laws providing family and medical leave still apply?

(a) Nothing in FMLA supersedes any provision of State or local law that provides greater family or medical leave rights than those provided by FMLA. The Department of Labor will not, however, enforce State family or medical leave laws, and States may not enforce the FMLA. Employees are not required to designate whether the leave they are taking is FMLA leave or leave under State law, and an employer must comply with the appropriate (applicable) provisions of both. An employer covered by one law and not the other has to comply only with the law under which it is covered. Similarly, an employee eligible under only one law must receive benefits in accordance with that law. If leave qualifies for FMLA leave and leave under State law, the leave used counts against the employee's entitlement under both laws. Examples of the interaction between FMLA and State laws include:

(1) If State law provides 16 weeks of leave entitlement over two years, an employee would be entitled to take 16 weeks one year under State law and 12 weeks the next year under FMLA. Health benefits maintenance under FMLA would be applicable only to the first 12 weeks of leave entitlement each year. If the employee took 12 weeks the first year, the employee would be entitled to a maximum of 12 weeks the second year under FMLA (not 16 weeks). An employee would not be entitled to 28 weeks in one year.

(2) If State law provides half-pay for employees temporarily disabled because of pregnancy for six weeks, the employee would be entitled to an additional six weeks of unpaid FMLA leave (or accrued paid leave).

(3) A shorter notice period under State law must be allowed by the employer unless an employer has already provided, or the employee is requesting, more leave than required under State law.

(4) If State law provides for only one medical certification, no additional certifications may be required by the employer unless the employer has already provided, or the employee is requesting, more leave than required under State law.

(5) If State law provides six weeks of leave, which may include leave to care for a seriously-ill grandparent or a "spouse equivalent," and leave was used for that purpose, the employee is still entitled to 12 weeks of FMLA leave, as the leave used was provided for a purpose not covered by FMLA. If FMLA leave is used first for a purpose also provided under State law, and State leave has thereby been exhausted, the employer would not be required to provide additional leave to care for the grandparent or "spouse equivalent."

(6) If State law prohibits mandatory leave beyond the actual period of pregnancy disability, an instructional employee of an educational agency subject to special FMLA rules may not be required to remain on leave until the end of the academic term, as permitted by FMLA under certain circumstances. (See Subpart F of this part.)

Section Number: 825.702

Section Name: How does FMLA affect Federal and State anti-discrimination laws?

(a) Nothing in FMLA modifies or affects any Federal or State law prohibiting discrimination on the basis of race, religion, color, national origin, sex, age, or disability (e.g., Title VII of the Civil Rights Act of 1964, as amended by the Pregnancy Discrimination Act). FMLA's legislative history explains that FMLA is "not intended to modify or affect the Rehabilitation Act of 1973, as amended, the regulations concerning employment which have been promulgated pursuant to that statute, or the Americans with Disabilities Act of 1990, or the regulations issued under that act. Thus, the leave provisions of the [FMLA] are wholly distinct from the reasonable accommodation obligations of employers covered under the [ADA], employers who receive Federal financial assistance, employers who contract with the Federal government, or the Federal government itself. The purpose of the FMLA is to make leave available to eligible employees and employers within its coverage, and not to limit already existing rights and protection." S. Rep. No. 3, 103d Cong., 1st Sess. 38 (1993). An employer must therefore provide leave under whichever statutory provision provides the greater rights to employees. When an employer violates both FMLA and a discrimination law, an employee may be able to recover under either or both statutes (double relief may not be awarded for the same loss; when remedies coincide a claimant may be allowed to utilize whichever avenue of relief is desired (Laffey v. Northwest Airlines, Inc., 567 F.2d 429, 445 (D.C. Cir. 1976), cert. denied, 434 U.S. 1086 (1978))).

(b) If an employee is a qualified individual with a disability within the meaning of the Americans with Disabilities Act (ADA), the employer must make reasonable accommodations, etc., barring undue hardship, in accordance with the ADA. At the same time, the employer must afford an employee his or her FMLA rights. ADA's "disability" and FMLA's "serious health condition" are different concepts, and must be analyzed separately. FMLA entitles eligible employees to 12 weeks of leave in any 12-month period, whereas the ADA allows an indeterminate amount of leave, barring undue hardship, as a reasonable accommodation. FMLA requires employers to maintain employees' group health plan coverage during FMLA leave on the same conditions as coverage would have been provided if the employee had been continuously employed during the leave period, whereas ADA does not require maintenance of health insurance unless other employees receive health insurance during leave under the same circumstances.

(c)(1) A reasonable accommodation under the ADA might be accomplished by providing an individual with a disability with a part-time job with no health benefits, assuming the employer did not ordinarily provide health insurance for part-time employees. However, FMLA would permit an employee to work a reduced leave schedule until the equivalent of 12 workweeks of leave were used, with group health benefits maintained during this period. FMLA permits an employer to temporarily transfer an employee who is taking leave intermittently or on a reduced leave schedule to an alternative position, whereas the ADA allows an accommodation of reassignment to an equivalent, vacant position only if the employee cannot perform the essential functions of the employee's present position and an accommodation is not possible in the employee's present position, or an accommodation in the employee's present position would cause an undue hardship. The examples in the following paragraphs of this section demonstrate how the two laws would interact with respect to a qualified individual with a disability.

(2) A qualified individual with a disability who is also an "eligible employee" entitled to FMLA leave requests 10 weeks of medical leave as a reasonable accommodation, which the employer grants because it is not an undue hardship. The employer advises the employee that the 10 weeks of leave is also being designated as FMLA leave and will count towards the employee's FMLA leave entitlement. This designation does not prevent the parties from also treating the leave as a reasonable accommodation and reinstating the employee into the same job, as required by the ADA, rather than an equivalent position under FMLA, if that is the greater right available to the employee. At the same time, the employee would be entitled under FMLA to have the employer maintain group health plan coverage during the leave, as that requirement provides the greater right to the employee.

(3) If the same employee needed to work part-time (a reduced leave schedule) after returning to his or her same job, the employee would still be entitled under FMLA to have group health plan coverage maintained for the remainder of the two-week equivalent of FMLA leave entitlement, notwithstanding an employer policy that part-time employees do not receive health insurance. This employee would be entitled under the ADA to reasonable accommodations to enable the employee to perform the essential functions of the part-time position. In addition, because the employee is working a part-time schedule as a reasonable accommodation, the employee would be shielded from FMLA's provision for temporary assignment to a different alternative position. Once the employee has exhausted his or her remaining FMLA leave entitlement while working the reduced (part-time) schedule, if the employee is a qualified individual with a disability, and if the employee is unable to return to the same full-time position at that time, the employee might continue to work part-time as a reasonable accommodation, barring undue hardship; the employee would then be entitled to only those employment benefits ordinarily provided by the employer to part-time employees.

(4) At the end of the FMLA leave entitlement, an employer is required under FMLA to reinstate the employee in the same or an equivalent position, with equivalent pay and benefits, to that which the employee held when leave commenced. The employer's FMLA obligations would be satisfied if the employer offered the employee an equivalent full-time position. If the employee were unable

to perform the essential functions of that equivalent position even with reasonable accommodation, because of a disability, the ADA may require the employer to make a reasonable accommodation at that time by allowing the employee to work part-time or by reassigning the employee to a vacant position, barring undue hardship.

(d)(1) If FMLA entitles an employee to leave, an employer may not, in lieu of FMLA leave entitlement, require an employee to take a job with a reasonable accommodation. However, ADA may require that an employer offer an employee the opportunity to take such a position. An employer may not change the essential functions of the job in order to deny FMLA leave. See Sec. 825.220(b).

(2) An employee may be on a workers' compensation absence due to an on-the-job injury or illness which also qualifies as a serious health condition under FMLA. The workers' compensation absence and FMLA leave may run concurrently (subject to proper notice and designation by the employer). At some point the health care provider providing medical care pursuant to the workers' compensation injury may certify the employee is able to return to work in a "light duty" position. If the employer offers such a position, the employee is permitted but not required to accept the position (see Sec. 825.220(d)). As a result, the employee may no longer qualify for payments from the workers' compensation benefit plan, but the employee is entitled to continue on unpaid FMLA leave either until the employee is able to return to the same or equivalent job the employee left or until the 12-week FMLA leave entitlement is exhausted. See Sec. 825.207(d)(2). If the employee returning from the workers' compensation injury is a qualified individual with a disability, he or she will have rights under the ADA.

(e) If an employer requires certifications of an employee's fitness for duty to return to work, as permitted by FMLA under a uniform policy, it must comply with the ADA requirement that a fitness for duty physical be job-related and consistent with business necessity.

(f) Under Title VII of the Civil Rights Act of 1964, as amended by the Pregnancy Discrimination Act, an employer should provide the same benefits for women who are pregnant as the employer provides to other employees with short-term disabilities. Because Title VII does not require employees to be employed for a certain period of time to be protected, an employee employed for less than 12 months by the employer (and, therefore, not an "eligible" employee under FMLA) may not be denied maternity leave if the employer normally provides short-term disability benefits to employees with the same tenure who are experiencing other short-term disabilities.

(g) For further information on Federal antidiscrimination laws, including Title VII and the ADA, individuals are encouraged to contact the nearest office of the U.S. Equal Employment Opportunity Commission. [60 FR 2237, Jan. 6, 1995; 60 FR 16383, Mar. 30, 1995]

Section Number: 825.800

Section Name: Definitions.

For purposes of this part:

Act or FMLA means the Family and Medical Leave Act of 1993, Public Law 103-3 (February 5, 1993), 107 Stat. 6 (29 U.S.C. 2601 et seq.)

ADA means the Americans With Disabilities Act (42 USC 12101 et seq.)

Administrator means the Administrator of the Wage and Hour Division, Employment Standards Administration, U.S. Department of Labor, and includes any official of the Wage and Hour Division authorized to perform any of the functions of the Administrator under this part.

COBRA means the continuation coverage requirements of Title X of the Consolidated Omnibus Budget Reconciliation Act of 1986, As Amended (Pub.L. 99-272, title X, section 10002; 100 Stat 227; 29 U.S.C. 1161- 1168).

Commerce and industry or activity affecting commerce mean any activity, business, or industry in commerce or in which a labor dispute would hinder or obstruct commerce or the free flow of commerce, and include "commerce" and any "industry affecting commerce" as defined in sections 501(1) and 501(3) of the Labor Management Relations Act of 1947, 29 U.S.C. 142(1) and (3).

Continuing treatment means: A serious health condition involving continuing treatment by a health care provider includes any one or more of the following:

(1) A period of incapacity (i.e., inability to work, attend school or perform other regular daily activities due to the serious health condition, treatment therefor, or recovery therefrom) of more than three consecutive calendar days, and any subsequent treatment or period of incapacity relating to the same condition, that also involves:

(i) Treatment two or more times by a health care provider, by a nurse or physician's assistant under direct supervision of a health care provider, or by a provider of health care services (e.g., physical therapist) under orders of, or on referral by, a health care provider; or

(ii) Treatment by a health care provider on at least one occasion which results in a regimen of continuing treatment under the supervision of the health care provider.

(2) Any period of incapacity due to pregnancy, or for prenatal care.

(3) Any period of incapacity or treatment for such incapacity due to a chronic serious health condition. A chronic serious health condition is one which:

(i) Requires periodic visits for treatment by a health care provider, or by a nurse or physician's assistant under direct supervision of a health care provider;

(ii) Continues over an extended period of time (including recurring episodes of a single underlying condition); and

(iii) May cause episodic rather than a continuing period of incapacity (e.g., asthma, diabetes, epilepsy, etc.).

(4) A period of incapacity which is permanent or long-term due to a condition for which treatment may not be effective. The employee or family member must be under the continuing supervision of, but need not be receiving active treatment by, a health care provider. Examples include Alzheimer's, a severe stroke, or the terminal stages of a disease.

(5) Any period of absence to receive multiple treatments (including any period of recovery therefrom) by a health care provider or by a provider of health care services under orders of, or on referral by, a health care provider, either for restorative surgery after an accident or other injury, or for a condition that would likely result in a period of incapacity of more than three consecutive calendar days in the absence of medical intervention or treatment, such as cancer (chemotherapy, radiation, etc.), severe arthritis (physical therapy), kidney disease (dialysis).

Eligible employee means:

(1) An employee who has been employed for a total of at least 12 months by the employer on the date on which any FMLA leave is to commence; and

(2) Who, on the date on which any FMLA leave is to commence, has been employed for at least 1,250 hours of service with such employer during the previous 12-month period; and

(3) Who is employed in any State of the United States, the District of Columbia or any Territories or possession of the United States.

(4) Excludes any Federal officer or employee covered under subchapter V of chapter 63 of title 5, United States Code; and

(5) Excludes any employee of the U.S. Senate or the U.S. House of Representatives covered under title V of the FMLA; and

(6) Excludes any employee who is employed at a work site at which the employer employs fewer than 50 employees if the total number of employees employed by that employer within 75 miles of that work site is also fewer than 50.

(7) Excludes any employee employed in any country other than the United States or any Territory or possession of the United States.

Employ means to suffer or permit to work.

Employee has the meaning given the same term as defined in section 3(e) of the Fair Labor Standards Act, 29 U.S.C. 203(e), as follows:

(1) The term "employee" means any individual employed by an employer;

(2) In the case of an individual employed by a public agency, "employee" means--

(i) Any individual employed by the Government of the United States--

(A) As a civilian in the military departments (as defined in section 102 of Title 5, United States Code),

(B) In any executive agency (as defined in section 105 of Title 5, United States Code), excluding any Federal officer or employee covered under subchapter V of chapter 63 of Title 5, United States Code,

(C) In any unit of the legislative or judicial branch of the Government which has positions in the competitive service, excluding any employee of the U.S. Senate or U.S. House of Representatives who is covered under Title V of FMLA,

(D) In a nonappropriated fund instrumentality under the jurisdiction of the Armed Forces, or

(ii) Any individual employed by the United States Postal Service or the Postal Rate Commission; and

(iii) Any individual employed by a State, political subdivision of a State, or an interstate governmental agency, other than such an individual--

(A) Who is not subject to the civil service laws of the State, political subdivision, or agency which employs the employee; and

(B) Who--

(1) Holds a public elective office of that State, political subdivision, or agency,

(2) Is selected by the holder of such an office to be a member of his personal staff,

(3) Is appointed by such an officeholder to serve on a policymaking level,

(4) Is an immediate adviser to such an officeholder with respect to the constitutional or legal powers of the office of such officeholder, or

(5) Is an employee in the legislative branch or legislative body of that State, political subdivision, or agency and is not employed by the legislative library of such State, political subdivision, or agency.

Employee employed in an instructional capacity. See Teacher.

Employer means any person engaged in commerce or in an industry or activity affecting commerce who employs 50 or more employees for each working day during each of 20 or more calendar workweeks in the current or preceding calendar year, and includes--

(1) Any person who acts, directly or indirectly, in the interest of an employer to any of the employees of such employer;

(2) Any successor in interest of an employer; and

(3) Any public agency.

Employment benefits means all benefits provided or made available to employees by an employer, including group life insurance, health insurance, disability insurance, sick leave, annual leave, educational benefits, and pensions, regardless of whether such benefits are provided by a practice or written policy of an employer or through an "employee benefit plan" as defined in section 3(3) of the Employee Retirement Income Security Act of 1974, 29 U.S.C. 1002(3). The term does not include non-employment related obligations paid by employees through voluntary deductions such as supplemental insurance coverage. (See Sec. 825.209(a)).

FLSA means the Fair Labor Standards Act (29 U.S.C. 201 et seq.).

Group health plan means any plan of, or contributed to by, an employer (including a self-insured plan) to provide health care (directly or otherwise) to the employer's employees, former employees, or the families of such employees or former employees. For purposes of FMLA the term "group health plan" shall not include an insurance program providing health coverage under which employees purchase individual policies from insurers provided that:

(1) No contributions are made by the employer;

(2) Participation in the program is completely voluntary for employees;

(3) The sole functions of the employer with respect to the program are, without endorsing the program, to permit the insurer to publicize the program to employees, to collect premiums through payroll deductions and to remit them to the insurer;

(4) The employer receives no consideration in the form of cash or otherwise in connection with the program, other than reasonable compensation, excluding any profit, for administrative services actually rendered in connection with payroll deduction; and,

(5) the premium charged with respect to such coverage does not increase in the event the employment relationship terminates.

Health care provider means:

(1) A doctor of medicine or osteopathy who is authorized to practice medicine or surgery by the State in which the doctor practices; or

(2) Podiatrists, dentists, clinical psychologists, optometrists, and chiropractors (limited to treatment consisting of manual manipulation of the spine to correct a subluxation as demonstrated by X-ray to exist) authorized to practice in the

State and performing within the scope of their practice as defined under State law; and

(3) Nurse practitioners, nurse-midwives and clinical social workers who are authorized to practice under State law and who are performing within the scope of their practice as defined under State law; and

(4) Christian Science practitioners listed with the First Church of Christ, Scientist in Boston, Massachusetts.

(5) Any health care provider from whom an employer or a group health plan's benefits manager will accept certification of the existence of a serious health condition to substantiate a claim for benefits.

(6) A health care provider as defined above who practices in a country other than the United States, who is licensed to practice in accordance with the laws and regulations of that country.

Incapable of self-care means that the individual requires active assistance or supervision to provide daily self-care in several of the "activities of daily living" (ADLs) or "instrumental activities of daily living" (IADLs). Activities of daily living include adaptive activities such as caring appropriately for one's grooming and hygiene, bathing, dressing and eating. Instrumental activities of daily living include cooking, cleaning, shopping, taking public transportation, paying bills, maintaining a residence, using telephones and directories, using a post office, etc.

Instructional employee: See Teacher.

Intermittent leave means leave taken in separate periods of time due to a single illness or injury, rather than for one continuous period of time, and may include leave of periods from an hour or more to several weeks. Examples of intermittent leave would include leave taken on an occasional basis for medical appointments, or leave taken several days at a time spread over a period of six months, such as for chemotherapy.

Mental disability: See Physical or mental disability.

Parent means the biological parent of an employee or an individual who stands or stood in loco parentis to an employee when the employee was a child.

Person means an individual, partnership, association, corporation, business trust, legal representative, or any organized group of persons, and includes a public agency for purposes of this part.

Physical or mental disability means a physical or mental impairment that substantially limits one or more of the major life activities of an individual. Regulations at 29 CFR Part 1630.2(h), (i), and (j), issued by the Equal Employment Opportunity Commission under the Americans with Disabilities Act (ADA), 42 U.S.C. 12101 et seq., define these terms.

Public agency means the government of the United States; the government of a State or political subdivision thereof; any agency of the United States (including the United States Postal Service and Postal Rate Commission), a State, or a political subdivision of a State, or any interstate governmental agency. Under section 101(5)(B) of the Act, a public agency is considered to be a "person" engaged in commerce or in an industry or activity affecting commerce within the meaning of the Act.

Reduced leave schedule means a leave schedule that reduces the usual number of hours per workweek, or hours per workday, of an employee.

Secretary means the Secretary of Labor or authorized representative.

Serious health condition entitling an employee to FMLA leave means:

(1) an illness, injury, impairment, or physical or mental condition that involves:

(i) Inpatient care (i.e., an overnight stay) in a hospital, hospice, or residential medical care facility, including any period of incapacity (for purposes of this section, defined to mean inability to work, attend school or perform other regular daily activities due to the serious health condition, treatment therefor, or recovery therefrom), or any subsequent treatment in connection with such inpatient care; or

(ii) Continuing treatment by a health care provider. A serious health condition involving continuing treatment by a health care provider includes:

(A) A period of incapacity (i.e., inability to work, attend school or perform other regular daily activities due to the serious health condition, treatment therefore, or recovery therefrom) of more than three consecutive calendar days, including any subsequent treatment or period of incapacity relating to the same condition, that also involves:

(1) Treatment two or more times by a health care provider, by a nurse or physician's assistant under direct supervision of a health care provider, or by a provider of health care services (e.g., physical therapist) under orders of, or on referral by, a health care provider; or

(2) Treatment by a health care provider on at least one occasion which results in a regimen of continuing treatment under the supervision of the health care provider.

(B) Any period of incapacity due to pregnancy, or for prenatal care.

(C) Any period of incapacity or treatment for such incapacity due to a chronic serious health condition. A chronic serious health condition is one which:

(1) Requires periodic visits for treatment by a health care provider, or by a nurse or physician's assistant under direct supervision of a health care provider;

(2) Continues over an extended period of time (including recurring episodes of a single underlying condition); and

(3) May cause episodic rather than a continuing period of incapacity (e.g., asthma, diabetes, epilepsy, etc.).

(D) A period of incapacity which is permanent or long-term due to a condition for which treatment may not be effective. The employee or family member must be under the continuing supervision of, but need not be receiving active treatment by, a health care provider. Examples include Alzheimer's, a severe stroke, or the terminal stages of a disease.

(E) Any period of absence to receive multiple treatments (including any period of recovery therefrom) by a health care provider or by a provider of health care services under orders of, or on referral by, a health care provider, either for restorative surgery after an accident or other injury, or for a condition that would likely result in a period of incapacity of more than three consecutive calendar days in the absence of medical intervention or treatment, such as cancer (chemotherapy, radiation, etc.), severe arthritis (physical therapy), kidney disease (dialysis).

(2) Treatment for purposes of paragraph (1) of this definition includes (but is not limited to) examinations to determine if a serious health condition exists and evaluations of the condition. Treatment does not include routine physical

examinations, eye examinations, or dental examinations. Under paragraph (1)(ii)(A)(2) of this definition, a regimen of continuing treatment includes, for example, a course of prescription medication (e.g., an antibiotic) or therapy requiring special equipment to resolve or alleviate the health condition (e.g., oxygen). A regimen of continuing treatment that includes the taking of over-the-counter medications such as aspirin, antihistamines, or salves; or bed-rest, drinking fluids, exercise, and other similar activities that can be initiated without a visit to a health care provider, is not, by itself, sufficient to constitute a regimen of continuing treatment for purposes of FMLA leave.

(3) Conditions for which cosmetic treatments are administered (such as most treatments for acne or plastic surgery) are not "serious health conditions" unless inpatient hospital care is required or unless complications develop. Ordinarily, unless complications arise, the common cold, the flu, ear aches, upset stomach minor, ulcers, headaches other than migraine, routine dental or orthodontia problems, periodontal disease, etc., are examples of conditions that do not meet the definition of a serious health condition and do not qualify for FMLA leave. Restorative dental or plastic surgery after an injury or removal of cancerous growths are serious health conditions provided all the other conditions of this regulation are met. Mental illness resulting from stress or allergies may be serious health conditions, but only if all the conditions of this section are met.

(4) Substance abuse may be a serious health condition if the conditions of this section are met. However, FMLA leave may only be taken for treatment for substance abuse by a health care provider or by a provider of health care services on referral by a health care provider. On the other hand, absence because of the employee's use of the substance, rather than for treatment, does not qualify for FMLA leave.

(5) Absences attributable to incapacity under paragraphs (1)(ii) (B) or (C) of this definition qualify for FMLA leave even though the employee or the immediate family member does not receive treatment from a health care provider during the absence, and even if the absence does not last more than three days. For example, an employee with asthma may be unable to report for work due to the onset of an asthma attack or because the employee's health care provider has advised the employee to stay home when the pollen count exceeds a certain level. An employee who is pregnant may be unable to report to work because of severe morning sickness.

Son or daughter means a biological, adopted, or foster child, a stepchild, a legal ward, or a child of a person standing in loco parentis, who is under 18 years of age or 18 years of age or older and incapable of self-care because of a mental or physical disability.

Spouse means a husband or wife as defined or recognized under State law for purposes of marriage in the State where the employee resides, including common law marriage in States where it is recognized.

State means any State of the United States or the District of Columbia or any Territory or possession of the United States.

Teacher (or employee employed in an instructional capacity, or instructional employee) means an employee employed principally in an instructional capacity by an educational agency or school whose principal function is to teach and instruct students in a class, a small group, or an individual setting, and includes athletic coaches, driving instructors, and special education assistants such as signers for the hearing impaired. The term does not include teacher assistants or aides who do not have as their principal function actual teaching or instructing, nor auxiliary personnel such as counselors, psychologists, curriculum specialists, cafeteria workers, maintenance workers, bus drivers, or other primarily noninstructional employees.

INDEX

Symbols

12-Month Employment Requirement 29, 123
  Calculation of 124
  DOL's regulations 123, 260
12-Week Minimum Leave Benefit 138
1250-Hour Employment Requirement 31, 257, 260
  Teachers 32, 261
50-Employee Threshold 19, 35, 225, 256
  Educational employees 24
75-Mile Rule 35
  Educational employees 24

A

Adoption 44, 128
  DOL Regulations 269
Adverse Employment Action 189
Age Discrimination In Employment Act 34, 212
Alcoholism 58, 62, 72
Americans With Disabilities Act 129, 145, 152
  Definition of impairment 69
  Relationship to FMLA 153
Anxiety 57
Arbitration Of FMLA Claims 145, 210
Asthma 57, 62
Attorney Fees 204

B

Back Conditions 57, 62
Benefits
  Accrual while on leave 164, 176
    DOL Regulations 277
  Loss of 243
Bereavement Leave 72
Bronchitis 63
Bus Drivers 130

C

Calculation Of 12-Month Period 124
Cancer 57, 127
Carpal Tunnel Syndrome 63

Certification For Return To Work 113, 243
Certification Of Leave Request 254
  Employer responsibility 85, 241
  Failure to request 110
  Intermittent leave 111
  Second opinion 108, 242
Chicken Pox 57
Childbirth 44, 128, 241
  DOL Regulations 269
Chiropractors 53, 73
Chronic Serious Health Condition 111
  Definition of 54
Civil Lawsuits 155, 248
Civil Rights Act 212
  Relationship to FMLA 154
  Title VII 34
Class Action Lawsuits 205
Colds 58, 63, 67
Collective Bargaining Agreements 144, 152, 172
Compensatory Time Off 139, 143
Constructive Discharge 189
Continuing Treatment 54
Covered Employers
  Definition of 18
Customized Notice To Employees
  Failure to give notice 91
  Required elements 86

D

Damages 198
  Educational employees 211
  Employment benefits 200
  Interest 201
  Liquidated damages 201
  Lost wages and salary 199, 246
  Penalties 251
Dentists 53
Depression 58, 127
Designating Leave As FMLA-Qualifying 141
Disability
  Definition of 69
Discipline Policies 146
Discrimination

Against employees using FMLA leave
182, 245
  DOL Regulations 306
  Gender 12
Doctor Of Medicine 53
DOL's Regulations
  Test of validity 13
Duration Of Leave 122
  12-week minimum 138
  Periods of a particular duration 131

E

Ear Infections 59, 64
Economic Damages 198
Economic Injury
  DOL Regulations 285
Educational Employers 24
Educational Employers/Employees 249
  1250-hour test 261
  DOL Regulations 302
  End-of-term leave 132
  Intermittent leave 129, 249
    DOL Regulations 303
  Job restoration rules 172, 250
    DOL Regulations 304
  Special liquidated damages 211
Emotional Conditions 59, 64
Employees
  Definition of "eligible employees" 30,
    237, 260
    Eductional employees 249
  Federal employees' FMLA rights 37
  Temporary 20
Employers
  Covered employers 18, 256
  Definiton of 237
  Educational 24
  Governmental bodies 19
  Joint employment 20
  Public agencies 23
  Successors 22
  Supervisors 22
  Temporary agencies 21
Employment Benefits
  Definition of 238
Enforcement Of FMLA Rights 183, 246

Epilepsy 59, 165
Equitable Estoppel
  Principles of 33
Equitable Relief 204
Equivalent Position
  DOL Regulations 282
  Educational employees
    DOL Regulations 304
  Restoration of jobs 254
Essential Functions Of The Job 165, 168
Evidence
  Of Incapacity 55

F

Fair Labor Standards Act 37
  Definition of "employer" 256
  Definition of "person" 18
  Hours worked 32, 261
  Joint employment 21
  Relationship with FMLA 152
Family Members
  Included within the FMLA 68
Federal Employees 37, 260
Fibromyalgia 59
Fitness For Duty Certification 113, 154,
    168
  DOL Regulations 296
Flu 67
Fluctuating Workweeks 153
FMLA
  Effective date 255
  Impact of 10
  Purpose of 11, 12, 236, 254
  Relationship to Civil Rights Act 154
  Relationship with ADA 153
  Relationship with FLSA 152
    DOL's regulations 153
Foster Care 44, 128
  DOL Regulations 269
Fraudulent Use Of FMLA Leave 188

G

Gender Discrimination 12

H

Health Care Provider
  Definition of 53, 238
Health Insurance Premiums 114
  DOL Regulations 278
  Maintenance of benefits 173, 244
Heart Attacks 59
Hepatitis 60
High Blood Pressure 60
Holidays 200
Hours Worked
  Under the FLSA 32
Hypertension 60, 65

I

Impairment
  Under the ADA 69
Incapacity
  Evidence of 55
  Requirements 55
Increments Of Leave 123
Independent Contractors 20
Interference Provisions 182
  DOL's regulations 184
Intermittent Leave 47, 123, 126, 128,
    239
  Certification for 107, 111
  DOL Regulations 267, 270
  For educational employees 129, 249
    DOL Regulations 303
  Rate of payment 153
  Transfer of employee 169
Investigative Authority 246

J

Joint Employment 20, 257
  Under the FLSA 21

K

Key Employees
  DOL Regulations 285, 286
  Exemption from job restoration rights
    170

Kidney Failure 60
Knee Injuries 60

L

Labor Management Relations Act 19
Lawsuits Under The FMLA 14
  Attorney fees 204
  By applicants 36
  Civil lawsuits 155
  Class action suits 205
  Concurrent jurisdictions 209
  Damages 198
    Liquidated damages 201
  Initiation of action by DOL 207
  Statutes of limitation 208
Leave Requirement
  Definition of 239
Legislative History 10, 13
Liability 22, 246
  Public agencies 23
Liquidated Damages 201, 247
  Educational employees 211

M

Maternity Leave 139
Medical Certification
  DOL Regulations 292
Midwives 53
Migraine Headaches 58, 61, 127
Miscarriage 56, 65
Monetary Damages 198
Multi-State Employers 126

N

National Labor Relations Act 184
Negative Employment Actions 186
Notice Requirements 80
  Denial of job restoration to key employ-
    ees 171
  DOL's regulations 82, 91, 141
  Notice of the intent not to return to
    work 168
  Requirements by employees 80
    DOL Regulations 290

Requirements by employers 85, 141
  DOL Regulations 288
  Posted notices on FMLA requirements
    222, 251
  Written notice 86
 Status reports 167
 Verbal notice 87
Nurse Practitioners 53

O

Optometrists 53
Osteopaths 53

P

Paid Leave
  DOL Regulations 273
  Substitution of 139
Parent
  Definition of 264
Part-Time Employment 45
Periods Of A Particular Duration 131
Personal Time Off 139, 240
Posting Requirements
  DOL Regulations 288
Pregnancy 51, 54, 111, 143
Prenatal Care 51, 54
Probationary Employees 165
Protection Of Employees
  DOL Regulations 287
Psychologists 53, 130
Public Agencies 259
  Definition of 259

Q

Qualifying Family Members 108, 115,
  122, 123, 140

R

Re-Evaluation Of Approved Leave 74
Reassignment 127
Recordkeeping Requirements 32, 225
  DOL Regulations 301
Reduced Leave Schedule 126
  Definition of 238

DOL Regulations 271
Reinstatement
  DOL Regulations 284
Religious Institutions 19
Remedies 198
  DOL Regulations 299
  Equitable relief 204
  Exhaustion of administrative remedies
    210
Respiratory Conditions 61, 65
Restoration Of Jobs 164, 243, 258
  Denial of 244
  Educational employees 172
  Equivalent position 166, 250, 254
  Key employees 170
  Refusal by employer 168
Restructured Jobs 168
Rights Upon Return To Work
  DOL Regulations 282

S

Serious Health Condition
  Certification of 100
    Blanket request 107
    DOL's regulations 101, 293
    Failure to request 110
    Intermittent leave 107
  Defintion of 52, 239
  DOL Regulations 53, 264
  Inclusions 55
  Non-qualifying 62
  Qualifying 56
Sickle Cell Anemia 61
Sick Leave 139, 200
Site Of Employment
  Definition of 262
Social Workers 53
Spouse
  Definition of 264
State Laws
  DOL Regulations 305
Status Reports 167
Statutes Of Limitations 208
Strep Throat 61
Subcontractors 37
Substance Abuse 72

Substitution Of Paid Leave 139
Successor Employers 22, 258

T

Teachers 24, 130
  1250-hour requirement 32
Temporary Agency
  As an employer 21
Temporary Employees 20
Termination
  Constructive discharge 189
  Employee obligation 129
  Employer rights and restrictions 129
Title VII Of Civil Rights Act 34
Transfer To Equivalent Job 127
  Intermittent leave 169

U

Ulcers 61

V

Vacation Time 139, 200, 240

W

Workers' Compensation 109, 122, 151
Written Notice
  Customized notice 86
  Of employees' rights and obligations
    33, 86